# The CCNA Cram Sheet

This Cram Sheet contains the distilled, key facts about Exams 641-821, 640-811, and 640-801. Review this information as the last thing you do before you enter the testing center, paying special attention to those areas where you feel that you need the most review. You can transfer any of these facts from your head onto a blank sheet of paper immediately before you begin the exam.

## INTRODUCTION TO CISCO NETWORKING TECHNOLOGIES (641-821)

1. The primary advantage of bridging is increased bandwidth available on a segment because of the decreased number of devices in the collision domain.
2. Switches have the same basic functionality as bridges but they usually have more ports. Each switch port is a separate collision domain, and each port provides dedicated bandwidth.
3. Virtual local area networks (VLANs) can be used to make a group of switch ports into a separate, isolated LAN. Routing is required for communication between VLANs.
4. VLANs can function across multiple switches when they are connected by a trunk connection. Inter-switch linking (ISL) is used to create a trunk connection between Fast Ethernet ports on Cisco switches.
5. Switches make it possible to run Ethernet devices in full-duplex mode. In full-duplex mode, two devices share the Ethernet wire simultaneously and exclusively, enabling faster throughput because very few collisions are possible.
6. Store-and-forward switching reads the entire frame before making a forwarding decision; cut-through switching reads only the first six bytes—the destination media access control (MAC) address—to make a forwarding decision. Store-and-forward switching performs error checking; cut-through switching does not.
7. The primary advantages of routers are
    - They allow you to connect dissimilar LANs
    - They provide multiple paths to a destination network
    - They allow the interconnection of large and complex networks
8. Connection-oriented communication uses a nonpermanent path for data transfer. It involves three steps: establish the connection, transfer the data, and terminate the connection. A practical example of a connection-oriented communication would be a walkie-talkie conversation where the connection has to be established each time to the receiver by pressing a button, and once you are finished talking you release the button until you want to talk again. Connectionless communication uses a permanently established link. An example of a connection-oriented protocol is TCP, and an example of connectionless communication protocol is UDP. Again, a practical example would be that of a telephone conversation where a connection is made and maintained throughout the duration of the call.
9. The layers of the OSI model are Application layer, Presentation layer, Session layer, Transport layer, Network layer, Data Link layer, and Physical layer.
    7. Application
    6. Presentation
    5. Session
    4. Transport
    3. Network
    2. Data Link
    1. Physical
10. Encapsulation, or tunneling, takes frames from one network system and places them inside frames from another network system.
11. The Presentation layer concerns itself with data representation, data encryption, and data compression. It supports different protocols for text, data, sound, video, graphics, and images, such as ASCII, MIDI, MPEG, GIF, and JPEG.

4. Interior Gateway Routing Protocol (IGRP) can be configured on a router with the following commands:

   `Router (config)# router igrp <autonomous system number>`

   `Router (config-router)# network <network>`

5. The most important basic commands used to monitor IP with Cisco routers are `show ip interface`, `show ip protocol`, and `show ip route`.

6. A list of the important access list numeric identifiers follows:
   - 1 through 99: IP standard access list
   - 100 through 199: IP extended access list
   - 800 through 899: IPX standard access list
   - 900 through 999: IPX extended access list
   - 1000 through 1099 Service Advertisement: Protocols (SAP) access list

7. Two rules for applying a wildcard mask to an IP address are

   A 1 bit in the wildcard mask indicates that the corresponding bit in the IP address can be ignored. Thus, the IP address bit can be either 1 or 0.

   A 0 in the wildcard mask indicates that the corresponding bit in the IP address must be strictly followed. Thus, the value must be exactly the same as specified in the IP address.

. The difference in the capabilities of IP-extended access lists in comparison with IP standard access lists is that standard access lists filter IP traffic based on source IP address or address range. IP extended access lists filter traffic based on source and destination addresses, ports, and many other fields.

. Know that the last line of any access list is `deny any any` (implicit).

. A single physical interface can be configured with several virtual subinterfaces. Each subinterface can be configured with different addressing information. Subinterfaces can be created and accessed using the serial interface number followed by a period and a number (such as serial 0.78).

. The commands to configure frame relay on a router are:
   - Router (config)# encapsulation frame-relay cisco
   - Router (config)# frame-relay lmi-type cisco
   - Router (config)# interface serial 0
   - Router (config-if)# frame-relay interface-dlci <dlci number>

. The basic commands to monitor frame relay activity on a router are `show frame-relay pvc`, `show frame-relay lmi`, `show frame-relay map`, and `debug frame-relay lmi`.

53. The commands to configure PPP on a router are:
    - Router (config)# username <name> password <password>
    - Router (config)# interface serial 0
    - Router (config-if)# encapsulation ppp
    - Router (config-if)# ppp authentication chap

54. The basic commands to monitor PPP activity on a router are `show interface` and `debug ppp chap`.

55. The commands to configure ISDN on a router are:
    - Router (config)# isdn switch-type <switch-type>
    - Router (config)# dialer-list <dialer-group> protocol <protocol-name> permit
    - Router (config-if)# interface bri 0
    - Router (config-if)# encapsulation PPP
    - Router (config-if)# dialer-group <number>
    - Router (config-if)# dialer map <protocol> <next-hop address>
    - name <hostname> speed <number> <dial-string>
    - Router (config-if) dialer idle-timeout <seconds>

56. The basic commands to monitor ISDN and DDR activity on a router are `show controller bri`, `show interface bri`, and `show dialer`.

29. Data link connection identifier (DLCI) serves as the addressing scheme within a frame relay network. Local Management Information (LMI) is a set of enhancements to frame relay that was developed by Cisco, StrataCom, Northern Telecom, and DEC. Cisco routers support LMI variations for American National Standards Institute (ANSI), Q933a, and Cisco.
30. DLCIs are mapped to network layer addresses through inverse ARP or by using the `frame-relay map` command.
31. Committed Information Rate (CIR) is the rate, in bits per second, at which data is transferred across the frame relay network.
32. Password Authentication Protocol (PAP) uses a two-way handshake to authenticate Point-to-Point Protocol (PPP) connections and transmits username/password information in clear text. Challenge Handshake Authentication Protocol (CHAP) uses a three-way handshake and relies on secret, encrypted passwords and unique IDs to authenticate PPP.
33. Integrated services digital network (ISDN) can be ordered as either basic rate interface (BRI) or primary rate interface (PRI). ISDN functions represent devices or hardware functions within ISDN. Reference points describe the logical interfaces between functions.
34. ISDN can be used to add bandwidth for telecommuting, improve Internet response time, carry multiple network layer protocols, and encapsulate other WAN services.
35. Dial-on-demand routing (DDR) works with ISDN to establish and terminate connections. It uses access lists to look for interesting traffic.

## INTERCONNECTING CISCO NETWORK DEVICES (640-811)

36. EXEC includes the following:
    - Context-sensitive help for syntax checking, command prompting, and keyword completion. Use the question mark (?) to activate context-sensitive help.
    - Command history that provides a record of recent commands. Use the Up and Down Arrow keys to scroll through the history list. Tab completes a partially entered command.
    - Enhanced editing that enables commands retrieved from the command history to be changed quickly then re-executed. The `terminal editing` and `terminal no editing` commands enable and disable enhanced editing.
    - Use the Tab key to allow the router to complete commands after you get a %incomplete command% message.
37. Examine the status of a router with the following commands: `show version`, `show memory`, `show protocols`, `show running-config` (or `write terminal`), `show startup-config` (or `show configuration`), `show interfaces`, and `show flash`.
38. The Cisco Discovery Protocol (CDP) displays summary information about directly connected devices and operates at the Data Link layer. The `show cdp neighbors` command displays ID, local and remote port, holdtime, platform, and capability information. The `show cdp entry <device id>` command displays information about a specific device, including all Layer 3 addresses and Internetwork Operating System (IOS) versions.
39. The command to back up a router configuration file (copy a configuration file from a router to a Trivial File Transfer Protocol [TFTP] server) is `copy running-config tftp`. The command to restore a configuration file (copy a configuration file from a TFTP server to a router) is `copy tftp running-config`.
40. The commands to set the enable secret, console, and auxiliary passwords on a router are as follows:

```
Router(config)#enable password

Router(config)#enable secret password

Router(config)#line aux 0
Router(config-line)#login
Router(config-line)#password password

Router(config)#line con 0
Router(config-line)#login
Router(config-line)#password password

Router(config)#line vty 0 4
Router(config-line)#login
Router(config-line)#password password
```

41. To create a banner for a router and a description for an interface, use the `banner motd` (message of the day) and `description` commands.
42. Router resource usage, bandwidth consumption, and update synchronization are problems for link state routing protocols. They can be eliminated or reduced by using the following techniques:
    - Lengthening update frequency
    - Exchanging route summaries
    - Using time stamps or sequence numbers
43. Routing Information Protocol (RIP) can be configured on a router with the following commands:

```
Router (config)# router rip

Router (config-router)# network
<network>
```

12. The Session layer establishes, manages, and terminates sessions between applications. Network file system (NFS), structured query language (SQL), and remote procedure calls (RPCs) are examples of Session layer protocols.
13. The Transport layer sits between the upper and lower layers of the OSI model. It performs flow control by buffering, multiplexing, and parallelization. It provides end-to-end data transport services by segmenting upper-layer applications, establishing an end-to-end connection, sending segments from one end host to another, and ensuring reliable data transport.
14. The primary functions of the Network layer of the OSI model are path determination and packet switching. In addition, remember that the Network layer is the domain of routing.
15. The primary functions of the Data Link layer of the OSI model are:
    - Allows the upper layers of the OSI model to work independently of the physical media
    - Performs physical hardware addressing
    - Provides optional flow control
    - Generates error notification
16. Convergence occurs when all routers in an internetwork agree on optimal routes. A routing loop occurs when a packet bounces back and forth between two or more routers.
17. Distance vector routing protocols send their entire routing tables to their neighbors. Link state protocols send the state of their own interfaces to every router in the internetwork.
18. Counting to infinity is a problem for distance vector routing protocols. It can be eliminated or mitigated by using the following techniques: maximum hop count, split horizon, route poisoning, and hold-down timers.
19. TCP provides a connection-oriented and reliable service to the applications that use its services with the use of acknowledgments, sequence number checking, error and duplication checking, and the TCP three-way handshake. User Datagram Protocol (UDP) provides a connectionless and best-effort service to the applications that use its services.
20. Well-known port numbers include:
    - File Transfer Protocol (FTP) 21
    - Telnet 23
    - Simple Mail Transfer Protocol (SMTP) 25
    - Domain Name System (DNS) 53
    - TFTP 69
    - Simple Network Management Protocol (SNMP) 161, 162
    - HTTP 80
21. Address Resolution Protocol (ARP) maps a known IP address to a physical address. Reverse Address Resolution Protocol (RARP) maps a known physical address to a logical address.
22. Understand the basic concepts of IP addressing. Dotted-decimal notation is the decimal representation of a 32-bit IP address. The dotted-decimal notation represents the four octets of bits by performing binary-to-decimal conversion for each octet and providing a decimal value for each octet.
23. You should know the decimal representation of classes A, B, and C addresses as well as the number of networks and nodes each supports as shown below:
    - Class A: 1 through 126
    - Class B: 128 through 191
    - Class C: 192 through 223
24. You should be able to recognize the default mask for each class of IP address as shown below:
    - Class A: 255.0.0.0
    - Class B: 255.255.0.0
    - Class C: 255.255.255.0
25. The network number and broadcast address for a given subnet are the first and last IP addresses, respectively. The range of usable IP addresses is all addresses between the network number and broadcast address. In binary format, the network number has all of the host bits of the address set to 0. The broadcast address has all of the host bits set to 1.
26. You should know how to do subnetting tasks very quickly. It will save you valuable time in the end.
27. The interface between the customer network and the WAN provider network occurs between the data terminal equipment (DTE) and the data communication equipment (DCE). DTE devices are usually routers. DCE devices are usually modems, channel service units/data service units (CSUs/DSUs), and terminal adapter/network terminations 1 (TA/NT1s).
28. Frame relay is a high-speed, packet-switching WAN protocol that operates at the Data Link layer. It runs on nearly any type of serial interface, uses frame check sequence (FCS) as its error-checking mechanism, and relies on a discard eligibility bit for congestion management. A virtual circuit must connect two DTE devices within a frame relay network. Permanent virtual circuits (PVCs) are more widely used than switched virtual circuits (SVCs) in frame relay networks.

# CCNA

James G. Jones

Sheldon Barry

**CCNA Exam Cram 2**



International Standard Book Number: 0-7897-3019-7

Library of Congress Catalog Card Number: 2003109248

Printed in the United States of America

First Printing: December 2003
Reprinted with corrections: April 2004

06 05 04 6 5 4

## Trademarks



## Warning and Disclaimer



## Bulk Sales

Que Publishing offers excellent discounts on this book when ordered in quantity for bulk purchases or special sales. For more information, please contact

**U.S. Corporate and Government Sales**
**1-800-382-3419**
**corpsales@pearsontechgroup.com**

For sales outside of the U.S., please contact

**International Sales**
**international@pearsoned.com**

**Publisher**
Paul Boger

**Executive Editor**
Jeff Riley

**Acquisitions Editor**
Carol Ackerman

**Development Editor**
Ginny Bess Munroe
Steve Rowe

**Managing Editor**
Charlotte Clapp

**Project Editor**
Dan Knott

**Production Editor**
Benjamin Berg

**Indexer**
Tom Dinse

**Proofreader**
Wendy Ott

**Technical Editors**
Michael Woznicki
Warren Wyrostek

**Team Coordinator**
Pamalee Nelson

**Multimedia Developer**
Dan Scherf

**Interior Designer**
Gary Adair

**Cover Designer**
Ann Jones

**Page Layout**
Michelle Mitchell
Ron Wise

Que Certification • 800 East 96th Street • Indianapolis, Indiana 46240

## A Note from Series Editor Ed Tittel

You know better than to trust your certification preparation to just anybody. That's why you, and more than two million others, have purchased an Exam Cram book. As Series Editor for the new and improved Exam Cram 2 series, I have worked with the staff at Que Certification to ensure you won't be disappointed. That's why we've taken the world's best-selling certification product—a finalist for "Best Study Guide" in a CertCities reader poll in 2002—and made it even better.

As a "Favorite Study Guide Author" finalist in a 2002 poll of CertCities readers, I know the value of good books. You'll be impressed with Que Certification's stringent review process, which ensures the books are high-quality, relevant, and technically accurate. Rest assured that at least a dozen industry experts have reviewed this material, helping us deliver an excellent solution to your exam preparation needs.

We've also added a preview edition of PrepLogic's powerful, full-featured test engine, which is trusted by certification students throughout the world.

As a 20-year-plus veteran of the computing industry and the original creator and editor of the Exam Cram series, I've brought my IT experience to bear on these books. During my tenure at Novell from 1989 to 1994, I worked with and around its excellent education and certification department. This experience helped push my writing and teaching activities heavily in the certification direction. Since then, I've worked on more than 70 certification-related books, and I write about certification topics for numerous Web sites and for *Certification* magazine.

In 1996, while studying for various MCP exams, I became frustrated with the huge, unwieldy study guides that were the only preparation tools available. As an experienced IT professional and former instructor, I wanted "nothing but the facts" necessary to prepare for the exams. From this impetus, Exam Cram emerged in 1997. It quickly became the best-selling computer book series since "*...For Dummies*," and the best-selling certification book series ever. By maintaining an intense focus on subject matter, tracking errata and updates quickly, and following the certification market closely, Exam Cram was able to establish the dominant position in cert prep books.

You will not be disappointed in your decision to purchase this book. If you are, please contact me at etittel@jump.net. All suggestions, ideas, input, or constructive criticism are welcome!

Ed Tittel

# About the Authors

**James G. Jones** has more than 30 years experience in the information technology industry and has held positions from technician to senior vice president of a Fortune 500 multinational. He holds a B.S. and M.B.A. from Michigan State University and numerous technical certifications including A+, MCSE, MCT, CNE, CCNA, and CCDA. He also holds certifications in the areas of fiber optics and network cabling, and is licensed by the FCC for installation and inspection of commercial radio and microwave applications. Today, in addition to writing books on technology, he regularly consults with leaders in the technology industry including Cisco, IBM, Hewlett Packard, Microsoft, and Oracle. Jim lives in Geneva, Illinois with his wife Sally and two sons Shaun and Chris.

Jim can be reached at `jim@jamesgjones.com`

**Sheldon Barry** (B.A., M.ED, CCNA, CCAI, MCSE, MCT) is a program specialist for e-learning, writer, and consultant in Newfoundland, Canada. He is currently employed as program specialist for e-learning at the Avalon West School District (`www.awsb.ca`). Some of his previous employment positions have included technical writing, educational content consulting, high school department head, and high school teacher.

Sheldon completed a bachelor of arts from Memorial University of Newfoundland in 1994 and then went on to complete a bachelor of education from Memorial in 1995. Since then Sheldon has completed a masters of education (information technology) degree. He currently enjoys life with his wife, Kelly; his two little girls, Sarah and Anna; and loves to play soccer and golf.

Sheldon can be reached at `sbarry@awsb.ca`.

# About the Contributing Author

**Orin Thomas**, BSc(Hons), MCSE, CCNA, CCDA, Linux+ is a writer, editor, and systems administrator who works for the certification advice Web site Certtutor.net. His work in IT has been varied: He's done everything from providing first level networking support at a university to acting in the role of systems administrator for one of Australia's largest companies. He holds a bachelor's degree in science with honors from the University of Melbourne and is currently working toward the completion of a Ph.D. in philosophy of science.

Orin has previously authored and contributed to several other certification publications, including *MCSA/MCSE Self-Paced Training Kit (Exam 70-290): Managing and Maintaining a Microsoft Windows Server 2003 Environment* (2003) and *MCSA/MCSE Self-Paced Training Kit (Exams 70-292 and 70-296): Upgrading Your Certification to Microsoft Windows Server 2003* (2003), both from Microsoft Press. He has authored several articles for technical publications as well as contributing to *The Insider's Guide to IT Certification*.

Orin resides in Melbourne, Australia with his beautiful wife Oksana and their wonderful son Rooslan. When he's not working, you can find him enjoying time with his family, playing Battletech, or reading a book by Terry Pratchett. You can visit him at `http://www.certtutor.net`.

# About the Technical Editors

**Michael J. Woznicki** spent seven and a half years in the United States Navy, where he earned an A.S. Degree in electronics. Over the past 14 years, Michael has worked for SunLife of Canada as a network analyst, CrossComm Corporation as the corporate network administrator, and for ExecuTrain as a technical instructor. He has worked in many facets of the computer industry, from help desk support supervisor and senior technical support engineer to network field service technician and network administrator.

Michael has over four years of technical training with both SunLife and CrossComm, as well as more than five and a half years of formal classroom instruction. He has taught classes in A+, Network+, iNet+, HTML, CSS, CIW Foundations, Cisco Routers, Novell NetWare 3.X and 4.X, and Microsoft operating systems from DOS to Windows XP Professional, as well as customized Windows 2000 Professional. Michael has more than 20 different certifications: Among them are Cisco Certified Network Associate (CCNA) and Cisco Certified Design Associate (CCDA), Certified Internet Webmaster (CIW), CompTIA INet+, Net+, Server+, Security+, A+, and the MCSA certification.

**Warren E. Wyrostek** is a graduate of Hunter College of C.U.N.Y with a B.A. in chemistry. He holds a master's in divinity from Union Theological Seminary and a master's in vocational-technical education from Valdosta State College. He is devoted to technology education as reflected by his list of certifications, which include Novell (MCNI, MCNE, and CDE), Microsoft (MCSE-NT 4.0 and MCSE-W2K), Prosoft (CIW CIW, MCIWD, and MCIWA), and Cisco (CCNA, CCDA, and CCNP). Warren has taught on the college and secondary school levels. Warren's main joy comes as a freelance writer and contract trainer in Novell, CompTia, Prosoft, and Microsoft technologies. At heart, he is a teacher who loves what education offers. You can reach Warren at `wyrostekw@msn.com`.

# Contents at a Glance

# Table of Contents

## Chapter 3
## Hardware and the OSI Model .....29



## Chapter 4
## Wide Area Network Protocols .....57



## Chapter 5
## TCP/IP .....77

## Chapter 10
## Configuring a Cisco Router ....................................179

# We Want to Hear from You!

As the reader of this book, *you* are our most important critic and commentator. We value your opinion and want to know what we're doing right, what we could do better, what areas you'd like to see us publish in, and any other words of wisdom you're willing to pass our way.

As an executive editor for Que Publishing, I welcome your comments. You can email or write me directly to let me know what you did or didn't like about this book--as well as what we can do to make our books better.

*Please note that I cannot help you with technical problems related to the topic of this book. We do have a User Services group, however, where I will forward specific technical questions related to the book.*

When you write, please be sure to include this book's title and author as well as your name, email address, and phone number. I will carefully review your comments and share them with the author and editors who worked on the book.


Email: feedback@quepublishing.com

Mail: Jeff Riley
Executive Editor
Que Publishing
800 East 96th Street
Indianapolis, IN 46240 USA


For more information about this book or another Que Publishing title, visit our Web site at `www.examcram2.com`. Type the ISBN (excluding hyphens) or the title of a book in the Search field to find the page you're looking for.

# Introduction

Welcome to the Cisco Certified Network Associate Exam Cram 2! Whether this is your first or your fifteenth *Exam Cram 2* series book, you'll find information here that will help ensure your success as you pursue knowledge, experience, and certification. This introduction explains Cisco's certification programs in general and talks about how the *Exam Cram 2* series can help you prepare for the Cisco Certified Network Associate exams. Chapter 1 discusses the basics of Cisco certification exams, including a description of the testing environment and a discussion of test-taking strategies. Chapters 2 through 16 are designed to remind you of everything you'll need to know in order to take—and pass—the CCNA 640-801 combined exam or the CCNA 640-821 background and 640-811 configuration exams. The three practice exams at the end of the book should give you a reasonably accurate assessment of your knowledge—and, yes, we've provided the answers and their explanations to the tests. Read the book and understand the material, and you'll stand a very good chance of passing the test.

*Exam Cram 2* books help you understand and appreciate the subjects and materials you need to pass Cisco certification exams. *Exam Cram 2* books are aimed strictly at test preparation and review. They do not teach you everything you need to know about a topic. Instead, we will present and dissect the questions and problems we have found that you're likely to encounter on a test. We have worked to bring together as much information as possible about Cisco certification exams.

Nevertheless, to completely prepare yourself for any Cisco test, we recommend that you begin by taking the Self-Assessment that is included in this book, immediately following this introduction. The Self-Assessment tool will help you evaluate your knowledge base against the requirements for a Cisco Certified Network Associate under both ideal and real circumstances.

Based on what you learn from the Self-Assessment, you might decide to begin your studies with some classroom training, some practice with configuration, or some background reading. On the other hand, you might decide to pick up and read one of the many study guides available from Cisco or third-party vendors on certain topics. We also recommend that you supplement your study program with visits to www.examcram2.com to receive additional practice questions, get advice, and track the CCNA program.

We also strongly recommend that you get some hands-on experience configuring Cisco routers and switches. If you do not have access to the appropriate equipment, you can log on to Cisco's Web site and practice with their configuration simulator. Book learning is essential, but without a doubt, hands-on experience is the best teacher of all!

# Taking a Certification Exam

After you've prepared for your exam, you need to register with a testing center. The combined exam (640-801) costs $125, and if you don't pass, you can retest for an additional $125 for each additional try. Exam 640-811 costs $100, and the cost of 640-821 was not available at time of publication but you can expect a cost of $100 to $125. Again, you can retest for either of these exams but you will have to pay a full exam fee each time you retest. In the United States and Canada, tests are administered by Prometric and by VUE. Here's how you can contact them:

- **Prometric**—You can sign up for a test through the company's Web site at www.prometric.com. Within the United States and Canada, you can register by phone at 800-755-3926. If you live outside this region, you should check the Prometric Web site for the appropriate phone number.
- **VUE**—You can sign up for a test or get the phone numbers for local testing centers through the Web at www.vue.com/ms.

To sign up for a test, you must possess a valid credit card or contact either Prometric or VUE for mailing instructions to send a check (in the United States). Only when payment is verified or your check has cleared can you actually register for the test.

To schedule an exam, you need to call the number or visit either of the Web pages at least one day in advance. To cancel or reschedule an exam, you must call before 7 p.m. Pacific standard time the day before the scheduled test time (or you might be charged, even if you don't show up to take the test). When you want to schedule a test, you should have the following information ready:

- Your name, organization, and mailing address.
- Your Cisco test ID. (Inside the United States, this usually means your Social Security number; citizens of other nations should call ahead to find out what type of identification number is required to register for a test.)

- The name and number of the exam you want to take.
- A method of payment. (As mentioned previously, a credit card is the most convenient method, but alternate means can be arranged in advance, if necessary.)

After you sign up for a test, you are told when and where the test is scheduled. You should try to arrive at least 15 minutes early. You must supply two forms of identification—one of which must be a photo ID—and sign a nondisclosure agreement to be admitted into the testing room.

All Cisco exams are completely closed book. In fact, you are not permitted to take anything with you into the testing area, but you are given a blank sheet of paper and a pen (or in some cases an erasable plastic sheet and an erasable pen). We suggest that you immediately write down on that sheet of paper all the information you've memorized for the test. In *Exam Cram 2* books, this information appears on a tear-out sheet inside the front cover of each book. You are given some time to compose yourself, record this information, and take a sample orientation exam before you begin the real thing. I suggest that you take the orientation test before taking your first exam, but because all the certification exams are more or less identical in layout, behavior, and controls, you probably don't need to do this more than once.

When you complete a Cisco certification exam, the software tells you immediately whether you've passed or failed. If you need to retake an exam, you have to schedule a new test with Prometric or VUE and pay another exam fee.

The first time you fail a test, you can retake the test 72 hours after the original.

After you pass the necessary set of exams, you are certified. Official certification is normally granted after three to six weeks, so you shouldn't expect to get your credentials overnight.

Many people believe that the benefits of CCNA certification go well beyond the knowledge gained by the newly anointed members of this elite group. We're starting to see more job listings that request or require applicants to have CCNA and other certifications, and many individuals who complete Cisco certification programs can qualify for increases in pay and/or responsibility.

# How to Prepare for an Exam

Preparing for any Cisco-related test requires that you obtain and study materials designed to provide comprehensive information about the product and its capabilities that will appear on the specific exam for which you are preparing. The following two sites can help you study and prepare:

- The Cisco Web site at `www.cisco.com` has an enormous amount of material available to CCNA candidates. Configuration simulators, practice tests, program updates, and career path guides are just a few of the resources available at this Web site.
- The exam-preparation advice, practice tests, questions of the day, and discussion groups on the `www.examcram2.com` e-learning and certification destination Web site.

In addition, you might find any or all of the following resources beneficial:

- **Classroom training**—Third-party training companies (such as Wave Technologies, Learning Tree, and Data-Tech) all offer classroom training on Cisco certifications. Although such training runs upward of $350 per day in class, most of the individuals lucky enough to partake find this training to be quite worthwhile. Cisco also offers classroom training through vocational schools and community colleges. If you have a school nearby that offers Cisco training, you should definitely explore the programs available.
- **Other publications**—There's no shortage of materials available about Cisco products and technologies. The "Need to Know More?" resource sections at the end of each chapter in this book give you an idea of where we think you should look for further discussion.

# What This Book Will Not Do

This book will *not* teach you everything you need to know about data communications, or even about a given topic. Nor is this book an introduction to computer technology. If you're new to Cisco products, technologies, and looking for an initial preparation guide, check out `www.quepublishing.com`, where you will find a whole section dedicated to the Cisco certifications. This book will review what you need to know before you take the test, with the fundamental purpose dedicated to reviewing the information needed on the CCNA certification exams.

This book uses a variety of teaching and memorization techniques to analyze the exam-related topics and to provide you with ways to input, index, and retrieve everything you'll need to know in order to pass the test. Once again, it is *not* an introduction to data communications.

## What This Book Is Designed To Do

This book is designed to be read as a pointer to the areas of knowledge you will be tested on. In other words, you may want to read the book one time, just to get an insight into how comprehensive your knowledge of computers is. The book is also designed to be read shortly before you go for the actual test and to give you a distillation of the entire field of Cisco router and switch configuration basics in as few pages as possible. We think you can use this book to get a sense of the underlying context of any topic in the chapters—or to skim-read for Exam Alerts, bulleted points, summaries, and topic headings.

We have drawn on material from Cisco's own listing of knowledge requirements, from other preparation guides, and from the exams themselves. We've also drawn from a battery of third-party test-preparation tools and technical Web sites as well as from our own experience with Cisco technologies and the exam. Our aim is to walk you through the knowledge you will need—looking over your shoulder, so to speak—and point out those things that are important for the exam (Exam Alerts, practice questions, and so on).

The CCNA exams make a basic assumption that you already have a strong background of experience with local and wide area networking. On the other hand, because the field is changing so quickly, no one can be a complete expert. We have tried to demystify the jargon, acronyms, terms, and concepts. Also, wherever we think you're likely to blur past an important concept, we have defined the assumptions and premises behind that concept.

# About This Book

If you're preparing for the CCNA exams for the first time, we have structured the topics in this book to build upon one another. Therefore, the topics covered in later chapters might refer to previous discussions in earlier chapters.

We suggest you read this book from front to back. You won't be wasting your time, because nothing we have written is a guess about an unknown exam. We have had to explain certain underlying information on such a regular basis that we have included those explanations here.

Once you've read the book, you can brush up on a certain area by using the index or the table of contents to go straight to the topics and questions you want to reexamine. We have tried to use the headings and subheadings to provide outline information about each given topic. After you've been certified, we think you'll find this book useful as a tightly focused reference for local and wide area networking.

# Chapter Formats

Each *Exam Cram* 2 chapter follows a regular structure, along with graphical cues about especially important or useful material. The structure of a typical chapter is as follows:

- **Opening hotlists**—Each chapter begins with lists of the terms you'll need to understand and the concepts you'll need to master before you can be fully conversant with the chapter's subject matter. We follow the hotlists with a few introductory paragraphs, setting the stage for the rest of the chapter.
- **Topical coverage**—After the opening hotlists, each chapter covers the topics related to the chapter's subject.
- **Alerts**—Throughout the topical coverage section, we highlight material most likely to appear on the exam by using a special Exam Alert layout that looks like this:

This is what an Exam Alert looks like. An Exam Alert stresses concepts, terms, software, or activities that will most likely appear in one or more certification exam questions. For that reason, we think any information found offset in Exam Alert format is worthy of unusual attentiveness on your part.

Even if material isn't flagged as a Exam Alert, *all* the content in this book is associated in some way with test-related material. What appears in the chapter content is critical knowledge.

- **Notes**—This book is an overall examination of computers. As such, we'll dip into many aspects of Cisco router and switch configuration issues. Where a body of knowledge is deeper than the scope of the book, we use notes to indicate areas of concern or specialty training.

Cramming for an exam will get you through a test, but it won't make you a competent IT professional. Although you can memorize just the facts you need in order to become certified, your daily work in the field will rapidly put you in water over your head if you don't know the underlying principles of Cisco networking.

- **Tips**—We provide tips that will help you to build a better foundation of knowledge or to focus your attention on an important concept that will reappear later in the book. Tips provide a helpful way to remind you of the context surrounding a particular area of a topic under discussion.

You should also read Chapter 1, "Cisco Certification Exams," for helpful strategies used in taking a test.

- **Practice questions**—This section presents a short list of test questions related to the specific chapter topic. Each question has a following explanation of both correct and incorrect answers. The practice questions highlight the areas we found to be most important on the exam.
- **Need To Know More?**—Every chapter ends with a section titled "Need To Know More?" This section provides pointers to resources that we found to be helpful in offering further details on the chapter's subject matter. If you find a resource you like in this collection, use it, but don't feel compelled to use all these resources. We use this section to recommend resources that we have used on a regular basis, so none of the recommendations will be a waste of your time or money. These resources may go out of print or be taken down (in the case of Web sites), so we've tried to reference widely accepted resources.

The bulk of the book follows this chapter structure, but there are a few other elements that we would like to point out:

- **Practice Exams**—The sample tests, which appear in the back of the book, are very close approximations of the types of questions you are likely to see on the current exams.
- **Answer keys**—These provide the answers to the sample tests, complete with explanations of both the correct responses and the incorrect responses.
- **Glossary**—This is an extensive glossary of important terms used in this book.
- **The Cram Sheet**—This appears as a tear-away sheet, inside the front cover of this *Exam Cram 2* book. It is a valuable tool that represents a collection of the most difficult-to-remember facts and numbers we think you should memorize before taking the test. Remember, you can dump this information out of your head onto a piece of paper as soon as you enter the testing room. These are usually facts that we've found require brute-force memorization. You only need to remember this information long

enough to write it down when you walk into the test room. Be advised that you will be asked to surrender all personal belongings before you enter the exam room itself.

You might want to look at the Cram Sheet in your car or in the lobby of the testing center just before you walk into the testing center. The Cram Sheet is divided under headings, so you can review the appropriate parts just before each test.

- **The CD**—The CD includes many helpful code samples that demonstrate all of the topics on the exam. If you work through the samples on the CD, you'll understand the techniques that you're likely to be tested on. The CD also contains the PrepLogic Practice Exams, Preview Edition exam simulation software. The Preview Edition exhibits most of the full functionality of the Premium Edition, but offers only questions sufficient for only one practice exam. To get the complete set of practice questions and exam functionality, visit `www.preplogic.com`.

# Contacting the Authors

We have tried to create a real-world tool that you can use to prepare for and pass the CCNA certification exams. We are interested in any feedback you would care to share about the book, especially if you have ideas about how we can improve it for future test-takers. We will consider everything you say carefully and will respond to all reasonable suggestions and comments. You can reach us via email at `jim@jamesgjones.com` or `sbarry@awsb.ca`.

Let us know if you found this book to be helpful in your preparation efforts. We would also like to know how you felt about your chances of passing the exam *before* you read the book and then *after* you read the book. Of course, we would love to hear that you passed the exam—and even if you just want to share your triumph, we would be happy to hear from you.

Thanks for choosing us as your personal trainers, and enjoy the book. We would wish you luck on the exam, but we know that if you read through all the chapters and work with the equipment or simulators, you won't need luck—you'll pass the test on the strength of real knowledge!

# Self-Assessment

We included a Self-Assessment in this *Exam Cram 2* to help you evaluate your readiness to tackle the Cisco Certified Network Associate program. It should also help you understand what you need to master the topic of this book—namely, the combined Cisco Certified Network Associate exam (640-801) or the two individual exams; Introduction to Cisco Networking Devices (640-821) and Interconnecting Cisco Network Devices (640-811). Before you tackle this Self-Assessment, however, we will talk about the concerns you might face when pursuing a CCNA certification and what an ideal candidate might look like.

## Cisco Certified Network Associates in the Real World

In the next section, we describe an ideal CCNA candidate, knowing that only a few actual candidates meet this ideal. In fact, our description of that ideal candidate might seem downright scary. But take heart; although the requirements for becoming a Cisco Certified Network Associate may seem formidable, they are by no means impossible to meet. However, you should be keenly aware that it does take time, requires some expense, and calls for a substantial effort.

You can get all the real-world motivation you need from knowing that many others have gone before you. You can follow in their footsteps. If you're willing to tackle the process seriously and do what it takes to gain the necessary experience and knowledge, you can take—and pass—the certification tests. In fact, the entire *Exam Cram 2* series is designed to make it as easy as possible for you to prepare for these exams, but prepare you must!

## The Ideal Cisco Certified Network Associate Candidate

Just to give you some idea of what an ideal CCNA candidate is like, here are some relevant statistics about the background and experience such an individual might have. Don't worry if you don't meet these qualifications (or, indeed, if you don't even come close) because this world is far from ideal, and where you fall short is simply where you'll have more work to do. The ideal candidate will have the following:

- Professional training and experience in networked Windows NT/Windows 2000/Windows XP and or Unix operating systems.
- Experience cabling and troubleshooting local area networks.
- Experience installing and configuring WAN links.
- Hands-on experience configuring bridges, switches, and routers.

We believe that well under a quarter of all certification candidates meet these requirements. In fact, most probably meet less than half of these requirements (that is, at least when they begin the certification process). However, because all those who have their certifications already survived this ordeal, you can survive it, too—especially if you heed what this Self-Assessment can tell you about what you already know and what you need to learn.

## Put Yourself to the Test

The following series of questions and observations is designed to help you figure out how much work you'll face in pursuing CCNA certification and what kinds of resources you can consult on your quest. Be absolutely honest in your answers, or you'll end up wasting money on exams you're not ready to take. There is no right or wrong answer, only steps along the path to certification. Only you can decide where you really belong in the broad spectrum of aspiring candidates.

Two things should be clear from the outset, however:

- Even a modest background in computer science will be helpful.
- Hands-on experience with networked systems and technologies is an essential ingredient for certification success.

## Educational Background

1. Have you ever taken any computer-related classes? (Yes or No)

   If yes, proceed to question 2; if no, proceed to question 4.

2. Have you taken any classes on networked Windows or the Unix operating system? (Yes or No)

   If yes, you probably have a good foundation for starting the CCNA program. If the answer is no, consider some basic reading in this area. To begin with, you should have a copy of Cisco's *Internetworking Technologies Handbook*. This is *the* resource for the CCNA program and many other Cisco certifications. In addition to the *Internetworking Technologies Handbook*, there are so many good books it is hard to recommend just one. Try stopping at one of the larger bookstores and peruse the shelves. If you do not have a bookstore in your area, check out Amazon.com. You should look for a practical book stressing networking and that starts where your experience leaves off. At the end of each chapter, we have included recommended resources for subjects covered in the chapter. We have read them all and they are good.

3. Have you taken any networking concepts or technology classes? (Yes or No)

   If yes, you will probably be able to handle the networking terminology, concepts, and technologies (but brace yourself for frequent departures from normal usage). If you're rusty, or your answer is no, we recommend you pick up a copy of Cisco Press's *Network Sales and Services Handbook* by Matthew Castelli. Each company has its own language (guess which one is used on the test). So, if you can find a book that uses the same terms, you will find on the test you will be that much further ahead.

4. Have you had experience cabling and troubleshooting networks? (Yes or No)

   If yes, you are one of the rare few with a golden future. If you answered no, pick up a copy of Sybex's *Cabling: The Complete Guide to Network Wiring* by David Groth and Jim McBee. Not only will this book provide a good conceptual foundation for the CCNA but it will also give you a leg up in the real world. Believe it or not, 70% of all network problems can be traced to the wire.

## Hands-On Experience

Another important key to success on all Cisco tests is hands-on experience. If we leave you with only one realization after taking this Self-Assessment, it should be that there's no substitute for time spent installing and configuring Cisco products.

5. Have you installed, configured, and worked with Cisco routers and switches? (Yes or No)

   If yes, exam 640-821 and the configuration portion of exam 640-801 should be easy for you.

   If you haven't worked with routers and switches, and do not have access to Cisco equipment, hop on the Cisco Web site at `www.cisco.com` and spend some time with the simulators. They are not as good as working with the real thing, but they are better than nothing.

You can obtain the exam objectives, practice questions, and other information about Cisco exams from the Cisco Web site at **www.cisco.com**.

If you have the funds or your employer will pay for it, consider taking a class at a Cisco authorized training and education center. You can find the locations of authorized centers at the Cisco Web site **www.cisco.com**.

## Testing Your Exam-Readiness

Whether you attend a formal class on a specific topic to get ready for an exam or use written materials to study on your own, some preparation for the CCNA exams is essential. At $125 a try, pass or fail, you want to do everything you can to pass on your first try. That's where studying comes in.

We have included several practice exam questions in each chapter and practice exams for each of the exams, so if you don't score well on the chapter questions, you can study more and then tackle the sample exams at the end of the book.

There is no better way to assess your test readiness than to take a good-quality practice exam and pass with a score of 70% or better. We usually shoot for 80+%, just to leave room for the "weirdness factor" that sometimes shows up on Cisco exams.

One last note: We hope it makes sense to stress the importance of hands-on experience in the context of the exams. As you review the material for the exams, you'll realize that hands-on experience with Cisco equipment and/or simulators is invaluable.

## Onward, Through the Fog!

After you've assessed your readiness, undertaken the right background studies, and obtained hands-on experience, you'll be ready to take a round of practice exams. Start with the ones at the back of this book. When you score 70% or better, you're ready to go after the real thing.

# Cisco Certification Exams

## Terms you'll need to understand:

✓ Radio button

✓ Check box

✓ Exhibit

✓ Multiple-choice/multiple-answer question formats

✓ Process of elimination

## Techniques you'll need to master:

✓ Preparing to take a certification exam

✓ Making the best use of the testing software

✓ Time management

✓ Question selection

This chapter is an introduction to the Cisco certification process and general information on the taking of the authorized examination. We feel that having prior knowledge of the method by which you will be tested will relax you and give you comfort in knowing that you will be ready to tackle the task at hand.

# Cisco Certified Network Associate Career Certification (CCNA) Changes

Recently, Cisco changed the requirements for their Cisco Certified Network Associate (CCNA) designation to allow for a more flexible path to certification. Candidates may still elect to take one exam (640-801) that will meet the requirements for certification, or they can meet the certification requirements in two steps with two exams (640-821 and 640-811). Many prefer the two-step approach because it reduces the content in each exam to a more manageable size. The first half of this book covers the material required by exam 640-821, and the second part covers material required by exam 640-811. Together, the sections cover everything required by exam 640-801. Therefore, this book can be an effective guide no matter which path you choose. However, even if you select the two-step approach, we strongly encourage you to read both sections of this book prior to sitting for any of the exams. Our experience has shown that topics that are confusing in one section will often become clear in the other. Furthermore, familiarity with the entire scope of material can often make the answer to a specific question more recognizable. The exam names are as follows:

- Introduction to Cisco Networking Technologies (640-821). If you elect the two-step approach, this will be the first exam you should take. It covers local area networking, wide area networking, and relevant Cisco equipment. The material is introductory level.
- Interconnecting Cisco Networking Devices (640-811). This is the second exam of the two-step approach. It assumes you are familiar with LAN/WAN technologies and moves directly into configuring and monitoring Cisco routers and switches.
- Cisco Certified Network Associate (640-801). This exam essentially combines exam 640-811 and exam 640-821. If you are recertifying or have had experience configuring Cisco equipment, this is probably the exam you want to take.

As long as we are making recommendations, here is one more. Monitor the Cisco Web site as you prepare for the CCNA exams. Things change, and at Cisco they change quickly. We made every effort to make this book the most up-to-date study guide available. However, without a doubt, something will change, and it may affect the test, so be sure to monitor the Web site, which is located at `http://www.cisco.com`.

# The Exam Situation

Exam taking is not something that most people anticipate eagerly, no matter how well prepared they are. In fact, if you really have trouble dealing with stress related to exams and tests, there are complete courses you could enroll in to help you better deal with it. For those of you who have already taken certification exams, you will not find anything substantially different about taking the CCNA exams.

Regardless of the number of exams you have completed, an understanding of how to deal with the exam (how much time to spend on questions, the environment you will be in, and so on) and the exam software that is provided will help you to concentrate on the task at hand, which of course is passing the exam. Also, experience has shown that mastering a few basic exam-taking skills should help you to recognize some of the tricks and gotchas you are bound to find in some of the exam questions.

Your first task is to find out where and when the exam is given and sign up for it. This is a lot easier than it sounds. There are two organizations providing Cisco certification testing:

- Vue Testing Service
  `www.vue.com`
  (877) 551-7587

- Thompson Prometric
  `www.prometric.com`
  (800) 776-4276

You can hop on their Web sites or call them directly. Either way, you will find a nearby testing facility and a time you can take the test. You will need to provide a credit card number because neither organization will test without payment up front. The cost of each exam at time of publication is $145 U.S. dollars and is subject to change. Now, the answer to your next three questions is "no." No, you will not get a refund if you do not show up. No, you will not get a refund if you are late (they will not let you take the test if you are late). Lastly, no, you will not get a refund if you do not pass the test, nor will you get a discount on the retest.

Okay, sounds kind of harsh, doesn't it? Well, it is only harsh if you are late or unprepared. Enough said?

When you arrive at the exam-testing center, you must sign in with an exam coordinator and show two forms of identification, one of which must be a photo ID. Please do not forget the photo ID. After you have signed in and your time slot arrives, you will be asked to deposit any books, bags, or other items you brought with you. Then, you will be escorted into a closed and hopefully quiet room. Typically, the room will be furnished with one to half a dozen computers, and each workstation will be separated from the others by dividers designed to keep you from seeing what is happening on someone else's computer.

Before the exam, be sure to make proper use of as much of the material that appears on the Cram Sheet (inside the front cover of this book) as you can. You will be supplied with a pen or pencil and a blank sheet of paper, or, in some cases, an erasable plastic sheet and an erasable felt-tip pen. Those are the only things you are allowed to take with you into the test room. However, you are allowed to write any information you want on both sides of this sheet once you enter the test room. Therefore, you might want to quickly write down any facts or figures you might forget, such as IP address ranges or configuration commands. When you are finished with the examination, any materials that you had in the room will stay in the room for exam confidentiality.

Most test rooms feature a wall with a large window or a security camera. This permits the exam coordinator standing behind it to monitor the room, to prevent exam takers from talking to one another, and to observe anything out of the ordinary that might happen. The exam coordinator will have preloaded the appropriate Cisco certification exam and you will be permitted to start as soon as you are seated in front of the computer and ready to begin. The timer on the exam does not start until you are ready to start, so do not rush anything.

All Cisco certification exams allow a certain maximum amount of time in which to complete the work (this time is indicated on the exam by an on-screen counter/clock, so you can check the time remaining whenever you like). The number of questions and amount of time allotted for each exam will vary.

- Exam 640-821 will have 55–65 randomly selected questions and you may take up to 90 minutes to complete the exam.
- Exam 640-811 consists of approximately 55–65 randomly selected questions and you may take up to 60 minutes to complete the exam.
- Exam 640-801 will have 55–65 randomly selected questions and allow 90 minutes for completion.

All Cisco certification exams are computer-generated and use a multiple-choice, multiple-answer question format. From time to time, you may be prompted to enter actual configuration commands as if you were at the command-line interface. It is important not to abbreviate the commands in any way when this type of question is posed; the simulator is usually looking for one correct answer, that being the full command. Although this may sound quite simple, the questions are constructed not only to check your mastery of basic facts and figures about Cisco router configuration, but also to require you to evaluate one or more sets of circumstances or requirements. Often, you will be asked to give more than one answer to a question. Likewise, you might be asked to select the best or most effective solution to a problem from a range of choices, all of which are technically correct. Taking the exam is quite an adventure, and it involves real thinking. This book will show you what to expect and how to deal with the potential problems and lead you on your way to being Cisco certified.

# Exam Layout and Design

Some exam questions require you to select a single answer, whereas others ask you to select multiple correct answers. The following multiple-choice question requires you to select a single correct answer. Following the question is a brief summary of each potential answer and why it is either right or wrong.

## Question 1

What is the key piece of information on which routing decisions are based?

❍ A. Source Network layer address

❍ B. Destination Network layer address

❍ C. Source MAC address

❍ D. Destination MAC address

Answer B is correct. The destination Network layer, or layer 3, address is the protocol-specific address to which this piece of data is to be delivered. The source Network layer address is the originating host and plays no role in getting the information to the destination; therefore, answer A is incorrect. The source and destination MAC addresses are necessary for getting the data to the router or to the next hop address, but they are not used in pathing decisions; therefore, answers C and D are incorrect.

This sample question format corresponds closely to the Cisco certification exam format—the only difference on the exam is that answer keys do not follow questions; too bad. To select an answer, position the cursor over the radio button next to the answer, and then click the mouse button to select the answer.

Now let us examine a question that requires choosing multiple answers. This type of question provides check boxes rather than radio buttons for marking all appropriate selections.

## Question 2

Which of the following services exist at the Application layer of the TCP/IP model? [Choose the three best answers]

❑ A. SMTP

❑ B. FTP

❑ C. ICMP

❑ D. ARP

❑ E. TFTP

Answers A, B, and E are correct. SMTP, FTP, and TFTP all exist at the Application layer of the TCP/IP model. Answer C is incorrect because ICMP exists at the Internet layer of the TCP/IP model. Answer D is incorrect because ARP exists at the Network Interface layer of the TCP/IP model.

For this type of question, more than one answer is required. These particular questions are scored as wrong unless all of the required selections are chosen. In other words, a partially correct answer does not result in partial credit when the test is scored. For Question 2, you have to select the corresponding check boxes next to items A, B, and E to obtain credit for a correct answer. These types of questions can be tricky and involves some process of elimination.

These two basic types of questions can appear in many forms; they constitute the foundation on which the entire Cisco certification exam questions rest. More complex questions include so-called *exhibits*, which are usually network scenarios, screen shots of output from the router, or diagrams. For some of these questions, you will be asked to make a selection by clicking on a check box or radio button on the screenshot itself. For others, you will be expected to use the information displayed therein to guide your answer to the question. Familiarity with the underlying utility is your key to choosing the correct answers.

Other questions involving exhibits use charts or network diagrams to help document a workplace scenario that you will be asked to troubleshoot or configure. Careful attention to such exhibits is the key to success. Be prepared to toggle frequently between the exhibit and the question as you work.

# Using Cisco's Exam Software Effectively

The bad news is that unlike some exams by Cisco and other companies, these particular exams do not allow you to mark questions for later review or skip questions. In fact, the test engine will not let you proceed if you have not selected an answer or if you have not chosen the correct number of answers.

With this in mind, *time management is essential during the test*. You cannot save difficult or lengthy questions to do at the end of the exam. For this reason, it will be helpful to monitor your progress by checking the clock periodically during the test. The test has approximately 55–65 questions and allows anywhere from 60 to 90 minutes. Because time is tight, we suggested previously that you quickly write down the quick facts, such as those provided on the cram sheet included in this book, before starting the exam. Believe me when I tell you that every minute will count and the exams are too expensive to fail because of a simple time management issue.

# Exam-Taking Basics

The most important advice about taking any exam is to *read each and every question carefully*. Some questions are deliberately ambiguous, some use double negatives, and others use terminology in incredibly precise ways. We may call them tricky while Cisco will say that they are problem solving questions; regardless, be aware.

Here are some suggestions for how to deal with the tendency to jump to an answer too quickly:

- Make sure you read every word in the question. If you find yourself jumping ahead impatiently, go back and start over, and be sure you have selected the answer you wanted to select, especially in the exhibit style questions.
- As you read, try to restate the question in your own terms. If you can do this, you should be able to pick the correct answers much more easily.
- Try to deal with each question by thinking through what you know about Cisco routers and their configuration—the characteristics, behaviors, facts, and figures involved. By reviewing what you know (and what you have written down on your information sheet), you will often recall or understand things sufficiently to determine the answer to the question.

We are confident that if you are comfortable with the content of this book, then you will be successful in your quest for certification.

# Question-Handling Strategies

Based on our experiences with certification exams, some interesting trends have stuck out over the years. For questions that require a single answer, two or three of the answers will usually be obviously incorrect, and two of the answers will be plausible—of course, only one can be correct. Unless the answer leaps out at you (if it does, reread the question to look for a trick; sometimes those are the ones you are most likely to get wrong), begin the process of answering by eliminating those answers that are most obviously wrong. To give you an idea of what we are saying here, consider a question that asks you about forwarding decisions of a switch. In all likelihood, two of the answers will be MAC address and Network address. The other answers will probably be really odd. Do not get too anxious and select the first one you see. Remember that a switch deals with MAC addresses.

Numerous questions assume that the default behavior of a particular utility is in effect. If you know the defaults and understand what they mean, this knowledge will help you cut through many questions rather quickly and again save valuable time for the less obvious questions.

As you work your way through the exam, another counter that Cisco thankfully provides will come in handy—the number of questions completed and questions outstanding. If you have fallen behind, use the last 5 minutes to guess your way through the remaining questions. Remember, guessing is potentially more valuable than not answering; blank answers are always wrong, but a guess may turn out to be right. If you do not have a clue about any of the remaining questions, pick answers at random. The important thing is to submit an exam for scoring that has an answer for every question. We say this as a tip, however we know that anyone who reads this book will never have to resort to that, right?

## Mastering the Inner Game

In the final analysis, knowledge breeds confidence, and confidence breeds success. If you study the materials in this book carefully and review all of the exam questions at the end of each chapter, you should become aware of those areas where additional learning and study are required.

Next, follow up by reading some or all of the materials recommended in the "Need to Know More?" section at the end of each chapter. The idea is to become familiar enough with the concepts and situations you find in the sample questions that you can reason your way through similar situations on a real exam. If you know the material, you have every right to be confident that you can pass the exam.

After you have worked your way through the book, take the practice exam at the end of the book. This will provide a reality check and help you to identify areas that you need to study further. Make sure that you follow up and review materials related to the questions you miss on the practice exam before scheduling a real exam. Take the real exam only when you have covered all of the ground and feel comfortable with the whole scope of the practice exam.

If you take the practice exam and do not score at least 70% correct, you need additional practice. Try to take as many practice exams as possible. If you have exhausted the questions at the end of this book, search the Web; you will be surprised at the number of questions available.

If you prepare seriously, you should do well. After all, if old guys like us can pass the tests, you should have no problem. Good luck and let us know how you did!

# Additional Resources

A good source of information about Cisco certification exams is Cisco itself. Because its products and technologies (and the exams that go with them) change frequently, the best place to go for exam-related information is online.

If you haven't already visited the Cisco certification site, do so right now at `http://www.cisco.com`.

## Coping with Change on the Web

Sooner or later, all the information we have shared with you about the Cisco Certified Professional pages and the other Web-based resources mentioned throughout the rest of this book will go stale or be replaced by newer information. In some cases, the URLs you find here might lead you to their replacements; in other cases, the URLs will go nowhere, leaving you with the dreaded "404 File not found" error message. When that happens, do not give up.

There's always a way to find what you want on the Web if you are willing to invest some time and energy. Most large or complex Web sites—and Cisco's qualifies on both counts—offer a search engine. As we have said earlier, as long as you can get to Cisco's site (**www.cisco.com**) you can use this tool to help you find what you need.

Finally, feel free to use general search tools—such as **www.google.com**, **www.altavista.com**, and/or **www.excite.com**—to search for related information.

# PART I

# Introduction to Cisco Technology (Exam 640-821)

# The Open Systems Interconnect Model (OSI)

## Terms you'll need to understand:

- ✓ Protocol Data Unit (PDU)
- ✓ Encapsulation
- ✓ De-encapsulation
- ✓ Media Access Control address
- ✓ Network address
- ✓ Connection-oriented communication
- ✓ Connectionless communications
- ✓ Logical Link Control sub-layer (LLC)
- ✓ Media Access Control sub-layer (MAC)
- ✓ The seven OSI layers

## Techniques you'll need to master:

- ✓ Understand the rationale behind the development of the OSI model
- ✓ Know the differences between connection-oriented and connectionless communications
- ✓ Learn the functions of each layer and sub-layer in the OSI model
- ✓ Understand how the OSI model passes between network nodes
- ✓ Describe the five steps of encapsulation and de-encapsulation

The *International Organization for Standardization (ISO)* developed the *Open Systems Interconnection (OSI)* reference model in 1984 for a host of reasons, including

- Increased interoperability between vendors
- Reduction of complex network operation to more easily understood pieces
- Simplification of future enhancements by keeping changes in one layer from affecting other layers
- Providing a method or model to understand network and internetwork communications

The good folks at Cisco can barely get out three sentences without referencing the OSI model. They use it to define their products, troubleshoot communications problems, and describe network operation, to name just a few. If you already know the OSI model, feel free to skim this chapter, but do not skip it. This is one of the areas where you definitely need to think "*the Cisco way.*"

As we go through the layers of the OSI model, we will italicize terms that Cisco uses in describing a particular layer. Pay attention to these italicized terms because you will run across them on the test and it is important you use them the way Cisco uses them. In most cases, we will give you a definition of the term the first time we use it, but in some cases we will defer the definition to a following section where it is better defined in context. (Yes, we will tell you when that occurs.)

# OSI Structure and Terms

The OSI reference model breaks network communication into seven distinct layers. These layers are then divided into upper layers and lower layers, and one layer is further divided into two sub-layers. To further confuse things, the layers are often referred to by their name, number, or a combination of both.

All of this can be a bit confusing, but if you keep the following points in mind, eventually it will become clearer:

- The OSI model is conceptual; it does not describe how things actually work.
- The OSI model is a universally accepted standard throughout the industry.
- The OSI model is a model based on theory, and it is an easier way to understand the functions of data transfer.

Before we get too far into the model, let's clarify something that took us a long time to appreciate: The OSI model is a reference model. It provides a structure for organizing functions of data communications, but does not necessarily address how those functions are physically performed. A physical device like a "brouter" performs both *bridging* and *routing*, which are functions found at different layers of the OSI model. (These devices and functions will be addressed in Chapter 3,"Hardware and the OSI Model.") Furthermore, the OSI model is not the only model used to describe data communications. *TCP/IP (Transmission Control Protocol/Internet Protocol)* is the most popular communication protocol in use today and it follows the Department of Defense (DoD) four-layer model. (We will discuss TCP/IP in Chapter 5, "TCP/IP.") So if you are thinking of the OSI model as *the* blueprint for developing communications equipment, *don't.* The OSI model provides a structure and organization for the functions of data communications; it may or may not accurately describe the functions of a piece of equipment or protocol. Also, not all companies describe the OSI model in the same way. In fact, you can even find the model described differently within the same company. Therefore, although you may already be familiar with the OSI model, there will probably be some subtle differences between your understanding of the model and the way Cisco defines the model. There is no need to elaborate on which definition will be marked correct on the test, so please do not skip this chapter.

The description of the OSI model in this chapter is consistent with what you will find on the test. Pay particular attention to any areas that conflict with your understanding of the model. If you are sure your understanding is correct, remember the two rules for passing a Cisco certification exam:

**Rule #1**—Cisco's interpretation is correct.

**Rule # 2**—If Cisco's interpretation is not correct, see rule number one.

# Layer One, the Physical Layer

The major function of this *Physical layer* is to place data on the network medium and ensure that the medium is capable of carrying that data. The type and gauge of wire, voltage levels, connectors, maximum distances, and other specifications for the medium are all found at this layer. The Physical layer is the lowest layer in the OSI model and as such is part of the OSI lower layers. (See Figure 2.1.)

Cisco originally defined Layer 4 as a transitional layer between the upper and lower layers of the OSI model. Later it was defined as part of the lower layers, as described in many current texts. However, Cisco is moving away from making a distinction between upper and lower layers, and this may well be reflected in the current exam. Therefore, if you see a question on the exam asking where Layer 4 resides, the safest answer would be the lower layers. After all, the test you will be taking has been extensively revised, so it should not define Layer 4 as transitional, and if the test reflects Cisco's move away from making a distinction between upper layer and lower layer groupings you will not get a question like this at all.

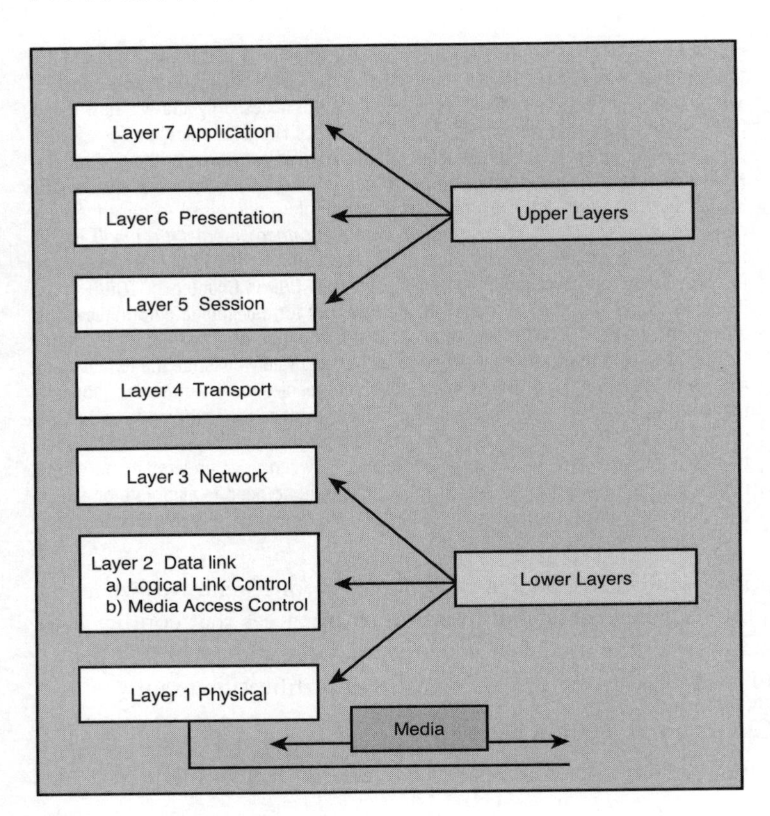


**Figure 2.1** The seven layers of the OSI model.

Figure 2.1 shows the seven layers of the OSI model as you will see it on the test. The Application layer or Layer 7 (the layer names and numbers are used interchangeably) is always at the top with the other layers listed in descending order. This figure also breaks the OSI model into *upper layers* and *lower layers*.

# Layer 2, the Data Link Layer

The *Data Link layer* or *Layer 2* is responsible for low-level error-free communication between two network devices or nodes. The Data Link layer is a part of the *lower layers* and the only layer that is broken into *sub-layers*. Sub-layers are always referred to by their name or initials and do not have a number.

The *Media Access Control (MAC)* sub-layer is the lower of these two sub-layers, and is extremely important because it defines the addressing used by the nodes of all networks. Every device or node attached to a network is required to have a unique *MAC address*. Fortunately each device also requires a *Network Interface Card (NIC)* to physically attach to a network and this is where the MAC address resides. The address is actually burned into a chip on the NIC by the manufacturer, which brings up an interesting question: How do the numerous manufacturers of NICs know that the MAC address they are using is unique? The MAC sub-layer specifies a way to ensure uniqueness. MAC addresses are 48 bits long and usually written as three groups of hexadecimal digits, like this:

```
081F.E453.5547
```

The first 24 bits (6 digits) are a unique vendor code assigned to the manufacturer by the IEEE. The last 24 bits (6 digits) are assigned by the manufacturer as a serial number. So long as everybody plays by the rules, any complete MAC address will be unique.

The *Logical Link Control (LLC)* sub-layer rests on top of the MAC sub-layer and provides the functionality required for *connectionless* and *connection-oriented* communication. LLC is the layer where protocol types are identified and where they can be encapsulated.

Connection-oriented communication is much like a telephone circuit, which is set up at the beginning of a conversation, maintained throughout the conversation, and then released at the end of the conversation. Connectionless communication is done on a frame-by-frame basis. Because each frame is autonomous, no link is established or maintained. Connectionless communication is faster than connection-oriented, but not quite as reliable. Each provides a way for upper-layer protocols to share transmission media, which is the main function of the LLC layer.

## Layer 3, the Network Layer

*Path determination* and *switching packets* between networks are the primary functions performed at Layer 3, which is also considered a lower layer. However, before these functions can be performed, a structure of network addressing must be established. Layer 2 already provides MAC addresses for every node on a network, so why do we need another addressing function at Layer 3? The reason is that MAC addressing uses a flat structure and is limited as to the number of addresses available. If we tried to use MAC addresses for communication across all networks, we would quickly run out of unique addresses or the addresses themselves would have to be so large as to be unusable. A higher level of addressing structure is clearly needed and that is provided by a Layer 3 *routable protocol.* There are several routable protocols available, including Internet Protocol (the IP portion of TCP/IP), Novell's Internet Packet Exchange (IPX), and AppleTalk from Apple

Computers. Each will provide a network addressing scheme and use packets that have a field for network addresses.

Do not confuse *routable protocols* with *routing protocols*, which also operate at Layer 3. Routable protocols such as IP, IPX, and AppleTalk provide a network addressing format and a packet structure that includes a field for the network address in addition to user data. Routing protocols are used by routers to exchange administrative information. Routing protocols do not include user data. *Routing Information Protocol (RIP)* and *Open Shortest Path First (OSPF)* are examples of some of the routing protocols we will discuss in Chapter 7, "Cisco Layer 3 Routing."

# Layer 4, the Transport Layer

The Transport layer is part of the *lower layers* of the OSI model. Establishing end-to-end connection-oriented communications, dividing upper layer communications into autonomous segments, and ensuring reliable data flow are all services provided by the Transport layer.

# Layer 5, the Session Layer

The Session layer establishes, manages, and terminates communications by coordinating service requests and responses between two or more stations. Sun's *Network File System (NFS)* and IBM's *Structured Query Language (SQL)* are representative of protocols used at the Session layer.

The *upper layers*—including *Session, Presentation,* and *Application*—provide standardization for applications to communicate. The functions of getting the data from one station to another are handled by the *lower layers.*

# Layer 6, the Presentation Layer

The Presentation layer ensures that information delivered to the Application layer is readable and in the proper format. This includes the functions of data encryption/decryption, data compression/decompression, and data representation. Examples of data formats used at the Presentation layer include ASCII, EBCDIC, MIDI, MPEG, JPEG, and GIF to name a few.

# Layer 7, the Application Layer

The Application layer is at the top of the OSI stack and closest to user applications. User applications providing communication functionality are considered part of the Application layer. A word processing application by itself would not be part of the Application layer. However, if the word processor provided email capabilities, it would definitely be included in Layer 7.

Be prepared to explain why the OSI model was developed, recognize the layers by number and name, and lastly be able to list the major functions or services provided at each layer. Remember that you are expected to answer questions "the Cisco way," so use terms as presented here, which in all likelihood may be slightly different than the way you learned the model.

# The OSI Model in Operation

There are four general rules that control the operation of the OSI model:

1. Data created at one layer must move down all layers below it before it can be transmitted to a receiving station. If that data was created at the Application layer, then it would move down through the six layers below it prior to transmission. If the data was created in the form of a network address at Layer 3, then it would move down through Layers 2 and 1 prior to transmission.
2. When data arrives at the receiving station, it must move up to the layer (peer layer) where it was created at the sending station. If the sending station created the data at the Application layer, then the data would have to move down through six layers of the sending station, be transmitted to the receiving station, and then move up through six layers at the receiving station until it arrived at the Application layer. If the data was generated at Layer 3, then it would only move up to the peer layer (Layer 3) at the receiving station.
3. A layer at the sending station can only communicate with its peer layer at the receiving station and vice versa. In other words, a packet of data that is assembled at the Network layer of the sending station can only be disassembled by the Network layer of the receiving station.
4. Each layer provides services to the layer directly above it in the OSI stack.

The OSI stack was presented previously in reverse order because it seems to be a little easier to understand that way. When you see the OSI stack in the real world, it will always be ordered from Layer 7 down to Layer 1. If you have trouble remembering the order, or the layers themselves, try saying; *"**A**ll **P**eople **S**eem **T**o **N**eed **D**ata **P**rocessing."* This should remind you of the layers and their order from Layer 7 (Application) to Layer 1 (Physical).

# Moving Through the OSI Model from the Application Layer

Let's follow a stream of data as it moves from the Application layer at a sending station to the Application layer at a receiving station. Remember that for a user application to be considered an application at Layer 7, it must require communications to another node or station. Email is an excellent example of a user application requiring communications, and as such is a Layer 7 application.

So, starting with an email message at Layer 7, the message is first passed to Layer 6 (Presentation). Layer 6 encrypts and/or compresses the message as required, and passes it to Layer 5 (Session).

Now the plot thickens. Starting with Layer 7, the message will move through *five steps of encapsulation.* Encapsulation is the process of putting something inside of something else, much like placing a letter in an envelope. Each layer from this point on will add information to the message. The additional information includes processing instructions for the same layer (Layer 5) at the receiving station. We say the message is encapsulated because the additional information is added as a *header* to the front of the message and often includes a *trailer* at the end of the message. So in our case, the now encrypted and/or compressed message is encapsulated at Layer 5 with information indicating that the message is part of a single session. When information is encapsulated, it becomes a *protocol data unit (PDU).* Each layer has its own PDU and the name of the PDU for Layer 5 is *"data"*.

Occasionally, the name of a PDU will be the only clue you have as to the correct answer for a question. You need to know protocol data units and the function of each layer of the OSI model backwards and forwards. Sounds simple right? Well, if the plot thickened in the previous paragraph, this is where it coagulates into an ugly goo! People in the industry (including the fine folks at Cisco) cannot agree on how to properly describe encapsulation in the OSI model. Older Cisco instructors, and a majority of industry documentation, describe five steps of encapsulation as we are doing here with the PDU for Layers 7 and 6 called an *"information unit."* We have seen test questions approach encapsulation both ways. Of course, current Cisco instructional material, at least the material we have seen, clarifies the matter by ignoring the issue completely. So, what should you do on the test? Well, everybody agrees that encapsulation occurs at Layers 5, 4, 3, 2, and 1. They also agree that the PDUs for these layers are respectively *"data"*, *"segment"*, *"packet"*, *"frame"*, and *"bits"* (we will discuss this in detail later). The only areas of uncertainty are whether Layers 7 and 6 are encapsulating levels, and should the protocol data units for these layers be called *"data"* or *"information unit"*. So here are our recommendations:

Read the question very carefully. It will probably provide a clue.

- There are two ways of looking at encapsulation. Think before answering any question dealing with encapsulation or PDUs.
- If there are equally correct responses for both views of encapsulation, GUESS. A guess may not be right, but no answer is definitely wrong.

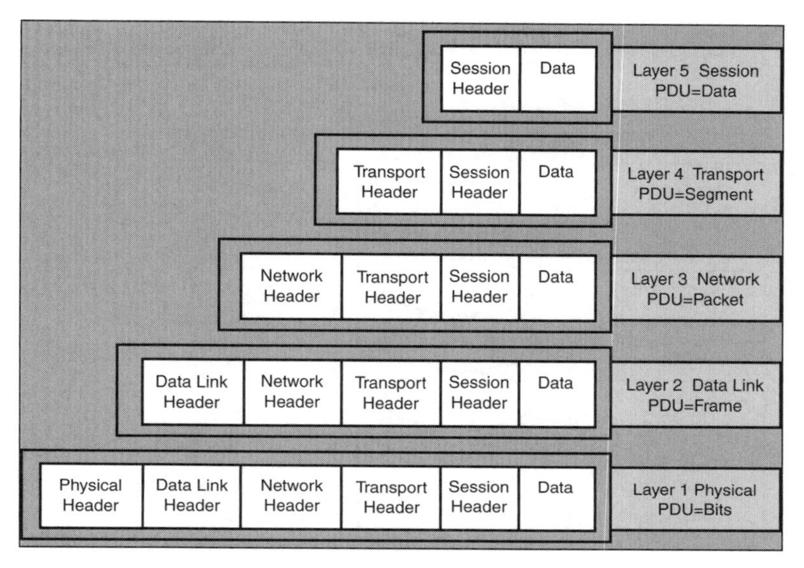


**Figure 2.2** Protocol data units and encapsulation.

Figure 2.2 shows five levels of encapsulation with associated protocol data units and OSI layers. There is still uncertainty as to whether Layers 6 and 7 should be viewed as encapsulating with a protocol data unit of "*data*" or as not encapsulating with a protocol data unit of "*information unit*".

When a layer formats information from the layer above and adds additional information, usually in the form of a header, the resulting assembly becomes a "Protocol Data Unit" (see Figure 2.2). In effect, the data from the higher layer (the letter) is encapsulated in data from the lower layer (the envelope). Layers 5 through 1 have PDUs with information specific to that layer. PDUs that are specific to a given layer are why only *peer layers* (layers at the same level) at the sending and receiving station can communicate. If all of this seems a bit murky, read on and it should become clearer.

The Transport layer takes the *Data PDU* from the Session layer, adds additional information as a header (encapsulating), and passes the resulting unit, now called a *Segment PDU*, to the Network layer. The Network layer in turn encapsulates the *Segment* into a *Packet PDU* with a logical source and destination address, and then passes the *Packet* to the Data Link layer, which encapsulates the *Packet* into a *Frame* with a physical source and destination address. The *Frame* is then passed to the Physical layer where it is turned into a *Bits PDU* and finally placed on the network medium.

If we have done everything right we will have used five steps of encapsulation, while passing through seven layers, and yes you will need to keep all of this straight for the test. Maybe Figure 2.3 will help.

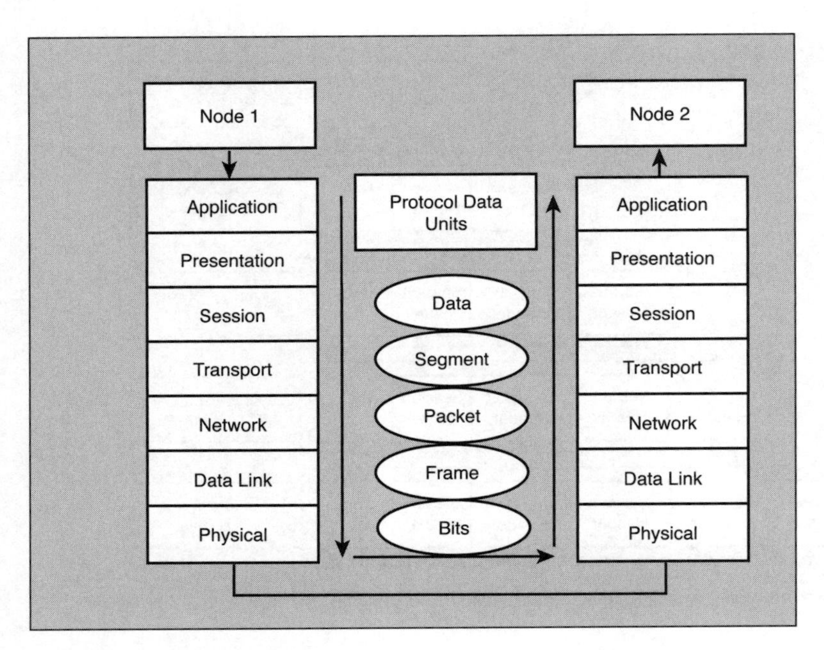


**Figure 2.3** Data flow between network stations.

Figure 2.3 shows the flow of data between two network stations. Five levels of encapsulation imply the PDUs for Layer 6 and Layer 7 would be an "information unit". Seven levels of encapsulation would use "Data" as the PDU for Layers 5, 6, and 7 and identify the upper two layers as encapsulating.

# Packet Handling at the Receiving Station (Reversing the Process)

Now that we have gone through seven layers and five steps of encapsulation, what do you think happens at the receiving station? Right, everything happens in reverse as the information flows up the OSI stack. The Physical layer of the receiving station senses voltage on the medium, converts it into *Bits*, and strips off any other signals placed there by the Physical layer of the sending station. The remaining *Frame* moves up to the Data Link layer where the physical source and destination address are removed and the resulting *Packet* is passed to the Network layer. There the logical source and destination address are removed and the remaining *Segment* is passed to the Session layer. Well, you get the idea. The process of moving up the OSI stack at the destination node is called *de-encapsulation* and when we finally get the information unit to the Application layer of the receiving station, we have successfully passed data from one node to another as described by the OSI model.

# Practice Exam Questions

## Question 1

Which layers of the OSI model are included in the lower layers?

- ❍ A. Application, Session, Presentation
- ❍ B. Physical, Transport, Data Link, Network
- ❍ C. Data link, Physical, Network
- ❍ D. Session, Data Link, Physical

Answer B is correct. Over time Cisco has defined upper and lower layers differently. At one time Layer 4 (Transport) was considered transitional and not a part of either the upper or lower groupings. Then it was included in the lower layers, and today Cisco is moving away from the distinction of upper and lower layers entirely. Despite the changing definitions, the safe answer is B. Answer A is incorrect because Application, Session, and Presentation have always been a part of the upper layers. D cannot be correct because again, Session is part of the upper layers. C is incorrect because it would require Layer 4 to be either transitional or part of the upper layers. Layer 4 has never been considered one of the upper layers, and as this exam has just been completely revised, the old definition of Layer 4 as transitional is highly unlikely.

## Question 2

Which layer uses the Segment as a Protocol Data Unit (PDU)?

- ❍ A. Layer 3, Network
- ❍ B. Layer 1, Physical
- ❍ C. Layer 2, Data Link
- ❍ D. Layer 4, Transport

Answer D is correct. The Transport layer uses the segment as its Protocol Data Unit (PDU). The Physical layer uses Bits as a PDU while the Data Link uses Frames and the Network layer uses Packets.

## Question 3

Select three reasons why the industry uses a layered model.

- ❑ A. A layered model allows developers to change the features of one layer without affecting the other layers.
- ❑ B. Interoperability is guaranteed because developers are required to comply with the standards established by the OSI model.
- ❑ C. Troubleshooting is easier if a layered model is used by all parties.
- ❑ D. A layered model reduces the complexity of networking to more manageable sub-layers.

Answers A, C, and D are correct. Answer B is incorrect because compliance with the OSI model is voluntary. A developer can certainly improve the ease of interoperability by adhering to the OSI model, but in no way is a developer required to use the model.

## Question 4

Which of the following are upper layers of the OSI model? (Check all correct answers.)

- ❑ A. Layer 4
- ❑ B. Network layer
- ❑ C. Session layer
- ❑ D. Presentation layer

Answers C and D are correct. The upper layers of the OSI model include Layer 7 (Application), Layer 6 (Presentation), and Layer 5 (Session). Answer A is incorrect because Layer 4 (Transport) sits between the upper layers and lower layers and is not considered a part of either. Answer B is incorrect because the Network layer (Layer 3) is part of the lower layers.

## Question 5

Which of the following are routable protocols? (Check all correct answers.)

- ❑ A. Ethernet
- ❑ B. AppleTalk
- ❑ C. RIP (Routing Information Protocol)
- ❑ D. IPX
- ❍ E. TCP/IP

Answers B, D, and E are correct. IPX from Novell, AppleTalk from Apple Computers, and TCP/IP all provide a place for a network address in their packets. RIP is used by routers to exchange path information and is considered a routing protocol, while Ethernet resides at Layer 2 and its frames have no place for a network address.

## Question 6

Which of the following could be a legitimate Media Access Control address?

❍ A. 192.168.254.3

❍ B. 3FA2.4756.F9A3

❍ C. A5514

❍ D. C1.3A.77.5B

Answer B is correct. A complete MAC address is composed of six octets or 12 hexadecimal characters. Answers C and D are incorrect because they do not have six octets or 48 bits. Answer A is a valid TCP/IP address but again, does not have six octets or 48 bits required by a MAC address.

## Question 7

Which of the following are valid Protocol Data Units? (Check all correct answers.)

❑ A. Packet

❑ B. Frame

❑ C. Bits

❑ D. Segment

All of the answers are correct. The PDU for Layer 3 (Network) is the *Packet*. *Frame* is the PDU for Layer 2, Data Link. The Physical layer (Layer 1) uses Bits for a PDU, and Layer 4 (Transport) uses the Segment as a PDU.

## Question 8

Where is encapsulation used in the OSI model?

❍ A. All seven layers of the receiving station

❍ B. At peer layers of both the sending station and receiving station

❍ C. Only at the Network layer

❍ D. At the sending station

Answer D is correct. Answers A and B are incorrect because *de-encapsulation* is used at the receiving station. Although encapsulation is used at the network layer of the sending station, it is also used at other layers of the sending station and not at all at the receiving station.

## Question 9

What is the serial number of a network interface card that has been given an address of 0365.FF32.A673?

- ❍ A. The serial number of a network interface card cannot be determined from its address.
- ❍ B. 0365
- ❍ C. FF32.A673
- ❍ D. 32A673

Answer D is correct. The last 24 bits (6 digits) of a network interface card's MAC address are a unique number (serial number) assigned by the manufacturer. The first 24 bits are a unique number assigned to the manufacturer as the manufacturer's identifier.

## Question 10

Which communications model best describes today's network operation?

- ❍ A. OSI
- ❍ B. TCP/IP
- ❍ C. OSPF
- ❍ D. DOD

Answer D is correct. The word "operation" is the key to this question. Answer A, OSI, is certainly the most commonly used model, but it is a theoretical model that rarely describes the actual operation of network or network equipment. TCP/IP is the most commonly used routable protocol, but it is not a communications model, which eliminates answer B. OSPF is a routing protocol, which eliminates answer C. Answer D, the Department of Defense Model (DoD), provided the specifications for TCP/IP. As such, it is the model which closest approximates how networks actually work today.

# Need to Know More?

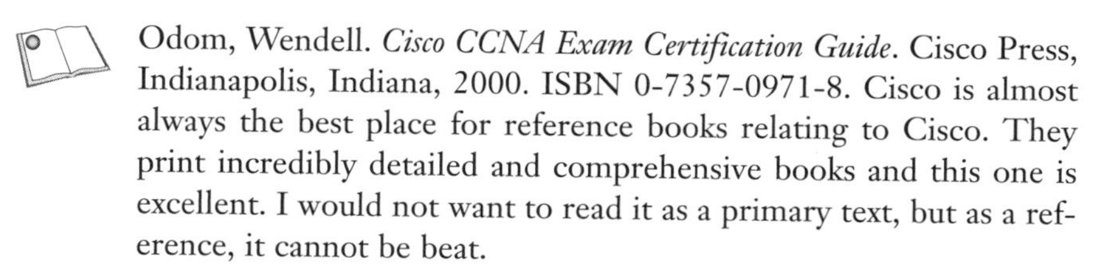

Odom, Wendell. *Cisco CCNA Exam Certification Guide*. Cisco Press, Indianapolis, Indiana, 2000. ISBN 0-7357-0971-8. Cisco is almost always the best place for reference books relating to Cisco. They print incredibly detailed and comprehensive books and this one is excellent. I would not want to read it as a primary text, but as a reference, it cannot be beat.

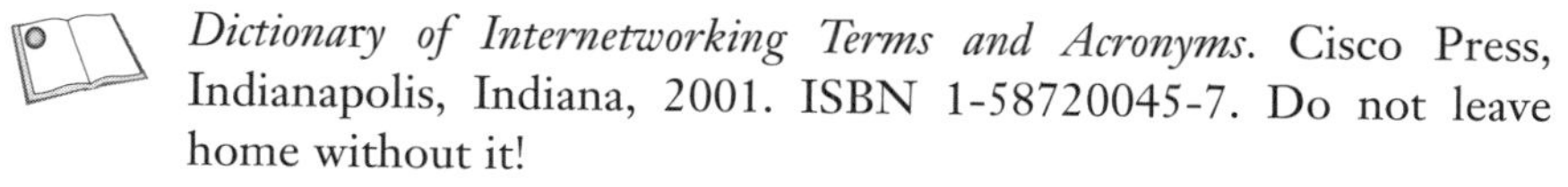

*Dictionary of Internetworking Terms and Acronyms*. Cisco Press, Indianapolis, Indiana, 2001. ISBN 1-58720045-7. Do not leave home without it!

Castille, Matthew J. *Network Sales and Services Handbook*. Cisco Press, Indianapolis, Indiana, 2003. ISBN 1-58705-090-0. This book is a lot like getting the time without the dissertation on how to make a watch. It is perfect for the CCNA exams.

# Hardware and the OSI Model

## Terms you'll need to understand

- ✓ Hub
- ✓ Bridge
- ✓ Layer 2 switch
- ✓ Router
- ✓ Layer 3 switch
- ✓ Repeater
- ✓ Star topology
- ✓ Bus topology
- ✓ Coaxial cable
- ✓ Twisted pair
- ✓ Collision domain
- ✓ Segment
- ✓ CSMA/CD

## Techniques you'll need to master:

- ✓ Ethernet operation
- ✓ Store and forward bridging
- ✓ Network segmentation
- ✓ Strengths and weaknesses of a star topology versus a bus topology
- ✓ Identify hardware typical of Layers 1 through 3 of the OSI model
- ✓ Understand the functions of and differences of bridges and Layer 2 switches
- ✓ Understand the operational differences and functions of Layer 1, 2, and 3 devices

When IBM released its first PC it started a veritable buying frenzy among corporations. What separated the IBM PC from others of the time was not so much technology as it was the IBM logo displayed prominently on the front of each PC. The IBM logos made the PC acceptable for deployment in a corporate environment, and deploy it they did! At the time, businesses were largely dependent upon timesharing vendors to run ad hoc analysis and simulations. The benefit of these real-time applications more than warranted the cost, which in many cases exceeded $40,000 to $50,000 per month. A PC, however, could often run the same application for a one-time cost of $6,000 to $12,000, making deployment a foregone conclusion.

### Why Are We Covering History?

You are probably asking yourself, why the history lesson? After all, Exam Crams are supposed to be "the facts, only the facts, and nothing but the facts" right? Well, there are really two reasons for this chapter. The first is that the CCNA exam covers far more material than can be memorized. Many of the questions will require you to determine the best answer based on your knowledge of how and why things work the way they do. Taking some time now to review the reasons behind the technology will not only pay big dividends at test time, but it will also provide a contextual framework for discussing some pretty complex equipment in the chapters to come. The second reason for the history lesson is that it provides a way to remember the low-level properties affecting the design and operation of today's equipment. The alternative is just listing electrical properties, physical design limitations, and the physics behind network operation, which can be drier than Oklahoma dirt. So put your feet up, relax, and let's go back to the time of short sleeve white shirts and pocket protectors.

"Give a man a fish and he will surely want a steak" is a parable that holds true for corporations as well as individuals, and it wasn't long before organizations were demanding even more savings from PC installations. It didn't take a rocket scientist to realize the major cost of PC deployment was in the peripherals, not the PCs. A letter-quality printer could cost as much as a PC and a really big hard drive, say 5MB, could exceed the cost of a PC. With the exception of running back and forth with 5 1/2-inch diskettes (sneaker-net) those peripherals were un-shareable and grossly underutilized. Ahh, if only peripherals could be shared, think of the savings!

## Early Bus Networks (10BASE-5 and 10BASE-2)

About this time a consortium of manufacturers working at Xerox's PARC (Pacific Area Research Center) released a really strange device called "Ethernet" that would do exactly what was needed—namely share PC resources. Ethernet used signaling that was well into the radio frequency spectrum and utilized a long coaxial cable (up to 500 meters) as a medium to connect PCs and peripherals. A coaxial cable consists of a single copper center conductor, covered by a dielectric material (insulator), which in turn is covered by a braid of copper wire, all of which is covered by a polyvinyl chloride (PVC) or Teflon jacket. (See Figure 3.1.)

**Figure 3.1** Coaxial Cable.

It is easy to see why installers preferred 10BASE-2 cable (right) over 10BASE-5 cable (left).

This type of cable is relatively immune to radio frequency interference from the outside, and also does a good job of containing radio frequency signals on the inside. Without these two properties, the cable would actually become a huge antenna, with all kinds of nasty consequences.

However, there is a downside to this type of cable, and all other cables, including fiber optics. The downside is that an impedance mismatch will reflect a signal. An impedance mismatch occurs where the properties of the cable change. Joining a cable to another with different properties will create an impedance mismatch. Nicking a cable will also create a mismatch, or we can go for the biggest mismatch of all and just whack the thing in half. Of course, all cables must end one way or another, so to avoid the resulting impedance mismatch, both ends of the coaxial cable were terminated with resistors (terminators). These terminators would dissipate the electrical energy rather than reflect it (see Figure 3.2). This assembly in its entirety is called a *backbone* or *bus topology*.

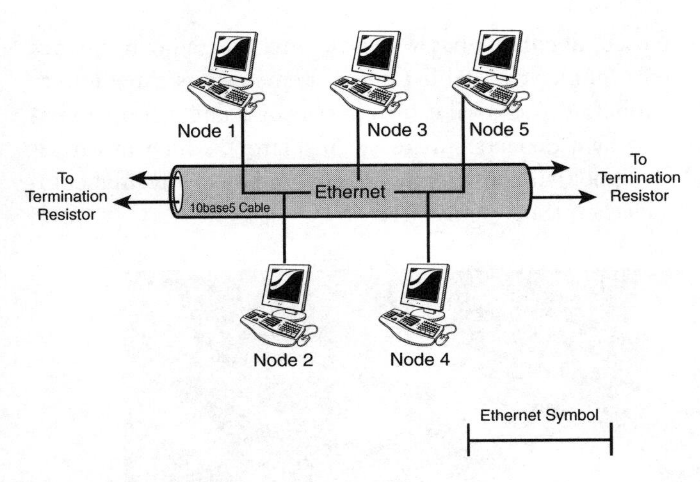


**Figure 3.2** Bus topology.

A bus topology provides a single transmission cable called a *bus*. Network nodes connecting to the bus share its transmission capacity. When coaxial cable is used for the bus, a terminator (resistor) must be installed at each end to eliminate reflections. Notice how the Ethernet symbol in the lower right resembles the bus design.

---

The resulting reflections from a cut or nicked coaxial cable or fiber-optic cable can bring an entire Ethernet system down. In fact, the nick or cut is located by launching a signal down the cable and then timing the reflection. The device used for this is called a *Time Domain Reflectometer (TDR)* for copper cable and an *Optical Time Domain Reflectometer* for fiber optics. Both will provide the distance from where the device is connected to the cut or nick by timing the reflected signal.

---

The backbone cable was a really good idea but without a way to attach stations or nodes it was useless, and this is where things got messy. Originally, nodes or stations were attached to the bus by way of a *tap*, which physically pierced the cable (see Figure 3.3).

These taps were quickly nicknamed *vampire taps* for obvious reasons, and the name has stayed with them ever since.

The tap included a transceiver (transmitter/receiver) for signaling, and was attached to the PC by an *attachment unit interface (AUI)* cable. The AUI cable was often called a *drop cable* and closely resembled today's serial cable. The PC itself was provided an interface card for attaching the drop cable and a piece of software called a *redirector* that routed resource requests either to the transceiver for transmission on the bus or to a locally attached resource, such as a printer or hard disk.

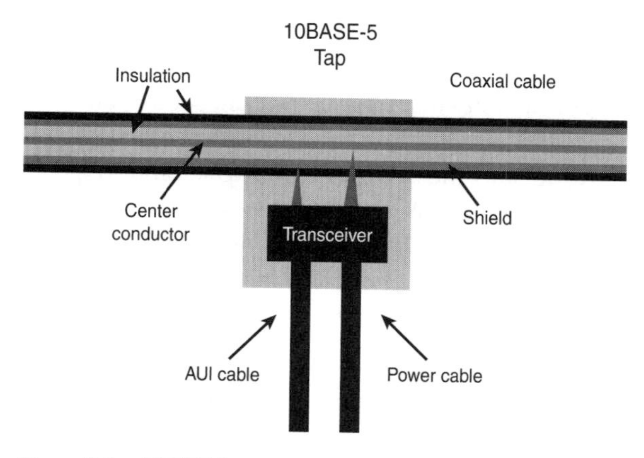


**Figure 3.3** 10BASE-5 taps.

We bet you are thinking that if a nick in the cable causes an impedance mismatch and reflections, the pins of the vampire tap piercing the cable would also cause reflections. Absolutely! That is why cable manufacturers marked Ethernet cable with a ring every 2.5 meters. The natural resistance of the cable could dampen the reflections from the pins, but it took 2.5 meters of cable to provide adequate resistance. So each tap had to be at least 2.5 meters for neighboring taps. That is why the cable was marked every 2.5 meters. If you always placed your taps on the marks, reflection problems would be eliminated.

The layout of a single transmission medium, like a coaxial cable, providing connectivity to a number of stations or nodes is referred to as a *bus topology* (actually, the proper name for the backbone is *bus* but in practice the terms are used interchangeably). Although multiple stations *(Multiple Access)* were connected to the bus, only one signal could traverse the bus at any one time (*Baseband*).

Multiple signals were eliminated because each of the network interfaces had a circuit that sensed voltage on the bus (*Carrier Sense*). If a voltage or carrier was present, the interface would delay transmission until the voltage again dropped to zero. So, a situation where two or more signals ended up on the bus at the same time would be highly unlikely.

In actual operation, having multiple signals on the bus can and does occur. Two or more interfaces, sensing zero voltage, could, in fact, transmit at the same time causing a *collision* on the bus. In fact, the stations did not necessarily have to transmit at exactly the same time.

A signal takes time to move from one end of the bus to the other, so it is quite possible a station on one end would transmit, not knowing there was already a signal on the other end of the bus. Two or more signals on the bus would create an over-voltage condition, which (you guessed it) would be sensed (*Collision Detection*) by the same circuit that was monitoring the voltage in the first place. When this occurred, the network interface would send a jam signal to busy out the entire bus, wait for a random time period of no carrier or voltage on the bus, and then retransmit the original signal. The random period of time was to prevent a second collision when the two or more network interfaces that originally caused the collision retransmit. Now you know why all Ethernets are categorized as *Carrier Sense, Multiple Access, Collision Detection (CSMA/CD)* networks.

## Pushing Distance Limitations (Repeaters)

The network we described previously was standardized as a 10BASE-5 (10Mbps, baseband, 500 meters) network and theoretically, if you stayed within the standards, everything would work fine. However, it was a lot cheaper to extend the bus a little over the 500 meter limit than to install a whole new bus, and that is what many people did. The problem was that as a signal travels down a medium, it loses a bit of its strength (attenuates) for every meter it travels. All standards tend to be conservative so in most cases this did not create a major problem. As people pushed the distance more and more, or used lower quality materials, attenuation began to cause problems. So it was not long before a nifty device called a *repeater* was developed to address signal attenuation.

A repeater is a Layer 1 (Physical layer) device installed between two segments of a bus (the bus is actually cut and then reconnected through the repeater). A repeater does not care about addresses, frames, packets, or any of the upper-layer protocols we have discussed. A repeater simply senses a voltage or signal on one side, rebuilds and retimes the signal, and then sends it out the other side (repeats). Do not make the assumption, however, that repeaters eliminate distance restrictions. Like railroads, all networks operate on a foundation of timing. It takes time for a signal to move down a cable and it takes even more time for a repeater to rebuild, retime, and retransmit a signal. So long as we stay within the established timing standards for our type of network, everything is fine. If we exceed those standards, things get ugly fast (see Figure 3.4).

More than one question will require knowing the difference between *segment* and *network*. Segments are part of the same network and are formed as the result of using a Layer 1 device such as a repeater or a Layer 2 device such as a bridge. A network is a single entity that can include several segments, but as a whole can be identified by a single Layer 3 address (see Figure 3.4).

# Pushing Station Limitations (Bridges)

So now we have a flexible network that can be easily expanded and provides sharing of expensive resources. The requirements have been met and everybody is happy. Well, not quite. The economies generated by shared resources provided a very real and tangible incentive for adding more stations to the network, and that is exactly what companies did. After all, an Ethernet segment could have as many as 1,024 nodes, which should be far more than anybody would ever need. The problem was that very few organizations made it to 1,024 nodes. Degradation in response time and throughput became a problem long before the magic number 1,024 was ever reached. Even more disturbing were traffic studies that revealed an incredibly high number of collisions with very little data transiting the network.

So what was happening? Well, it turns out that every node or station added to an Ethernet network increases the probability of a collision. When a collision occurs, the node interface sends out a jam signal that stops all transmission on the network. The interface then waits for a random period of silence before retransmitting the original frame of data. All of this takes time, and although the network is busy, very little data is moving across the network. At some point the network reaches its capacity of 10Mbps with the majority of that capacity used for collision recovery. Depending on the type of traffic, that ceiling is usually reached when approximately 4Mbps of data are moving across the network. Furthermore, if we attempt to push even more data through a saturated Ethernet, the total capacity available to data will decrease as the number of collisions increase. In short, Ethernet has the remarkable characteristic of providing excess capacity when you don't need it and reduced capacity when you do.

Well, no engineer can tolerate this kind of situation so it was not long before another nifty device called a *bridge* was developed. A bridge allows you to cut the Ethernet cable and then reattach it using the bridge. The bridge, like a repeater, has two network interfaces, with each attached to a segment of the cable. When a frame is launched on one segment (let's call it "A"), the bridge copies the entire frame into a buffer, reads the source address and destination address, and performs a *Cyclical Redundancy Check (CRC)* to ensure the frame is complete and accurate.

A repeater segments an Ethernet network but does not create separate collision domains. A bridge both segments a network and creates separate collision domains (see Figure 3.4).

A *Cyclical Redundancy Check* is a number attached to the end of a frame that was derived by running the digits of the frame through a specific computation. The bridge performs the same computation and if the resulting number is equal to the one stored in the CRC field, then the frame is considered accurate and complete.

Because the bridge reads the entire frame, it is considered a *Store and Forward* device. The bridge then writes the source address of the frame to a reference table for segment "A" and checks to see if the destination address has also been logged as a source address on segment "A". If the destination address is in fact listed in the table, the bridge then knows that both the source and destination addresses are on segment "A" and the frame is discarded. However, if the destination address is not already listed in the table, the bridge assumes the address must be located on segment "B" and the frame is passed on through the second interface to segment "B". Of course the same thing is happening at the interface for segment "B". Within a few seconds the bridge will have compiled tables for the stations on both segments of the network and frames will either be checked and passed or stopped and discarded based on destination address and completeness of the frame. The ability of bridges to automatically build and update network tables led many to call them *learning bridges.*

So, what did all of this really accomplish? First, traffic that is moving between stations on the same segment stayed on that segment and did not tie up the resources of the other segment. It was like gaining the capacity of two networks with all of the benefits of a single network. Secondly, because a CRC was performed on each frame needing transit across segments, only good frames were actually passed. This effectively limits collisions to a single segment which also frees the other segment to carry traffic. When a network is segmented with a bridge, each of the segments is considered a separate *collision domain* (see Figure 3.4). Prior to segmentation, the entire network was one collision domain. We can also add multiple bridges, and create multiple collision domains, which would greatly expand our capacity for additional stations.

The collision domain is another one of those concepts that may not be questioned directly, but will be at the core of several questions. Remember that a collision domain is a group of nodes or stations that is connected in such a way that if any two transmit at the same time, the resulting collision will affect the entire group. A repeater is a Layer 1 device that will rebuild, retime, and retransmit any voltage pattern down the wire. Although a repeater does break a network into segments, it does not create separate collision domains. A bridge is a Layer 2 device that also segments a network, but because it stops collisions from passing from one segment to the other, it does create separate collision domains. If you understand collision domains to the point where you can easily identify the problems of cut through switches discussed later in this chapter, then you are ready.

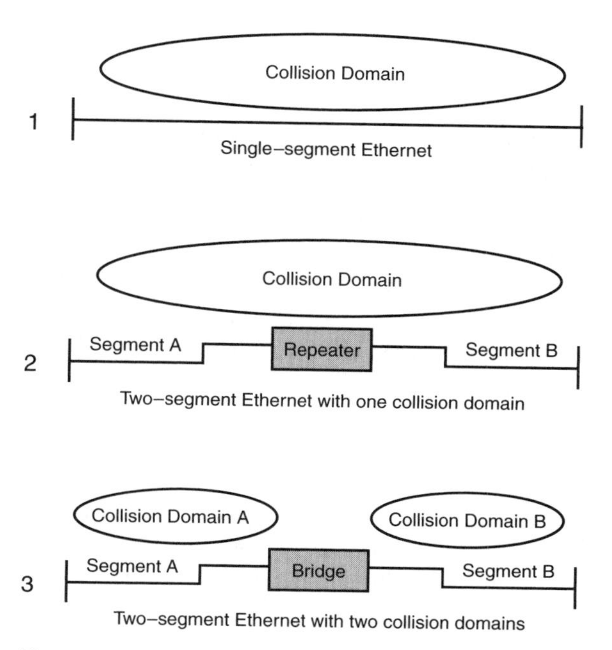


**Figure 3.4** A segment is always a subset of a network (1). Both a repeater and a bridge will divide a network into segments (2 & 3). However, only a device with bridging functionality will create separate collision domains as well as segments (3).

So, with all of these benefits, was there a downside to using bridges? Of course, it took time for a bridge to read and analyze each frame. Multiple bridges could easily exceed the timing restrictions of a network. When this happened, stations or entire segments at one end of the network would be completely unaware that stations at the other end of the network had begun transmitting. The resulting collisions storms could and did shut down entire networks. It was also possible to accidentally create a loop with multiple bridges that would cause frames to endlessly race around the loop until the network got so clogged it could no longer function. The *Spanning Tree Protocol (STP)* was eventually developed so that bridges could communicate with each other to determine which bridges would be active and which would be held in reserve. This not only eliminated loops but also allowed for redundancy in the network. Even with these drawbacks, the bridge solved many more problems than it created and greatly advanced the capabilities of networking.

## Layer 3 Expansion (Routers)

However (you knew this was coming didn't you?), there was one limitation to bridges that could not be overcome. That limitation had to do with scalability or size. I am sure you noticed how many times the term "frame" was used in the previous paragraphs.

You already know from Chapter 2 that in the OSI model, "frame" is the PDU for Layer 2, and Layer 2 is where MAC addresses are defined. So it would not be unreasonable to assume that bridge functions were based on the MAC address of the network interface attached to stations in the network. If you made that assumption you are absolutely correct!

You will likely get at least one "recall type" question relating directly to Protocol Data Units (PDUs). However, many questions will use a PDU name without calling attention to it, much like the way we used "frame" in the previous paragraphs. This may be your only clue as to how to answer a specific question. So be sure you can recognize PDU names, the layer of the OSI model where they operate, and the functions of that layer. If you have been a bit sloppy with the way you have applied PDU names in the past (all of us have), start disciplining yourself right now to only use the name of a PDU in exact context of its definition. That will go a long way toward making some of the test questions intuitively obvious.

Bridges are Layer 2 devices and the foundation of their operation is the MAC address. You will probably also recall from Chapter 2 that MAC addresses have a problem with scalability. Maintaining a unique address across many networks required going to a higher level (Layer 3) where a logical network address was defined.

The MAC address is physical because it is burned into a chip on the network interface. There is nothing virtual about it. What is on the chip is what you get and only what you get, period. The network address is "logical" in that it is derived from a routing protocol and assigned to a network. The network address is not burned into a chip or physically attached to a device in any way. It is a part of the software in use and can be readily changed. The concept is identical to logical drives on a PC. You may have only one physical drive, but that drive could, and usually is, configured as several logical drives.

The need for a different address scheme was not the only problem encountered when data was passed across or between different networks. There was almost always a change in media type, signaling requirements, and interface hardware. The whole issue of network overhead also became a major problem. Network stations needed a way to identify the addresses of other stations on the network. One popular network software package accomplished this by having each station broadcast its MAC address every three seconds. Now imagine you bridged the networks of two remote corporate divisions over a 56Kb leased line that costs $100,000 a month. With every station broadcasting its address across that link every three seconds, how much real data could get through? Some other device was clearly needed and that device was called a *router*.

Routers and bridges differ in that bridges use the MAC address (Layer 2) to perform their functions while routers use the network address (Layer 3). That, folks, "is the difference, the whole difference, and nothing but the difference"! Routers rely on a routing protocol for the definition and establishment of network addresses, and there is more than one protocol.

You are already familiar with at least one routable protocol named IP, which is a part of TCP/IP and stands for Internet Protocol. Others include Novell's IPX and Apple's AppleTalk. However, regardless of protocol, all routers fall into one of two types: *static* or *dynamic*. Most smaller, single site applications use static routers.

A static router, or fixed configuration router, is initially configured by the user and then it stays that way until the user goes back and manually changes the configuration. Configuring a router is done using a command-line interface or a Web-based interface developed by the manufacturer. Most static routers today have a Web-based interface with very limited options so it will be easier for the end user to configure. Simplicity is good in a static router because most of those end users have little if any computer training. The good news is that once a static router is configured it will merrily chug away forever, which is great for single location with a stable network environment. The bad news is that every time the environment changes, somebody has to physically change the operating parameters of the router. The really bad news is that if the environment changes and the organization has multiple sites, somebody, hopefully not you, has to reconfigure each router individually. This reconfiguration can usually be done through a utility such as telnet, but in many cases requires a personal visit. So if you get into a situation which uses static routers in multiple locations, keep your bags packed and be prepared to make house calls.

The limitations of static routers were a major problem for big decentralized companies with "big bucks" budgets, so it did not take long for a new type of router to arrive on the scene. A router that could automatically adjust to changes in the network environment, be configured and managed remotely, and provide even more filtering capability would be perfect, and that folks is exactly what a *dynamic router* or flexible configuration router does.

A major hurtle to development of dynamic routers was finding a way to make the router aware of changes in the network and then provide it with a method for determining the best route to a given address. Therefore, it should not be surprising that the advent of dynamic routers coincided with advent of *routing protocols*. A routing protocol provides a way for routers to exchange information from their *routing tables* and then determine the best route to a network given that information. Each protocol handles this function slightly differently, and each has its own set of benefits and drawbacks. *RIP (Routing Information Protocol)* and *IGRP (Interior Gateway Routing Protocol)* are examples of protocols that use a *distance vector algorithm* for determining the best route. A distance vector routing protocol requires each router to exchange information with its direct neighbors. In this way, information travels from router by router throughout the network. Some refer to this approach as "routing by rumor." *OSPF (Open Shortest Path First)* and *IS-IS (Intermediate System to Intermediate System)* are examples of protocols that use link state routing. Link state routing requires each router to exchange information with every other router in the network. We will be going into each of these approaches in Chapter 7. However, for now it is enough to know that:

- Routable protocols provide a framework for addressing networks and a structure (Packet) to carry user data across networks.
- Routing protocols provide a way for routers to exchange routing table data and a method for determining the best route to a given address.

Configuring a static router or fixed configuration router can be intimidating, and they are designed for simplicity. Configuration of a dynamic router or flexible configuration router can be downright otherworldly. Initial configuration of a dynamic router is usually done through a command-line interface. However, instead of having a dozen or so parameters like a static router, a dynamic router can easily have thousands. The scary part is that not only do you have to find where a parameter is set in a complex command-line interface, but you also have to know the ramifications that setting will have on all of the other parameters that interact with it. We are not trying to scare you here (well maybe a little). The real thing we want to get across is that setting up large dynamic routers is not a task to be taken lightly. Becoming a Cisco Certified Network Associate (CCNA) is your first step to joining the elite few who can really handle these complex systems.

We have arrived at a point where we have large bridged coaxial cable-based networks connected by dynamic routers that are talking to each other and keeping the whole system running like a top. In fact, the new coaxial cable standard called 10BASE-2 (see Figure 3.1) largely replaced the bulky 10BASE-5 systems. 10BASE-2 installations use a much thinner coaxial cable and replaced the dreaded vampire tap with a simple "T" connector (see

Figure 3.5). So now everybody should be ecstatic, right? The problems of installation were greatly reduced, networks could be segmented with bridges to allow more users, and routers provided long distance connectivity. What more could possibly be needed? The answer is something other than coax.

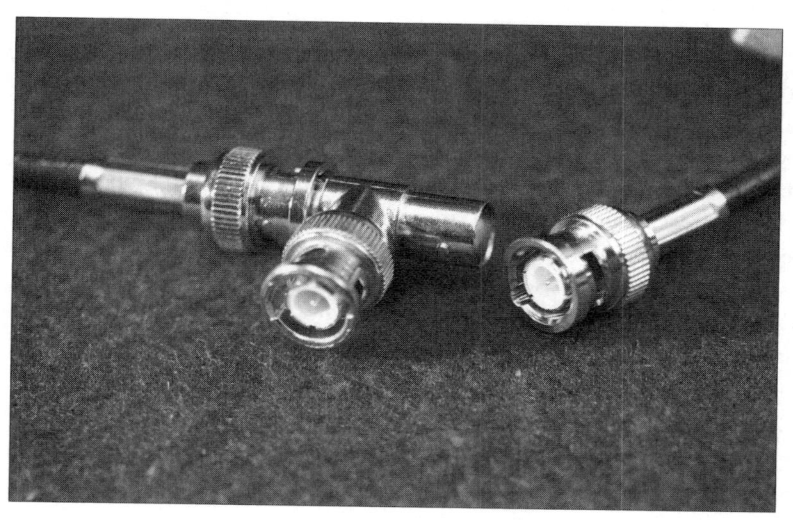

**Figure 3.5** 10BASE-2 Networking.

Figure 3.5 shows the "T" connector used to attach the bus to the station. The leg of the "T" (facing forward) attaches to the interface card in the station, while the top of the "T" provides a straight through connection for the cable.

# Development of 10BASE-T Wiring

Even though 10BASE-2 made coaxial networks a little easier to work with, the installations were still prone to catastrophic failures when the cable was nicked, expensive to install and maintain, and difficult to work with. However, what was the alternative? Well, a lot of people were asking why networking could not be more like telephones and utilize a simple pair of wires. Actually, there were some good reasons why networks could not use paired wires. Networks operated at frequencies that were well into the radio spectrum. At those frequencies a pair of wires would act like a giant antenna and radiate all over the place. The pair of wires would also receive the signals of other radio frequency devices such as fluorescent lights, monitors, and CPU units. All in all not a good thing, and the very reason coaxial cable was used in the first place.

It would be nice to use paired wire in networks, but it just wasn't going to happen. And it did not happen until a couple of engineering types figured out that if the wires were twisted the radiation would be cancelled out, and that sending two signals down the wires 180 degrees out of phase and then measuring the difference would make other sources of radio frequency noise irrelevant.

The world of networking changed overnight. The twisted-pair cable required by the new network was later standardized as Category 5 cable, and the whole configuration was standardized as 10BASE-T (10 megahertz, base band, twisted pair). Ethernet would remain a bus topology, but the coaxial cable that formed the bus was shrunk to about a foot long. The taps, which included repeaters, were attached to the bus at the factory, and each tap/repeater was terminated in a modular receptacle much like the RJ-45 jack used by the telephone company. The whole assembly was encased in a box with the receptacles mounted on the outside. Today we call that box a hub (see Figure 3.6) and its use created a topology called a *star wired bus.*

---

The new topology was called a star wired bus because the bus remained within the cabinetry of the hub. Of course, the coaxial cable was replaced by traces on a printed circuit board, but the functionality of the bus was still there. 10BASE-T cables radiated out from the hub to each station on the network, which is why it is called "star wired."

---

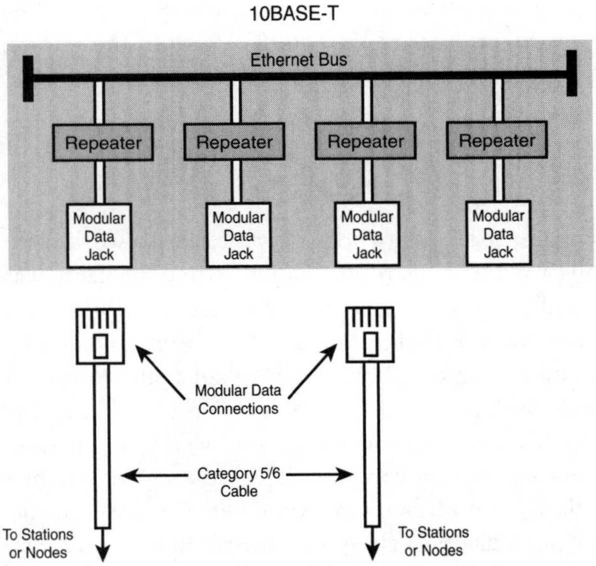

**Figure 3.6** A typical star wired bus topology.

The advent of the hub and 10BASE-T wiring eliminated most of the problems inherent in a coaxial cable based bus network. The hub cabinetry protected the physical bus, taps, and repeaters, eliminating damage from nicks, cuts, and leaky tap connections. The difficult job of tapping into the bus was performed and tested at the factory, which allowed field connections to be as simple as snapping a Category 5 connector into the jack on the hub. That plagued coaxial cable-based networks. Because each station had a dedicated cable connecting it to a repeater in the hub, individual cable runs could be up to 100 meters with cable faults like cuts isolated to a single station. The dedicated hub connection also isolated damage caused by cable faults to a single station. Lastly, when compared to coaxial cable, 10BASE-T cable was extremely easy and inexpensive to install.

# Enter the Switch

Today, Layer 1 repeaters and hubs and Layer 3 routers are used extensively in networking, but we do not hear much about Layer 2 bridges. The reason is that to a large extent bridges have been replaced. Remember that bridges read the entire frame, check it for accuracy, and then forward or drop it depending on the bridge's address tables. Also remember that this took time, and in highly populated networks a store and forward device like the bridge could actually become a bottleneck. So a couple of engineering types reasoned that to perform a bridging function it was only necessary to read the source and destination address from the beginning of the frame.

Based on this, a decision to drop or forward could be made and address tables could be populated. Well, the cost of high-speed memory and processors had dropped so much that rather than apply this approach to existing bridges and gain an incremental speed advantage, it was decided that the time was right to come out with a whole new class of device.

The new device read the source and destination address of the frame, populated its bridging tables, and either passed or dropped the frame based on this information. Sounds just like a bridge doesn't it? Well, here is where the plot thickens. Instead of connecting just two segments, the new device connected six or more. Forwarding a frame entailed building a virtual circuit between two segments and then once the frame was passed the circuit could be used to connect two other segments. Now if you had six segments you would only need to run three virtual circuits to connect all of the segments. Or, if you only had one virtual circuit, you could switch it between segments at three times LAN speed and accomplish the same thing, namely a *non-blocking switch*. (See why the high-speed processors and memory were needed?)

The term *non-blocking* means a device has the capacity to forward frames between all possible segments at the same time. In short, if there is a bottleneck in the network it won't be the switch. Each port connecting to a segment maintained its own bridging table and when forwarding to another segment, the frame was moved to what is often called the switching matrix. The switching matrix established a virtual circuit between the two segments for just enough time for the frame to transit the matrix to the destination segment. The device was called a *Layer 2 switch* and its meteoric rise in popularity was only exceeded by a plummet in popularity of the bridge.

But was there a downside to the capacity of the Layer 2 switch? At first the answer appeared to be no, but then it was noticed that when a switched network began to reach capacity, its operation became strangely erratic. It turned out the key to the erratic behavior was linked to the very thing that gave the Layer 2 switch its awesome capacity and speed.

The bridge read the entire frame and checked the CRC to ensure the frame was complete and accurate before passing it on. The switch, however, only read the source and destination address from the beginning of the frame. So only the first few bytes of the frame would need to survive a collision to be passed on to another segment. This did not become a problem until the segment approached saturation. As the number of collisions rose, the switch would begin passing a significant number of damaged frames. In essence, the switch was creating a different collision domain every time it set up a virtual circuit and those collision domains were changing so fast it was almost impossible to diagnose.

Most switches were put in environments that would never get close to saturation, and in these situations they performed beautifully. Unfortunately, the erratic performance usually occurred in large complex networks and it became enough of a problem to prompt a redesign of the switch.

The first generation of switches became known as *cut-through switches*. The second generation switch implemented a full store and forward operation identical to the original bridges and accordingly was called a *store and forward switch*. However, the store and forward technology came at the expense of speed and price. So you could have a fast and cheap switch that would work fine in some situations or a slow expensive switch that would work in all situations. Seems like a compromise was needed, doesn't it? The compromise, which was developed by Cisco, is called a *fragment-free switch*. A fragment-free switch reads the first 64 bytes of the frame. Statistically, there is over a 90% chance the remainder of the frame is intact if the first 64 bytes are. Cisco takes the best of all three approaches by offering switches that can be configured to operate in any of the three modes.

Everybody knows a switch is a Layer 2 device. A switch works with MAC addresses so the only thing it could be is a Layer 2 device. However, Cisco has a very popular line of products that apply the fast switching matrix of Layer 2 to the routing of packets at Layer 3. Do you know what Cisco calls those devices? You guessed it, "switches"!

Terms are always evolving at Cisco. The term "switch," in this case, is moving from the generic name of a device to the description of a technology. So be careful of the assumptions you bring with you to the test. Your assumptions are probably not wrong, but they may be very different from the way Cisco sees the world. Enough said?

# Token Passing Topologies

We have already covered a lot in this chapter, but we really can't move on without going over one last network technology. That technology is Token Ring, a la IBM. You will not see Token Ring questions on the CCNA test per se, but you will need to know about wide area token passing networks, and they are easier to understand if you know about their LAN counterparts.

The Token Ring network architecture has become closely identified with IBM and for good reason. Way back in 1972, IBM announced a Token Ring control method for LANs which was remarkably similar to one developed by a Mr. Willemjin. The IBM announcement sparked a host of license and patent disputes which resulted in Mr. Willemjin becoming a very rich man. This was an apt beginning for IBM's long and painful journey into local area networking.

At the time, IBM owned the global mainframe computing market with few able to compete. Others realized there was no way to take on IBM in the mainframe market, but the new interest in distributed computing held promise. Distributed computing utilized small computers tied together in a network and offered user groups a level of control not possible in mainframe computing. Although IBM now had the Token Ring Architecture free and clear sitting on a back shelf, it viewed the whole trend toward distributed computing as detrimental to continued expansion of the mainframe and as a result nothing happened for more than 10 years. Finally, as IBM watched companies like Digital, Network General, and Wang grow, they decided to act. Of course IBM was not about to legitimize the technologies these upstart companies were using, so something different was needed, and something that was really different had been sitting on a back shelf for over 10 years.

Token Ring was released as a whole new architecture, including special cables, hardware, and even different terms to describe its operation. The concept was sold to large IT departments and while the DP guys didn't especially like the idea, it did give them a way to offer additional services to the user communities and reclaim some of the budget and control they had lost to distributed processing.

Token ring, as the name implies, used a ring structure where each node was physically attached to its neighbors (see Figure 3.8). Data passes from one node to the next in a counterclockwise direction as it traverses the ring. Typically, IBM type one cable was used, which was not much smaller than the old 10BASE-5 cable. The cable contained heavy gauge twisted pairs of wires wrapped in one or more shields of high density braid and foil. The cable was terminated in a complex connector measuring about 2 inches square, which would allow cables to be joined together or attached to devices such as *Multi-Station Access Units (MSAU)*, which provided a central attachment point for the ring.

The operation of the ring began when the first station was attached or started. That station would send a query over to the ring to see if any other stations were active. If not, the station would assume the role of active monitor and release a token (see Figure 3.7).

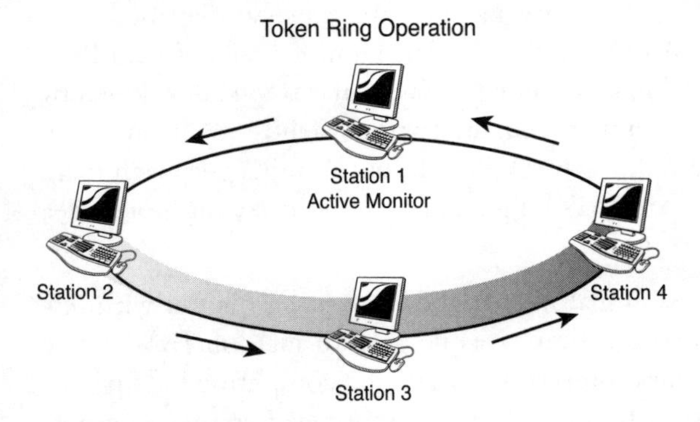


**Figure 3.7** Token Ring Operation.

Unlike a bus where each node attaches to one shared cable, Token Ring uses a dedicated cable between neighboring nodes. Data must flow from the upstream neighbor, through a dedicated cable to the next downstream node. That node repeats the frame and launches it on the cable attaching it to its next downstream node.

A token is like a data frame but only has a starting delimiter, access control field, and ending delimiter (see Figure 3.8). It is used to notify a node that it may now send data. If the node has data to send, it will change the ID bit in the token to indicate it is now a data frame, attach the data, and transmit the data frame to the next downstream neighbor (see Figures 3.7, 3.8, and 3.9). If there is no data to transmit, the token will be repeated and sent to the next downstream neighbor as is.

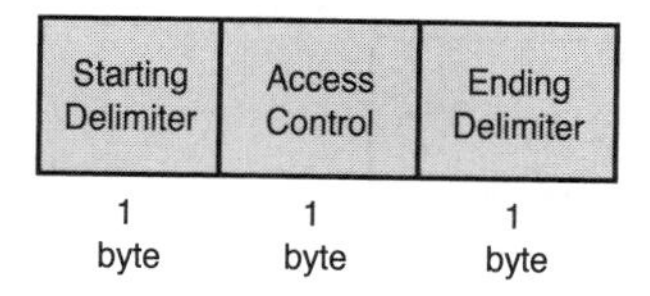


**Figure 3.8** The Token in Token Ring

If the frame is not addressed to the next downstream neighbor, that node retransmits it to the next downstream node. This process continues until the data frame arrives at the node it is addressed to. That node reads the data frame, changes the frame status field to indicate the frame has been received, and then retransmits the updated frame on to the sending node. At the sending node, the frame is compared to the frame that was sent originally, and if they are identical the node releases a token frame and the whole process starts over. This is the process followed by the standard 4 megabit Token Ring network. A variation of this process has the receiving station release a token after it has read, updated, and sent the original data frame. This variation is called "early token release" and it is used in 16 megabit Token Ring networks. No matter what variation is in use, there can only be one token on the ring at any one time. I think you can see why IBM liked this approach: no collisions, few if any retransmits, and control of cable quality.

So, what happens when a cable is severed? That should stop ring operation, shouldn't it? Well, yes, but even in this situation Token Ring offers some benefits over Ethernet. Each node monitors traffic from its *nearest active upstream neighbor (NAUN)*. There is always a Token frame or Data frame on the ring so there is always traffic. When traffic stops coming from a node's NAUN, that node goes into beacon mode, which will be heard and repeated by all of the downstream nodes. The presence of a beacon on a ring indicates the ring has stopped functioning and a serious problem exists. In addition, the address of the beaconing node indicates the problem is somewhere between it and its NAUN. So not only are serious problems reported, but their location is also identified. Neat eh?

Traffic that moves from one ring to another is handled somewhat differently than Ethernet. To begin with, each ring is a network in its own right, so routing and bridging get a bit mixed. This is one architecture that definitely stretches the OSI model. Notice the routing information field, which is a part of the data frame in Figure 3.9. When data is bridged in a Token Ring environment, a process called *source route bridging* is used. The initiating node sends several special frames to the receiving node, which echoes the frames back. The route of the frame that returns first is added to the routing information frame of the data frame and the frame is sent to the bridge.

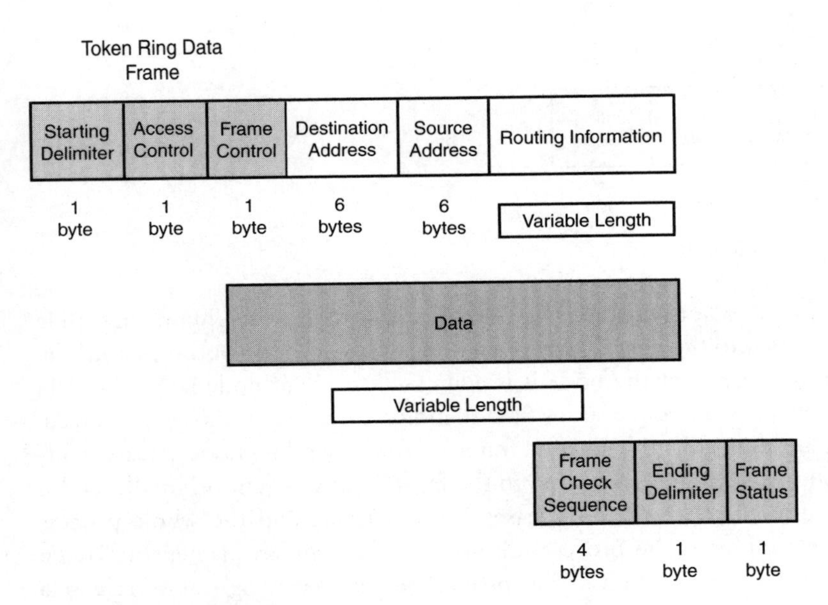


**Figure 3.9** The Token Ring Data frame.

Although Token Ring is a Layer 2 architecture, its frame has a large field for routing information. In this case, the field is used to store instructions for source route bridging.

The bridge does not have to check any tables or determine any routes because the routing instructions are included with the data frame in the routing information field; hence, source route bridging. Data frames can also be encapsulated in routable protocols and follow a more traditional way of moving between networks. This procedure would have to be adopted if the route passed across non-Token Ring networks.

This is as far as we are going to go in Token Ring. Introducing Token Ring earlier in the chapter would have really confused things; we mention it here because it will help build a foundation for things to come. On the test, assume you are dealing with Ethernet unless told otherwise. Speaking of tests, why don't you try the following questions and see how you do?

# Exam Prep Questions

## Question 1

Your company has upgraded all of its hubs to switches. One of the switches appears to be working overly hard, with its overall traffic indicator lit continuously, as are the port lights. Your boss is afraid there is a bottleneck and dispatches you with one of the company's $70,000 protocol analyzers to diagnose the problem. However, when you plug the analyzer into an open port, it reports extremely light and sporadic traffic. What, if anything, is the problem?

❍ A. Indicator lights on networking equipment are notoriously inaccurate. If the protocol analyzer reports light traffic then the switch is well below capacity and there is no problem.

❍ B. The switch probably has address filtering activated on the analyzer's port. Deactivating the filtering option will give the analyzer access to all traffic.

❍ C. Switches build virtual circuits between two ports. If the analyzer's port is not part of the current circuit, it will not see activity.

❍ D. There is no problem. Unlike a hub, activity lights on a switch should be on constantly.

Answer C is correct. Okay, this was a nasty way to start because we haven't even mentioned activity lights and protocol analyzers. Nevertheless, if you know how a switch works, it should not be hard to deduce the answer. Switches do create virtual circuits between two ports. If a port were not part of the circuit, it would not be aware of the activity. That makes answer C a likely candidate. Activity indicator lights are not accurate, but if every port's indicator is lit constantly, that switch has to be really working. Therefore, A is probably not correct. Filtering sounds good, but even without filtering, the analyzer would still only see activity broadcast or addressed to its port. That rules out B as a correct answer. Lastly, if every port activity indicator is constantly lit, it would be logical to assume there is activity. A switch only connects two ports at a time, so having all of the port activity lights continually on is probably not normal. Therefore D is questionable as a correct answer.

## Question 2

Which type of switch can create multiple temporary collision domains when segments approach saturation?

❍ A. Cut-through switches

❍ B. Non-blocking switches

❍ C. Switches running in fragment-free mode

❍ D. Store-and-forward switches

Answer A is correct. Early cut-through switches read the source and destination addresses and dropped or forwarded frames based on that information alone. As segments approached saturation and the number of collisions escalated, cut-through switches could and did pass the remains of collisions provided the source and destination address fields survived intact. When this occurred, both segments would essentially be in the same collision domain connected by the switch. Answer B is incorrect because non-blocking means the switch has the capacity to switch frames between all segments at the same time. Answer C could be correct because a fragment-free switch examines only the first 64 bytes of the frame. However, it has been shown that if the first 64 bytes of a frame are correct then there is greater than a 90% chance the remainder of the frame is also correct, so few if any damaged frames would be passed. Answer D is incorrect because a store-and-forward switch is the only type of switch that will stop all damaged frames by performing a cyclical redundancy check (CRC) prior to passing the frame on.

## Question 3

How did the 10BASE-T standard put an end to the cumbersome bus structure of early Ethernets?

❍ A. 10BASE-T eliminated the bus in favor of star wiring that was far less expensive and more reliable.

❍ B. Networks using the 10BASE-T standard moved the signaling frequency below the radio spectrum so common twisted-pair wire could be used.

❍ C. A network using the 10BASE-T standard was far more reliable than a bus network because severing a cable only brought down a segment of the network.

❍ D. A network using the 10BASE-T standard is a bus network.

Answer D is correct. Networks using the 10BASE-T standard did not require coaxial cable. The bus structure however remained as a part of the Hub. The correct way of describing an Ethernet using the 10BASE-T standard is a "star wired, bus network." Answer A is incorrect because the 10BASE-T standard did not eliminate the use of a bus. Answer B is incorrect because signaling remained in the radio spectrum despite the use of cabling meeting the 10BASE-T standard. Answer C is incorrect because severing a cable would only bring down the node or station using the station.

## Question 4

Your uncle has a problem with his 10BASE-2 Ethernet and he has asked for your help. He has several geographically dispersed offices in a shared tenant office building. There are only 10 stations connected to the network but 2 of the stations located in adjoining offices experience erratic network behavior when communicating with each other. With the exception of these 2 stations, the network performs well. You take a look at each of the problem stations and find that each station has the network cable attached to only one side of the "T" connector. The other side of the "T" connector has a 3-inch black plug attached. Knowing your uncle is short on cash, what would you recommend he buy to remedy the problem with the 2 adjoining stations?

❍ A. A patch cable to connect the stations in the adjoining offices and complete the network path.

❍ B. A 10BASE-2 repeater.

❍ C. A non-filtering bridge.

❍ D. A static or fixed configuration router.

Answer B is correct. Okay, this question really rambles but so will some of the questions on the exam. The key to the question is seeing the 10BASE-2 cable attached to only one side of each station's "T" connector. The plug attached to the other side of the "T" connector should be a giveaway. Although these stations are in adjoining offices, they are each at the end of the network cable. Even if you have never seen one, you could probably guess that the black plug is actually a terminating resistor, which confirms these stations as the ends of the network. To communicate, these stations must send data across the entire network. While we don't know the exact length of the cable, we do know it streams off to connect the other geographically diverse offices and then loops back almost to the starting point. That is probably a "pretty good distance" (technical term). As only the end stations are having problems, this is most likely an attenuation problem, which is a Layer 1 (Physical) issue. The most efficient way to deal with Layer 1 attenuation is with a Layer 1 repeater. Okay, there are a lot of assumptions here and not much in the way of cold hard facts, but that's the way it is in the real world and, of course, it did make you think. Answer A is incorrect because it would create a loop. Signals introduced to a loop would continue around the loop until dissipated by attenuation, which would effectively bring down the network. Answer C could be correct because bridges provide a Layer 1 repeater function, but they are really designed to provide Layer 2 capabilities, which would not be used. Besides, bridges are more expensive than repeaters and your uncle is strapped for cash. Answer D is incorrect because routers are even more expensive than bridges and they operate at Layer 3. Of course routers could be made to work, but you would need a pair of them and you would end up with two separate networks. Definitely a square peg in a round hole approach.

## Question 5

How does a transmitting station on an Ethernet recognize a collision when it takes place?

- ❍ A. A CRC is performed and if results do not match then a collision has occurred.
- ❍ B. The transmitting station cannot determine that a collision has taken place while it is transmitting. It must wait until the receiving interface recognizes the collision and sends an error report in the form of a jam signal.
- ❍ C. The interface does not monitor network errors. That is done at Layer 2 when the frame is checked for accuracy.
- ❍ D. A voltage comparator on the transmitting interface senses an over-voltage condition on the line.

Answer D is correct. This is an area where there are a lot of old wives' tales and any one of them will get you in trouble. Collision detection is a Layer 1 issue for Ethernet dealing with voltage levels on the line. A voltage comparator on the interface (it is really a $.22 chip) monitors the voltage of the line even when the interface is transmitting. So long as the voltage stays within a predetermined range, everything is okay. However, when two or more signals are on the line at the same time, the combined voltage exceeds this level. The comparator senses the over voltage and it initiates the recovery process. Answer A is incorrect because the Cyclical Redundancy Check is performed at Layer 2 and indicates a fault with the data, which may not have been caused by a collision. Answer B is incorrect because the voltage is monitored during transmission. Answer C is incorrect because the question is asking about a Layer 1 collision, not Layer 2 error detection.

# Question 6

What is the Protocol Data Unit (PDU) used at Layer 4?

❍ A. Frame

❍ B. Segment

❍ C. Packet

❍ D. Data

Answer B is correct. Layer 4 is the Transport layer and Segment is the name of its PDU. Answer A, Frame, is the PDU for Layer 2, Data Link. Answer C, Packet, is the PDU for Layer 3, Network. Answer D, Data, generally describes the PDUs for Layers 5 through 7.

# Question 7

A network administrator is charged with connecting LANs from the Memphis production site to LANs at the Detroit headquarters. The administrator leases a 56Kb line between the locations and terminates the line with bridges to make the link as maintenance free and as transparent as possible. The link meets all expectations but it is carrying far more traffic than anticipated. In fact, the administrator is growing increasingly concerned about degradation of response times. What would you recommend?

❍ A. Replace the bridges with cut through switches to increase throughput.

❍ B. Lease a second line to cover peak loads.

❍ C. All of the above.

❍ D. None of the above.

Answer D is correct. The administrator is linking networks at Layer 3 with a bridge, which is a Layer 2 device. Bridges would pass all of the administrative traffic from both networks across the link, which could easily fill whatever bandwidth was available. Although there are special purpose bridges that could work in this situation, the real solution would be to use routers. Routers would eliminate Layer 2 administrative traffic from the link and free up bandwidth for data traffic. Answer A is incorrect because a switch would also pass administrative traffic only faster. Answer B is incorrect because it is addressing the symptom not the problem. And now, will the administrator and all those choosing A, B, or C please report to your new job in Marketing tomorrow morning.

## Question 8

Which protocols are Layer 3 routable protocols? (Choose all that apply.)

- ❑ A. Internet Protocol (IP)
- ❑ B. Routing Information Protocol (RIP)
- ❑ C. Internet Packet Exchange (IPX)
- ❑ D. AppleTalk.

Answers A, C, and D are routable protocols that carry data between networks. Answer B is a distance-vector routing protocol that is used by routers to exchange routing table information and determine optimum paths for packets.

## Question 9

People working at the end stations of a 10BASE-5 network are constantly complaining that information they send each other is slow and often has errors. Which devices may alleviate the problem? (Choose all that apply.)

- ❑ A. A bridge
- ❑ B. A hub
- ❑ C. A repeater
- ❑ D. A static or fixed configuration router

Answers A and C are correct. The most likely cause of the problem is attenuation of the signal as it crosses the cable. The end stations would experience a majority of the problems because they have the most cable between them. A repeater which rebuilds, retimes, and then retransmits the signal would be the ideal short-term solution. Although a bridge is designed to separate collision domains, its operation includes rebuilding, retiming, and retransmitting frames just like a repeater. The bridge provides more than is needed, but its repeater function would fix the problem. Hubs are not used in a 10BASE-5 network so answer B is wrong and answer D could go either way. If you could find a router with both ports configured for 10BASE-5 networks, it could conceivably work in this situation by rebuilding the signal as it was sent between networks. The user, however, would have to be willing to accept the higher costs of the router and the need to readdress many of the stations and configure them all to use the router as a gateway. Certainly not an elegant solution, and if this were the test I would not select it as a viable solution.

# Question 10

A wiring technician was directed to extend a 10BASE-2 network cable to provide service to a new suite of offices. The existing cable was too short so the technician spliced a piece of cable that looked exactly like the network cable but had different numbers printed on the jacket. When the network was initialized the following morning, the entire network experienced erratic operation. What would be the most likely problem?

❍ A. 10BASE-2 cable cannot be cut without introducing a high level of attenuation. This attenuation can be great enough to stop all but the strongest signals.

❍ B. Joining even slightly dissimilar cables (the numbers didn't match) would almost certainly create an impedance mismatch. The resulting reflected signals would create erratic performance and could bring the whole network down.

❍ C. 10BASE-2 cable is extremely tolerant of mismatches so it is doubtful the extension cable, even with a less than perfect splice, would cause erratic operation. A more likely culprit would be a malfunctioning vampire tap on the new cable.

❍ D. None of the above.

Answer B is correct. We know that even a slight impedance mismatch will reflect signals on any cable. Dissimilar cables, joined with a splice, would be an invitation for disaster. So answer B would be the most likely candidate. A splice would have to be unbelievably awful to create an attenuation problem. Impedance mismatch yes, attenuation, not very likely, which would make answer A incorrect. No cable is tolerant of mismatched characteristics and besides that, vampire taps are not used on 10BASE-2 cable so C is also incorrect. Answer B is related to the material presented in the chapter and consistent with other examples. So answer D can be ruled out.

# Need to Know More?

It is a very good idea to have several books on basic networking. However, there are so many good books coming out each day it is impossible to recommend the one or two that are most relevant at any given time. A search on the Internet followed by a visit to Amazon.com has always produced results. However, you do have to be careful that the materials are consistent with Cisco or at least be aware of any differences. One of the books we like for Ethernet is *Ethernet Tips and Techniques* by Byron Spinney, CRM books, Fort Washington, PA. ISBN 1-878956-43-4. We are not going to recommend it here because it does not track closely with the CCNA program. Besides, Byron sees routing as a Layer 4 function. (See what I mean?)

The three books listed below track well with Cisco and the material in this chapter. They are also applicable to the entire CCNA curricula and as such are good to have.

Castelli, Matthew. *Network Sales and Services Handbook.* Cisco Press, Indianapolis, Indiana, 2003. ISBN 1-58705-090-0. Although this book is targeted at sales, it does a very good job of explaining technologies and Cisco products without getting into mind-boggling minutia. A good book to have!

Odom, Wendell. *Cisco CCNA Exam Certification Guide.* Cisco Press, Indianapolis, Indiana, 2000. ISBN 0-7357-0971-8. Cisco is almost always the best place for reference books relating to Cisco. They print incredibly detailed and comprehensive books and this one is excellent. I would not want to read it as a primary text but as a reference it cannot be beat.

*Dictionary of Internetworking Terms and Acronyms.* Cisco Press, Indianapolis, Indiana, 2001. ISBN 1-58720045-7. Don't leave home without it!

# Wide Area Network Protocols

## Terms you'll need to understand:

- ✓ Frame relay
- ✓ Data Link Connection Identifier (DLCI)
- ✓ Local Management Interface (LMI)
- ✓ Integrated Services Digital Network (ISDN)
- ✓ Basic Rate Interface (BRI)
- ✓ Primary Rate Interface (PRI)
- ✓ Data terminal equipment (DTE)
- ✓ Data communications equipment (DCE)
- ✓ Point-to-Point Protocol (PPP)
- ✓ High-Level Data Link Control (HDLC)

## Techniques you'll need to master:

- ✓ Switched services
- ✓ Point-to-point and Point-to-multipoint connections
- ✓ Peer-to-peer connections
- ✓ Authentication

Wide area networking is a core business at Cisco. You will need to demonstrate knowledge of major protocols and services inherent to wide area networking when you sit for the CCNA test. This chapter will provide an overview of the *Point-to-Point Protocol*, *Frame Relay* network operation, and *Integrated Services Digital Network* components. While these are not the only protocols and services included in wide area networking, they are representative, and provide a foundation for presenting the protocols and services required by the test.

# WAN Services

Because WANs cover long distances, organizations typically subscribe to an outside provider for WAN services. These services (usually telephone and data) are routed from an interface at one end of the customer's network through the provider's network to the other end of the customer's network.

It is the provider's responsibility to provide the customer with the parameters necessary to connect to its network. The WAN provider's network appears as a cloud to the customer, who simply makes a point-to-point connection to the remote site.

The main interface between the customer and provider networks occurs between the *data terminal equipment (DTE)* and the *data communications equipment (DCE)*.

Be sure you are comfortable with the following terms as laid out in Figure 4.1:

- *Customer Premise Equipment (CPE):* Devices that are physically located on the subscriber's premises. These devices are usually owned by the customer or leased from the WAN provider.
- *Demarcation (Demarc):* The point where CPE ends and the local loop begins, usually in the customer's main data closet.
- *Local Loop (Last Mile):* Cabling that extends from the demarc to the WAN service provider's central office.
- *Central Office (CO):* The WAN service provider's switching facility, which provides the nearest point of presence (POP) for the service. The service provider's switching facility can also be called a POP.
- *Data Terminal Equipment (DTE):* Usually a router or bridge at the customer's location that connects to the local loop through the DCE.
- *Data Communications Equipment:* A device at the end of the local loop that attaches to the DTE. The DCE provides clocking and conversion of data into a suitable format for transmission across the local loop. Examples of Data Communications Equipment include modems, terminal adapters (TA), network termination (NT1), and channel service unit/data service unit (CSU/DSU).

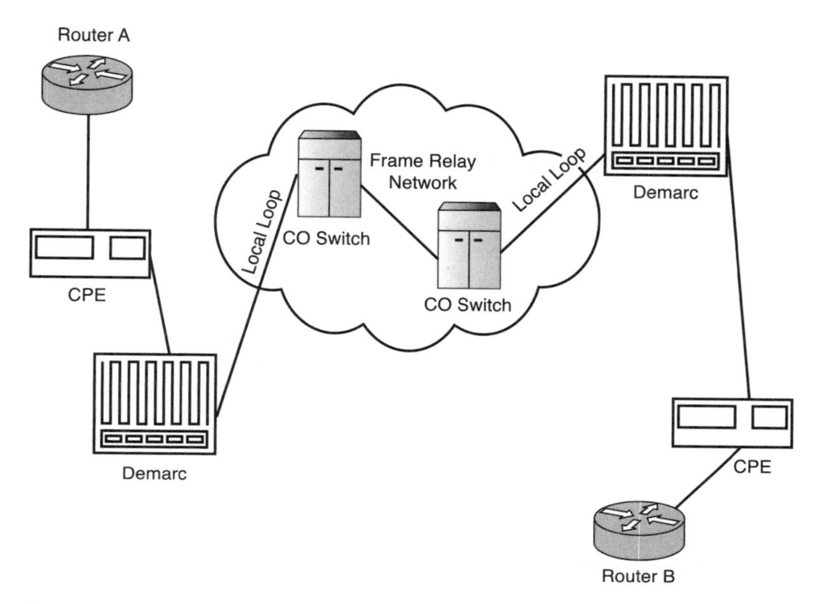


**Figure 4.1** Connecting to the WAN service provider's network.

The customer's router usually serves as the DTE device and performs the packet-switching function. Sometimes, DTE devices are bridges or terminals. The DCE attaches to the DTE and provides clocking, converts the data into a suitable format, and switches the data across the provider's network. DCE devices include modems, a channel service unit/data service unit (CSU/DSU), and a terminal adapter/network termination 1 (TA/NT1). The DTE/DCE interface serves as the boundary where responsibility for the network traffic shifts from the customer's network to the WAN provider's network. It can support several common types of WAN service connections when the DTE is a Cisco router.

The first type involves *switched services*. Switches within the provider's network transmit data from one customer DTE to that customer's other DTEs. Frame Relay and ISDN are examples of packet-switched and circuit-switched services, respectively.

The second type involves connecting remote devices to a central mainframe. Synchronous Data Link Control (SDLC) is the protocol used in these types of point-to-point or point-to-multipoint connections. SDLC is a bit-synchronous data link protocol that supports legacy IBM networks.

A third type involves connecting peer devices. HDLC and PPP can be used to encapsulate the data for transmission to peer DTE devices.

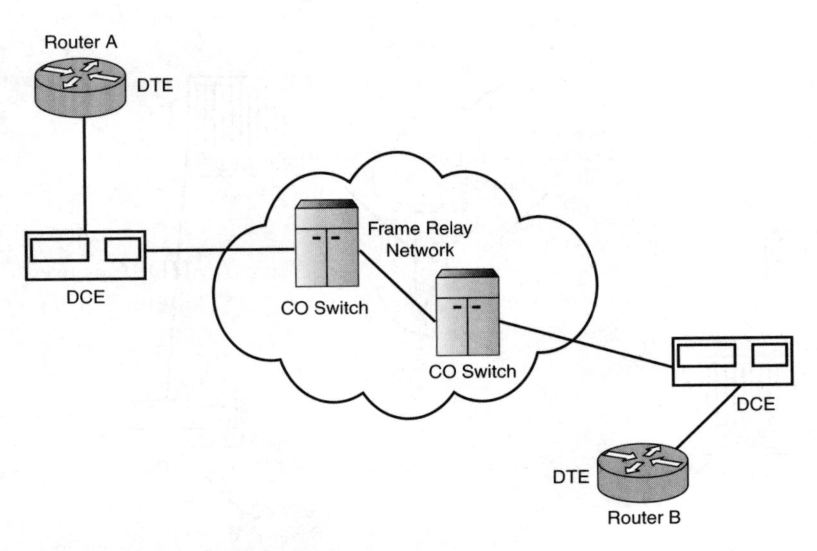


**Figure 4.2** Placement of DTE and DCE in a wide area network.

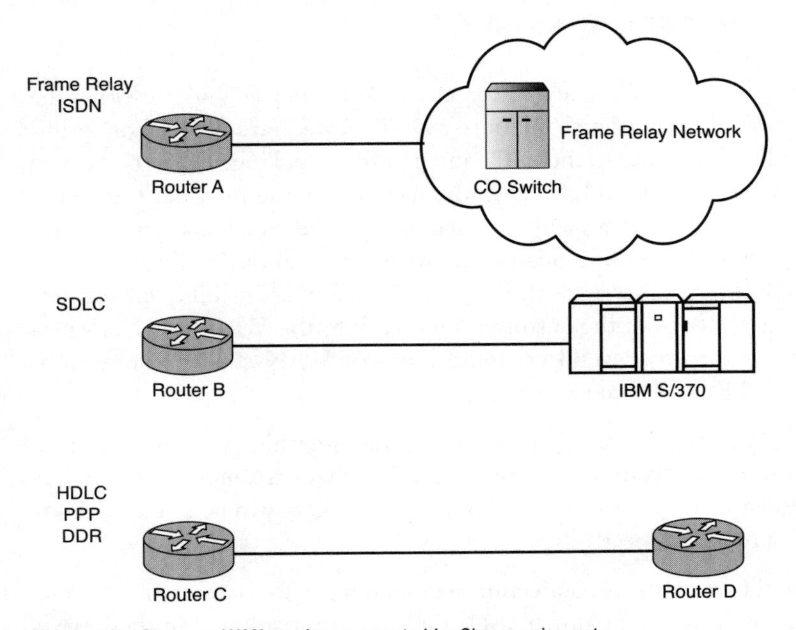


**Figure 4.3** Common WAN services supported by Cisco equipment.

This chapter is full of *acronyms* and you will need to know them *all* for the test. We will use them repeatedly to help you remember, but it would still be a good idea to re-read this chapter prior to the test, just to be sure you feel comfortable with the terminology.

# HDLC Overview

*High-Level Data Link Control (HDLC)* is the default encapsulation used by Cisco routers over synchronous serial links. HDLC is an ISO standard data link protocol. It specifies a method to encapsulate data over synchronous serial links using frame characters and checksums.

Cisco routers use a proprietary version of HDLC. Typically, HDLC is used on leased lines between two Cisco devices. If you need to establish a link between a Cisco router and a non-Cisco device, you must use PPP encapsulation instead of HDLC.

The ISO standard HDLC does not support multiple protocols on a single link. However, Cisco's proprietary HDLC adds a field that allows it to support multi-protocol environments.

# PPP Overview

*Point-to-Point Protocol (PPP)* encapsulates Network layer information for transmission over point-to-point links. It was designed by developers on the Internet and is described by a series of documents called *Request for Comments (RFCs)*—namely, 1661, 1331, and 2153.

PPP consists of two main components:

- *Link Control Protocol (LCP)*—Establishes, configures, and tests the connection
- *Network Control Program (NCP)*—Configures many different Network layer protocols

## PPP Physical Layer

PPP can operate on a variety of DTE/DCE physical interfaces, including

- Asynchronous serial
- Synchronous serial
- High-Speed Serial Interface (HSSI)
- ISDN

Other than what is required by a particular physical interface, PPP makes no special transmission rate requirements.

## PPP Connections

It is the responsibility of the Link Control Protocol (LCP) within PPP to establish, configure, test, maintain, and terminate the point-to-point connection. Four phases occur during the LCP process:

- Link establishment
- Link quality determination
- Network layer protocol negotiation
- Link termination

During link establishment, LCP opens the connection and negotiates configuration parameters. Acknowledgment frames must be sent and received before this phase can be considered completed successfully.

The link quality determination phase involves testing the connection to determine whether the line quality is sufficient to support the Network layer protocols. Although this phase seems very important, it is optional.

In the third phase, the appropriate Network layer protocols are configured. *Network control programs (NCPs)* configure PPP to support different Network layer protocols, including Internet Protocol (IP), Internetwork Packet Exchange (IPX), and AppleTalk. The PPP devices transmit NCP packets to select and configure one or more Network layer protocols. After each selected Network layer protocol has been configured, data can begin to be transmitted across the link. If the LCP terminates a link, it notifies the NCP, which takes appropriate action.

The link termination phase can be initiated by the LCP at any time. Link termination can occur from events such as a user request, a loss of carrier, or the expiration of a timeout parameter.

## PPP Authentication

PPP authentication occurs during the link quality determination phase; therefore, authentication is optional. The calling side of the link must transmit information to ensure that the sender is authorized to establish the connection. This is accomplished by a series of authentication messages being sent between the routers. PPP supports two types of authentication: *Password Authentication Protocol (PAP)* and *Challenge Handshake Authentication Protocol (CHAP)*.

## PAP

PAP uses a two-way handshake to allow remote hosts to identify themselves. After the link has been established and the link establishment phase is complete, PAP performs the following steps:

1. The remote host initiates the call, sends a username and password to the local host, and continues to send the information until it is accepted or rejected.

2. The local host receives the call and accepts or rejects the username and password information. If the local host rejects the information, the connection is terminated.

## CHAP

CHAP uses a three-way handshake to force remote hosts to identify themselves after the link establishment phase. CHAP performs the following steps after the link establishment phase is complete:

1. The local router that received the call sends a challenge packet to the remote host that initiated the call. The challenge packet consists of an ID, a random number, and either the name of the local host performing the authentication or a username on the remote host.

2. The remote host must respond with its encrypted unique ID, a one-way encrypted password, the remote hostname or a username, and a random number.

3. The local router performs its own calculation on the response values. It accepts or rejects the authentication request based on whether the value it received from the remote host matches the value it calculated.

Like PAP, CHAP terminates the connection immediately if the local host rejects the authentication request.

During the PAP process, the username and password information is sent from the remote host in clear text, so PAP is not a recommended protocol. It offers no protection from a network analyzer capturing the information and using it. Because CHAP uses secret, encrypted passwords and unique IDs, it is a much stronger protocol than PAP. You can choose only one type of authentication, so CHAP is definitely recommended; however, PAP is better than no authentication at all.

# ISDN Overview

*ISDN* refers to the call-processing system that enables voice, data, and video to be transmitted over our existing telephone system. ISDN offers several advantages over existing analog modem lines. For example, ISDN connection speeds begin at 64Kbps, whereas typical modem speeds hover between 28.8Kbps and 56Kbps. The call setup time for an ISDN call is also much quicker. ISDN can transmit data packets, voice, or video. ISDN is a viable solution for remote connectivity (telecommuting) and access to the Internet. ISDN also supports any of the Network layer protocols supported by the Cisco Internetwork Operating System (IOS) and encapsulates other WAN services, such as PPP.

ISDN can be used to

- Add bandwidth for telecommuting
- Improve Internet response times
- Carry multiple Network layer protocols
- Encapsulate other WAN services

# Basic Rate Interface and Primary Rate Interface

ISDN can be ordered as either BRI or PRI. An ISDN BRI service contains two bearer channels (or B channels) of 64Kbps and one data channel (or D channel) of 16Kbps. The B channel carries user data, and the D channel carries signaling and control information. The maximum throughput for BRI is 128Kbps (two B channels at 64Kbps). In North America and Japan, an ISDN PRI service uses a T1 line that contains 23 B channels and one D channel, enabling a maximum throughput of 1.544Mbps. In Europe, PRI service uses an E1 line that contains 30 B channels and 1 D channel, enabling a throughput of 2.048Mbps.

ISDN, like other communications services, requires *Data Terminal Equipment (DTE)* and *Data Communications Equipment (DCE)*. In most cases you will be connecting a router to the ISDN BRI service and that router will have an ISDN BRI interface. The interface can either be built in to the router's circuitry or take the form of a module added to the router. Sometimes you will see the term "TE1" (terminal equipment one) applied to routers with an interface and "TE2" used for routers without the interface. In either case, that interface is the Data Terminal Equipment (DTE) and in the world of ISDN BRI it is called a *Terminal Adapter (TA)*. The Data Communications Equipment that connects to the local loop of the service provider is called a *Network Termination One (NT1)*. The NT1 provides clocking and conversion of data into a suitable format for transmission across the local loop. In North America, the service provider usually provides the NT1 (but not always) and the user is responsible for providing power to the NT1. Physically, the router's Terminal Adapter connects to the NT1 via a cable and the NT1 connects to the local loop (see Figure 4.4).

ISDN PRI service has 23 bearer channels so it uses a larger ISDN PRI specific DCE called a Data Service Unit and Channel Service Unit (DSU/CSU). The DSU provides clocking and conversion of data while the CSU splits out the channels for use by the Data Communications Equipment.

In North America, ISDN BRIs can be provisioned without an NT1. In this case, the customer is responsible for providing the NT1 and power for the NT1. Unlike analog telephone lines, if you want a BRI to stay up during a power outage, you must supply uninterrupted power to the NT1. This is not a problem for large companies where wiring closets are supplied with a UPS or UPS service. However, small firms and remote offices may not have a UPS, which can be a problem. If IP telephony is used the problem becomes major.

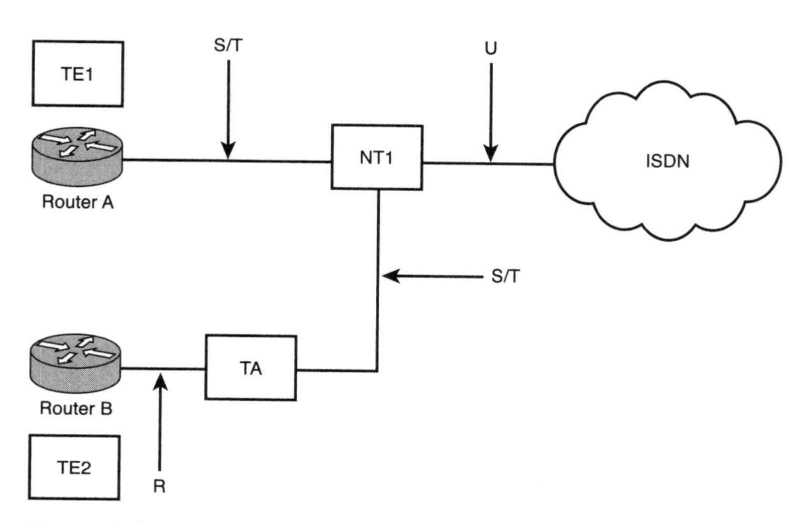


**Figure 4.4** Interface devices used with ISDN.

DCE, DTE, CSU, and DSU are generic terms that apply to many types of services. The TA is a type of DTE specific to ISDN, just like NT1 is a type of DCE specific to ISDN BRI. These generic terms will come up over and over again so be sure you understand the functions of each.

# DDR

*Dial-on-demand routing (DDR)* works with ISDN to establish and terminate network connections, as traffic dictates. DDR configuration commands define host and ISDN connection information. An access list and DDR dialer group define what type of traffic should initiate an ISDN call. You can configure multiple access lists to look for different types of "interesting" traffic—network traffic that, when it arrives at the router, triggers the router to initiate the ISDN connection.

When the router notices interesting traffic, it refers to its ISDN information and initiates the setup of the ISDN call through its BRI or PRI and NT1 device. It should also be noted here that 56Kbps dial-up interfaces can also be used with DDR. When the connection is established, normal routing occurs between the two end devices. After interesting traffic stops being transmitted over the ISDN connection, the connection idle timer begins. When the idle timer expires, the connection is terminated.

# Frame Relay

*Frame Relay* is a high-speed, packet-switching WAN protocol. Packet-switching protocols enable devices to share the available network bandwidth. As its name implies, Frame Relay operates at Layer 2 of the Open Systems Interconnection (OSI) model and runs on nearly any type of serial interface. Frame Relay encapsulates packets from the upper layers of the OSI model and switches them through the provider's network.

Frame Relay services have been streamlined to gain more throughput. Services such as flow control, robust congestion management, and error checking are left to upper-layer protocols such as Transmission Control Protocol (TCP); however, Frame Relay does include some error checking and congestion management.

Frame Relay uses *cyclic redundancy checking (CRC)* to perform error checking quickly. CRC produces a frame check sequence (FCS), which is appended to each frame that is transmitted. When a node receives the frame, it calculates a new FCS (based on the data portion of the frame) and compares it with the one contained in the frame. If the values are different, the frame is dropped.

Frame Relay manages congestion through the use of a discard eligibility bit. This bit is set to a value of 1 if the frame has lower importance than other frames; the DTE device is responsible for setting the bit and sets the bit to 1 for frames that have lower importance than other frames. Switches within the WAN provider's network may discard frames to manage congestion.

However, the switches only discard frames with the discard eligibility bit set to 1; frames with bits set to 0 are still transmitted. This feature protects against critical data being dropped during periods of network congestion.

## Virtual Circuits

Communication in a Frame Relay network is connection oriented, and a defined communication path must exist between each pair of DTE devices. *Virtual circuits* provide the bidirectional communication within Frame Relay networks. In essence, a virtual circuit is a logical connection established between two DTE devices. Many virtual circuits can be multiplexed into one physical circuit, and a single virtual circuit can cross multiple DCE devices within the Frame Relay network.

Virtual circuits can be grouped into two categories: *switched virtual circuits (SVCs)* and *permanent virtual circuits (PVCs)*. SVCs are temporary connections and can be used when only sporadic data communication is necessary between DTE devices. SVCs require the connection to be set up and terminated for each session. Conversely, PVCs are permanent connections. They support frequent and consistent data communications across a Frame Relay network. When the PVC is established, DTE devices can begin transmitting data when they are ready. PVCs are used more widely in Frame Relay networks than SVCs.

## DLCI

A *data link connection identifier (DLCI)* serves as the addressing scheme within a Frame Relay network. The service provider assigns a DLCI for each PVC, and the DLCI is locally significant within the network. In other words, the DLCI must be unique within the network like an Internet Protocol (IP) address. Two DTE devices that have a PVC established between them may or may not use the same DLCI value.

Two methods can be used to map a DLCI to a Network layer address (such as an IP address)—dynamically via inverse ARP or manually using the **map** command. Both methods are discussed in the "Configuring Frame Relay" section of Chapter 8. For now it is sufficient to know that DLCIs can be configured manually or dynamically.

## LMI

*Local Management Interface (LMI)* is a set of enhancements to the Frame Relay protocol specifications. Developed in 1990 by four companies (nicknamed the "*Gang of Four*"), LMI extensions offer several features for better management of complex Frame Relay networks. These extensions include global addressing, virtual circuit status messaging, and multicasting.

The "Gang of Four" includes Cisco Systems, StrataCom, Northern Telecom, and Digital Equipment Corporation.

The LMI global addressing extension enables a DLCI to have global instead of local significance. With LMI, DLCI values are unique within a Frame Relay network, and standard address resolution protocols, such as Address Resolution Protocol (ARP) and reverse ARP (or inverse ARP), as well as discovery protocols can be used to identify nodes within the network. Virtual circuit status messaging improves the communication and synchronization between DTE and DCE devices. The status messages, which are similar to hello packets, report on the status of PVCs. LMI multicasting enables multicast groups to be assigned. Multicasting reduces overhead by allowing route updates and address resolution messages to be sent to specific groups of DTE devices.

Cisco supports the following Frame Relay LMI protocol variations:

- *ANSI*—American National Standards Institute
- *q933a*—International Telecommunication Union–Telecommunication standardization sector
- *Cisco*—Gang of Four

# Exam Prep Questions

## Question 1

Which protocol is responsible for establishing, configuring, testing, maintaining, and terminating PPP connections?

❍ A. BRI

❍ B. PRI

❍ C. LCP

❍ D. NCP

The correct answer is C. LCP has the primary responsibility for a PPP connection. Answers A and B are incorrect because BRI and PRI are not components within PPP. Answer D is incorrect because NCP is responsible for the configuration supporting Network layer protocols.

## Question 2

Which of the following is an authentication type that would be appropriate for an environment that requires strong encrypted passwords?

❍ A. PAP

❍ B. CHAP

❍ C. LCP

❍ D. NCP

The correct answer is B. CHAP uses encrypted passwords, making it a much stronger protocol than PAP. Answer A is incorrect because PAP uses clear text to send passwords. Answers C and D are incorrect because neither is an authentication type.

## Question 3

Which of the following physical interfaces will PPP operate on?

❍ A. Asynchronous serial

❍ B. Synchronous serial

❍ C. HSSI

❍ D. ISDN

❍ E. All of the above

The correct answer is E. PPP can operate on a variety of DTE/DCE physical interfaces, including asynchronous serial, synchronous serial, HSSI, and ISDN.

## Question 4

Which PPP authentication protocol uses a three-way handshake?

- ❍ A. PAP
- ❍ B. CHAP
- ❍ C. LCP
- ❍ D. NCP1

The correct answer is B. The CHAP three-way handshake includes the local host requesting authentication, the remote host sending an encrypted response, and the local host comparing the received information and then accepting or rejecting the connection. PAP only uses a two-way handshake. Therefore, answer A is incorrect. LCP and NCP1 are not authentication protocols. Therefore, answers C and D are incorrect.

## Question 5

If your router does not have an ISDN BRI interface, which devices will you need to connect to ISDN services? (Choose the two best answers.)

- ❑ A. NT1
- ❑ B. TA
- ❑ C. TE1
- ❑ D. TE2

The correct answers are A and B. You need a TA to convert the serial signal from your router into a BRI signal, and you need an NT1 to convert the BRI signal for use by the ISDN digital line. A TE1 is a device that *has* a built-in BRI and already transmits BRI signals. Therefore, answer C is incorrect. Answer D is incorrect because a device that does *not* have a built-in BRI is considered a TE2.

## Question 6

How can you use ISDN? (Choose all that apply.)

- ❑ A. To improve Internet response times
- ❑ B. To encapsulate other WAN services
- ❑ C. To add bandwidth for telecommuting
- ❑ D. To carry multiple Network-layer protocols

The correct answers are A, B, C, and D.

## Question 7

DCE devices provide which of the following functions?

- ❍ A. Provides a clock to the DTE
- ❍ B. Converts data into a suitable format
- ❍ C. Switches data across the provider's network
- ❍ D. All of the above

The correct answer is D. Answers A, B, and C are all functions of DCE devices.

## Question 8

Frame Relay operates at which layer of the OSI model?

- ❍ A. Transport
- ❍ B. Network
- ❍ C. Data Link
- ❍ D. Physical

The correct answer is C. Frame Relay operates at the Data Link layer. Answers A and B are incorrect because Frame Relay does not include any specifications for Layer 4 (Transport) or Layer 3 (Network). Although Frame Relay can operate on several different physical media, it does not include specifications for Layer 1 (Physical). Therefore, answer D is incorrect.

## Question 9

Which of the following devices can serve as a DTE device? (Choose the two best answers.)

- ❑ A. Router
- ❑ B. Terminal
- ❑ C. Modem
- ❑ D. CSU

The correct answers are A and B. Routers and terminals can be configured to act as DTE devices. Modems and CSUs cannot be configured as DTE devices, but they can be configured as DCE devices. Therefore, answers C and D are incorrect.

## Question 10

Which of the following are common WAN services supported by Cisco? (Choose the five best answers.)

- ❑ A. ISDN
- ❑ B. Frame Relay
- ❑ C. PPP
- ❑ D. BGP
- ❑ E. HDLC
- ❑ F. SDLC

The correct answers are A, B, C, E, and F. ISDN, Frame Relay, PPP, HDLC, and SDLC are all WAN services supported by Cisco equipment. Although BGP is supported by Cisco equipment, it is an exterior routing protocol. Therefore, answer D is incorrect.

## Question 11

Which of the following can be used to establish bidirectional communication between two DTE devices? (Choose the two best answers.)

- ❑ A. CVC
- ❑ B. DVC
- ❑ C. PVC
- ❑ D. SVC

The correct answers are C and D. A permanent virtual circuit (PVC) remains established between two DTE devices, even when data is not being transmitted. A switched virtual circuit (SVC) is established only when two DTE devices need to transmit data; it is disconnected when the transmission is over. CVC and DVC are not related to virtual circuits between DTE devices. Therefore, answers A and B are incorrect.

## Question 12

Which of the following serves as the addressing scheme within a Frame Relay network?

- ❍ A. DLCI
- ❍ B. LMI
- ❍ C. NBMA
- ❍ D. SVC

The correct answer is A. A DLCI number serves as the addressing scheme and is assigned to each PVC. LMI provides several enhancements to Frame Relay specifications. Therefore, answer B is incorrect. Answer C is incorrect because NBMA describes how a router must send broadcasts within a Frame Relay network. An SVC is established to enable DTE to communicate. Therefore, answer D is incorrect.

## Question 13

Cisco supports which of the following Frame Relay LMI protocol variations? (Choose the three best answers.)

- ❑ A. IETF
- ❑ B. ANSI
- ❑ C. Q933A
- ❑ D. Cisco

The correct answers are B, C, and D. Cisco supports LMI extensions from American National Standards Institute (ANSI), International Telecommunication Union–Telecommunication standardization sector (Q933A), and Cisco's "Gang of Four." Answer A is incorrect because IETF is a type of frame encapsulation supported by Cisco that enables Cisco devices to communicate with non-Cisco devices across a Frame Relay network.

## Question 14

Frame Relay uses what mechanism to perform error checking?

- ❍ A. CRC
- ❍ B. LMI
- ❍ C. TA/NT1
- ❍ D. Inverse ARP

The correct answer is A. Frame Relay uses CRC to derive the FCS, which is a calculated value based on the data portion of each frame. If a device calculates an FCS value that is different from the FCS value it receives, the frame is dropped. LMI is communicated between DTE and DCE devices and contains the status of the virtual circuit. Therefore, answer B is incorrect. Answer C is incorrect because a TA/NT1 is a DCE device and has nothing to do with error checking. Answer D is incorrect because inverse ARP is the method by which DTE devices discover Layer 3 protocol address information about each other.

# Need to Know More?

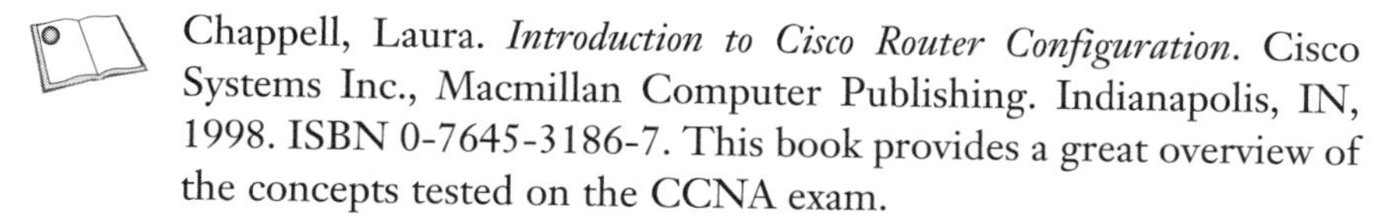

Chappell, Laura. *Introduction to Cisco Router Configuration*. Cisco Systems Inc., Macmillan Computer Publishing. Indianapolis, IN, 1998. ISBN 0-7645-3186-7. This book provides a great overview of the concepts tested on the CCNA exam.

Ford, Merilee, H. Kim Lew, Steve Spanier, and Kevin Downes. *Internetworking Technologies Handbook, 2nd Edition*. Macmillan Computer Publishing. Indianapolis, IN, 1998. ISBN 1-56205-102-3. This book is full of resourceful information on internetworking technologies.

Lammle, Todd, Donald Porter, and James Chellis. *CCNA Cisco Certified Network Associate*. Sybex Network Press. Alameda, CA, 1999. ISBN 0-7821-2381-3. This book is a great supplement for learning the technologies tested on the CCNA exam.

Syngress Media, with Richard D. Hornbaker, CCIE. *Cisco Certified Network Associate Study Guide*. Osborne/McGraw-Hill. Berkeley, CA, 1998. ISBN 0-07882-487-7. Another great book for review before taking the CCNA exam.

*Dictionary of Internetworking Terms and Acronyms*. Cisco Press, Indianapolis, Indiana, 2001. ISBN 1-58720045-7. Cisco has its own language for technologies used in its products. You will need to use and understand that language for the test. This book will help.

`www.cisco.com`, the official Cisco Web site, contains several Cisco white papers on topics such as PPP configuration and troubleshooting.

`www.cis.ohio-state.edu/hypertext/information/rfc.html`, the Computer and Information Science Web site at Ohio State University, provides information about Internet RFC documents. You can review detailed information on PPP in RFCs 1661, 1331, and 2153.

5

# TCP/IP

## Terms you'll need to understand:

✓ TCP
✓ IP
✓ FTP
✓ UDP
✓ ARP
✓ RARP
✓ DNS
✓ Application layer
✓ Transport layer
✓ Internet layer
✓ Network Access layer
✓ Subnetting
✓ Dotted decimal notation
✓ Well-known port numbers

## Techniques you'll need to master:

✓ Subnetting
✓ Identifying the various layers of the TCP/IP model
✓ Identifying the different classes of IPs
✓ Performing a conversion from binary to dotted decimal notation

The *Transmission Control Protocol/Internet Protocol (TCP/IP)* is the foundation of the Internet and the single most widely used protocol suite in the world today. A detailed working knowledge of TCP/IP is required for the CCNA exam, so it is very important you feel comfortable with everything presented in this chapter.

TCP/IP is not just a protocol, it is an entire suite of protocols which, together, provide comprehensive rules and standards for communications (interdependent protocols are called a *protocol suite* or *protocol stack*). Most presentations of TCP/IP begin by showing how these protocols fit into the OSI model. The only problem with this approach is that TCP/IP does not fit into the OSI model (and you thought we were kidding in Chapter 3, "Hardware and OSI Model," when we said the OSI model is good, it just does not describe how anything really works).

TCP/IP was developed under a four-layer model called the *Department of Defense model* or *DoD model*. We will show you how these two models map to each other as well as how the protocol suite fits into either model, because you will need to know this for the test. However, if integrating TCP/IP into the OSI model seems a bit awkward to you, it is only because it is.

# Background and History of TCP/IP

In the late 1960s, Stanford University received funding from the Defense Advanced Research Projects Agency (DARPA) to create and deliver a protocol meeting the requirements of the four-layer Department of Defense model for data communication. The specification further required full utilization of packet-switching technology, ability to communicate between dissimilar networks, and, as this was the height of the cold war, complete survivability despite the end of civilization.

The project was successful and the resulting protocols (collectively called TCP/IP) became the cornerstone of the Defense Department's data communications network called *ARPAnet*. ARPAnet expanded to include universities participating in Defense Department research, and as more people became accustomed to efficient global data communications, the pressure to extend the capabilities also grew. Eventually, segments of the network branched off into non-military areas. Two of the larger branches became The National Science Foundation network (NSFnet) and a series of loosely defined networks called the Internet.

# Four Layers of the DoD Model and the TCP/IP Protocol Suite

Before we get into layers and protocols, you need to know about *ports*, a concept that will come up repeatedly in TCP/IP. A port number identifies a sending or destination application. Every application running on a host uses certain ports or ranges of ports to communicate with applications running on other hosts. It is by these port numbers that TCP or UDP determines which application to pass the data to in the Application layer. The well-known ports have a value between 0 and 1,023. When an application on one device wants to communicate with an application on another device, it must specify the address of the device (IP address) and identify the application (port number).

| Port # | Process |
|---|---|
| 21 | FTP |
| 23 | Telnet |
| 25 | SMTP |
| 69 | TFTP |
| 80 | HTTP |
| 110 | POP3 |

Be on the lookout for these port numbers and applications in the following paragraphs. You will need to have them memorized for the exam!

Also, be sure to check out: **http://www.iana.org/assignments/port-numbers** for information on other port numbers.

Let's start by looking at the specific functions and protocols of each of the four layers. In Figure 5.1, we will look at how those layers and protocols map to the OSI model later in the chapter.

## Process/Application Layer

The first layer of the model is the Process/Application layer. This layer is where applications actually have to do something with the data once it is received. It is important to note than any software application that uses the TCP/IP suite—such as Internet Explorer, Outlook Express, or Adobe Acrobat Reader—needs to communicate with the correct port for that application process on a receiving computer. That is why these processes use well-known public port numbers. Noteworthy to mention is that the sending port and receiving port do not have to be the same, and generally are not the same. This layer also consists of a set of services that provides access to all types of networks. Applications utilize the services to communicate with other devices and remote applications. A large number of TCP/IP services is provided at the Application layer, some of which were mentioned previously. In the following sections, you will see a list of several Application layer protocols and their associated port numbers.

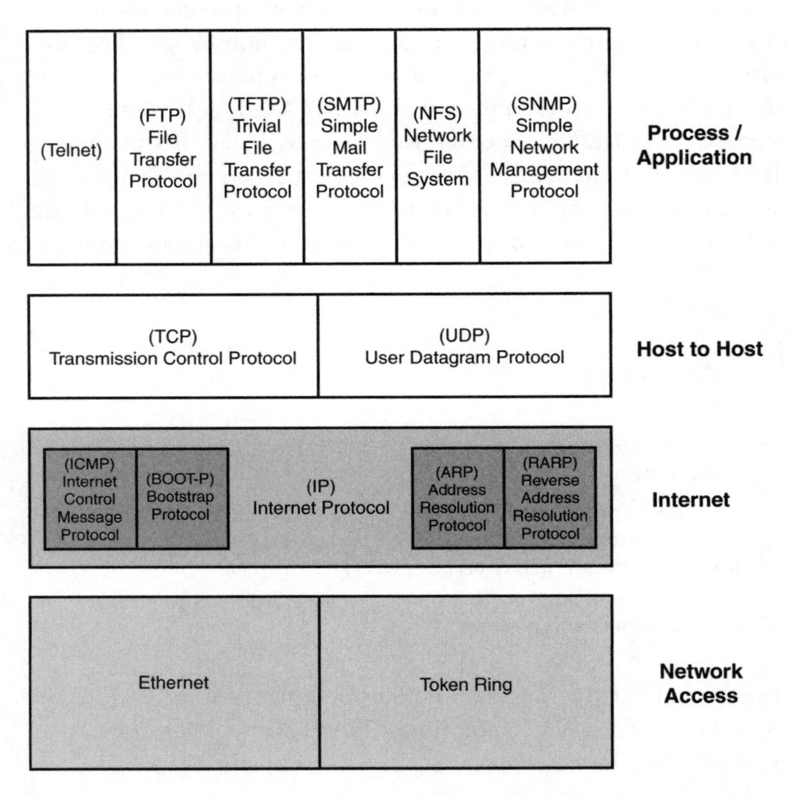


**Figure 5.1** The four layers of the DoD model and associated protocols from the TCP/IP suite.

## File Transfer Protocol (FTP)

FTP is used to copy a file from one host to another host, regardless of the physical hardware or operating system (OS) of each device. FTP identifies a client and server during the file transfer process. In addition, it provides a guaranteed transfer by using the services of TCP. The services that TCP provides are explained in more detail in the "Transport Layer" section of this chapter. FTP uses port 20 or 21 to deliver files.

## Trivial File Transfer Protocol (TFTP)

TFTP was built to be a small, robust FTP service. The original goal was to develop a protocol that could fit into the limited read-only memory (ROM) space of diskless machines. TFTP is a connectionless protocol that uses the services of UDP for transport. TFTP is used to copy files from one host (server) to another host (client). In many cases, TFTP is used to copy software to a device as it boots up. A common use of a TFTP server is to upgrade the IOS of a Cisco router, which you hopefully have already done or will be doing soon. TFTP uses port 69.

## Telnet

The Telnet service allows users to act as though their terminals are attached to another device. This process is referred to as terminal emulation. Telnet is a very useful protocol in internetworking because it allows network administrators to view and configure remote devices in the network from one location. Telnet uses the services of TCP to provide a connection-oriented session. Telnet uses port 23.

## Simple Mail Transfer Protocol (SMTP)

SMTP is used to pass mail messages between devices. It uses TCP connections to pass the email we've all grown to love between two mail servers. SMTP uses port 25. More specifically, SMTP is what allows email to get from the mail client to the mail server, whereas POP3 or Post Office Protocol is what gets mail from the mail server to the mail client.

## Simple Network Management Protocol (SNMP)

SNMP is used to obtain data on remote devices, such as a configurable switch. Typically, a network-management station uses SNMP to poll the devices in a network and to retrieve data regarding the devices' current and past conditions. Each of the agents maintains a management information database (MIB) locally that constantly stores information about that device. The manager systematically polls each of its agents, requesting information from their databases. It then manipulates and organizes the data into a useful format for reporting or displaying on the network-management monitor. SNMP has become the de facto standard for device management and is widely used today.

## Domain Name Service

DNS is a service that is used to translate hostnames or computer names into IP addresses, such as `www.awsb.ca`. DNS is a hierarchical database of names and their associated IP addresses. DNS allows people to enter a word-based address for any device on the Internet. When this occurs, that person's device requests a DNS lookup from a DNS server. The DNS server replies with the IP address associated with that hostname. Can you imagine if this service never existed? You would have to know the IP address of every Web site, effectively a nightmare, so be happy. DNS uses port 53. DNS has some security issues as well because it uses port 53 for both UDP and TCP traffic.

## Transport Layer

The next layer for us to look into is the Transport layer. The Transport layer passes data between the Application layer and the Internet layer. It consists of two protocols, *Transmission Control Protocol (TCP)* and *User Datagram Protocol (UDP)*. This layer provides an end-to-end connection between two devices, otherwise referred to as host-to-host communications, during communication by performing sequencing, acknowledgments, checksums, and flow control. The Transport layer allows the Application layer to ignore the complexities of the network and focus on its primary job. This layer is also responsible for sending data that it receives from the Network layer to the appropriate application.

### TCP

TCP provides a connection-oriented, reliable service to the applications that use its services. TCP was designed to add some reliability into the world of IP networking. A description of the main functions of TCP follows:

- *Initiates connection with three-way handshake*—TCP uses the concept of the three-way handshake to initiate a connection between two devices. A TCP connection begins with device A sending a request to synchronize sequence numbers and initiate a connection (a SYN message). Device B receives the message and responds with a SYN message with the sequence number increased by one. Device A responds by sending an acknowledgement message (an ACK) to device B, indicating that the device received the sequence number it expected.

- *Performs error and duplication checking*—TCP uses a checksum to identify packets that have changed during transport. If a device receives a packet with a bad checksum, it drops the packet and does not send an acknowledgment for it. Therefore, the sending device resends the packet (hopefully, it will not change during transport this time). In addition, any time TCP receives a duplicate packet, it drops the duplicate.

- *Performs acknowledgment windowing to increase efficiency of bandwidth use*—Any time a TCP device sends data to another device, it must wait for the acknowledgment that this data was received. To increase the efficiency of bandwidth utilization, TCP can change the window size. If the window size is increased to 2, the sending device requires only one acknowledgment for every two packets sent. TCP sets the window size dynamically during a connection, allowing either device involved in the communication to slow down the sending data rate based on the other device's capacity. This process is often referred to as *sliding windows* because of TCP's ability to change the window size dynamically.

- *Segments Application layer data stream*—TCP accepts data from applications and segments it into a desirable size for transmission between itself and the remote device. The segment size is determined while TCP is negotiating the connection between the two devices. Either device can dictate the segment size; however, the receiving station is given priority.
- *Provides acknowledgment timers*—TCP maintains timers to identify when packets have taken too long to get to their destination. When an acknowledgment is not received for an IP packet before the expiration of the timer, TCP resends the packet to the destination.
- *Enables sequence number checking*—TCP/IP uses sequence number checking to ensure that all packets sent by an application on a sending node are read in the correct order by an application on the receiving node. The packets might not be received at the Transport layer in the correct order, but TCP sequences them in their original order before passing them to the Application layer.
- *Provides buffer management*—Any time two devices are communicating, the possibility exists that one device can send data faster than the other can accept it. Initially, the receiving device puts the extra packets into a buffer and reads them when it gets a chance. When this data overflow persists, however, the buffer is eventually filled and packets begin to drop. TCP performs some preventive maintenance called *flow control* to avoid this scenario.

Do not get too bogged down and overwhelmed by the amount of information on TCP and its functions. Merely understand what it does and that the main point to know is that TCP is connection-oriented and a reliable service.

## UDP

UDP is a connectionless protocol that will run on top of an IP network. One of the disadvantages of UDP is that it provides very few error recovery services. However, one's disadvantage is another's advantage. Because there is no error checking, UDP is considerably faster than TCP. The primary purpose of UDP is to broadcast messages over a network. UDP simply receives data from the Application layer, applies the proper header, and sends the datagram on its merry way. This is why UDP is referred to as a best-effort protocol.

# Internet Layer

The Internet layer is responsible for path determination and packet switching. The Internet layer utilizes a logical addressing scheme to make intelligent decisions regarding path determination and packet switching. The Internet layer performs the actual relay of packets from an originating network to a destination network in an efficient manner. Every packet is viewed by IP, which determines its destination by using a routing table. The routing table helps establish the best path for the packet to be sent.

## IP

*Internet Protocol (IP)* is the transport for TCP, UDP, and Internet Control Message Protocol (ICMP) data. IP provides an unreliable service and is effectively a connectionless protocol. I know this is hard to imagine, but remember that the transport layer above it does all the error checking, so this layer does not have to worry about it. It lets the upper-layer protocols, such as TCP, or application-specific devices worry about reliability. In addition, IP performs as a connectionless service because it handles each datagram as an independent entity. IP performs packet switching and path determination by maintaining tables that indicate where to send a packet based on its IP address.

## Address Resolution Protocol (ARP)

ARP is a TCP/IP protocol that is used to convert an existing IP address into a physical address. Consider a computer that wants to know the address of another computer. The computer sends out (broadcasts) an ARP request to the network. The receiving computer that owns the physical address being sought replies to the original computer that was looking for its address. Sound rather simple? It is.

## Reverse Address Resolution Protocol (RARP)

RARP provides the exact opposite type of mapping from ARP—that is, RARP maps a known physical address to a logical address. A diskless machine that does not have a configured IP address when started typically uses RARP.

These devices send a broadcast requesting an IP address. In such a scenario, a device on the same local area network (LAN) is designed to respond to this broadcast request and supply the IP address for that physical address.

### Internet Control Message Protocol (ICMP)

ICMP communicates error messages and control messages between devices. The ICMP protocol allows devices to check the status of other devices, query the current time, and perform other functions. The most popular use of ICMP is the use of the PING command. The PING command uses ICMP to test an Internet connection. The Ping command is an excellent command used for troubleshooting, but you probably already know that by now, don't you? The most common ICMP messages are as follows:

- *Destination unreachable*—Indicates that a certain device cannot be contacted
- *Time exceeded*—Indicates that a certain device could not be reached within a specified time limit
- *Echo*—Requests an echo reply to determine device reachability
- *Echo reply*—Replies to an echo request indicating that a host is reachable

## Network Interface Layer

The Network Interface Layer does just as its name implies: It works at the hardware level to define the physical transmission of signals along the network. It effectively encapsulates information into frames (remember encapsulation?) that can be transmitted across the network. This layer provides access to the LAN. The physical addressing and network-specific protocols exist at this layer. Token Ring, Ethernet, and Fiber Distributed Data Interface (FDDI) are some examples of Network Interface layer protocols, as can be seen in Figure 5.2.

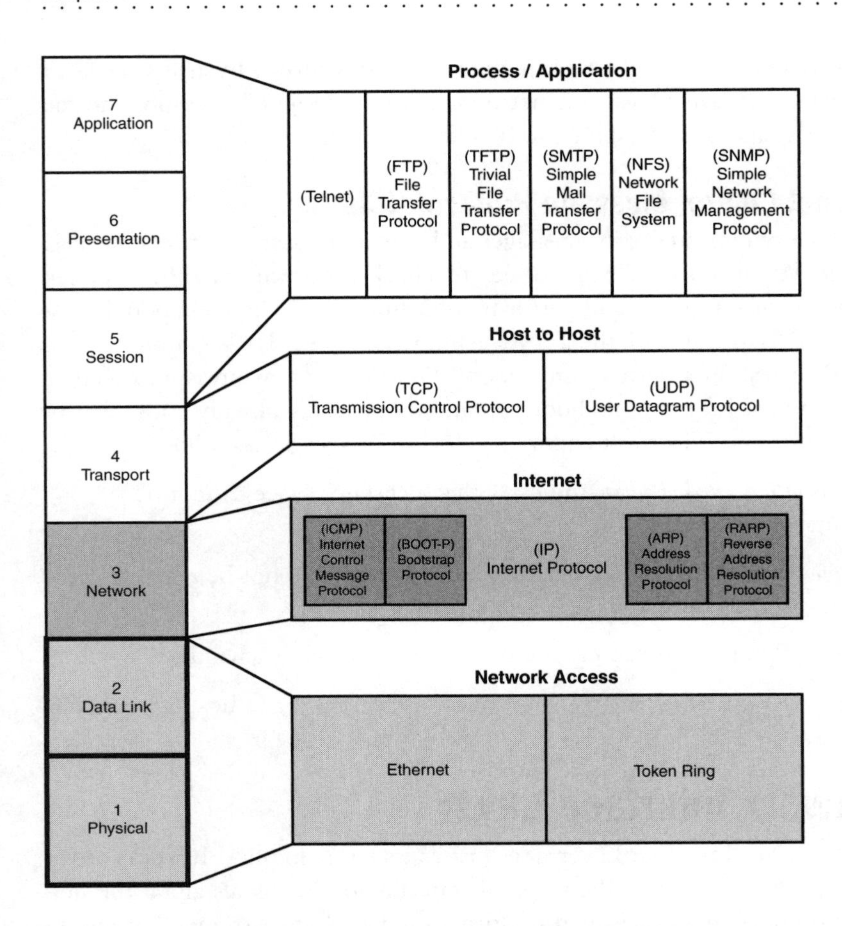


**Figure 5.2** This graphic shows how the OSI model (left) maps to the DoD model (right). You should be familiar with how these two models relate for the test.

# IP Addressing

Every computer that communicates on the Internet is assigned a unique IP address that identifies the device and distinguishes it from other computers on the Internet. This section looks at the various classes of IP addressing and pays great attention to examples of each, as you will be required to know the various classes by heart for a Cisco examination.

## Binary Notation

Let's start right off by making an unbelievable claim: IP addressing is a simple, straightforward, easy-to-remember method for uniquely identifying a device to the rest of an IP network. Nobody seems to have a problem with the part about uniquely identifying devices, but as far as being "simple and easy to remember"...no way! Actually, IP addressing is only complex because it is invariably presented as a mix of base 2 math, base 10 math, a little hexadecimal for interest, and a seemingly endless number of arbitrary rules. Instead of adopting this approach, let's look at IP addressing as it was developed.

The people who developed IP were real geeks. They coded in base 2, were comfortable using base 2, and, of course, the native language of computers was base 2 machine language. Why would they develop IP in anything other than base 2? 32 digits could be grouped into four octets, which easily fit in computer registers and provided a reasonable range of addresses. However, 32 digits only provided a reasonable range if organized in a hierarchical structure, and this is where it got interesting. If all 32 digits were used in a linear address, there could be 1 network with a little more than four trillion stations, or slightly over four trillion networks with 1 station each. Either scenario made a good argument for dividing the digits, with some identifying the network and some identifying the station. The big question would be where to make the division. If the 32 digits were allocated evenly (16 to network address and 16 to station address), there could be up to 65,535 networks with each having up to 65,535 stations each. Sounds reasonable, but wouldn't it be neat if the division could be variable depending on need? Geeks like neat and these geeks worked with the Defense Department so a little cryptography produced the ideal solution; the address would become a code within a code. If the first bit (the leftmost or most significant bit) of the address was zero, then the first octet would be the network address and the remaining three octets would form the station or host address. This would yield up to 126 networks (2 are reserved for testing and broadcast) and more than 65 million hosts on each network. If the first 2 bits were "10", then the first two octets would be the network address and the last two octets would be the host address. This provided more than 16 thousand networks and more than 65,000 hosts on each network. If the first three digits were "110" then the first three octets would be network addresses and the last octet would be host addresses. More than 2 million network addresses, with 256 host addresses on each network, would be provided with this structure. Of course, special use addresses are required for any network, so addresses where the first four digits were "1110" were reserved for multicast/broadcast, and addresses starting with "11110" were reserved for experimentation.

This in a nutshell is IP addressing: simple, straightforward, and easy to remember (so long as you work with it in binary). Later the four address structures would be labeled A, B, C, and D, and binary would be converted to base 10 and formatted as dotted decimal notation. Unfortunately, the relations that are so easy to see in binary are unrecognizable in dotted decimal notation.

You should be able to quickly perform conversions between decimal and binary for the exam. If you are the least bit unsure, spend a few hours practicing before the exam (no calculators are allowed). If you get stuck while taking the exam, work the problem out in binary and then convert to decimal.

# Dotted Decimal Notation

IP addresses are typically shown in *dotted decimal notation*, which was developed so that people could easily read and write IP addresses. You already know that an IP address in its native form is binary. You also know that the address is composed of 32 bits that have been divided into 8-bit groups, referred to as *octets* or *bytes*. An IP address in dotted decimal notation specifies the decimal equivalents of each of the four octets, separated by dots. An example of a dotted decimal IP address is 209.128.50.98.

Each octet can have a decimal value between 0 and 255. Why would there be such a limitation, you ask? The total number of possible values for a binary number with 8 bits can be written mathematically as $2^8$. Although $2^8$ has a total value of 256, IP addresses begin with the number 0 instead of 1; therefore, the decimal range starts at 0 and ends with 255, for a total of 256 possible values.

# IP Classes

The number of bits assigned to the network ID and the host ID depends on the number of hosts required on a given network and the number of networks required in an environment. Before the idea of classful addressing was in place, it was the network administrator's responsibility to determine which bits in the 32-bit address to assign to the network ID and which bits to assign to the host ID. If the number of hosts required on a given network was enormous, the network administrator assigned a large portion of the 32 bits available to host IDs and used a small portion for network IDs. If a large number of networks were required with only a few hosts per network, the network administrator used a small portion of the bits for host IDs and a large number for network IDs.

This method of allocating address space was inefficient, often giving small organizations the right to a large number of IP address spaces. Therefore, IP address space was divided into three classes in the attempt to meet the needs of large and small organizations. (Actually, the IP address was divided into five classes; however, we will focus on the three more commonly used classes.) With the class system, it is possible to assign a corporation address space based on the number of hosts and networks it requires. This system is referred to as *classful addressing*. Classful addressing divides the 4,294,967,296 ($2^{32}$) possible IP addresses into five different classes.

The first 3 bits of the address indicate a class A, B, or C IP address. After a while, you will only need to look at the first octet of an IP address in decimal format to determine its class. The class of an IP address governs the number of bits that can be used for network IDs and the number of bits that can be used for host IDs. For example, an organization that is allocated a class B address must use 16 bits to identify its network ID and 16 bits to identify its host ID. It is important to note that this strict rule can be avoided, and most often is, through a process known as *subnetting*.

## Class A

Class A addresses are typically assigned to very large organizations, universities, and the military. It is extremely difficult—if not impossible—to get a class A address today. These addresses are identified in binary by the first bit having a value of 0 or in decimal by having a *value between 1 and 126*. Class A addresses use the first 8 bits to specify the network ID and the last 24 bits to designate the host ID.

A maximum of 126 class A network IDs are available. This value is arrived at by taking the number of bits used for the network ID to the power of 2. In this case, $2^7$ equals a total of 128 (only 7 bits are available because the first bit must be 0). However, the network ID 0.0.0.0 is reserved for the default route, and the network ID 127.0.0.0 is reserved for the loopback function. Therefore, the range of possible class A network IDs in decimal is 1 to 126.

Although you may never need to know the exact number, each class A network ID can support a total of 16,777,214 ($2^{24}$–2) host IDs. The purpose of subtracting 2 from the possible number of hosts is to remove two special host IDs. Any time every bit in the host ID portion of an IP address has a value of 1, it is considered a *broadcast IP address*, meaning that all hosts in the network should read a message sent to this address, like an ARP request. Obviously, no device should have an address that is used for broadcasting information. The second consideration is when every bit in the host ID's binary value is 0. This value is used to denote a network ID number.

## Class B

Class B addresses are typically assigned to medium and large organizations. These addresses are identified in binary by the first 2 bits having a value of 10, or in decimal by having a *value between 128 and 191*. Class B addresses use the first 16 bits to specify the network ID and the last 16 bits to designate the host IDs. Because the first 2 bits of all class B addresses are always 10, however, only 14 bits are available to be used for network IDs. This allows a total of 16,384 ($2^{14}$) class B network addresses. Each network ID supports a total of 65,534 ($2^{16}$–2) host IDs.

### Class C

Class C addresses are typically assigned to small and medium organizations. These addresses are identified in binary by the first 3 bits having a value of 110, or in decimal by having a *value between 192 and 223*. Class C addresses use the first 24 bits to specify the network ID and the last 8 bits to designate the host IDs. Because the first 3 bits of a class C address are 110, however, only 21 bits are available to be used for network IDs. This allows a total of 2,097,152 ($2^{21}$) class C network addresses. Each network ID supports a total of 254 ($2^8$–2) host IDs.

You will see several questions relating to classful addresses. If you memorize the dotted decimal ranges for A, B, and C class addresses, you will be able to quickly answer these questions. You can always work them out in binary, but the time taken to do that cannot be used on other questions.

## Other Classes

Two other classes of addresses are also available but generally not used in the public address space; these have been reserved for specific functions. Class D addresses are identified in binary by the first 4 bits having a value of 1110, or in decimal by having a value between 224 and 239. Class D addresses have been reserved to support IP *multicasting*, which is the process of using one address to send a message to a group of people. The main benefit of sending a chunk of data headed for multiple destinations is that it has to be sent between the transit routers only once, and therefore a ton of bandwidth is conserved. Class E addresses are identified in binary by the first 5 bits having a value of 11110, or in decimal by having a value between 240 and 247. Class E addresses have been reserved for experimental or research use.

## Subnetting

One of the major goals of classful addressing is the ability to assign one and only one address to an organization. However, few organizations can function with just one network address. Subnetting provides a solution for this problem.

### Default Mask

A *default mask* is a 32-bit number divided into four octets, just like an IP address. A default mask indicates the number of bits used to identify the network ID, and it's implied with all class A, B, and C addresses. Class A addresses imply an 8-bit default mask because the first 8 bits in these addresses designate the network ID. Therefore, the default mask (the number of bits that indicate the network ID) can be represented in decimal format as 255.0.0.0.

Why do we need a default mask if we can already determine this by the class of the IP address? As mentioned previously, organizations often have the need to increase the number of networks in their intranet. However, when an organization has only one block of IP addresses it can advertise to the Internet but wishes to have many subnetworks in its environment, the organization can indicate that it has used some of the host ID bits as network ID bits by providing a subnet mask.

## Subnet Mask

A *subnet mask* is an extension to the default mask. It indicates the number of bits in addition to the default mask that should be used to identify network IDs. What does this do for an organization? It increases the number of networks an organization can create from one class A, B, or C network ID.

For example, if an organization has a registered class C address and needs to create two networks, it must somehow get more network IDs. The organization can accomplish this by using some of the bits designated as host IDs as network IDs. However, the organization must indicate that this class C address is no longer using the default 24 bits as a network ID. The organization can indicate this by applying a subnet mask to represent the additional bits that are to be used as network IDs versus host IDs. The subnet mask can be represented in various ways; in this chapter, we will refer to the subnet mask as the default mask plus any additional bits used for network IDs.

## Logical ANDing

How should the subnet mask be used to determine the network ID for an IP address? To determine the network ID and the host ID for an IP address, it is necessary to perform a process known as *logical ANDing*. When information is sent to a router and is destined for a remote location, the router cares only about which network to send the information to. The router knows the subnet mask and the destination IP, so the ANDing process is used with these two addresses to determine the network portion of an IP address and then a routing table is used to determine the remote network to send the information to. This indicates which bits to use as network bits and which bits to use as host bits when the IP address is deciphered. When the subnet mask is applied to an IP address, each bit starting from the most significant bit to the least significant bit is compared between the IP address and the subnet mask. For example, the first bit of the first octet of the IP address is compared with the first bit of the first octet of the subnet mask. The resulting value from this bit-by-bit comparison is the network ID. The rule set to apply is listed as follows:

- If the subnet mask and the IP address both have values of 1, the resulting network ID bit is 1.
- If the subnet mask has a value of 1 and the IP address has a value of 0, the resulting network ID bit is 0.
- If the subnet mask has a value of 0, the resulting network ID bit is 0.

So far, you have learned that IP addresses are divided into classes to allocate the IP address space to varying sizes of organizations efficiently. Efficient allocation of address space also minimizes the number of entries that need to be maintained in the routing tables of Internet routers. Because organizations required more networks than the InterNIC believed reasonable to assign due to wasted IP address space, a subnet mask was created, giving organizations a tool for increasing the number of networks they had by borrowing bits from the host IDs of their assigned IP address space. A subnet mask uses the logical AND process to distinguish between the network ID and the host ID of an IP address.

Next, we'll discuss some of the items to consider when determining the number of bits to use for the subnet mask. A bad decision on a subnet mask can place constraints on an organization's future addressing choices.

## Subnetting Consideration

Remember that the purpose of the subnet mask is to give an organization the flexibility to increase the number of networks in its environment. So, you might think that an organization should give itself the maximum number of networks possible with its assigned IP address space. Any time a bit is added to the network ID, however, a bit is removed from the host ID. Therefore, if the number of networks is increased, the number of host IDs available per network is decreased.

Organizations need to determine the happy medium between sufficient host IDs and network IDs for their specific needs. The cost of changing the subnet mask on thousands of computers because of a scaling issue is not a welcome thought for network administrators. Here are some of the questions that must be asked before a subnet addressing scheme is developed:

- What is the total number of network IDs the organization needs today?
- What is the total number of host IDs the largest network requires today?
- What is the total number of network IDs the organization will need in the future?
- What is the total number of host IDs the largest network will require in the future?

The answers to these questions will determine how an organization subnets its assigned IP address space. The purpose of asking about current and future requirements is to get an understanding of what is absolutely needed today and what should be planned for the future. To illustrate the process of classful IP addressing, subnetting, and logical ANDing as well as IP addressing considerations, examples using class A and C addresses are provided in the following sections.

The next few sections will give some real good examples of subnetting. If you are comfortable with this concept, congratulations, you may proceed to another section. If you are not comfortable, please read on. Beware, you will be tested extensively on this section for the CCNA exam.

## Class A Network Example

This example uses a fictitious company named AWSB to illustrate the process of determining the proper subnetting for an organization. AWSB has been allocated the class A IP address 114.0.0.0 by the InterNIC. AWSB must determine the proper way to use this IP address space to support its current and future needs. To determine these needs, we must answer the four questions suggested previously. These questions are repeated here, along with AWSB's responses to them:

- What is the total number of network IDs AWSB needs today? *Answer: 5,000.*
- What is the total number of network IDs AWSB will need in the future? *Answer: 9,000.*
- What is the total number of host IDs AWSB requires on its largest network today? *Answer: 1,000.*
- What is the total number of host IDs AWSB will require on its largest network in the future? *Answer: 2,000.*

AWSB has been assigned only one network ID; however, it needs lots more to support its current and future requirements. AWSB plans to use subnetting to create more network IDs. As mentioned previously, by default, 24 bits are allocated for host IDs with a class A IP address space. We know that AWSB requires 5,000 networks today and 9,000 in the future. Therefore, to create enough network IDs, we have to take bits from the host IDs and use them for network IDs. How many bits have to be taken from the host ID bits to provide 5,000 network IDs?

AWSB requires a total of 13 bits to provide 5,000 network IDs. The number of bits required can be determined by taking $2^{13}$ (for a total of 8,192 possible networks). A subnet mask of 255.255.248.0 is used to represent the 13 bits of subnetting. However, 13 bits provide only 8,192 total possible networks, which is not enough to support AWSB's expected growth. A total of 14 bits is required to ensure that 9,000+ networks can be supported in the future. If AWSB uses 14 bits as the subnet mask (a subnet mask of 255.255.252.0), it has a total of 16,384 ($2^{14}$) possible network IDs. AWSB would prefer to use 14 bits of the host ID to subnet the current 114.0.0.0 class A address; however, taking 13 bits from the host ID would provide a sufficient number of network IDs (subnets) to provide for today's needs.

AWSB must determine whether enough bits still remain to provide an adequate number of host IDs. AWSB requires 1,000 host IDs per network today and expects to need 2,000 host IDs per network in the future. How many bits are required to provide 1,000 host IDs? How many bits are required to provide 2,000 host IDs? How many bits are still available to be used as host IDs?

The number of bits required for 1,000 host IDs is 10, which provides a total combination of 1,022 ($2^{10}$–2). Remember that we subtract 2 to represent the broadcast (all 1s) and the zero (all 0s) value in each network. However, AWSB requires 11 bits to provide sufficient host IDs to support its future requirement of 2,000 hosts.

AWSB has only 24 bits of host IDs in its class A 114.0.0.0 IP address to use for both hosts and networks. To get enough host IDs for 2,000 users per network and 9,000+ network IDs, however, it would take 14 network ID bits and 11 host ID bits, for a total of 25 bits. AWSB is short 1 bit, so it has to decide whether to limit the number of hosts or networks to have in the future. In this case, AWSB would probably opt to use only 13 bits (8,192 networks) for network IDs and 11 bits for host IDs (2,046 host IDs per network). The decision can become more difficult, however, when an organization doesn't have the luxury of owning an entire class A IP address.

## Class C Network Example

In this example, we will define the actual subnets and host IDs. If an organization named AWSB has been assigned the IP address space 210.14.12.0, it has been assigned a class C address with a default mask of 255.255.255.0. This organization requires five networks today and expects to need eight in the future. In addition, AWSB expects the largest number of hosts on a given network now and in the future to be 30 users.

AWSB requires more networks and must subnet the 8 bits allocated to host IDs to provide these networks. To do so, AWSB must subnet 3 bits to provide eight more networks ($2^3$). The subnet mask of this IP address is now 255.255.255.224. The value of the last octet has changed to represent the 3 bits (128 + 64 + 32 = 224) that are now used to identify networks instead of hosts. However, AWSB must make sure that it will have enough host IDs left to identify all 30 devices on its largest network. AWSB has 5 bits remaining for host IDs, giving it a total of 30 ($2^5$–2) host IDs per network.

# Summary of Subnetting

You have seen that flexibility has been built into IP addressing via a process known as *subnetting*, which allows organizations to divide up classful network IDs into a number of other networks. Any device can determine how an IP address is divided by looking at the IP address's subnet mask. This mask indicates which bits have been used for subnetting and which bits are still being used to identify hosts. Of course, each class of IP address has a default mask. Furthermore, we identified some important questions to consider when setting up an addressing scheme. Specifically, you need to know the number of hosts and networks an organization requires in the present and the future.

The ability to do subnet masks on the fly for the CCNA exam is crucial. The good news is that this ability is also crucial to being proficient at networking in general. Therefore, feel good about spending a significant amount of time practicing the art of subnetting.

# Exam Prep Questions

## Question 1

The following IP address is listed in dotted decimal format. What is the corresponding binary value of this IP address?

**112.14.12.8**

- ❍ A. 01100000.00110000.01101111.10110111
- ❍ B. 0.11.0.11
- ❍ C. 01110000.00001110.00001100.00001000
- ❍ D. 01110000.00001110.11000000.00110011

The correct answer is C. The conversion of these binary bits yields a decimal value of 112.14.12.8. Answer A can be identified quickly as incorrect by noting that the fourth octet begins with 1, but its value is not greater than 128. Answer B can be eliminated immediately because it is not in the format of a binary IP address. Answer D can be judged to be incorrect by determining the decimal value of either the third or fourth octet. It is important to note that it is not necessary to convert each one of the possible answers into decimal format. It is much quicker to eliminate the obviously wrong answers (such as B) and then isolate reasons to remove other answers before converting any values.

## Question 2

Which of the following statements is not true concerning the deciphering of a subnet ID from an IP address and subnet mask using the ANDing process?

- ❍ A. If the subnet mask and the IP address both have values of 1, the resulting network ID bit is 1.
- ❍ B. If the subnet mask has a value of 1 and the IP address has a value of 1, the resulting network ID bit is 0.
- ❍ C. If the subnet mask has a value of 1 and the IP address has a value of 0, the resulting network ID bit is 0.
- ❍ D. If the subnet mask has a value of 0, the resulting network ID bit is 0.

The correct answer is B. It specifies that a network ID bit of 0 is the result when comparing a subnet mask bit with a value of 1 and an IP address with a value of 1. This is *not* one of the rules used to decipher network IDs.

Therefore, answer B is the correct answer. Answers A, C, and F are the three rules presented in this chapter for deciphering network IDs from an IP address with a subnet mask. Therefore, these answers are incorrect.

## Question 3

Which of the following tools can be utilized to test IP connectivity between two devices? (Choose the three best answers.)

- ❑ A. **Ping**
- ❑ B. **Telnet**
- ❑ C. **Traceroute**
- ❑ D. **show ip interface**
- ❑ E. **show ip protocol**

The correct answers are A, B, and C. Ping, Telnet, and Traceroute are all tools mentioned in this chapter for testing IP connectivity between two devices. Answers D and E are incorrect because `show ip interface` and `show ip protocol` are used to monitor IP addresses and the functioning of IP within a local router.

## Question 4

Which of the following tools will identify the address of intermediate hops between two destinations?

- ❍ A. Traceroute
- ❍ B. Telnet
- ❍ C. Ping
- ❍ D. Rlogin
- ❍ E. TCP

The correct answer is A. The `traceroute` command can be used to identify the address of every intermediate hop between two locations. Answer B is incorrect because the `telnet` command is used to obtain remote control of a destination device. Answer C is incorrect because the `ping` command only tells users whether they have IP connectivity. Answer D is incorrect because `rlogin` is a command used for remote access on Unix machines. Finally, answer E is incorrect because TCP is a Layer 4 protocol, and it is not used for testing IP connectivity.

## Question 5

Which of the following is the default mask of a class A IP address?

❍ A. 255.0.0.255

❍ B. 255.255.0.0

❍ C. 255.0.0.0

❍ D. 255.255.255.0

The correct answer is C. Class A addresses have a default mask of 8 bits, or 255.0.0.0. Answer A is incorrect because all default masks are made up of contiguous bits. Answer B is incorrect because 255.255.0.0 is the default mask of a class B IP address, not a class A IP address. Answer D is incorrect because 255.255.255.0 is the default mask of a class C IP address, not a class A IP address.

## Question 6

Which of the following terms does not identify a layer of the TCP/IP model?

❍ A. Application

❍ B. Transport

❍ C. Presentation

❍ D. Internet

❍ E. Network access

The correct answer is C. Only the OSI model uses the Presentation layer; therefore, this term does not identify a layer of the TCP/IP model. Answers A, B, D, and E all identify separate layers of the TCP/IP model.

## Question 7

Which of the following services exist at the Application layer of the TCP/IP model? (Choose the best answers.)

❑ A. SMTP

❑ B. FTP

❑ C. ICMP

❑ D. ARP

❑ E. TFTP

The correct answers are A, B, and E. SMTP, FTP, and TFTP all exist at the Application layer of the TCP/IP model. Answer C is incorrect because ICMP exists at the Internet layer of the TCP/IP model. Answer D is incorrect because ARP exists at the Internet layer of the TCP/IP model.

## Question 8

If you wanted to locate the hardware address of a local device, which protocol would you use?

- ❍ A. ARP
- ❍ B. RARP
- ❍ C. ICMP
- ❍ D. PING

The correct answer is A. If you know the IP address and you are trying to find the hardware (MAC) address, ARP is the choice. Answers C and D are incorrect because a `ping` command is used to verify network connectivity and sends ICMP packets to determine this. RARP, answer B, is incorrect because it will find the IP address, given the hardware address.

## Question 9

Which of the following services is used to translate hostnames into IP addresses?

- ❍ A. SNMP
- ❍ B. SMTP
- ❍ C. IP
- ❍ D. UDP
- ❍ E. DNS

The correct answer is E. DNS is used to translate word-based addresses into IP addresses, or vice versa. SNMP and SMTP are TCP/IP Application layer services, but they do not perform address translation. SNMP is used to monitor remote devices, and SMTP is used to send email between devices. IP is not a service but rather a protocol used for logical addressing and routing. Therefore, answers A, B, and C are incorrect. Finally, UDP is a Transport layer protocol used for packet sequencing, which makes answer D incorrect.

## Question 10

Which of the following functions is not performed by TCP?

- ❍ A. Flow control
- ❍ B. Sequencing
- ❍ C. Error checking
- ❍ D. Subnetting

The correct answer is D. Subnetting is not a function performed by TCP; it is a process used to create more networks out of classful IP addresses. Answer A is incorrect because TCP does indeed provide flow control in the form of sliding windows and buffer management. Answer B is incorrect because TCP provides sequencing to ensure that datagrams are read in the correct order on the receiving side. Finally, answer C is incorrect because TCP provides error checking by applying a checksum to the TCP header and encapsulated data.

# Need to Know More?

Sportack, Mark A. *IP Addressing Fundamentals.* Cisco Press, Indianapolis, Indiana, 2003. ISBN 1-58705-067-6. IP addressing can be extremely confusing. This book covers the topic from every angle possible. While IP addressing is presented in far more detail than required for the CCNA, it is a good reference to have for the entire Cisco certification program.

Osterloh, Heather. *TCP/IP Primer Plus.* Sams Publishing, Indianapolis, Indiana, 2002. ISBN 0-672-32208-0. Written clearly and concisely, this one book can answer almost any question relating to TCP/IP. It is a good book to have for both this certification and future Cisco certifications.

Castelli, Matthew. *Network Sales and Services Handbook.* Cisco Press, Indianapolis, Indiana, 2003. ISBN 1-58705-090-0. Although this book is targeted at sales, it does a very good job of explaining technologies and Cisco products without getting into mind bogging minutia. A good book to have!

Odom, Wendell. *Cisco CCNA Exam Certification Guide.* Cisco Press, Indianapolis, Indiana, 2000. ISBN 0-7357-0971-8. Cisco is almost always the best place for reference books relating to Cisco. They print incredibly detailed and comprehensive books and this one is excellent. I would not want to read it as a primary text but as a reference it cannot be beat.

# Cisco Layer 2 Switching

## Terms you'll need to understand:

- ✓ Spanning Tree Protocol
- ✓ Store-and-forward switching
- ✓ Fragment-free switching
- ✓ Cut-through switching
- ✓ Virtual Local Area Network (VLAN)
- ✓ VLAN ID
- ✓ VLAN Trunking Protocol (VTP)

## Techniques you'll need to master:

- ✓ Filtering and forwarding frames
- ✓ Preventing loops
- ✓ Discovering MAC addresses
- ✓ Frame tagging
- ✓ Inter-switch link

Chapter 3, "Hardware and the OSI Model," presented the evolution of the switch, as we know it today. Here, we will present switching technology, as Cisco views it. Many of the features and protocols we will be talking about are proprietary to Cisco or pioneered by Cisco. Therefore, even if you feel you know the technology, read this chapter carefully. Switching is a major product technology for Cisco and you will see more than a few questions on the test that relate directly to this chapter.

# Layer 2 Switching Technology

Remember from earlier chapters that switches operate at Layer 2 of the Open Systems Interconnection (OSI) model.

Cisco has applied switching technology to some of their Layer 3 and Layer 4 products. Because of this, you will sometimes hear people refer to Layer 3 and Layer 4 switches. The CCNA exam, however, only covers Layer 2 switches. Therefore, when you see the term "switch," assume it is a Layer 2 device.

The technology upon which Layer 2 switches operate is the same as that provided by Ethernet bridges. The basic operation of a switch involves the following:

- Discovering Media Access Control (MAC) addresses
- Filtering or forwarding frames
- Preventing loops

# Discovering MAC Addresses

Like a bridge, a switch monitors all frames that pass through it to learn the MAC addresses of each device connected to its ports. This information is stored in the MAC Address Table also known as the CAM (Content Addressable Memory). The switch consults the filter table each time it receives a frame to determine whether to forward the frame to a different port or to drop it.

When the switch is initially booted up, the filter table is empty. Forwarding or filtering decisions cannot be made with an empty database, so initially each incoming frame is forwarded through all the switch's ports. This is called *flooding the frame*. As flooding occurs, the switch begins to learn the MAC addresses and associate them with one of its ports.

This address-learning process is a continual operation of the switch. Each MAC database entry is stored in memory and is valid only for a preset interval. If a new frame does not refresh the entry, the entry is discarded.

## Filtering and Forwarding

Each time the switch receives a frame, it examines the destination MAC address. If this address exists in the MAC database, the frame is forwarded only through the switch port associated with the address. This process frees all the segments connected to different ports of the excess bandwidth taken by the frame. This is known as *frame filtering*.

Whenever the destination MAC address is unknown, the frame is flooded to all switch ports. This is undesirable because it wastes bandwidth.

## Preventing Loops

Both bridges and switches introduce the possibility of creating a bridged network with multiple paths to a single destination. Typically, this type of redundancy is considered favorable, but for switches and bridges it can cause problems in the form of *bridging loops*, which occur when circular connections exist in a bridged network. Figure 6.1 illustrates a bridged network with bridging loops.

Bridges and switches provide a bridging function. Although we will use the term "bridge" in this discussion, the concept of bridging loops applies equally to switches.

For example, if someone sends a broadcast message from segment 2, the message would be forwarded to physical segment 3 by bridges B and C. Bridge A would then receive two broadcasts and forward both broadcasts to physical segment 1. Bridge D would have forwarded this broadcast to physical segment 1 as well. Subsequently, bridge D will receive the two broadcasts forwarded by bridge A and forward these frames to physical segment 2. This continuous forwarding of broadcast packets wastes bandwidth. With more complex bridged networks, the broadcast packets can be forwarded exponentially, leading to what is termed a *broadcast storm*. This occurs when so many broadcasts are being continuously forwarded that they consume all the available bandwidth. The Spanning Tree Protocol, which implements an algorithm that removes all circular connections in a bridged network, eliminates bridging loops.

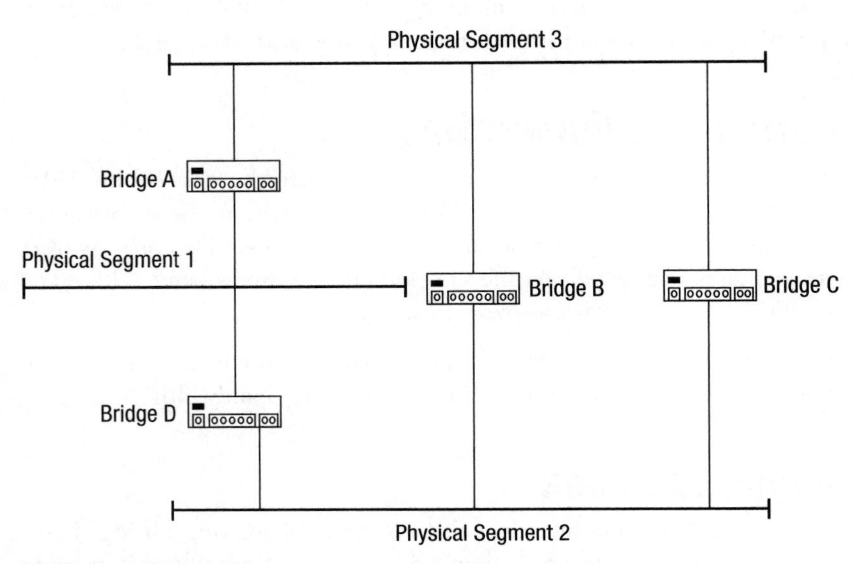


**Figure 6.1** Switches and bridges can create loops if improperly positioned.

## Spanning Tree Protocol

The Spanning Tree Protocol creates a loop-free network topology by placing connections that create loops in a blocking state. It is important to note that this protocol does not eliminate loops but rather only blocks the connections that create the loops. Loops in a network often provide needed redundancy in the case of a physical connection being disconnected. The Spanning Tree Protocol maintains the benefits of redundancy while eliminating the disadvantages of looping. To illustrate how the Spanning Tree Protocol functions, we will use the bridged network shown earlier in Figure 6.1.

The Spanning Tree Protocol selects a root bridge in the network (in this case, bridge A).

### Determining the Root Bridge

When a network using multiple bridges and spanning tree protocol starts, the bridges automatically broadcast their ID numbers. The ID number is actually a combination of the MAC address and an assigned priority value. In most cases, the bridge with the lowest priority number assumes the role of root bridge. If two or more bridges have the same priority number, the one with the lowest MAC address becomes the root bridge.

Next, every other bridge selects one of its ports with the least path cost to the root bridge. The *least path cost* is the sum of the cost to traverse every network between the indicated bridge and the root bridge. The root path cost can be determined in multiple ways; in this case, we have arbitrarily assigned costs to each path. Next, designated bridges are determined. A *designated bridge* is the bridge on each LAN with the lowest aggregate root path cost. It's the only bridge on a LAN allowed to forward frames. Figure 6.2 illustrates our network with the root path cost assigned to each bridge interface.

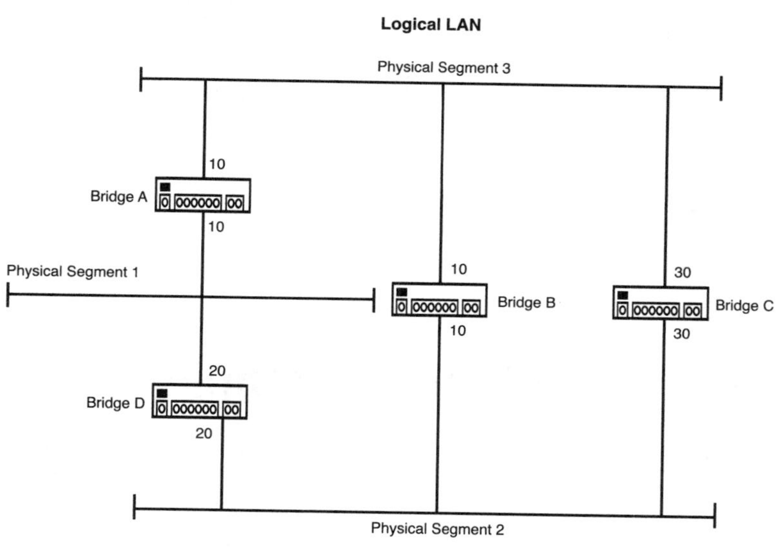


**Figure 6.2** The root path cost for each bridge interface.

By applying the Spanning Tree Protocol, we block the connection between bridge C and physical segments 2 and 3, because bridge D and bridge B both have lower aggregate root path costs to the root bridge (bridge A). We also block the connection between bridge D and physical segment 2, because bridge B has a lower root path cost than bridge D. Figure 6.3 illustrates our bridged network after the Spanning Tree Protocol has been applied. Note that the connections between bridge C and physical segments 2 and 3 are blocked, as well as the connection between bridge D and physical segment 2.

We now have no circular paths in our network, but we maintain redundancy, because the Spanning Tree Protocol is applied whenever a bridge is powered up or a topology change occurs. Therefore, if the connection between bridge B and physical segment 2 is broken, the Spanning Tree Protocol would run and the connection between bridge D and physical segment 2 would be enabled.

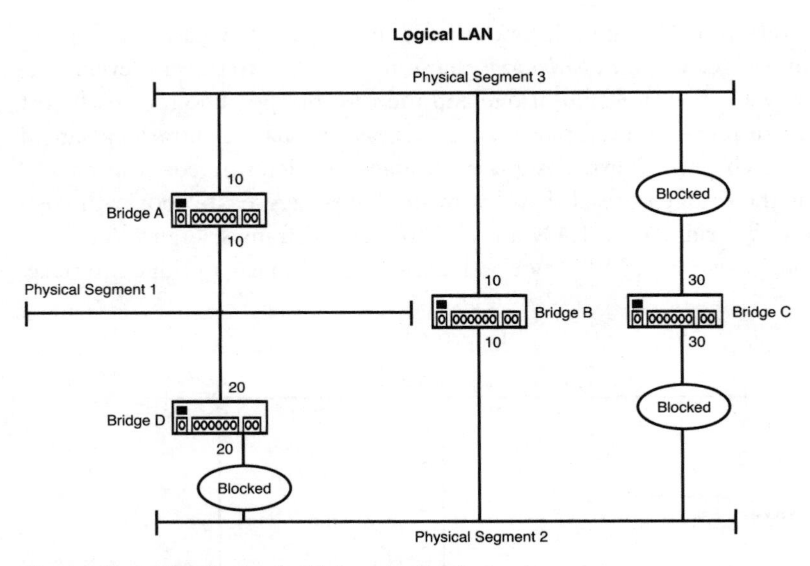


**Figure 6.3** A bridged network with Spanning Tree Protocol.

# Cisco LAN Switching Methods

All the switching methods used by Cisco switches provide increased throughput in comparison to bridges. The hardware-based architectures of switches allow them to make decisions at wire speeds. The primary difference between the various methods is the process each uses to switch frames.

Frames have been consistently used to represent Layer 2 data messages in this chapter. The term *cells* can also be used to identify Layer 2 data messages. This term is used when referring to data traffic using the Asynchronous Transfer Mode (ATM) technology. The CCNA exam does not cover this technology, so only frames have been presented in this chapter to simplify the concepts.

## Store-and-Forward Switching

In store-and-forward switching mode, the switch reads the entire incoming frame and copies the frame into its buffers. After the frame has been completely read, the switch performs the Layer 2 cyclical redundancy check (CRC) to determine whether an error occurred during transmission. If the frame has an error, the switch drops the frame. If no error is identified, the switch checks its forwarding table to determine the proper port (in the case of a unicast) or ports (in the case of a multicast) to which the frame must be forwarded.

Store-and-forward switches have the highest latency of any switching mode, because the switch must read the entire frame before making a forwarding decision. The added error checking of store-and-forward switching, however, reduces the number of erred frames that are forwarded.

## Cut-Through Switching

Cut-through switches introduce a lower level of latency during the switching process than store-and-forward switches do, mainly because the frame is forwarded as soon as the destination address and outgoing interface are determined. They achieve increased performance by eliminating the error checking and making forwarding decisions based only on the first six bytes of the incoming frame. (These first six bytes contain the destination MAC address of the frame.) Cut-through switches read the destination address of the incoming frame and immediately check the forwarding table to determine the proper destination ports. This increased performance does, however, allow erred frames to be forwarded more often than store-and-forward switches do.

## Fragment-Free Switching

Fragment-free switching is a modification to the cut-through switching method. Like cut-through switches, fragment-free switches read only a portion of the frame before beginning the forwarding process. The difference is that fragment-free switches read the first 64 bytes, which is enough to check the frame for collisions. This allows for better error checking than with cut-through switches, with a minimal loss in latency.

Cisco has incorporated switching technology into devices operating at layers other than Layer 2. Be very careful when answering exam questions to determine how the term "switch" is used. The features and functions we are presenting in this chapter apply to Cisco layer two switches exclusively.

# Virtual Local Area Networks (VLANs)

A VLAN is a group of switched ports that acts as a separate, isolated LAN. There can be several VLANs defined on a single switch (see Figure 6.4). A VLAN can also span multiple switches. Workstations in separate VLANs will never encounter traffic from or share bandwidth with other VLANs unless the data is routed. In other words, a router or switch with routing capabilities is required if devices on different VLANs need to communicate. It should be noted that VLAN configuration is done through the switch and its software.

Remember from earlier chapters that one of the main benefits to switches is that they segment a network into many collision domains. Each port represents a single collision domain, and devices share bandwidth only with other devices on the same switch port. Unless a switch is segmented into VLANs, however, all the devices on the switch are still in the same broadcast domain; that is, all broadcasts are sent to each port throughout the switching fabric.

VLANs introduce a way to limit the broadcast traffic in a switched network (a job normally associated with routers). When you create a VLAN by defining which ports belong to it, you are really just creating a boundary for broadcast traffic. This has the effect of creating multiple, isolated LANs on a single switch.

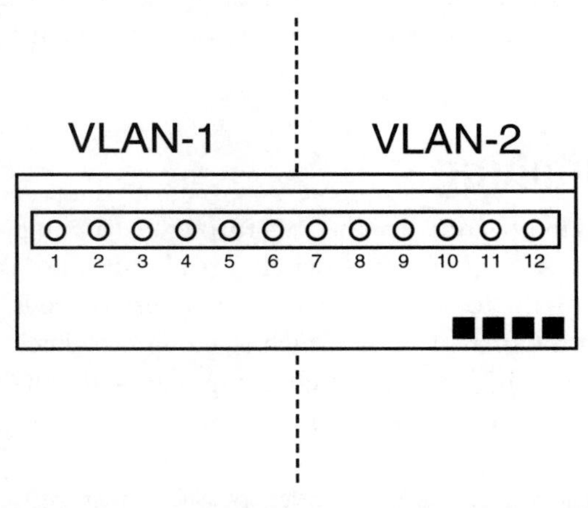


**Figure 6.4** This figure shows a 12-port switch that has been divided into two VLANs. Ports 1 through 6 are VLAN 1, and ports 7 through 12 are VLAN 2.

It is important to understand the need for routers in a switched network. If devices on different VLANs need to communicate, routing is required to facilitate this exchange of data. Many of today's network systems are collections of routers *and* switches.

What happens when a device on one VLAN needs to communicate with a device on another VLAN? Because a VLAN is a closed Layer 2 network, traffic must cross a Layer 3 device to communicate with other VLANs.

This means a router is required to facilitate the exchange of packets between VLANs.

It is possible for a device to participate in more than one VLAN by using a special type of network card that performs ISL, which is discussed later in this chapter.

The real benefit to using VLANs is that they can span multiple switches. Figure 6.5 shows two switches that are configured to share VLAN information.

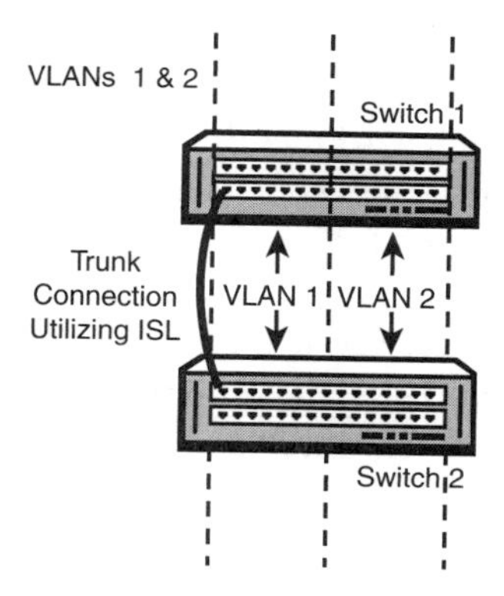


**Figure 6.5** VLANS can span multiple switches.

A large campus network may have hundreds of switches spread throughout several buildings. Users can be put on the appropriate VLANs easily, no matter where they are physically located. Users on the same VLAN do not have to be connected to the same device. Therefore, LANs are no longer tied to the physical location of users but rather can be assigned based on department, functional area, or security level. By isolating users according to department or functional area, network administrators can keep the majority of data traffic within one VLAN, thereby maximizing the amount of traffic switched at hardware speeds versus what is routed at slower software speeds.

The ability to assign a user to a VLAN on a port-by-port basis makes adding, moving, or deleting users simple. For example, let's say a user changes from the accounting department to the marketing department. If the network administrator designed the network and VLANs by functional department, this user would have changed VLANs. To accommodate this change, the administrator only has to make a software configuration change in the switch by assigning that user's port to the new VLAN.

In addition, VLANs provide the flexibility necessary to group users by security level. This can greatly simplify applying a security policy to a network. In summary, here are the benefits of VLANs:

- They simplify security administration.
- They allow users to be grouped by functional area versus physical location.
- They simplify moving and adding users.

# Frame Tagging

Frame tagging is the method used by Cisco switches to identify to which VLAN a frame belongs. As a frame enters the switch, the switch encapsulates the frame with a header that "tags" the frame with a VLAN ID. Any time a frame needs to leave one switch for another, the tagged frame is sent throughout the switching fabric. When the frame arrives at the destination switch, the tag tells the switch to which VLAN the frame belongs. This process is illustrated in Figure 6.6 using the VLAN IDs 10, 20, and 30.

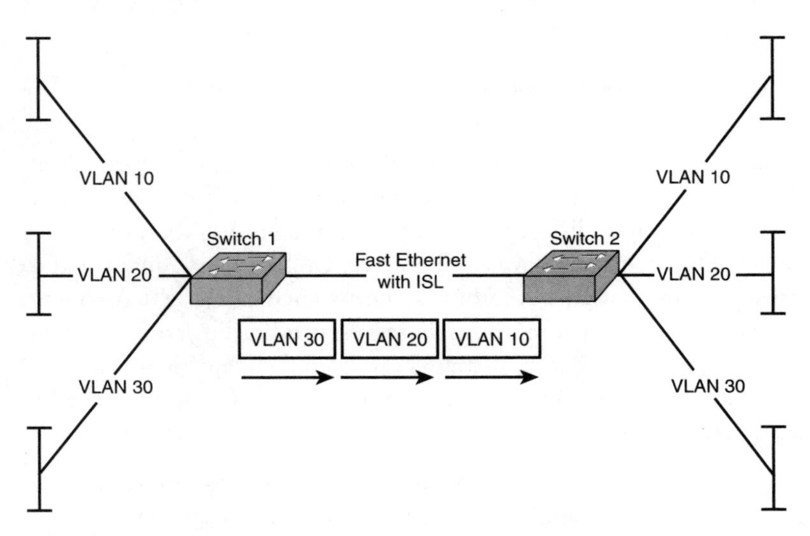


**Figure 6.6** Frame tagging in a VLAN environment.

The tag is stripped off of the frame before the frame is sent out to the destination device. This process gives the illusion that all ports are physically connected to the same switch.

Be sure to understand the function of frame tagging, which "tags" a frame with a user-defined VLAN ID.

# Trunk Connections

Under normal circumstances, a switch port can carry traffic for a single VLAN only. For VLANs to span multiple switches, a trunk connection must be created. This trunk connection transports data from multiple VLANs. Trunk connections allow VLANs to be used throughout the switching fabric of large networks.

Any Fast Ethernet or Asynchronous Transfer Mode (ATM) port on a switch can be designated as a trunk port. This port typically connects to another switch via a crossover 100BASE-T cable in the case of a Fast Ethernet trunk.

For the trunked port to transport multiple VLANs, it must understand frame tags.

# Interswitch Link (ISL)

ISL is a technology developed by Cisco that allows a single Ethernet interface to participate in multiple VLANs. When a trunk connection is made on a Catalyst switch's Ethernet port, ISL is used. ISL is also available on Ethernet cards that can be used in servers or routers.

A device utilizing an ISL Ethernet card will appear to have many physical cards, each connected to a different segment. ISL allows this single Ethernet card to have many logical (virtual) addresses. The user must configure each logical interface with an address that reflects the VLAN to which it belongs.

ISL works by allowing the frame-tagging information to be passed along to the Ethernet card. The Ethernet card then reads the frame tag, which identifies the VLAN to which the frame belongs. Conversely, the ISL Ethernet card creates the frame tags when transmitting frames.

ISL is a technology proprietary to Cisco and, therefore, is not supported on equipment made by other vendors. However, in mid-1998, the Institute of Electrical and Electronics Engineers (IEEE) standardized a frame-tagging process similar to Cisco's ISL. The new standard is a protocol called 802.1Q. With 802.1Q, switches from multiple vendors can coexist in the same switching fabric.

# VLAN Trunking Protocol (VTP)

VTP is a protocol used between switches to simplify the management of VLANs. Configuration changes that are made to a VTP server are propagated across trunks to all connected switches.

All switches that are to be managed in this way must be members of the same *management domain*. A VTP management domain is the entire group of switches that share configuration information.

For example, when you add a new VLAN to a member switch, the VLAN is available in all the network switches automatically. VTP allows switched networks to scale to larger environments; otherwise, VLAN configuration would have to be maintained manually on individual switches.

By default, Catalyst switches are set to a no-management-domain state. The switches remain in a no-management state until a user configures the management domain or the switches receive an advertisement for a domain over a trunk link.

## VTP Modes

When it has a management domain, a switch operates in one of three VTP modes: server, client, or transparent. The default mode is server.

In VTP server mode, a switch can create, modify, or delete VLAN and other configuration parameters for the entire VTP domain. VTP messages are sent over all trunk links, and configuration changes are propagated to all switches in the management domain.

In VTP client mode, the switch receives VTP messages and applies configuration changes made from any VTP server. However, a client cannot create, change, or delete VLAN information.

In VTP transparent mode, the switch forwards all VTP messages to other switches in the domain but does not use the configuration from VTP advertisements. A VTP transparent switch can create, modify, or delete VLANs, but the changes apply only locally and are not transmitted to other switches.

## VTP Pruning

VTP can detect whether a trunk connection is carrying unnecessary traffic. By default, all trunk connections carry traffic from all VLANs in the management domain. In many cases, however, a switch does not need a local port configured for each VLAN. In this event, it is not necessary to flood traffic from VLANs other than the ones supported by that switch (see Figure 6.7). VTP pruning enables the switching fabric to prevent flooding traffic on trunk ports that do not need it.

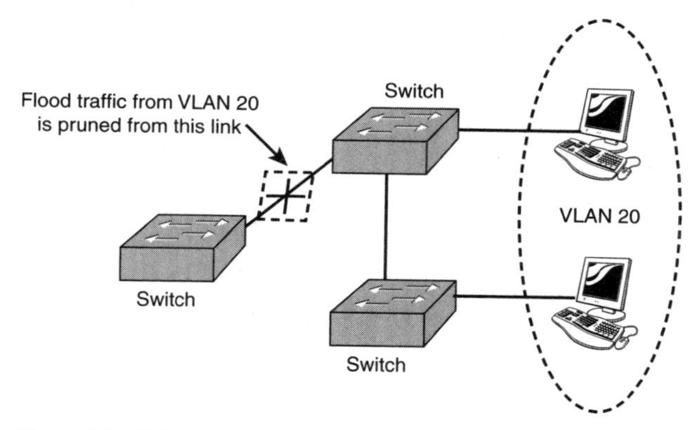


**Figure 6.7** VTP pruning.

# Configuring VLANs

Three methods can be used to assign a switch port to a particular VLAN: *port-centric*, *static*, and *dynamic*. In a port-centric configuration, all nodes that are connected to ports within the same VLAN are given the same VLAN ID. In this type of configuration, the network administrator's job is much easier because of the ease of administering the VLAN. In a static VLAN configuration, the ports on a switch are hard-coded and remain in effect until the administrator changes them. This type of configuration is typical of a network that is very well monitored and where changes are unlikely. The third type of port configuration is dynamic. This type of configuration involves more overhead on setup for the administrator because of the database configuration. The ports on these switches automatically determine their assigned VLAN. The VLAN assignment is determined by the type of protocol (within a frame), MAC address, and logical addressing. A major benefit of this type of configuration is that the administrator will notice when any unauthorized or new user is on the network. If a workstation happens to be connected to a port that is unassigned, the switch will record the MAC address of the workstation and check its database to determine which VLAN to assign the workstation to.

# Exam Prep Questions

## Question 1

What is maintained in a switch's forwarding table?

- ❍ A. A device's IP address and the IP network on which the device resides
- ❍ B. A device's MAC address and the physical segment on which that device resides
- ❍ C. The MAC addresses and the best interfaces to use to forward a frame to a destination MAC address
- ❍ D. The IP network and MAC address of devices

The correct answer is C. Forwarding tables maintain MAC addresses. In addition, forwarding tables maintain the best interfaces to use to forward a frame to a destination MAC address. Answer A is incorrect because a bridge does not maintain IP addresses in its forwarding table. IP is a Layer 3 protocol and is used by routers, not bridges. Answer B is a trick answer because it is partially correct. However, bridges do not maintain the physical segment on which a device resides. Bridges only maintain the next physical segment to forward a frame en route to the device's physical segment. In some cases, the device will exist on this physical segment, but not in all cases. Answer D is incorrect because bridges do not maintain IP network information.

## Question 2

What is the name of the protocol used to eliminate loops?

- ❍ A. Switching
- ❍ B. ISL
- ❍ C. Frame tagging
- ❍ D. Spanning Tree Protocol

The correct answer is D. The Spanning Tree Protocol is used to remove circular routes in bridged and switched networks. Answer A is incorrect because switching is a Layer 2 technology, not a protocol. Answer B is incorrect because interswitch link (ISL) is used to allow VLANs to span multiple physical switches. Answer C is incorrect because frame tagging is a process used to identify the VLAN of a frame between switches.

# Question 3

Which of the following switching methods provides the greatest frame throughput?

- ❍ A. Store-and-forward switching
- ❍ B. Frame-tag switching
- ❍ C. Cut-through switching
- ❍ D. ISL switching

The correct answer is C. Cut-through switching provides high-throughput frame switching because it reads only a portion of the frame before making the forwarding decision. Cut-through switching does not provide error checking. Answer A is incorrect because store-and-forward switching has slower frame throughput rates than cut-through switching because of its error-checking capabilities and because it reads the entire frame before making a forwarding decision. Answer B is incorrect because frame-tag switching does not exist; frame tagging is a process used to identify a frame's VLAN between switches. Answer D is incorrect because it is used to allow VLANs to span multiple switches as well.

# Question 4

Which of the following are advantages of VLANs? (Choose the two best answers.)

- ❑ A. They reduce switching overhead.
- ❑ B. They increase switching throughput.
- ❑ C. They simplify the adding, moving, and changing of users.
- ❑ D. They allow users to be grouped by functional area, not physical location.

The correct answers are C and D. VLANs increase the flexibility of assigning users to LANs. This increased simplicity allows users to be grouped by functional area rather than physical location, because VLANs can span multiple switches. Answer A is incorrect because VLANs do not reduce the amount of overhead required to switch a frame. Answer B is incorrect because VLANs do not provide any increased switching throughput.

## Question 5

What must you do to allow a VLAN to span two or more switches?

- ❍ A. Set up a VTP domain.
- ❍ B. Set up a trunk connection.
- ❍ C. Configure the duplex setting on the ports.
- ❍ D. Configure port security on the switch.

The correct answer is B. A trunk connection must be established in order for a VLAN to span multiple switches. Trunk ports recognize frame tags and are therefore able to carry information on multiple VLANs. Answer A is incorrect because a VTP domain is not necessary for switches to share VLAN information. Answer C is incorrect because the duplex setting does not have to be configured manually to connect two switches. Answer D is incorrect because port security is not necessary for a VLAN to span switches.

## Question 6

Which of the following are advantages of using VTP in a switching environment? (Choose the two best answers.)

- ❑ A. It enables VLANs to span multiple switches.
- ❑ B. It simplifies the management of VLANs.
- ❑ C. It simplifies the scalability of the switched network.
- ❑ D. It allows switches to read frame tags.

The correct answers are B and C. VTP simplifies the management of VLANs because configuration information is propagated automatically throughout the switching fabric when changes are made. Without VTP, each switch would have to be configured manually; therefore, VTP makes it easier to scale to a larger switched environment. Answer A is incorrect because VTP is not necessary for VLANs to span multiple switches. Answer D is incorrect because VTP does not allow the switch to read frame tags.

## Question 7

What is ISL used for?

- ❍ A. To allow an Ethernet interface to understand frame tags
- ❍ B. To make two Ethernet interfaces appear as one
- ❍ C. To connect an Ethernet switch with a high-speed core switch such as ATM
- ❍ D. To allow simultaneous routing and switching

The correct answer is A. ISL allows an Ethernet interface to understand frame tags, which identify the VLAN to which a packet belongs. For this reason, an ISL interface can participate in multiple VLANs, which is necessary for a trunk connection. Answer B is incorrect because ISL can actually have the opposite effect of this—a single Ethernet interface may appear to be several by having multiple Layer 3 addresses. Answers C and D are incorrect because these are not functions of ISL.

## Question 8

What is the purpose of VTP pruning?

- ❍ A. To detect loops in the switching fabric
- ❍ B. To disable a trunk connection that creates a bridging loop
- ❍ C. To simplify the management of VLANs
- ❍ D. To prevent flooding unnecessary traffic across trunk connections

The correct answer is D. VTP pruning is used to prevent flooding of unnecessary traffic across trunk connections. Answer A is incorrect because this is a function of the Spanning Tree Protocol. Answer B is incorrect because this is not the purpose of VTP pruning. Answer C is incorrect because this is the purpose of the VTP, not VTP pruning.

## Question 9

When a network has multiple bridges and is using Spanning Tree Protocol, how is the root bridge determined?

- ❍ A. The first bridge to initiate service becomes the root bridge.
- ❍ B. The bridge with the lowest ID number assumes the root bridge role.
- ❍ C. The bridge with the lowest MAC address is always the root bridge.
- ❍ D. The bridge with the highest serial number is the root bridge.

The correct answer is B. The bridge's ID number is a combination of its MAC address and its assigned priority number. The bridges broadcast their ID numbers and the one with the lowest ID becomes the root. If two bridges have the same priority number then the one with the lower MAC address becomes the root. Answer A is not correct because the first bridge to enter service may or may not be an appropriate root bridge. C is incorrect because the root bridge ID number is determined by a combination of the MAC address and priority number. Answer D is incorrect for the same reason.

## Question 10

A network administrator wants to pass traffic between two VLANs on the same switch. What will he need to accomplish this?

- ❍ A. Nothing. If VLANs are on the same switch, the administrator can simply turn on cross filtering by MAC address.
- ❍ B. A bridge running Spanning Tree Protocol.
- ❍ C. A router.
- ❍ D. A second switch connecting the two VLANs.

Answer C is correct. A router is required for two VLANs to pass traffic, even if they are on the same switch. Answer A is incorrect because there is no cross filtering option on a Layer 2 switch. Answer B is incorrect because a single bridge in this configuration would pass all traffic between the two VLANs, negating the entire purpose of the VLANs. The spanning tree protocol would make no difference where only one bridge is employed. Answer D is incorrect for the same reason answer B is incorrect.

# Need to Know More?

Chappell, Laura. *Introduction to Cisco Router Configuration.* Cisco Systems Inc., Macmillan Computer Publishing. Indianapolis, IN, 1998. ISBN 0-7645-3186-7. This book provides a great overview of the concepts tested on the CCNA exam.

Ford, Merilee, H. Kim Lew, Steve Spanier, and Kevin Downes. *Internetworking Technologies Handbook, 2nd Edition.* Macmillan Computer Publishing. Indianapolis, IN, 1998. ISBN 1-56205-102-3. This book is full of resourceful information on internetworking technologies.

Lammle, Todd, Donald Porter, and James Chellis. *CCNA Cisco Certified Network Associate*. Sybex Network Press. Alameda, CA, 1999. ISBN 0-7821-2381-3. This book is a great supplement for learning the technologies tested on the CCNA exam.

Syngress Media, with Richard D. Hornbaker, CCIE. *Cisco Certified Network Associate Study Guide*. Osborne/McGraw-Hill. Berkeley, CA, 1998. ISBN 0-07882-487-7. Another great book for review before taking the CCNA exam.

*Dictionary of Internetworking Terms and Acronyms*. Cisco Press. Indianapolis, IN, 2001. ISBN 1-58720045-7. Cisco has its own language for technologies used in their products. You will need to use and understand that language for the test. This book will help.

Castelli, Matthew. *Network Sales and Services Handbook*. Cisco Press. Indianapolis, IN, 2003. ISBN 1-58705-090-0. Although this book is targeted at sales, it does a very good job of explaining technologies and Cisco products without getting into mind bogging minutia. A good book to have!

# Cisco Layer 3 Routing

## Terms you'll need to understand:

- ✓ Routing protocols
- ✓ Routing algorithms
- ✓ Distance vector
- ✓ Link state
- ✓ Network discovery
- ✓ Routing metrics
- ✓ RIP
- ✓ IGRP

## Techniques you'll need to master:

- ✓ Understand path determination
- ✓ Determine strengths of link state and distance vector protocols in differing configurations
- ✓ Describe ways of increasing stability of link state and distance vector protocols
- ✓ Describe the goals of routing protocols
- ✓ List routing protocols and path determination
- ✓ Describe convergence as impacted by different protocols
- ✓ Be able to compare and contrast the following types of routing protocols:
  - Static versus dynamic
  - Single path versus multi-path
  - Flat versus hierarchical
  - Interior versus exterior
  - Distance vector versus link state

Now that you have mastered the art of IP addressing and subnetting, it is time to take you to a new level: the wonderful world of routing. Cisco is a company that has the world's most famous routers, but you already know that and this is why you want to be successful when taking your CCNA exams. In a nutshell, routing occurs in the Network layer (Layer 3) of the OSI reference model. By sending packets from the source network to the destination network, the Network layer gives its best effort in the delivery of end-to-end services. In this chapter we will be describing the intricacies of that process.

# Routing Activities

Getting packets to their next hop requires a router to perform two basic activities: path determination and packet switching. These activities are very basic, but you need to have a thorough understanding of how they are accomplished.

*Path determination* involves reviewing all available paths to a destination network and choosing the optimal route on which to send a packet. Network topology information used to determine optimal routes is collected and stored in routing tables, which contain information such as the destination network, the next hop, and an associated metric (the cost of sending packets to that next hop).

*Packet switching* involves changing a packet's physical destination address to that of the next hop. However, the packet's destination logical address remains constant during the packet-switching process.

# Routing Algorithms and Protocols

Routers choose the optimal or best route based on the available route information. A *routing algorithm* aids in the collection of route information and the determination of the best path. These algorithms may vary in several aspects. They may differ based on the goals they were designed to achieve within an internetwork. In addition, several types of routing algorithms exist to suit specific internetwork requirements. The metrics used by different routing algorithms also vary.

A *routing protocol* is a standard method of implementing a particular routing algorithm. For the purpose of our discussions, *routing protocols* mean the routing algorithms or the protocols that implement them. Please do not confuse them with routed protocols; they are very different.

## Goals of Routing Protocols

Technology and internetworks change on a regular basis and because of this change, new needs arise and thus new routing protocols are created. For example, a routing protocol that functioned well in a small internetwork two years ago may certainly experience problems in the large internetworks in use today.

Routing protocols have been designed to meet one or more of the following design goals:

- Flexibility
- Optimization
- Rapid convergence
- Robustness
- Simplicity

### Flexibility

A routing protocol has to be flexible. It should be able to adapt quickly to its ever-changing network environment. If a network segment goes down, a flexible routing protocol is able to detect that event and determine the next best path to use while the segment is down. When the network segment becomes available, the routing protocol should also update its route table to reflect that event. Flexible routing protocols can also adapt to changes in network variables, such as network bandwidth and delay.

### Optimization

The optimization of a routing protocol gauges its capability to choose the best route correctly. The metrics used by the protocol affect its optimality. For example, one protocol may heavily weight the number of hops as its metric, whereas another may use a combination of a number of hops and network delay.

### Rapid Convergence

Convergence occurs when all routers within an internetwork agree on the optimal routes through the internetwork. In other words, an update has been disseminated throughout the internetwork and all routers are working with the same updated table.

Network events, such as routes going down or becoming available, cause routers to recalculate optimal paths and distribute update messages about network routes. These messages permeate the entire network until all routes converge and agree on optimal routes. Slow convergence of the routing protocol can cause problems, such as a routing loop.

A *routing loop* occurs when two or more routers have not yet converged and are broadcasting their inaccurate route tables. In addition, they are most likely still switching packets based on their inaccurate route tables. Figure 7.1 illustrates this case. An event has just occurred within the network—router A lost its path to network 5. While router A is updating its route table, it receives an update from router B that says network 5 is one hop away.

Router A increases the counter by 1 and adds this new information to its route tables. In turn, router A broadcasts its updated route table to router C, which updates its table and broadcasts the erroneous information to router D. Router D updates its table and propagates the misinformation to router B.

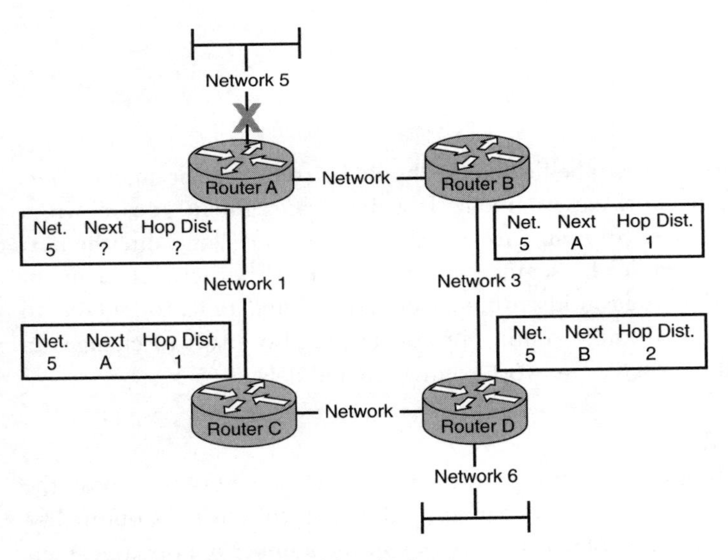


**Figure 7.1** Illustration of a potential routing loop.

This cycle will continue ad infinitum. If packets traversing the network are destined for network 5, they will loop between router A and router B until the packet becomes too old and is discarded. Figure 7.2 illustrates this situation.

## Robustness

Robust and stable routing protocols perform correctly during unusual and unpredictable network events. High utilization, hardware failures, and incorrect configurations can create significant problems within a network. A robust routing protocol is stable during a variety of network situations.

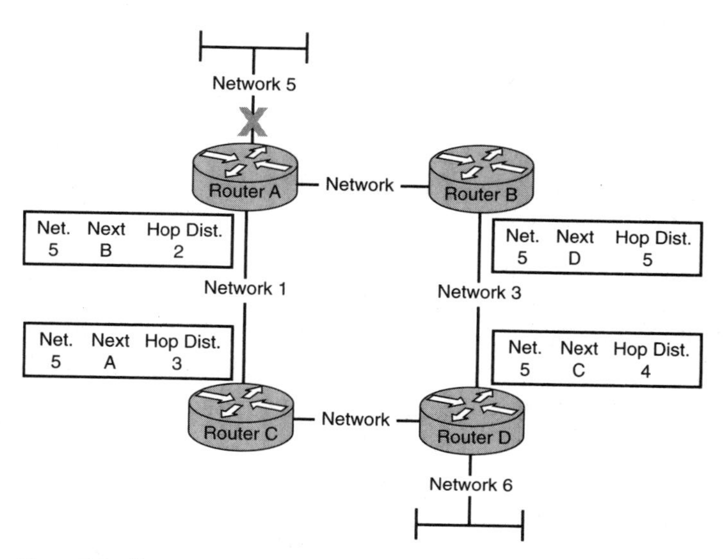


**Figure 7.2** Illustration of the end result of a routing loop.

### Simplicity

The simplicity of a routing protocol refers to its ability to operate efficiently. Because routing protocols collect and store route information, a protocol is competing for the router's limited physical resources. A routing protocol must perform its functions with minimal administrative overhead.

## Types of Routing Protocols

It is very common in technology reference materials for routing protocols to be categorized by type. The type of routing protocol deployed within an internetwork should be based on the organizational requirements.

Types of routing protocols include

- Static or dynamic
- Single path or multipath
- Flat or hierarchical
- Interior or exterior
- Distance vector or link state

## Static or Dynamic

A network administrator configures a static route manually. When defining a *static route*, the administrator configures the destination network, next hop, and appropriate metrics. The route does not change until the network administrator changes it. Static routes function well in environments where the network is simple and network traffic is predictable.

*Dynamic routes* change and adjust to changes within the internetwork environment automatically. When network changes occur, routers begin to converge by recalculating routes and distributing route updates. The route-update messages permeate the network, which causes more routers to recalculate their routes. This route-update process continues until all routers have converged.

Occasionally, static routes augment dynamic routes. In a dynamically routed environment, a router discards a packet if the destination network does not appear in the route table. To avoid this, a static route called a default route can be configured. The default route points to a router that has been specifically configured to receive and process packets that do not have routes listed in the routing tables.

## Single Path or Multipath

When calculating the optimal path for a particular network, some routing protocols simply choose the best *single path* to a destination network. Others allow more than one optimal path if the paths have equal metric values. A *multipath protocol* enables traffic load-balancing using the multiple paths and offers additional advantages over single-path protocols, such as reliability.

## Flat or Hierarchical

A routing environment is considered *flat* if all routers are peers to each other. Routers that use a flat routing protocol may communicate with any other router in the network as directly as possible. Like static routing, a flat routing protocol functions well in simple and predictable network environments.

Alternatively, a *hierarchical* routing environment contains several routers that compose a backbone. Most traffic from non-backbone routers usually traverses the backbone routers (or at least travels to the backbone) in order to reach another non-backbone router. Within a hierarchical routing environment, autonomous systems (sometimes referred to as *domains* or *areas*) can be established. Being part of the same autonomous system enables a group of routers to share network topology information with each other, but that same information is not shared outside the group. Although several layers or tiers may exist within the hierarchy, the routers at the highest level comprise the backbone. Cisco, as of publication of this book, is eager to promote a three-tier system. The Cisco system has a backbone, distribution, and access layer. Equipment is being manufactured and marketed according to these layers. The backbone must provide the fastest throughput possible, without making any routing decisions (or as few as possible). Those are high-end expensive and complex routers and switches. Distribution level is where most of the routing is happening. Those are mid-level boxes. Access level is where hosts are connected to the network, and they are mostly 2000 series of switches and routers.

While it is not very important to know the model numbers for the CCNA exam, the three-level architecture that Cisco uses is a must-know for any Cisco test. Typically, the network backbone comprises its own autonomous system or domain.

## Interior or Exterior

An *interior* routing protocol operates within a single autonomous system or domain. These protocols are typically implemented within an organization's private network. Routers that are running interior routing protocols are considered *intradomain routers*; they only need to know about other routers within their domain. Conversely, an *exterior* routing protocol conveys routing information between domains. Exterior routing protocols are in use within the Internet. *Interdomain routers* need to know how to route traffic between autonomous systems and can protect against errors or problems with one domain affecting another.

## Distance Vector or Link State

*Distance vector protocols* require each router to send all or a large part of its route table to its neighboring routers. *Link state protocols* require each router to send the state of its own interfaces to every router in the internetwork. Distance vector protocols are simple and straightforward, but they converge slowly and consume a significant amount of bandwidth because they have to send updates every set amount of time, and they send entire tables as opposed to the updated entries, which can cause routing loops. Link state protocols converge quickly, but they require more of the router's central processing unit (CPU) and memory resources.

Each routed protocol can be implemented in one or more routing protocols. The routing protocols (or standard set of rules) actually enable the router to determine the best path. Common routing protocols include

- Routing Information Protocol (RIP)
- Interior Gateway Routing Protocol (IGRP)

- Open Shortest Path First (OSPF)
- Enhanced Interior Gateway Routing Protocol (EIGRP)
- Border Gateway Protocol (BGP)
- Exterior Gateway Protocol (EGP)

**Table 7.1 Interior Routing Protocols**

| Routing Protocol | Static or Dynamic | Single-Path or Multipath | Flat or Hierarchical | Interior or Exterior | Distance Vector or Link State |
|---|---|---|---|---|---|
| RIP | Dynamic | Single-path | Flat | Interior | Distance vector |
| IGRP | Dynamic | Multipath | Flat | Interior | Distance vector |
| OSPF | Dynamic | Multipath | Hierarchical | Interior | Link state |
| EIGRP | Dynamic | Multipath | Flat | Interior | Advanced distance vector |

IGRP and EIGRP are Cisco proprietary routing protocols. They are only supported on Cisco routers.

## Routing Metrics

Routing protocols use many different metrics to determine the optimal route. These variables can be used individually or in combination with one another to create the metric defined within a given routing protocol.

Metrics used in routing protocols include

- Bandwidth
- Delay
- Load
- Path length or hops
- Reliability

### Bandwidth

The available capacity of a network link is known as its *bandwidth*. Typically, a 10Mbps Ethernet link is preferable to a 56Kbps Frame Relay link. However, if other metrics such as delay are considered, the Ethernet link may not be the optimal path.

### Delay

*Network delay* refers to the amount of time necessary to move a packet through the internetwork from source to destination. Delay is a conglomeration of several other variables, including physical distance between source and destination, bandwidth and congestion of intermediate links, and port queues of intermediate routers.

### Load

*Load* is an indication of how busy a network resource is. CPU utilization and packets processed per second are two valuable factors when calculating the load.

### Path Length

In some routing protocols, *path length* refers to the sum of the costs of each link traversed up to the destination network. Other routing protocols refer to path length as the *hop count*, which is the number of passes through a router that a packet makes on its way to the destination network.

### Reliability

This metric allows the network administrator to assign a numeric value arbitrarily to indicate a reliability factor for the link. Some network links go down more than others do; some are easily repaired and become available relatively quickly. The reliability metric is simply a method used to capture an administrator's experience with a given network link.

A routed protocol such as IP is concerned with the movement of user traffic. A routing protocol such as RIP or OSPF is concerned with maintaining route tables.

## Distance Vector Versus Link State

This section highlights the similarities and differences between two types of widely used routing protocols: distance vector and link state.

# Distance Vector Overview

A *distance vector routing protocol* sends all or part of its route table across the network, but only to its neighbors. The route table contains the distance and direction to any network within its domain. Figure 7.3 provides an overview of the distance vector process.

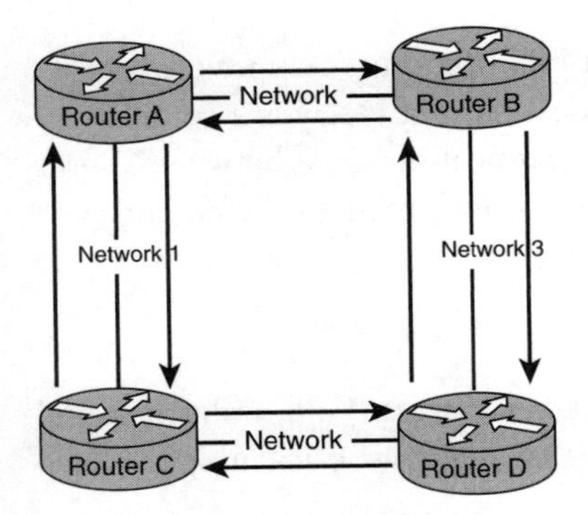


**Figure 7.3** Illustration of the distance vector process.

Periodically, router A broadcasts its entire route table to its neighbors, router B and router C. Router B updates the route information it received by increasing the metric value, which is usually the hop count, by 1. Router B then compares the route information it just received and updated with the existing route information from its route table. Router B replaces existing route information with an updated entry only if the updated route information has a lower calculated metric. Router B then broadcasts its route table to its direct neighbors, router D and router A. This process occurs regularly and in all directions for all directly connected neighbors. Although this process enables routers to accumulate network distance information, the routers do not know the network's exact topology.

# Link State Overview

A *link state routing protocol* (sometimes referred to as *shortest path first*) sends only the state of its own network links across the network, but it sends this information to every router within its domain. This process enables routers to learn and maintain full knowledge of the network's exact topology and how it is interconnected. Figure 7.4 provides an overview of the link state process.

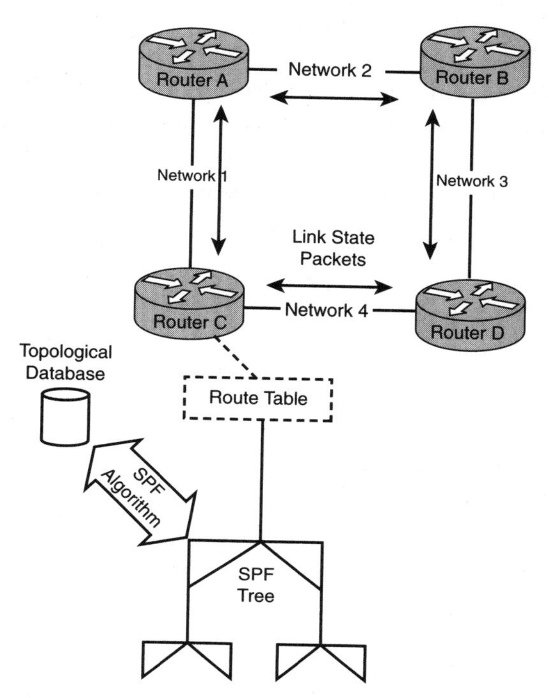


**Figure 7.4** Illustration of the link state process.

Link state routing protocols rely on several components to acquire and maintain knowledge of the network. The following process is typical of routers using a link state protocol:

- A router broadcasts and receives link state packets to and from other routers via the network. Link state packets contain the status of a router's links or network interfaces.
- The router then builds a topology database of the network.
- After building a topology database the router runs a Shortest Path First (SPF) algorithm against the database to generate an SPF tree of the network, with itself as the root of the tree.
- Lastly, the router populates its route table with optimal paths and ports to transmit data through to reach each network.

# Network Discovery

When a router starts up, it must undergo a *network discovery* process, which enables the router to begin communicating with other routers on the network. Figure 7.5 illustrates the network discovery process for distance vector protocols. Router A has just started up and is configured to run a distance vector.

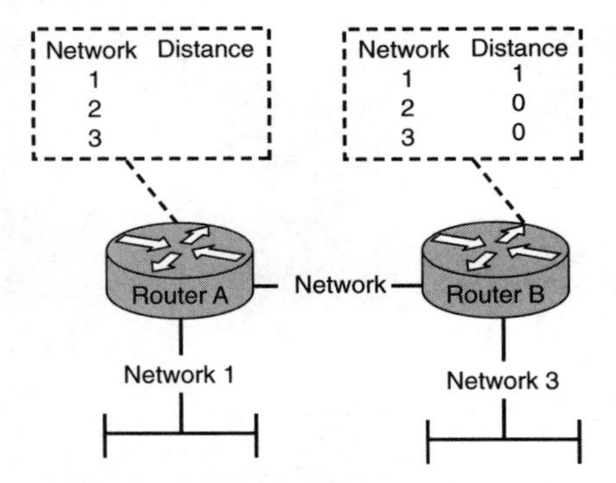


**Figure 7.5** Illustration of the network discovery process.

Router A begins the discovery process by identifying its neighbor, router B. Router A begins populating its route table with its directly connected networks, networks 1 and 2, which receive a metric of 0. It passes its route table to router B and receives router B's entire route table. Router A increases the distances of each entry by one hop. After the distances have been updated, router A will already have better routes to networks 1 and 2, but not network 3. Router A increases the distance to network 3 by one hop and stores this in its route table.

The network discovery process for link state protocols is similar to that of distance vector protocols. Instead of route tables, routers exchange link state packets and use that information to build their topology databases, SPF trees, and route tables.

Regardless of whether a router uses a distance vector or link state routing protocol, the router dynamically discovers its network environment. It can then use its route table to perform the packet-switching function.

# Topology Changes

After the router has discovered the network, it must also keep up with network topology changes. Depending on the protocol used, a router transmits route information periodically or when a network event occurs. Routers detect changes in the network topology via these updates.

Most distance vector protocols handle topology changes through regularly scheduled updates. After a specified interval, a router broadcasts its route table to its neighbor. Route recalculation occurs, if necessary, and updates in the network topology are broadcast. The route distribution timers are not synchronized across routers.

Link state protocols rely on network events to address topology changes. If a router detects a network event (such as one of its neighbors is no longer reachable or a new neighbor appears), it triggers an update. The router broadcasts the state of its links to all other routers within the domain. Upon receiving the update, other routers update their topology database and broadcast the state of their links also. When all updates have been received, each router updates its SPF tree and route tables accordingly. At this point, the network has converged. Event-triggered updates have a ripple effect within a network.

## Distance Vector Problems

The fact that route updates with a distance vector protocol occur after a specified interval can become problematic. With RIP, route updates are broadcast every 30 seconds by default. As a result, distance vector protocols converge slowly. Routing loops and the problems they create were discussed previously in this chapter. Routing loops create a condition known as *counting to infinity*, where the distance metric is continually increased because the network has not fully converged.

## Distance Vector Remedies

One technique to remedy a count-to-infinity situation involves a maximum hop count. Although this count will not prevent a routing loop, it does reduce the time that the routing loop exists. A maximum hop count, when reached, forces a router to mark a network unreachable rather than increase the distance metric.

Routing loops also occur when information that contradicts information sent previously is broadcast back to a router. Router A sends information about network 5 to router B. *Split horizon* prevents a router from sending information it received about a network back to the neighbor that originally sent the information. For example, split horizon prohibits router B and router C from sending any information about network 5 back to router A.

*Route poisoning* occurs when a router detects that a network is down and immediately marks it as unreachable. This route update is broadcast throughout the network. While the other routers slowly converge, the router maintains this poisoned route in its route table and ignores updates from other routers about better routes to the network. The poisoned route is removed after several update cycles. Route poisoning works well with hold-down timers.

A *hold-down timer* indicates that no updates to a particular route should be accepted until the timer expires. A hold-down condition is triggered when a router receives an update from its neighbor indicating that a reachable network has just gone down. The router marks the network as unreachable and starts its hold-down timer. While the timer is active, updates from any other router are ignored. Updates about the unreachable network are accepted only from the neighboring router that initially indicated the unreachable network while the timer is active. If the neighboring router indicates that the network is reachable again, the router stops the hold-down timer and updates its route table. When the hold-down timer expires, the router marks the network reachable and receives updates from any router.

## Link State Problems

Because link state routing protocols have knowledge of the entire network and converge quickly, they do not suffer from the same problems as distance vector protocols. One problem that affects link state protocols is the significant memory and processor resources required from the router itself when acquiring and maintaining full knowledge of large networks. As updates move through the network, each router must receive the update, recalculate its information, and send its own link information. Of course, this type of overhead affects the ability of the router to move user data packets through the network.

A second shortcoming of link state protocols is the amount of network bandwidth that can be consumed while the network converges. Routers flood updates about the state of their links to every other router in the network, so the amount of bandwidth consumed is significant. As routers collect link information from each other, the amount of bandwidth available for end-user communications is reduced. This high level of bandwidth utilization typically occurs on initialization of the network or when several routers start up simultaneously.

Additional problems can occur during the link state update process itself. It is imperative that each router receive all the packets in a timely manner and that the updates are synchronized. For example, if one part of the network receives route information before another part, convergence may take longer, or SPF trees and route tables may store inaccurate information. Additionally, as routers attempt to move link state packets through the network, they may be doing so without fully constructed SPF trees or route tables.

## Link State Remedies

One remedy for link state problems involves minimizing the resources required to build and maintain route tables. The time between periodic updates can be lengthened to reduce the processing resources required. Also, routers can be identified to serve as border routers. The border routers can then exchange route summaries with other border routers and each core router to reduce the bandwidth consumed during the update process, and to isolate update processes to hierarchical areas. The border router then passes updates to the routers within its area.

Another technique involves coordinating link state updates. Timestamps and sequence numbers can be attached to the link state packet. Routers then realize when they receive inaccurate or old link state packets.

The following techniques help to stabilize link state protocols:

- Minimize router resource usage by lengthening the update frequency or exchanging route summaries.
- Coordinate updates with timestamps or sequence numbers.

Both distance vector and link state routing protocols have demonstrated their worth over time. Each has advantages that may suit a particular network design perfectly. Several factors must be considered when choosing a routing protocol, including business policies and operational issues. Table 7.2 provides a quick comparison of distance vector and link state routing protocols.

**Table 7.2 Distance Vector Versus Link State Routing Protocols**

| Distance Vector | Link State |
|---|---|
| Sees the network from its neighbor's perspective | Sees the entire network from its own perspective |
| Distance metrics accumulate from router to router | Calculates shortest path to other routers |
| Route updates occur periodically | Route updates are event-triggered |
| Convergence is slow | Convergence is fast |
| Broadcasts entire route table to neighbors | Broadcasts link status information to all other routers |

# Exam Prep Questions

## Question 1

Which of the following are basic functions of a router? (Choose the two best answers.)

❑ A. Packet switching

❑ B. Packet filtering

❑ C. Path determination

❑ D. Rapid convergence

The correct answers are A and C. Routers packet switch when they have determined the best path. Path determination is the process of choosing the best network path from all available network paths. Packet filtering is a technique used to control inbound and/or outbound packets to or from a router. Therefore, answer B is incorrect. Rapid convergence is a design goal of some routing protocols. Therefore, answer D is incorrect.

## Question 2

Network routing information distributed among routers is stored in which of the following?

❍ A. Flash memory

❍ B. Route table

❍ C. Metric table

❍ D. NVRAM

The correct answer is B. Route tables contain information about destination networks and the next hop along the optimal path to get there. Flash memory contains the operating system images used by the router. Therefore, answer A is incorrect. Metric information is contained within a router's route table. Therefore, answer C is incorrect. NVRAM contains the router's active configuration files. Therefore, answer D is incorrect.

## Question 3

Which of the following conditions is a problem experienced by distance vector routing protocols?

❍ A. Split horizon

❍ B. Route poisoning

❍ C. Counting to infinity

❍ D. Maximum hop count

❍ E. Hold-down timers

The correct answer is C. Counting to infinity can result from the slow convergence inherent in distance vector protocols. Split horizon, route poisoning, maximum hop count, and hold-down timers are techniques/items used to reduce the occurrence and impact of the counting-to-infinity situation. Therefore, answers A, B, D, and E are incorrect.

## Question 4

Which of the following routing protocols communicates route information by sending the state of its links to all routers in its domain?

❍ A. BGP

❍ B. OSPF

❍ C. IGRP

❍ D. RIP

Answer B is correct. The question is describing a link state protocol and OSPF is an excellent example. Both RIP and IGRP are distance vector protocols, so answers C and D are incorrect. BGP is an exterior routing protocol optimized for passing routing information between domains. Therefore answer A is correct.

## Question 5

Which of the following help to mitigate the shortcomings of link state protocols? (Choose the two best answers.)

❑ A. Maximum hop count

❑ B. Minimize router resource usage

❑ C. Coordinate updates

❑ D. Route poisoning

The correct answers are B and C. Lengthening the update frequency or exchanging router summaries at specific border routers helps to minimize router resource usage. Therefore, answer B is correct. Also, attaching time-stamps or sequence numbers on link state packets helps to coordinate update information between routers. Therefore, answer C is correct. A maximum hop count and route poisoning address problems with distance vector protocols. Therefore, answers A and D are incorrect.

## Question 6

Which of the following are not problems inherent to link state routing protocols? (Choose two.)

- ❑ A. High router resource usage
- ❑ B. Split horizon
- ❑ C. High network bandwidth consumption
- ❑ D. Hold-down timers
- ❑ E. Unsynchronized updates

The answer is B and D. Split horizons and hold down timers are techniques used to reduce problems in distance vector protocols. High network bandwidth usage and router resource usage are typical of link state protocols when packets are flooding the network during convergence. Therefore, answers C and A are not correct. If link state updates are not synchronized inaccurate SPF trees and route tables can result. This would make answer E incorrect.

## Question 7

A friend of yours is implementing a "Just in Time" inventory policy and linking her company network to the networks of several suppliers. Based on just this information, which of the following protocols would you recommend using?

- ❍ A. EIGRP
- ❍ B. OSPF
- ❍ C. BGP
- ❍ D. IP

Answer C is correct. The key to this question is your friend's decision to connect autonomous domains. Exterior routing protocols are optimized for this task and the only exterior routing protocol available is answer C, Border

Gateway Protocol (BGP). Answers A and B are incorrect because they are interior routing protocols. Answer D is incorrect because IP is a routable protocol, not a routing protocol.

## Question 8

A large company network is operating at or near capacity. The administrator is about to change routing protocols from EIGRP to OSPF to gain the additional efficacies of a hierarchical protocol. Based on just this information, is this a good idea?

- ❍ A. Yes, EIGRP is a flat routing protocol and not optimized for large implementations.
- ❍ B. Yes, a multipath routing protocol would balance loads in a saturated network and better utilize the bandwidth available.
- ❍ C. No, OSPF typically uses more bandwidth and processor power than EIGRP.
- ❍ D. No, a hierarchical routing protocol is not efficient.

The correct answer is C. OSPF is a link state routing protocol. Link state protocols are notorious for using large amounts of bandwidth and processor power when coming to convergence. When a network is running at or near capacity, bandwidth and processor power are usually not available. Therefore, transitioning from a distance vector protocol like EIGRP, which uses bandwidth and processing power efficiently, to a link state protocol like OSPF would not be advisable in this situation. Answers A, B, and D are incorrect for the same reason.

## Question 9

Why is IP one of the most popular routing protocols available?

- ❍ A. IP provides a flexible addressing structure that is highly scalable.
- ❍ B. IP is the routing protocol of the Internet. As such, its use reduces compatibility issues faced by other routing protocols.
- ❍ C. IP uses a four-layer process which is more efficient than the OSI's seven-layer process.
- ❍ D. None of the above.

Answer D is correct. IP is not a routing protocol. It is a routable protocol. Therefore, A, B, and C are incorrect and answer D is the only acceptable option.

# Need to Know More?

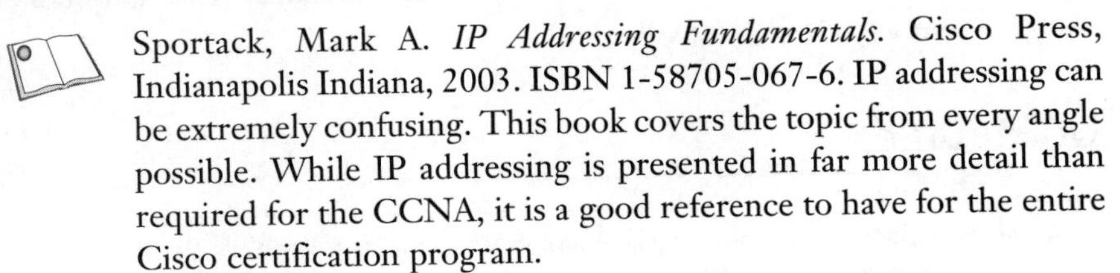

Sportack, Mark A. *IP Addressing Fundamentals.* Cisco Press, Indianapolis Indiana, 2003. ISBN 1-58705-067-6. IP addressing can be extremely confusing. This book covers the topic from every angle possible. While IP addressing is presented in far more detail than required for the CCNA, it is a good reference to have for the entire Cisco certification program.

Osterloh, Heather. *TCP/IP Primer Plus.* Sams Publishing, Indianapolis, Indiana, 2002. ISBN 0-672-32208-0. Written clearly and concisely, this one book can answer almost any question relating to TCP/IP. It is a good book to have for both this certification and future Cisco certifications.

Castelli, Matthew. *Network Sales and Services Handbook.* Cisco Press, Indianapolis, Indiana, 2003. ISBN 1-58705-090-0. Although this book is targeted at sales, it does a very good job of explaining technologies and Cisco products without getting into mind bogging minutia. A good book to have!

Odom, Wendell. *Cisco CCNA Exam Certification Guide*. Cisco Press, Indianapolis, Indiana, 2000. ISBN 0-7357-0971-8. Cisco is almost always the best place for reference books relating to Cisco. They print incredibly detailed and comprehensive books and this one is excellent. I would not want to read it as a primary text, but as a reference it cannot be beat.

# PART II

# Interconnecting Cisco Networking Devices (Exam 640-811)

# Configuration

## Terms you'll need to understand:

✓ Random Access Memory (RAM)
✓ Non Volatile Random Access Memory (NVRAM)
✓ Read-only memory (ROM)
✓ Flash electrically erasable programmable memory (flash memory or flash EEPROM)
✓ Startup configuration file
✓ Running configuration file
✓ User mode
✓ Privileged mode
✓ Global configuration mode
✓ Setup mode
✓ Rxboot mode

## Techniques you'll need to master:

✓ Connecting to routers
✓ Learning the startup sequence
✓ Understanding the update process
✓ Understanding the configuration change process

Although Cisco has added many products and technologies through acquisition, they do attempt to maintain a uniform philosophy of design. Nowhere is this philosophy more pronounced than in their core product area of routers. This is a very short, but important chapter because it covers the operational design of Cisco routers. You will be expected to know each memory area, the type of memory used, and the function of programs stored in that memory region. You will also need to know which operational mode provides access to a given region or function.

## Router Memory Components

Cisco routers utilize four different types of memory, with each type providing different functions. RAM, NVRAM, Flash memory, and ROM are the four types of memory used. Their functions are discussed in the following sections (see Figure 8.1).

### RAM

RAM serves as a working storage area for the router and contains data such as routing tables, various types of cache and buffers, as well as input and output queues. RAM also provides temporary memory for the router's active IOS and configuration file (the running configuration file). However, all the contents of RAM are lost if the router is powered down or restarted.

### NVRAM

Unlike RAM, nonvolatile RAM (NVRAM) retains its contents when the router is powered down or restarted. NVRAM stores permanent information, such as the router's backup configuration file. The startup configuration file is retrieved from NVRAM during startup, at which time it is loaded into RAM.

### Flash

Flash memory stores the Cisco IOS image and associated microcode. Flash memory is erasable, electronically reprogrammable ROM that retains its contents when the router is powered down or restarted. Flash memory allows software to be upgraded without chips being added, removed, or replaced.

### ROM

Like Flash memory, ROM contains a version of IOS—usually an older version with minimal functionality. It also stores the bootstrap program and power-on diagnostic programs. However, software upgrades can be performed only by replacing the ROM chip.

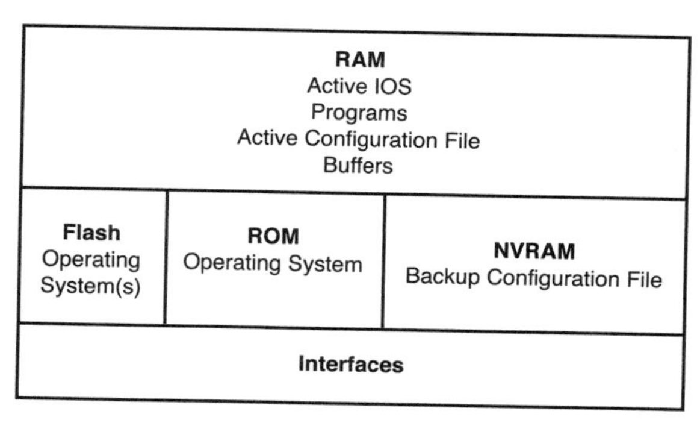


**Figure 8.1** Standard memory configuration for a Cisco router.

# Types of Configuration Files

Cisco IOS software uses and requires a configuration file to determine how a router is to function. Typically, network administrators enter the commands needed by the configuration file. Only two types of configuration files exist for the context of the CCNA exam:

- The *running configuration* file exists in RAM and contains the commands that Cisco IOS uses to drive the actions of the router.
- The *startup configuration* file exists in NVRAM and is the backup for the running configuration file. *Startup configuration files reside in NVRAM; running configuration files exist in RAM.*

As noted previously, RAM is erased when a router is powered down. Therefore, the running configuration file is erased as well.

The router will always use the running configuration file to execute. However, any time a router is restarted (cycling power or reloading the software), the running configuration file is erased and the startup configuration file is the only remaining configuration file. Therefore, during the boot sequence of a router, the router copies the startup configuration file to the running configuration file (NVRAM to RAM). Therefore, it is paramount that any time a change is made to a running configuration, the change is also copied to the startup configuration.

Be sure to know the following main operating files and where they reside:

| Operating File | Memory |
|---|---|
| Basic IOS | ROM |
| Boot Strap | ROM |
| Diagnostics | ROM |
| Current IOS | FLASH |
| Startup configuration* | NVRAM |
| Running configuration | RAM |

*Also called backup configuration file

# Router Modes

Accessing a router can be done through a console port, a modem connection, or through one of the operational interfaces. Once accessed, a router can be placed in one of five primary modes:

- User
- Privileged
- Setup
- Rxboot
- Global configuration

There are more than five operational modes. However, additional modes are used for very specific functions and are invariably lumped together in a category called "other." The CCNA exam will only cover the five primary modes.

Each of these modes provides access to specific memory areas and functions, as described in the following sections.

## User Mode

User mode provides a display-only environment. You can view limited information about the router but you cannot change the configuration of the router.

## Privileged Mode

Privileged mode enables you to perform an extensive review of the router. This mode supports testing commands, debugging commands, and commands to manage the router configuration files.

## Setup Mode

Setup mode is triggered on router startup when no configuration file resides in nonvolatile random access memory (NVRAM). This mode executes an interactive prompted dialog box to assist in creating an initial router configuration.

## RXBOOT Mode

A router's maintenance mode is called *RXBOOT mode* or *ROM monitor mode*. This mode facilitates recovery functions when the router password is lost or the IOS file stored in Flash memory has been erased or is corrupt. Pressing the Break key (from a console terminal directly connected to the router) within the first 60 seconds of startup also allows you to place the router in this mode.

## Global Configuration Mode

You perform simple configuration tasks that permeate all aspects of the router in global configuration mode. For example, router names, router passwords, and router banners are all configured in this mode.

# Exam Prep Questions

## Question 1

Which of the following router components contain versions of the router's configuration file? (Choose the two best answers.)

- ❑ A. Flash memory
- ❑ B. NVRAM
- ❑ C. RAM
- ❑ D. ROM

The correct answers are B and C. NVRAM contains the backup configuration file for the router, whereas RAM contains the router's active configuration file. Flash memory and ROM do not contain a configuration file; they contain the router's IOS image files. Therefore, answers A and D are incorrect.

## Question 2

Where does the running configuration file exist in a Cisco router?

- ❍ A. NVRAM
- ❍ B. ROM
- ❍ C. RAM
- ❍ D. Flash memory

The correct answer is C. The running configuration file exists in RAM. This file is erased when a router is reloaded or its power is cycled. Answer B cannot be correct because ROM is a read-only device, and configuration files are constantly being updated. Answer A is incorrect because NVRAM is used to maintain the startup configuration file, not the running configuration file. Answer D is incorrect because Flash memory stores a copy of the IOS software, not the running configuration files.

## Question 3

What mode is triggered when a router is powered up for the first time?

- ❍ A. User Mode
- ❍ B. Priority Mode
- ❍ C. Startup Mode
- ❍ D. Setup Mode

Answer D is correct. A router goes into setup mode when power is applied for the first time. Once the administrator has entered the basic configuration requirements, a running configuration file is generated, which in turn provides the user mode and priority mode for additional configuration. Therefore, answers A and B are incorrect. Startup Mode sounds correct, but there is no startup mode in the five basic modes of operation.

## Question 4

What are three possible ways to connect to a router?

- ❑ A. Through a console port
- ❑ B. Remotely via a modem
- ❑ C. Through the maintenance interface
- ❑ D. Through an active router interface

Answers A, B, and D are correct. You can connect locally through a serial cable connected to the console port or Telnet through an active interface from a terminal. Most routers also allow for a modem connection when the network is down and you cannot physically go to the router location. There is no maintenance interface on a router.

## Question 5

Power is restored after a major power outage. Your router, however, has lost all of the configuration updates you made over the past month. What has most likely happened?

- ❍ A. The battery powering NVRAM could not maintain memory for the length of the power outage.
- ❍ B. The running configuration file did not have sufficient time to back itself up to NVRAM when the power failed.
- ❍ C. Power fluctuations inherent in power outages probably purged the flash memory.
- ❍ D. You forgot to save your changes.

Answer D is correct. When you change a running configuration file, you must also save the changes to the startup configuration file in NVRAM. Otherwise, when power is restored, the startup configuration file will be copied to RAM and your changes will be lost. The running configuration file does not back itself up. Therefore, B is incorrect. Answer A is incorrect because NVRAM does not use a backup battery. Flash memory could be purged as a result of power fluctuations, but it is a very remote possibility. If flash memory were purged, the router would use the IOS version from ROM, which would be very noticeable.

## Question 6

What, if any, are the differences between the IOS stored in ROM and the IOS stored in EEPROM?

- ❍ A. They are both the same; the ROM version is a backup for the version in EEPROM.
- ❍ B. The EEPROM version is a full version of IOS. The ROM version contains only the basics required for initial operation.
- ❍ C. The EEPROM version contains all of the configuration changes input by the administrator. The ROM version is a basic unmodified version of IOS.
- ❍ D. ROM contains the running version of IOS, EEPROM contains downloaded updates for the IOS.

Answer B is correct. The EEPROM contains the most current full version of IOS used for day-to-day operation. ROM contains a scaled down version of the IOS, which will get the router running in the event no other operating system is available. Answer A is incorrect because the versions are very different. Answer C is incorrect because "flashing" and then downloading another version of IOS is the only way to change the IOS version in EEPROM. The administrator cannot make changes to the IOS configuration in EEPROM. Lastly, answer D is incorrect because the current or running version of IOS resides in EEPROM.

## Question 7

Why do Cisco routers maintain a basic version of IOS in ROM?

❍ A. ROM is easy to change and provides an ideal way of updating the router software.

❍ B. Storing IOS in ROM prevents the users from modifying or stealing the non-compiled version of IOS.

❍ C. ROM contains the core operating code for IOS. Without it, the router could not function.

❍ D. ROM does not require power to maintain data. Therefore, if all else fails, the scaled down version of IOS stored in ROM is capable of getting the router up and running with basic functionality.

Answer D is correct. A basic version of IOS is stored in ROM so that the router will always be able to be started with basic functionality. Answer A is not correct because downloading to an EEPROM is far easier than distributing and installing ROM chips. Answer B is incorrect because the code in ROM is compiled and theft and/or tampering is really not a concern. Lastly, C is not correct because the EEPROM stores a complete version of IOS. The ROM version is a scaled down backup.

## Question 8

After four hours of work, you finally have the new Cisco router running perfectly. When you return from lunch your boss mentions he made a few simple changes and now it does not work. What would be the best way to rectify the situation?

❍ A. Purge the memories and start over.

❍ B. Flash the EEPROM, download a clean IOS, and rebuild the running configuration file.

❍ C. Walk your boss back through what he remembers of the changes and try to undo each change.

❍ D. Turn the router off and then turn it on again.

Answer D is correct. Your boss has changed the running configuration file. Chances are very good he did not save the running configuration file to the startup file in NVRAM. Therefore, turning the router off and then on again will erase the running configuration file and replace it with a copy of the startup file. So long as you saved your work (you did save your work, didn't you?), the router should come back up and work just like it did before lunch. Answer A is incorrect because if you purged the memories, you would lose the startup file and any hope of recovering your prior work. Answer B is incorrect because your boss's actions only affected the running configuration file. He could not compromise the operating system so nothing would be accomplished by reloading the IOS. Answer C is incorrect because he would probably not remember exactly what he did, and even if he did, cycling the power would be much faster and easier.

## Question 9

With regard to the situation in question 8, you must have done one of the following for the situation to develop as it did. What would that most likely be?

- ❑ A. Went to lunch and left the console running in user mode.
- ❑ B. Left the console running in global mode when you went to lunch.
- ❑ C. Left the console running in setup mode while you went to lunch.
- ❑ D. Went to lunch and left the console running in privileged mode.

Answers B and D are correct. Question 8 states that the router was running perfectly prior to going to lunch. The router needs a running configuration file to operate. The presence of a running configuration file indicates setup mode had completed and will not run again until both the running configuration file and startup file are lost. Answer C is therefore eliminated as an option. User mode is a display only mode, so if the console was left in that mode, your boss could only view parts of the configuration, not change it. Therefore, answer A is incorrect. That leaves D as a correct answer. Only privileged mode provides access to the running configuration file. You must have gone to lunch and left the console running in privileged mode. Answer B is also correct. If you went to lunch and left your router in Global Configuration mode anyone could sit down and configure anything he or she wanted.

## Question 10

Now that the router in question 8 is up and running again, your boss confides that what he was really trying to do was name the router after his wife. He is now too embarrassed to try it himself so he asks you to rename the router. What mode must the router be in to change its name?

- ❍ A. Global mode
- ❍ B. Privileged mode
- ❍ C. Setup mode
- ❍ D. RXBOOT mode

Answer A is correct. The name of a router is one of those global parameter changes that really does not affect the configuration files. Answer C is a possibility, but the router is already running, so you are not going to have access to setup mode. Privileged mode, answer B, is for access to the configuration files. Router name is really not a part of the configuration. Lastly, RXBOOT mode is maintenance and recovery, not setting global parameters.

The exam will ask about the five modes of operation and the settings that can be accessed in each mode. Although the previous three questions make it sound like there is an underlying logic behind these terms, they are in reality arbitrary. For you to answer these questions correctly on the test you are probably going to have to memorize the modes and their subsets. We will be going into the modes and their subsets in more detail in the configuration chapters that follow.

# Need to Know More?

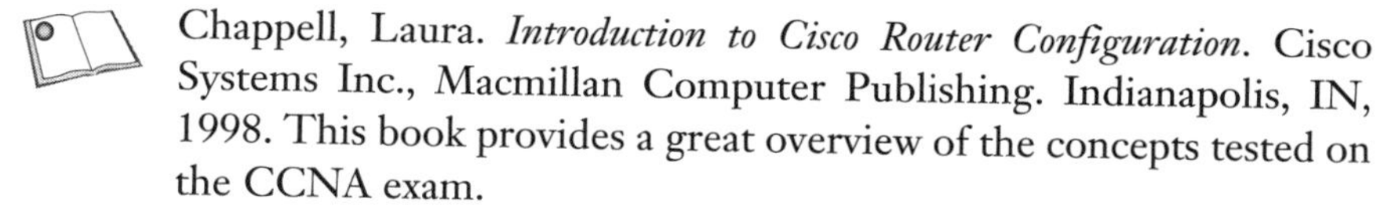

Chappell, Laura. *Introduction to Cisco Router Configuration*. Cisco Systems Inc., Macmillan Computer Publishing. Indianapolis, IN, 1998. This book provides a great overview of the concepts tested on the CCNA exam.

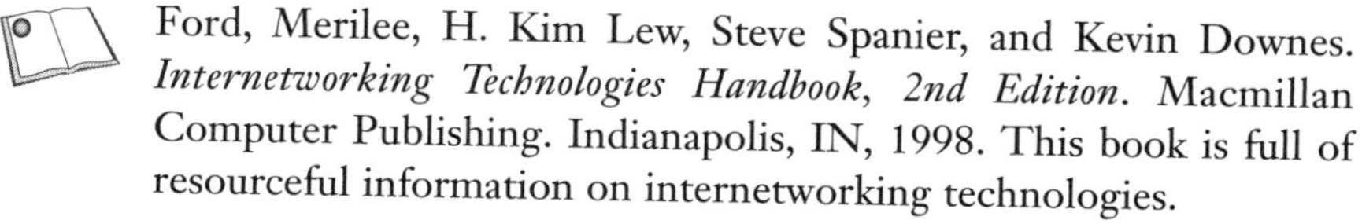

Ford, Merilee, H. Kim Lew, Steve Spanier, and Kevin Downes. *Internetworking Technologies Handbook, 2nd Edition*. Macmillan Computer Publishing. Indianapolis, IN, 1998. This book is full of resourceful information on internetworking technologies.

Lammle, Todd, Donald Porter, and James Chellis. *CCNA Cisco Certified Network Associate*. Sybex Network Press. Alameda, CA, 1999. This book is a great supplement for learning the technologies tested on the CCNA exam.

Syngress Media, with Richard D. Hornbaker, CCIE. *Cisco Certified Network Associate Study Guide*. Osborne/McGraw-Hill. Berkeley, CA, 1998. Another great book for review before taking the CCNA exam.

*Dictionary of Internetworking Terms and Acronyms*. Cisco Press. Indianapolis, IN, 2001. Cisco has its own language for technologies used in their products. You will need to use and understand that language for the test. This book will help.

Castelli, Matthew. *Network Sales and Services Handbook*. Cisco Press. Indianapolis, IN, 2003. Although this book is targeted at sales, it does a very good job of explaining technologies and Cisco products without getting into mind bogging minutia. A good book to have!

# Configuring a Cisco Switch

## Terms you'll need to understand:

- ✓ Virtual local area network (VLAN)
- ✓ Trunking
- ✓ Inter-switch link (ISL)
- ✓ VLAN Trunking Protocol (VTP)

## Techniques you'll need to master:

- ✓ Configuring a Cisco Switch
- ✓ Creating and configuring VLANs
- ✓ Assigning a VLAN to switched ports
- ✓ Establishing a trunk connection between switches
- ✓ Understanding and enabling VTP

A skill that few people possess is the ability to correctly configure a Cisco switch. As you already know, newer applications increase demand for a switched network. In this chapter, we walk you through the process of configuring a switch.

## Switch Startup

The startup process for a Cisco switch can be monitored in the following ways:

- Observing the light-emitting diodes (LEDs) on the switch chassis
- Examining the Cisco Internetwork Operating System (IOS) output by connecting a terminal to the switch's console port

Cisco catalyst switches have several LEDs that give a convenient visual indicator of the switch's operational status. These LEDs are green when the switch is functioning properly and amber when there's any sort of problem.

The Catalyst 1900 series switch executes a power-on-self-test (POST) each time the switch is powered on, which can be monitored by watching the LEDs on the switch chassis. The typical sequence is as follows:

1. Initially, all LEDs are green.
2. Each LED is associated with a specific POST. Each LED turns off after its task is complete or turns amber if there's a problem.
3. The system LED turns amber if any test fails.
4. When the POST is complete, the LEDs blink, then turn off.

In addition to monitoring LEDs, any errors encountered during startup can be checked by attaching a terminal to the console port of the switch and observing the text output. The initial output from a Catalyst 1900 switch with no errors looks similar to the following:

```
Catalyst 1900 Management Console
Copyright (c) Cisco Systems, Inc.1993-1999
All rights reserved.

Standard Edition Software
Ethernet address:   00-E0-1E-7E-B4-40

PCA Number: 73-2239-01
PCA Serial Number: SAD01200001
Model Number: WS-C1924-A
System Serial Number: FAA01200001
--------------------------------

User Interface Menu
```

```
[M] Menus
[K] Command Line
[I] IP Address
[P] Console Password

Enter Selection:
```

## Configuring the Switch

There are three different options for configuring a new Catalyst 1900 switch:

- ➤ Menu-driven interface
- ➤ Command-line interface (CLI) (only available on Enterprise Edition IOS software)
- ➤ Web-based interface

These configuration options may vary depending on which model of switch you have and which version of software it is running. Using the menu-driven interface may seem like the easiest and quickest way to get your switch running. It is important, however, that you learn how to configure the switch through the CLI as well.

The CLI is the standard interface used to configure any Cisco device running the IOS, Cisco's proprietary OS. In addition, Cisco simulates some commands through the CLI in the certification exam so beware.

The Web-based interface is another easy visual way to monitor and configure the switch. It is important to note, however, that before you can use the Web-based interface, the switch must have a valid Internet Protocol (IP) address. For this reason, you must first configure at least an IP address using one of the other two configuration methods.

## Default Configuration

Cisco switches come with a default configuration that is actually usable in many cases without any additional customization. Table 9.1 shows the default configuration settings of a Catalyst 1900 switch. For most situations, you will want to configure at least some basic options on the switch, such as an IP address, default gateway, and duplex options. An example of where you would use the default configuration would be an environment where

VLANs, port filtering, and so on are not an issue and you merely want the functionality of a switch, albeit an expensive one.

**Table 9.1 Catalyst 1900 Default Configuration**

| Option | Default Value |
|---|---|
| IP Address | 0.0.0.0 |
| CDP | Enabled |
| Switching mode | Fragment-free |
| 100BASE-T port | Auto-negotiate duplex mode |
| 10BASE-T port | Half duplex |
| Spanning tree protocol | Enabled |
| Console password | None |

# Using the Menu-Driven Interface

Using the menu-driven interface to configure a Catalyst 1900 switch is a simple and straightforward process. You must first connect to the switch through the console port using a PC with terminal emulation software or Telnet into the switch. As soon as the switch starts up, a menu that you use to select the option to configure appears. The initial management console logon screen looks like this:

```
User Interface Menu

[M] Menus
[K] Command Line
[I] IP Address
[P] Console Password

Enter Selection:
```

You may want to give the switch a password by pressing P and following the instructions about setting the console password. You can enter the IP Configuration menu by pressing I. You will see this once you enter the IP Configuration menu:

```
Catalyst 1900 - IP Configuration

Ethernet Address:00-E0-1E-7E-B4-40

----------Settings----------
[I] IP address                 0.0.0.0
[S] Subnet mask                 0.0.0.0
[G] Default gateway               0.0.0.0
[B] Management Bridge Group1 (fixed)
[M] IP address of DNS server 1       0.0.0.0
[N] IP address of DNS server 2       0.0.0.0
```

```
[D] Domain name
[R] Use Routing Information Protocol    Enabled

----------Actions----------
[P] Ping
[C] Clear cached DNS entries
[X] Exit to previous menu

Enter Selection:
```

You can access the Management Console Main Menu by pressing M, which shows you the following:

```
Catalyst 1900 - Main Menu

[C] Console Settings
[S] System
[N] Network Management
[P] Port Configuration
[A] Port Addressing
[D] Port Statistics Detail
[M] Monitoring
[B] Bridge Group
[R] Multicast Registration
[F] Firmware
[I] RS-232 Interface
[U] Usage Summaries
[H] Help

[X] Exit Management Console

Enter Selection:
```

Almost every option that you may need to configure for a Catalyst switch has an associated menu command.

# Using the CLI

The Command Line Interface (CLI), while slightly more difficult to learn than the menu-driven interface, is important to know because it is used for configuration across the entire Cisco product line. The CLI is available on switches that are running the Enterprise Edition of Cisco's IOS. From the initial management console logon screen, press K to enter the CLI. You will get a prompt that looks similar to the following:

```
1900>
```

Enter privileged mode by using the `enable` command. Then, enter configuration mode by using the `config terminal` command.

```
1900>enable
Enter Password: <enable password>
1900#config terminal
1900(config)#
```

# Configuring TCP/IP Options

Giving the switch an IP address is one of the first things that should be done. The command used to do so is `ip address {ip address} {subnet mask}`. The default gateway should also be specified by using the `ip default-gateway {ip address}` command. The following is an example:

```
ip address 192.168.1.10 255.255.255.0
ip default-gateway 192.168.1.1
```

You may also need to configure a domain name for the switch and tell it how to resolve names by giving it a name-server address, as shown in the following:

```
ip domain-name cisco.com
ip name-server 192.168.1.20
```

Now, we can view the TCP/IP information by using the `show ip` command:

```
hostname# show ip

IP Address:192.168.1.10
Subnet Mask:255.255.255.0
Default Gateway:192.168.1.1
Management VLAN: 1
Domain name: cisco.com
Name server 1:192.168.1.20
Name server 2:198.92.30.32
HTTP server :Enabled
HTTP port : 80
RIP :Enabled
```

In the previous code, you will see various components of a TCP/IP configured device with all the relevant information such as the address, subnet mask, gateway, and also that there is a Web server configured for port 80.

# VLANs

A *VLAN* is a group of switched ports that acts as a separate, isolated LAN. There can be several VLANs defined on a single switch. A VLAN can also span multiple switches. Workstations in separate VLANs will never encounter traffic or share bandwidth from other VLANs unless the data is routed. In other words, a router or switch with routing capabilities is required if devices on different VLANs need to communicate. It should be noted that VLAN configuration is done through the switch and its software.

Remember that one of the main benefits of switches is that they segment a network into many collision domains. Each port represents a single collision domain, and devices share bandwidth only with other devices on the same switch port. Unless a switch is segmented into VLANs, however, all of the devices on the switch are still in the same broadcast domain; that is, all broadcasts (and multicasts) are sent to each port throughout the switching fabric.

VLANs introduce a way to limit the broadcast traffic in a switched network (a job normally associated with routers). When you create a VLAN by defining which ports belong to it, you are really just creating a boundary for broadcast traffic. This has the effect of creating multiple, isolated LANs on a single switch.

Figure 9.1 shows a 12-port switch that has been divided into two VLANs. Ports 1 through 6 are VLAN 1, and ports 7 through 12 are VLAN 2.

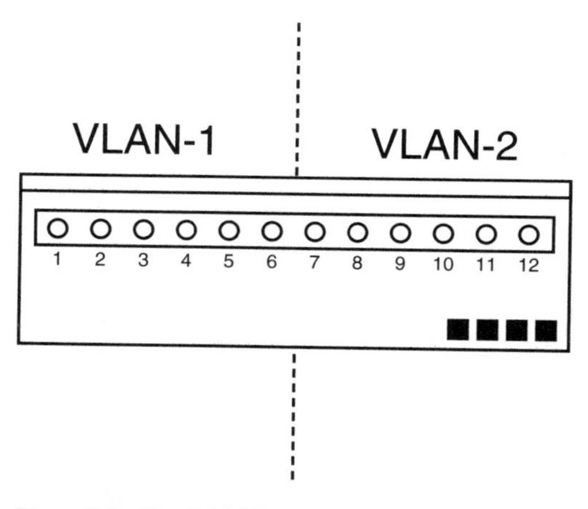


**Figure 9.1** Simple VLAN.

It is important to understand the need for routers in a switched network. If devices on different VLANs need to communicate, routing is required to facilitate this exchange of data. Many of today's network systems are a collection of routers *and* switches.

What happens when a device on one VLAN needs to communicate with a device on another VLAN? Because a VLAN is a closed Layer 2 network, traffic must cross a Layer 3 device to communicate with other VLANs. This means that a router is required to facilitate the exchange of packets between VLANs.

The behavior we're describing here is that of Layer 2 switching. There are Layer 3 switches on the market that perform routing, but these are beyond the scope of this book.

It is possible for a device to participate in more than one VLAN by using a special type of network card that performs ISL (Inter-switch link). ISL is discussed further in the "ISL" section in this chapter.

The real benefit to using VLANs is that they can span multiple switches. Figure 9.2 shows two switches that are configured to share VLAN information.

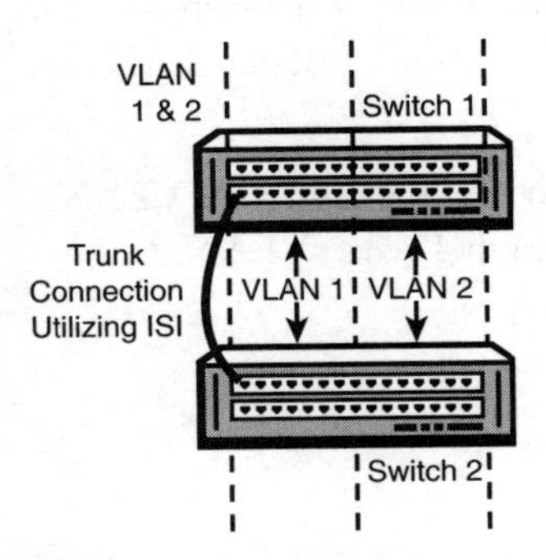


**Figure 9.2** VLANs spanning multiple switches.

A large campus network may have hundreds of switches spread throughout several buildings. A user can be put on the appropriate VLAN easily, no matter where he or she is physically located. Users on the same VLAN do not have to be connected to the same device. Therefore, LANs are no longer tied to the physical location of users, but can be assigned based on department, functional area, or security level. By isolating users according to department or functional area, network administrators can keep the majority of data traffic within one VLAN, thereby maximizing the amount of traffic switched at hardware speeds versus what is routed at slower software speeds.

The ability to assign a user to a VLAN on a port-by-port basis makes adding, moving, or deleting users simple. For example, let's say a user changes from the accounting to the marketing department. If the network administrator designed the network and VLANs by functional department, this user would have changed VLANs. To accommodate this change, the administrator only has to make a software configuration change in the switch by assigning that user's port to the new VLAN.

In addition, VLANs provide the flexibility necessary to group users by security level. This can greatly simplify applying a security policy to a network. In summary, the benefits of VLANs are that they:

- Simplify security administration.
- Allow users to be grouped by functional area versus physical location.
- Simplify moving and adding users.

# Frame Tagging

*Frame tagging* is the method used by Cisco Catalyst switches to identify to which VLAN a frame belongs. As a frame enters the switch, the switch encapsulates the frame with a header that "tags" the frame with a VLAN ID. Any time a frame needs to leave one switch for another, the tagged frame is sent throughout the switching fabric. When the frame arrives at the destination switch, the tag tells the switch to which VLAN the frame belongs. This process is illustrated in Figure 9.3 using the VLAN IDs 10, 20, and 30. The tag is stripped off of the frame before the frame is sent out to the destination device. This process gives the illusion that all ports are physically connected to the same switch.

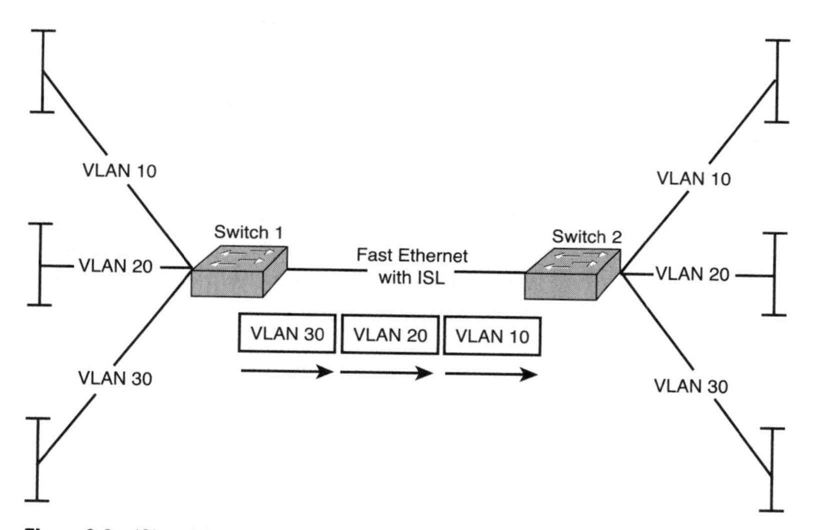


**Figure 9.3** ISL and frame tagging.

Be sure to understand the function of frame tagging, which "tags" a frame with a user-defined VLAN ID.

# Trunk Connections

Under normal circumstances, a switch port can carry traffic for a single VLAN only. For VLANs to span multiple switches, a *trunk connection* must be created. This trunk connection transports data from multiple VLANs. Trunk connections allow VLANs to be used throughout the switching fabric of large networks.

Any FastEthernet or asynchronous transfer mode (ATM) port on a Catalyst switch can be designated as a trunk port. This port typically connects to another switch via a crossover 100BASE-T cable in the case of a Fast Ethernet trunk.

For the trunked port to transport multiple VLANs, it must understand frame tags.

# ISL

*ISL* (Inter-switch link) is a technology developed by Cisco that allows a single Ethernet interface to participate in multiple VLANs. When a trunk connection is made on a Catalyst switch's Ethernet port, it utilizes ISL. ISL is also available on Ethernet cards that can be used in servers or routers.

A device utilizing an ISL Ethernet card will appear to have many physical cards, each connected to a different segment. ISL allows this single Ethernet card to have many logical (virtual) addresses. The user must configure each logical interface with an address that reflects the VLAN to which it belongs.

ISL works by allowing the frame-tagging information to be passed along to the Ethernet card. The Ethernet card then reads the frame tag, which identifies the VLAN to which the frame belongs. Conversely, the ISL Ethernet card creates the frame tags when transmitting frames.

ISL is a technology proprietary to Cisco and, therefore, is not supported on equipment made by other vendors. However, in mid-1998, the Institute of Electrical and Electronics Engineers (IEEE) standardized a frame-tagging process similar to Cisco's ISL. The new standard is a protocol called 802.1Q. With 802.1Q, switches from multiple vendors can coexist in the same switching fabric.

# VTP

*VTP* (VLAN Trunking Protocol) is a protocol used between switches to simplify the management of VLANs. Configuration changes that are made to a VTP server are propagated across trunks to all connected switches.

All switches that are to be managed in this way must be members of the same *management domain*. A VTP management domain is the entire group of switches that share configuration information.

For example, when you add a new VLAN to a member switch, the VLAN is available in all of the network switches automatically. VTP allows switched networks to scale to larger environments; otherwise, VLAN configuration would have to be maintained manually on individual switches.

By default, Catalyst switches are set to a no-management-domain state. The switches remain in a no-management state until a user configures the management domain or they receive an advertisement for a domain over a trunk link. The default VTP configuration parameters are shown in Table 9.2

**Table 9.2 Default VTP Configuration**

| Option | Default Value |
|---|---|
| VTP Domain Name | None |
| VTP Mode | Server |
| VTP Password | None |
| VTP Pruning | Disabled |
| VTP Trap | Enabled |

## VTP Modes

When it has a management domain, a switch operates in one of three VTP modes: server, client, or transparent. The default mode is server.

In *VTP server mode*, a switch can create, modify, or delete VLAN and other configuration parameters for the entire VTP domain. VTP messages are sent over all trunk links, and configuration changes are propagated to all switches in the management domain.

In *VTP client mode*, the switch receives VTP messages and applies configuration changes made from any VTP server. However, a client cannot create, change, or delete VLAN information.

In *VTP transparent mode*, the switch forwards all VTP messages to other switches in the domain, but does not use the configuration from VTP advertisements. A VTP transparent switch can create, modify, or delete VLANs, but the changes apply only locally and are not transmitted to other switches.

## VTP Pruning

VTP can detect if a trunk connection is carrying unnecessary traffic. By default, all trunk connections carry traffic from all VLANs in the management domain. In many cases, however, a switch does not need a local port configured for each VLAN. In this event, it is not necessary to flood traffic from VLANs other than the ones supported by that switch. VTP pruning enables the switching fabric to prevent flooding traffic on trunk ports that do not need it. This is illustrated in Figure 9.4.

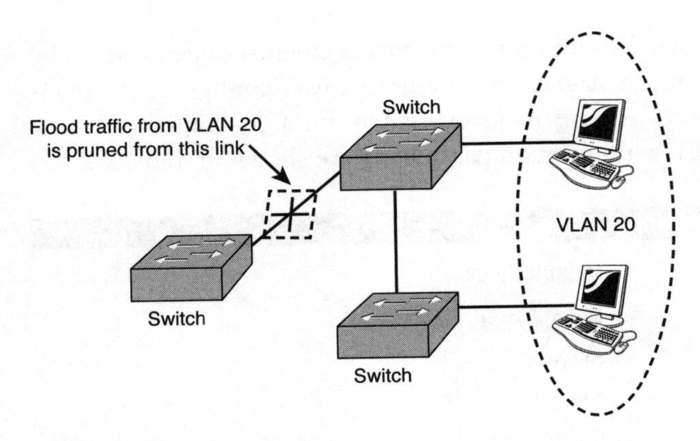


**Figure 9.4** VTP pruning.

# Configuring VLANs

There are three methods that can be used to assign a switch port to a particular VLAN. They are port-centric, static, and dynamic. In a *port-centric configuration*, all nodes that are connected to ports within the same VLAN are given the same VLAN ID. In this type of configuration, the network administrator's job is much easier because of the ease of administering the VLAN.

In a *static VLAN configuration* the ports on a switch are hard coded and remain in effect until the administrator changes them. This type of configuration is typical of a network that is very well monitored, where changes are unlikely.

The third type of port configuration is *dynamic*. This type of configuration involves more overhead on setup for the administrator because of the database configuration. The ports on these switches automatically determine their assigned VLAN. The VLAN assignment is determined by the type of protocol (within a packet), MAC address, and logical addressing. A major benefit of this type of configuration is that the administrator will notice any unauthorized or new user is on the network. If a workstation happens to be connected to a port which is unassigned, the switch will record the MAC address of the computer and check its database to determine which VLAN to assign the workstation to.

In the rest of this chapter, we look at the Cisco commands used to configure, monitor, and maintain VLANs and trunk connections.

Before you begin creating VLANs, you must determine whether the switch will participate in a VTP domain that will synchronize VLAN configuration with the rest of the network. Also, if you want to use VLANs across multiple switches, a trunk connection must be made to interconnect the switches.

The steps required to configure VLANs are as follows:

1. Enable VTP (optional).
2. Enable trunking (optional).
3. Create VLANs.
4. Assign VLANs to ports.

## Enabling VTP

When adding a new switch to an existing domain, it is good practice to add it in VTP client mode initially. This way, you can prevent the switch from propagating incorrect VLAN information to other switches. In the following example, however, we are setting up a new VTP domain and will place the switch into server mode. The commands to do so are as follows:

```
1900#conf terminal
Enter configuration commands, one per line. End with CNTL/Z
1900(config)#vtp server
1900(config)#vtp domain ccnalab
```

To verify VTP information, use the `show vtp` command from EXEC privileged mode:

```
hostname# show vtp

VTP version: 1
   Configuration revision: 3
   Maximum VLANs supported locally: 1005
   Number of existing VLANs: 5
   VTP domain name      : ccnalab
   VTP password       : vtp_server
   VTP operating mode   : Server
   VTP pruning mode    : Enabled
   VTP traps generation  : Enabled
   Configuration last modified by: 0.0.0.0 at 00-00-0000 00:00:00
```

## Enabling Trunking

The next step is to create a trunk connection to other switches that will be sharing VLAN information. In the following example, assume that we are connecting two Catalyst 1900 switches via their 100BASE-T ports using a crossover category 5 Ethernet cable. We are using the FastEthernet ports known in the IOS as f0/26.

The trunk command has five options: on, off, desirable, auto, and non-negotiate. Table 9.3 shows the function of each trunk mode.

**Table 9.3 Trunk Command Options**

| Option | Function |
|---|---|
| On | Port goes into permanent ISL trunk mode. Negotiates with the connected device to convert the link to a trunk. |
| Off | Disables trunking on this port. Negotiates with the connected device to convert the link to non-trunk. |
| Desirable | Port will enter trunk mode if the connected device is set to on, desirable, or auto; otherwise, port is a non-trunk. |
| Auto | Port will enter trunk mode if the connected device is set to on or desirable; otherwise, port is a non-trunk. |
| Non-Negotiate | Port goes into permanent ISL trunk mode, but no negotiation takes place with the connected device. |

To enable trunking on a port, enter interface configuration mode for the desired port first, and then use the trunk command with the appropriate option, as shown here:

```
1900#conf terminal
Enter configuration commands, one per line. End with CNTL/Z
1900(config)#interface f0/26
1900(config-if)#trunk on
```

The same configuration must be executed for the appropriate port on the connected device. Because we set the trunk to on mode in the previous example, the corresponding port must be set to on, auto, or desirable for the trunk connection to be established.

To verify the trunk operation, use the show trunk command. Its syntax is as follows:

```
show trunk [a ¦ b]
```

A Catalyst 1900 switch has two FastEthernet ports that can act as trunk connections. They are known as interfaces f0/26 and f0/27. When using the show trunk command, option A refers to the first trunk port (in this case, f0/26). Option B is for port f0/27. So, to see the trunking status for FastEthernet port A (f0/26), use the following command:

```
1900#show trunk a
DISL state: On, Trunking: On, Encapsulation type: ISL
```

# Creating VLANs

To create a new VLAN, use the `vlan` command from global configuration mode. This command has several options that can be specified, but for our purposes, all we need to have is a four-digit number to identify the VLAN and a name for it. Each VLAN must have a unique numeric ID, which can be any number from 1 to 1005.

We will create a VLAN called Engineering and make it VLAN 2:

```
hostname(config)# vlan 2 name Engineering
```

To verify the configuration of the VLAN, use the `show vlan` *`vlan#`* command:

```
1900#show vlan 2

VLAN Name       Status      Ports
---------       ------      -----
2 Engineering     Enabled
-------------     -------

VLAN Type      SAID   MTU  Parent RingNo BridgeNo Stp  Trans1 Trans2
---------      ----   ---  ------ ------ -------- ---  ------ ------
2 Ethernet     100009 1500 0      1      1        Unkn 0      0
```

# Assigning VLAN to Ports

Now that the VLAN has been created, you can statically assign which ports will be members of the VLAN. A port can belong to only one VLAN at a time. By default, all ports are members of VLAN 1.

To assign a VLAN to a port, enter interface configuration mode for the appropriate port, then use the `vlan-membership` command:

```
1900#conf terminal
Enter configuration commands, one per line. End with CNTL/Z
1900(config)#interface ethernet 0/8
1900(config-if)#vlan-membership static 2
```

To verify VLAN membership and to see which ports belong to what VLAN, use the `show vlan-membership` command:

```
hostname# show vlan-membership
Port  VLAN Membership Type  Port VLAN Membership Type
----  ---- ---------------  ---- ---- ---------------
 1    1    Static           14   2    Static
 2    1    Static           15   2    Static
 3    1    Static           16   2    Static
 4    1    Static           17   2    Static
 5    1    Static           18   2    Static
```

```
6    1    Static           19   2    Static
7    1    Dynamic          20   2    Static
8    1    Dynamic          21   2    Static
9    1    Dynamic          22   2    Static
10   1    Dynamic          23   2    Static
11   1    Dynamic          24   2    Static
12   1    Dynamic          AUI  2    Static
13   1    Dynamic
A    1    Static
B    2    Static
```

## Using the Web Interface

Catalyst 1900 and 2820 switches come with a built-in Web server that can be used for monitoring and configuring the switch. It is very visually oriented and allows you to change configuration options in a point-and-click environment. All you have to know is the IP address of the switch, and you can point your Web browser to the switch's IP address. If the switch has been configured with a password, you will have to enter it to use the Web interface.

# Exam Prep Questions

## Question 1

What must be done to allow a VLAN to span two or more switches?

- ❍ A. Set up a VTP domain
- ❍ B. Set up a trunk connection
- ❍ C. Configure the duplex setting on the ports
- ❍ D. Configure port security on the switch

Answer B is correct. A trunk connection must be established in order for a VLAN to span multiple switches. Trunk ports recognize frame tags and are therefore able to carry information on multiple VLANs. Answer A is incorrect because a VTP domain is not necessary for switches to share VLAN information. Answer C is incorrect because the duplex setting does not have to be configured manually to connect two switches. Answer D is incorrect because port security is not necessary for a VLAN to span switches.

## Question 2

What is ISL used for?

- ❍ A. To allow an Ethernet interface to understand frame tags
- ❍ B. To make two Ethernet interfaces appear as one
- ❍ C. To connect an Ethernet switch with a high-speed core switch such as ATM
- ❍ D. To allow simultaneous routing and switching

The correct answer is A. ISL allows an Ethernet interface to understand frame tags, which identify the VLAN to which a packet belongs. For this reason, an ISL interface can participate in multiple VLANs, which is necessary for a trunk connection. Answer B is incorrect because ISL can actually have the opposite effect of this—a single Ethernet interface may appear to be several by having multiple Layer 3 addresses. Answers C and D are incorrect because these are not functions of ISL.

## Question 3

What is the purpose of VTP pruning?

❍ A. To detect loops in the switching fabric

❍ B. To disable a trunk connection that creates a bridging loop

❍ C. To simplify the management of VLANs

❍ D. To prevent flooding unnecessary traffic across trunk connections

The correct answer is D. VTP pruning is used to prevent flooding of unnecessary traffic across trunk connections. Answer A is incorrect because this is a function of the spanning tree protocol. Answer B is incorrect because this is not the purpose of VTP pruning. Answer C is incorrect because this is the purpose of the VTP, not VTP pruning.

## Question 4

Which of the following is a valid command to create a VLAN on a Catalyst 1900 switch and name it Accounting?

❍ A. **switch(config)#create vlan 10 name Accounting**

❍ B. **switch#create vlan 10 name Accounting**

❍ C. **switch(config)#vlan 10 name Accounting**

❍ D. **switch#vlan 10 name Accounting**

The correct answer is C. The correct syntax to create a VLAN in command mode is `vlan {number} name {name}` from global configuration mode. Answers A and B are incorrect because the word "create" is not a part of this command. Answer D has the correct syntax for the command, however, the switch is not in configuration mode; therefore, answer D is incorrect.

## Question 5

Which of the following commands will assign Ethernet port 9 on a Catalyst 1900 to VLAN 20?

❍ A. **interface Ethernet 0/9 and vlan-membership static 20**

❍ B. **vlan-membership interface Ethernet 0/9 static 20**

❍ C. **interface Ethernet 0/9 and vlan 20**

❍ D. **vlan 20 interface Ethernet 0/9**

The correct answer is A. To assign an interface to a VLAN, you must first enter port configuration mode by using the `interface Ethernet 0/9` command from global configuration mode. Then, use the `vlan-membership` command to assign a VLAN to the port. Answers B, C, and D are all invalid syntax.

## Question 6

Which VLAN port configuration option requires more up-front administration because of database configuration?

❍ A. Static

❍ B. Port-centric

❍ C. Dynamic

❍ D. Dynamic-relational

The correct answer is C. The dynamic configuration requires more initial overhead because the administrator has to configure the switches database. Answer A is incorrect because static is also labor intensive up front, but not as much as dynamic. Answer B is incorrect because port-centric is the easiest of the three to administer. Answer D is incorrect because there is no such thing as a dynamic-relational configuration for Cisco's switch ports. The only configuration options are static, port-centric, and dynamic.

## Question 7

Which VLAN port configuration option states that no other packets will flow over into other workstation's domains?

❍ A. Static

❍ B. Port-centric

❍ C. Dynamic

❍ D. Static filtered

The correct answer is B. Port-centric is the correct choice because of the ability to assign VLAN IDs to ports in the same VLAN. Answer A, static, and B, dynamic, are incorrect because neither has the capability of assigning IDs to specific ports within the same VLAN. Answer D is incorrect because static filtered is not a VLAN port configuration option.

## Question 8

Which of the following commands could be used to assign an IP address to a Catalyst 1900 switch?

- ❍ A. **ip-address 10.1.1.10 255.0.0.0**
- ❍ B. **ip address 10.1.1.10 and subnet-mask 255.0.0.0**
- ❍ C. **ip 10.1.1.10/255.0.0.0**
- ❍ D. **ip address 10.1.1.10 255.0.0.0**

The correct answer is D. The command for assigning an IP address to a switch from the command prompt is `ip address` *`{address}{subnet-mask}`*. Answers A and C are incorrect because these are invalid commands. Answer B is incorrect because `subnet-mask` is not a valid command.

## Question 9

What command can be used on a Catalyst 1900 switch to view it's TCP/IP configuration information?

- ❍ A. **show tcp/ip**
- ❍ B. **show ip**
- ❍ C. **show network**
- ❍ D. **display network**

The correct answer is B. The `show ip` command will display information about the TCP/IP settings the switch is using. Answers A, C, and D are all invalid commands.

# Question 10

A marketing department has 15 stations on the fourth floor connected to a Cisco 1900 switch. The department has an additional 12 stations on the second floor connected to a second Cisco 1900 switch. The two switches are connected via standard 100BASE-T ports using a crossover cable. The department head has stated that she wants everybody on the same department LAN. Which trunk command option would you use for the port connected to the crossover cable on the fifth floor to ensure communications between the two groups?

❍ A. On

❍ B. Off

❍ C. Desirable

❍ D. Auto

Answer B is correct. Trunking is used when VLANs span more than one switch. In this case, the department head wants a single LAN so trunking would not be needed or desired. Traffic will automatically flow across the crossover cable as needed. Answer A is not correct because it would force the port into permanent ISL trunk mode. Answer C is not correct because if the port on the second floor were set to anything other than "off", both ports would immediately go into trunk mode. Answer D is not correct because if the port on the second floor was set to "desirable" or "on", both ports would again go into trunk mode.

# Need to Know More?

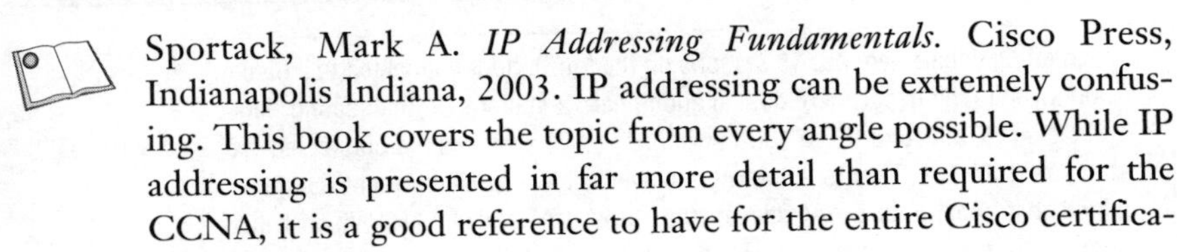

Sportack, Mark A. *IP Addressing Fundamentals.* Cisco Press, Indianapolis Indiana, 2003. IP addressing can be extremely confusing. This book covers the topic from every angle possible. While IP addressing is presented in far more detail than required for the CCNA, it is a good reference to have for the entire Cisco certification program.

Osterloh, Heather. *TCP/IP Primer Plus.* Sams Publishing, Indianapolis, Indiana, 2002. Written clearly and concisely, this one book can answer almost any question relating to TCP/IP. It is a good book to have for both this certification and future Cisco certifications.

Castelli, Matthew. *Network Sales and Services Handbook.* Cisco Press, Indianapolis, Indiana, 2003. Although this book is targeted at sales, it does a very good job of explaining technologies and Cisco products without getting into mind bogging minutia. A good book to have!

Odom, Wendell. *Cisco CCNA Exam Certification Guide.* Cisco Press, Indianapolis, Indiana, 2000. Cisco is almost always the best place for reference books relating to Cisco. They print incredibly detailed and comprehensive books and this one is excellent. I would not want to read it as a primary text, but as a reference it cannot be beat.

# Configuring a Cisco Router

## Terms you'll need to understand:

- ✓ Running and startup configuration files
- ✓ TFTP (Trivial File Transfer Protocol)
- ✓ Configuration register
- ✓ Standard access Lists
- ✓ **enable secret** password command
- ✓ **service password-encryption** command
- ✓ Boot field
- ✓ Link Control Protocol (LCP)
- ✓ Point-to-Point Protocol (PPP)
- ✓ ISDN (Integrated Services Digital Network)
- ✓ Frame relay
- ✓ IP extended access lists

## Techniques you'll need to master:

- ✓ Copying and moving configuration files
- ✓ Configuring a router during initial setup
- ✓ Identifying main Cisco IOS commands for router startup
- ✓ Loading and backing up of Cisco IOS
- ✓ Configuring a router to use PPP, ISDN, and/or frame relay
- ✓ Configuring routing protocols
- ✓ Configuring standard and extended access list for IP

If you ever wanted some hands-on experience to help you in your CCNA preparation (of course you do), then this chapter is for you. This chapter focuses on a number of very important and often-applied skills in networking. The ability to manage configuration files, to load and copy Cisco software, and to understand the impact of these types of commands is vital for your success. More importantly, you need to master these crucial skills to avoid causing a disaster in your company's network and pass the exam of course. Understanding the many password types and security levels used on Cisco routers is equally important. Finally, this chapter describes and illustrates the steps required to set up a router via the initial setup sequence. However, let's start with a review of key concepts from Chapter 8, where we first introduced router configuration.

# Router Elements

This section describes the various interface modes in which you can work on a router. It also provides an overview of the different components within a router and explains how to examine the status of each of those components.

## Router Modes

Regardless of how you access a router (through the console port, a modem connection, or a router interface), you can place it in one of several modes. Other router modes exist beyond the user and privileged modes in previous chapters. Each router mode enables specific functions to be performed. The different types of router modes include user, privileged, setup, RXBOOT, global configuration, and other configuration modes, as shown in Table 10.1.

**Table 10.1 Router Modes**

| Mode | Function | How Accessed | Prompt |
|---|---|---|---|
| User | Limited display | Log in to the router | **Router>** |
| Privileged | Display, testing, debugging, configuration file manipulation | From user mode, enter theenable command | **Router#** |
| Setup | Create initial router configuration | During router startup, if the configuration file is missing from NVRAM (console dialog) | Interactive dialog prompts |
| RXBOOT | Perform router recovery | Press the Break key during router startup (console access only) | **>** |

*(continued)*

**Table 10.1 Router Modes *(continued)***

| Mode | Function | How Accessed | Prompt |
|---|---|---|---|
| Global | Perform simple configuration | From EXEC privileged mode, enter the **configure** command | **Router (config)#** |
| Others | Perform complex and multiline configuration | From within global configuration mode, the command entered varies | **Router (config-<mode>)#** |

## User Mode

As stated earlier, user mode provides a display-only environment. You can view limited information about the router but cannot change the configuration.

## Privileged Mode

Privileged mode enables you to perform an extensive review of the router. This mode supports testing commands, debugging commands, and commands to manage the router configuration files.

## Setup Mode

Setup mode is triggered on router startup when no configuration file resides in nonvolatile random access memory (NVRAM). This mode executes an interactive prompted dialog box to assist in creating an initial router configuration.

## RXBOOT Mode

A router's maintenance mode is called *RXBOOT mode* or *ROM monitor mode*. This mode facilitates recovery functions when the router password is lost or the IOS file stored in Flash memory has been erased or is corrupt. Pressing the Break key (from a console terminal directly connected to the router) within the first 60 seconds of startup also allows you to place the router in this mode.

## Global Configuration Mode

You perform simple configuration tasks in global configuration mode. For example, router names, router passwords, and router banners are configured in this mode.

## Other Configuration Modes

You perform complex router-configuration tasks in several other configuration modes. You enter interface, subinterface, controller, and routing protocol configurations from within these other modes. Table 10.2 provides a summary of the syntax for each router mode.

**Table 10.2 Router Configuration Summaries**

| Configuration Mode | Router Prompt |
|---|---|
| Interface | **NFLD(config-if)#** |
| Subinterface | **NFLD(config-subif)#** |
| Router | **NFLD(config-router)#** |
| IPX-Router | **NFLD(config-ipx-router)#** |
| Line | **NFLD(config-line)#** |
| Controller | **NFLD(config-controller)#** |
| Map-List | **NFLD(config-map-list)#** |
| Router-Map | **NFLD(config-route-map)#** |

# Router Components

Every router contains several components that compose its configuration. These components are RAM, NVRAM, Flash memory, ROM, and interfaces.

## RAM

RAM serves as a working storage area for the router and contains data such as routing tables, various types of cache and buffers, and input and output queues. RAM also provides storage for temporary memory for the router's active IOS and configuration file (the running configuration file). However, all the contents of RAM are lost if the router is powered down or restarted.

## NVRAM

Unlike RAM, nonvolatile RAM (NVRAM) retains its contents when the router is powered down or restarted. NVRAM stores permanent information, such as the router's backup configuration file. The startup configuration file is retrieved from NVRAM during startup and loaded into RAM.

## Flash

Flash memory stores the Cisco IOS image and associated microcode. Flash memory is erasable, electronically reprogrammable ROM that retains its contents when the router is powered down. Several copies or versions of an IOS image can be contained in Flash memory. Flash memory allows software to be upgraded without chips on the processor being added, removed, or replaced.

## ROM

Like Flash memory, ROM contains a version of IOS—usually an older version with minimal functionality. It also stores the bootstrap program and power-on diagnostic programs. However, software upgrades can be performed only by replacing the ROM chip itself.

### Interfaces

Interfaces provide the network connections where packets move in and out of the router. Depending on the model of router, interfaces exist either on the motherboard or on separate, modular interface cards.

## Router Status

Routine administration of a router involves examining the status of the router. The `show` command enables you to view the status of the router's components. You can execute `show` from either user or privileged mode. However, the keywords used with the `show` command are different in the user and privileged modes.

Figure 10.1 illustrates some of the more common `show` command keywords and the router components with which they are associated

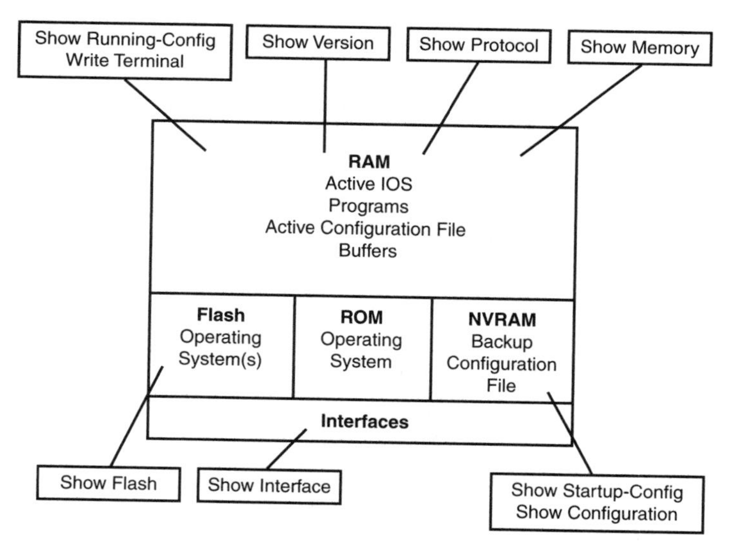


**Figure 10.1** The **show** commands and associated router components.

The `show version` command displays hardware and software version numbers relating to a specific router, as shown here:

```
NFLD#show version
Cisco Internetwork Operating System Software
IOS (tm) 2500 Software (C2500-IS-L), Version 11.3(7)T,
RELEASE SOFTWARE (fc1)
Copyright (c) 1986-1998 by Cisco Systems, Inc.
```

```
Compiled Tue 01-Dec-98 10:21 by ccai
Image text-base: 0x0303A9D8, data-base: 0x00001000

ROM: System Bootstrap, Version 11.0(10c)XB1, PLATFORM SPECIFIC
RELEASE SOFTWARE
(fc1)
BOOTFLASH: 3000 Bootstrap Software (IGS-BOOT-R),
Version 11.0(10c)XB1, PLATFORM
SPECIFIC RELEASE SOFTWARE (fc1)

NFLD uptime is 2 days, 7 hours, 17 minutes
System restarted by reload
System image file is "flash:c2500-is-l_113-7_T",
booted via flash

cisco 2500 (68030) processor (revision M) with
6144K/2048K bytes of memory.
Processor board ID 06972781, with hardware revision 00000000
Bridging software.
X.25 software, Version 3.0.0.
1 Ethernet/IEEE 802.3 interface(s)
1 Token Ring/IEEE 802.5 interface(s)
2 Serial network interface(s)
32K bytes of non-volatile configuration memory.
8192K bytes of processor board System flash (Read ONLY)

Configuration register is 0x2102

NFLD#
```

The show memory command displays statistics about the router's memory, as shown here:

```
NFLD#show memory
            Head Total(b) Used(b)  Free(b) Lowest(b) Largest(b)
Processor  87510  5733104  809476  4923628   4872780    4890708
      I/O 600000  2097152  488444  1608708   1476032    1532904


     Processor memory

Address Bytes Prev. Next Ref PrevF NextF Alloc PC What
87510    1068 0     87968  1         31A0B86 List Elements
87968    2868 87510 884C8  1         31A0B86 List Headers
884C8    3884 87968 89420  1         314B0E0 TTY data
89420    2000 884C8 89C1C  1         314D52E TTY Input Buf
89C1C     510 89420 89E48  1         314D55E TTY Output Buf
89E48    3000 89C1C 8AA2C  1         31B31BA Interrupt Stack
8AA2C      44 89E48 8AA84  1         36C16D8 *Init*
8AA84    1068 8AA2C 8AEDC  1         31A0B86 messages
8AEDC      88 8AA84 8AF60  1         31AFBAC Watched Boolean
8AF60      88 8AEDC 8AFE4  1         31AFBAC Watched Boolean
8AFE4      88 8AF60 8B068  1         31AFBAC Watched Boolean
8B068      88 8AFE4 8B0EC  1         31AFBAC Watched Boolean
8B0EC    1032 8B068 8B520  1         31B796A Process Array
8B520    1000 8B0EC 8B934  1         31B7D1C Process Stack
8B934     480 8B520 8BB40  1         31B7D2E Process
8BB40     108 8B934 8BBEC  1         31AFDBC Process Events
8BBEC      44 8BB40 8BC44  1         36C16D8 *Init*
8BC44    1068 8BBEC 8C09C  1         31A0B86 List Elements
 --More--
```

The `show protocols` command displays the Network layer protocols and addresses that are configured on the router, as shown here:

```
NFLD#show protocols
Global values:
 Internet Protocol routing is enabled
Ethernet0 is up, line protocol is up
 Internet address is 172.16.57.1/24
Serial0 is administratively down, line protocol is down
Serial1 is administratively down, line protocol is down
TokenRing0 is administratively down, line protocol is down
NFLD#
```

The `show running-config` command displays the active configuration file. Use the `write terminal` command if the router's IOS version is 10.3 or earlier. The `write terminal` command is also supported in later versions of the IOS:

```
NFLD#show running-config
Building configuration...
Current configuration:
!
version 11.3
service timestamps debug uptime
service timestamps log uptime
no service password-encryption
!
hostname NFLD
!
interface Ethernet0
 description Engineering LAN Segment
 ip address 172.16.57.1 255.255.255.0
!
interface Serial0
 no ip address
 no ip mroute-cache
 shutdown
 no fair-queue
!
interface Serial1
 no ip address
 shutdown
!
interface TokenRing0
 no ip address
 shutdown
!
ip classless
!
!
line con 0
line aux 0
line vty 0 4
 login
!
end

NFLD#
```

The `show startup-config` command displays the backup configuration file. Use the `show configuration` command if the router's IOS version is 10.3 or earlier. The `show configuration` command is also supported in later versions of the IOS:

```
NFLD#show startup-config
Using 424 out of 32762 bytes
!
version 11.3
service timestamps debug uptime
service timestamps log uptime
no service password-encryption
!
hostname NFLD
!
interface Ethernet0
 description Engineering LAN Segment
 ip address 172.16.57.1 255.255.255.0
!
interface Serial0
 no ip address
 no ip mroute-cache
 shutdown
 no fair-queue
!
interface Serial1
 no ip address
 shutdown
!
interface TokenRing0
 no ip address
 shutdown
!
ip classless
!
!
line con 0
line aux 0
line vty 0 4
 login
!
end

NFLD#
```

The `show interface` command displays statistics for all the interfaces on the router. The `show` command can also be used to display statistics for a specific interface, if that interface is included as a keyword when issuing the command.

```
NFLD#show interface ethernet 0
Ethernet0 is up, line protocol is up
 Hardware is Lance, address is 00e0.1e60.9d9f
(bia 00e0.1e60.9d9f)
 Description: Engineering LAN Segment
 Internet address is 172.16.57.1/24
 MTU 1500 bytes, BW 10000 Kbit, DLY 1000 usec,
   reliability 255/255, txload 1/255, rxload 1/255
 Encapsulation ARPA, loopback not set, keepalive set (10 sec)
 ARP type: ARPA, ARP Timeout 04:00:00
 Last input 00:00:01, output 00:00:03, output hang never
```

```
  Last clearing of "show interface" counters never
  Queueing strategy: fifo
  Output queue 0/40, 0 drops; input queue 0/75, 0 drops
  5 minute input rate 0 bits/sec, 0 packets/sec
  5 minute output rate 0 bits/sec, 0 packets/sec
     42 packets input, 9697 bytes, 0 no buffer
     Received 42 broadcasts, 0 runts, 0 giants, 0 throttles
     0 input errors, 0 CRC, 0 frame, 0 overrun, 0 ignored, 0 abort
     0 input packets with dribble condition detected
     80 packets output, 16167 bytes, 0 underruns
     0 output errors, 0 collisions, 2 interface resets
     0 babbles, 0 late collision, 0 deferred
     0 lost carrier, 0 no carrier
     0 output buffer failures, 0 output buffers swapped out
NFLD#
```

The `show flash` command displays information about the Flash memory device, as shown here:

```
NFLD#show flash

System flash directory:
File Length  Name/status
 1  7181580 c2500-is-l_113-7_T
[7181644 bytes used, 1006964 available, 8388608 total]
8192K bytes of processor board System flash (Read ONLY)

NFLD#
```

# Managing Configuration Files

The process of managing configuration files is straightforward; however, it is increasingly difficult because of the different versions of Cisco software and the wide variety of architectures used in Cisco hardware. This section will bring light to these subjects; present an overview of the different types of configuration files and the commands used to move, display, and copy these files; and, finally, highlight some of the areas that can cause confusion when managing configuration files.

## Types of Configuration Files

Cisco IOS software uses and requires a configuration file to determine how a router is to function. Typically, network administrators enter the commands necessary for their environment into a router configuration file. Only two types of configuration files exist for the context of the CCNA exam:

- The running configuration file exists in RAM and contains the commands that Cisco IOS uses to drive the actions of the router.

RAM is erased during power cycles or software reloads. Therefore, the running configuration file is erased as well. Startup configuration files, which provide a backup for the running configuration files, reside in NVRAM and are not erased with a power down.

- The startup configuration file exists in NVRAM and is the backup for the running configuration file.

The router will always use the running configuration file to execute. However, any time a router is restarted (cycling power or reloading the software), the running configuration file is erased and the startup configuration file is the only remaining configuration file. During the boot sequence of a router, the router copies the startup configuration file to the running configuration file (NVRAM to RAM). Therefore, it is paramount that any time a change is made to a running configuration, the change is also copied to the startup configuration. The many ways of preventing the loss of changes made are discussed in this chapter.

# Displaying the Running and Startup Configuration Files

The purpose of displaying a running or startup configuration file is to determine the configuration commands being executed on a router. Use the `show running-config` and `show startup-config` commands to show the running configuration and startup configuration files, respectively. Displaying the running configuration file shows the commands being executed at the time that the `show` command is executed, as shown here:

```
Router#show running-config
Building configuration...
Current configuration:
Last configuration change at 03:25:38 UTC Sat Jan 1 2000
version 11.2
no service password-encryption
no service udp-small-servers
no service tcp-small-servers
hostname Router
enable secret 5 $1$2uUP$2I.L0xxD3wnX.7WDMHzb60
enable password cisco
no ip domain-lookup

interface Serial0
 ip address 138.144.2.2 255.255.255.0
 encapsulation frame-relay
 bandwidth 2000
 frame-relay lmi-type cisco

interface Serial1
```

```
 no ip address
 shutdown
!
interface TokenRing0
 ip address 138.144.3.1 255.255.255.0
 ring-speed 16
!
interface TokenRing1
 ip address 138.144.4.1 255.255.255.0
 ring-speed 16
!
router igrp 1
 network 138.144.0.0
!
no ip classless
!
snmp-server community public RO
!
line con 0
line aux 0
line vty 0 4
password cisco
login
!
end
```

The **Router#** prompt indicates that the command is initiated from the EXEC privileged (**enable**) command line. It is important to know in what mode a command should be executed.

## Configuring the Running and Startup Configuration Files

The running configuration file often requires changes while the router is functioning. Cisco IOS is designed to accept changes to a running or startup configuration file without restarting (reloading) or cycling the power of the router. The following commands are used to manipulate the configuration files:

- `Router# configure terminal`—Allows a user to add, change, or delete commands in the running configuration file while the router is executing.
- `Router# configure memory`—Allows a user to add, change, or delete commands in the startup configuration file.

Making changes to the running configuration file will immediately affect the behavior of a router.

# Backing Up and Restoring Configuration Files

Configuration files are copied and moved constantly in most networks. One common method of copying files is with the use of a Trivial File Transfer Protocol (TFTP) server. Most Unix machines have built-in TFTP support. Also, TFTP server programs are available for Windows-based PCs. Cisco makes a TFTP server program that is available to registered users on its Web site at the following Web address: `www.cisco.com/pcgi-bin/tablebuild.pl/tftp`. Cisco routers use a TFTP server to load IOS and to copy software and configuration files. To copy a file using TFTP, one device needs to be executing TFTP server software and the other device needs to be executing the client software. Cisco routers are equipped with both functions. Network administrators often need to back up a running or startup configuration file on a central server. The following command sequence accomplishes this goal:

```
Router# copy running-config TFTP
Remote host []? 172.15.10.2 (IP Address of TFTP Server)
Name of configuration file to write [router-confg]? <Return>
Write file Router-confg on host 172.15.10.2? [confirm] <Return>
Building configuration...
Writing Router-confg !!!!!!!!!!!!!!!!![OK]
```

Pay attention to the order and syntax of commands during the test. The function of a command can completely change, depending on the syntax. Also be aware that Cisco networking devices accept the short form of commands, for example **config t** instead of **configure terminal**. We use the long forms exclusively in this book because they are easier to remember.

The reverse process occurs when a configuration file is copied from a central server to an executing router. This process is most often used when a router has gone dead or someone has accidentally deleted the configuration file on the router. If the running configuration was backed up on a TFTP server, it is really simple to restore the configuration file. The first step for restoring the configuration file on a router is to determine Internet Protocol (IP) connectivity from the central server to the router. This might require the use of a ping test and/or the configuration of an IP address on the router. The following command sequence is used for restoring a running configuration file:

```
Router# copy TFTP running-config
Host or network configuration file [host]? <Return>
Address of remote host [255.255.255.255]? 172.15.10.2 (TFTP Server)
Name of configuration file [Router-confg]?Router-confg  -
(File name)
Configure using Router-confg from 172.15.10.2? [confirm] <Return>
Loading Router-confg from 172.15.10.2 (via serial 1): !!!!!
[OK - 875/32723]
Router#
```

Exercise caution when performing configuration file changes across networks, especially to remote sites. Visit the Cisco Web site (**www.cisco.com**) and utilize the search engine to identify anything you might need to be aware of while performing configuration file backups or restores in your network. Always be sure to find hardware-specific features before changing configuration files or Cisco IOS software.

Another method of backing up a running configuration is to save it to NVRAM. You should complete this process after every change to the running configuration file, unless a good reason exists to keep the startup configuration different. By copying the running configuration to NVRAM, you are ensuring that if the router is reloaded or the power is cycled, it will boot with the same configuration you are currently executing. The following command sequence is required for this process:

```
Router#copy running-config startup-config
Building configuration...
[OK]
```

The startup configuration file can also be copied into RAM, thereby overwriting the running configuration file, by performing the following command:

```
Router# Copy startup-config running-config
```

It is necessary to know all the backup and restore commands for the CCNA exam. Be sure to pay special attention to the syntax of these commands. It is easy to forget the sequence of words for the different commands.

Finally, the startup configuration file can be completely erased. When this occurs, the router boots into setup mode the next time it is reloaded:

```
Router#erase startup-config
```

# Router Passwords

The router passwords on the Cisco router provide security against unwanted users; Cisco IOS passwords were never intended to resist a determined, intelligent attack. Many programs exist (Cisco is aware of these programs) that can crack the MD5 encryption algorithm Cisco IOS employs. Cisco always recommends that some type of user-authentication protocol be used to enhance the security of Cisco routers. RADIUS and TACACS are two of the more popular authentication methods that major corporations use today. Cisco routers utilize five different password types to provide security.

# The enable password and enable secret Password Commands

The `enable password` and `enable secret` password commands are designed to provide an additional layer of security for passwords. Both commands allow you to establish an encrypted password that must be entered for the user to access privileged exec mode. The `enable secret` command was developed to use an improved encryption algorithm. The `enable secret` password overrides the password for `enable password` when it is present. An `enable secret` password can be entered by issuing the following command:

```
Router(config)#enable secret NFLD
Router#
```

The `enable password` and `enable secret` commands also provide for security levels. These options are not part of the objectives set by the CCNA exam and are not, therefore, presented in this book.

# The console and auxiliary Password Commands

The `console` and `auxiliary` password commands restrict user mode access via the console or auxiliary ports on the router:

```
Router(config)#line aux 0
Router(config-line)#login
Router(config-line)#password NFLD
```

The `login` command designates that you want users to have to enter their passwords every time they connect to the router via the auxiliary port. The `login` command can be added to the console port to require a password login as well. The `console` password is set with the same command format as the `aux` password, except that the keyword `aux` is changed to `con`.

# The virtual terminal Password Command

The `virtual terminal` (or `vty`) password restricts user modes accessed via a Telnet session. The `virtual terminal` password must be set; otherwise, a user will not be able to log in to the router with a Telnet session. Multiple virtual terminal sessions can be engaged at one time. A separate password can also be specified for each virtual terminal session, as shown in the following:

```
Router(config-line)#line vty 0 4
Router(config-line)#login
Router(config-line)#password NFLD
```

The Cisco IOS allows five simultaneous Telnet connections. Notice that the syntax is *line* then *line type* and *line number*. Cisco interface numbers always start with 0. For this example, we are specifying all five ports, numbers 0 through 4, to designate five virtual terminals that all use the password "NFLD."

Of the five different types of passwords, only the `enable secret` password is encrypted by default. For the remaining passwords, you must use the `service password-encryption` command. This command encrypts the `enable`, `console`, `auxiliary`, and `virtual terminal` passwords:

```
Router(config)#service password-encryption
```

Passwords that have already been set in the configuration file will not become encrypted; only plain text passwords that are entered prior to configuring `service password-encryption` are converted to encrypted passwords. The `service password-encryption` command does not provide a high level of network security, but it helps to keep unauthorized individuals from viewing a password in a configuration file.

# Router Identification and Banner

A router's name is referred to as the *hostname*. The default hostname for all Cisco routers is "Router." You can change the hostname of a router in global configuration mode by entering the `hostname` command. The hostname is changed with the following commands:

```
Router(config)#hostname NFLD
NFLD(config)#
```

Notice that the hostname changed from "Router" to "NFLD" immediately after executing the command.

The `banner motd` command allows you to display a message-of-the-day (MOTD) banner every time you log in to the router. Even though the banner message was designed to convey day-to-day messages, it is typically used for displaying security messages for legal reasons:

```
NFLD(config)#banner motd * Authorized Access Only,
 All Violations Will Be Prosecuted *
NFLD(config)#
```

The asterisk (*) before the word "Authorized" and after the word "Prosecuted" represents the start and finish of the text to be displayed as the banner.

In this scenario, the next time you Telnet into the router, the MOTD banner will display the following message:

```
Authorized Access Only, All Violations Will Be Prosecuted.
User Access Verification
Password:
```

A description can be added to every interface using the `description` command. Typically, an interface description, which is limited to 80 characters, is used to describe the function of the interface, as shown in the following:

```
NFLD(config)#interface s0
NFLD(config-if)#description 56K between NFLD and San Diego
NFLD(config-if)#
```

The next time someone views the running configuration file, she will see the following description:

```
interface Serial0
description 56K connection between NFLD and San Diego
ip address 138.144.2.2 255.255.255.0
encapsulation frame-relay
bandwidth 2000
frame-relay lmi-type cisco
```

# Initial Configuration of a Cisco Router

The first time a Cisco router is powered on, the startup configuration file is blank, so it will boot into the initial configuration dialog. This dialog is designed to walk a novice through the basic steps and requirements of configuring a Cisco router.

The initial configuration dialog is a menu-driven command-and-response query designed to configure a router with a bare-bones configuration. The dialog will start anytime a configuration file is not found in NVRAM during the boot sequence, as described previously. The two instances in which a configuration file will not exist in NVRAM are when the router is powered on for the first time and when the router is reloaded subsequent to the startup configuration file being erased.

The following code is a sample initial router configuration phase:

```
Would you like to enter the initial configuration
dialog? [yes] <Return>
First, would you like to see the current interface
summary? [yes] <Return>
Any interface listed with OK? Value "NO" does not have a
valid configuration
```

```
Interface     IP-Address   OK?  Method    Status  Protocol
Serial 0      unassigned   NO   not set   up      down
Serial 1      unassigned   NO   not set   up      down
Ethernet 1    unassigned   NO   not set   up      down
Ethernet 2    unassigned   NO   not set   up      down
Configuring global parameters:
```

Notice that in the configuration dialog, many of the questions have answers in brackets following them. These are the default values or answers for the questions. To accept a default value, simply press Enter and move on to the next question. If you don't want to use the default value, simply enter your own. Also, if at any time you are stumped as to the proper syntax to use, you can always type **?** at the prompt for help or press the Tab key, which will finish your syntax for you.

The preceding interface summary indicates that the router has two serial and two Ethernet interfaces. In this example, we will configure both serial interfaces and neither of the Ethernet interfaces. None of the four interfaces has been assigned an IP address, which is indicated by the "unassigned" designation, listed under the IP-Address column. The status of the interface is set to "up" because this is the default value. We must manually shut down the interface to turn it off. However, the protocol is listed as "down" because no active connections are on the interface. After the interface summary is displayed, the next step in the initial configuration dialog is to configure the hostname, passwords, routing protocols, and IP addressing, as shown here:

```
Enter host name [Router] NFLD
The enable secret is a one-way cryptographic secret used instead
 of the enable password when it exists.
Enter enable secret: NFLD
The enable password is used when no enable secret exists and when
Using older software and some boot images.
Enter enable password: Cisco
Enter the virtual terminal password: Telnet
Configure SNMP Network Management? [yes]: no
Configure IP? [yes] <Return>
       Configure IGRP Routing? [yes]: no
       Configure RIP Routing? [yes]: no
Configure Interfaces:
       Configuring interface Ethernet 0:
       Is this interface in use? [yes] no
       Configuring interface Ethernet 1:
       Is this interface in use? [yes] no
       Configuring interface Serial 0:
       Is this interface in use? [yes] <Return>
Configure IP on this interface? [yes] <Return>
Configure IP unnumbered on this interface? [no] : <Return>
IP Address for this interface: 172.29.3.4
       Number of bits in subnet field [8]: <Return>
Class B network is 172.29.0.0, 8 subnet bits; mask is
     255.255.255.0
       Configuring interface Serial 1:
       Is this interface in use? [yes] <Return>
Configure IP on this interface? [yes] <Return>
Configure IP unnumbered on interface? [no] : <Return>
```

```
        IP Address for this interface: 172.29.4.3
        Number of bits in subnet field [8]: <Return>
Class B network is 172.29.0.0, 8 subnet bits; mask is
     255.255.255.0
```

Now we have configured the two serial interfaces, set up our passwords, and chosen any routing protocols we want to utilize. For the sake of simplicity, however, we did not turn on either the Routing Information Protocol (RIP) or the Interior Gateway Routing Protocol (IGRP). The router will then show us the configuration that we created:

```
The following configuration command script was created:
Hostname NFLD
Enable secret 5 09371034073401823
Enable password Cisco
Line vty 0 4
Password Telnet
No snmp-server
!
ip routing
!
interface Ethernet 0
Shutdown
No ip address
Interface Ethernet 1
Shutdown
No ip address
Interface Serial 0
Ip address 172.29.3.4 255.255.255.0
Interface Serial 1
Ip address 172.29.4.3 255.255.255.0
!
end
Use this configuration? [yes/no]: yes
```

We have now completed the initial configuration dialog and successfully configured the NFLD router with IP addressing.

# PPP Overview

Point-to-Point Protocol (PPP) encapsulates Network layer information for transmission over point-to-point links. It was designed by developers on the Internet and is described by a series of documents called *Request for Comments (RFCs)*—namely, 1661, 1331, and 2153. Figure 10.2 shows how PPP's layered architecture relates to the Open Systems Interconnection (OSI) model.

PPP consists of two main components:

- *Link Control Protocol (LCP)*—Establishes, configures, and tests the connection
- *Network Control Program (NCP)*—Configures many different Network layer protocols

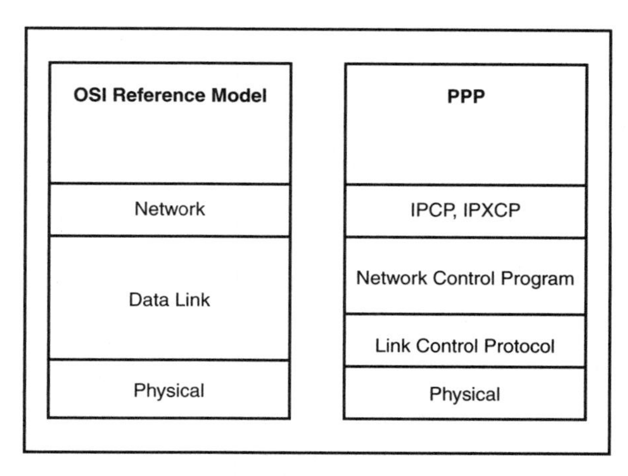


**Figure 10.2** The OSI reference model and PPP.

# Configuring PPP

Configuring PPP on a Cisco router requires that both global and interface configuration commands be executed on both the local and remote routers. Figure 10.3 presents an example of two routers that need to establish a PPP link.

**Figure 10.3** Point-to-Point Protocol (PPP).

A username and password must be set, so the following global configuration command must be executed:

```
Username name password secret-password
```

In this command, `name` and `secret-password` indicate the name of the remote host and the password to use for authentication. The password must be the same on both the local and remote routers. Table 10.3 lists the interface commands that must be executed to configure PPP. Figure 10.4 presents the global and interface configuration commands for router A and router B.

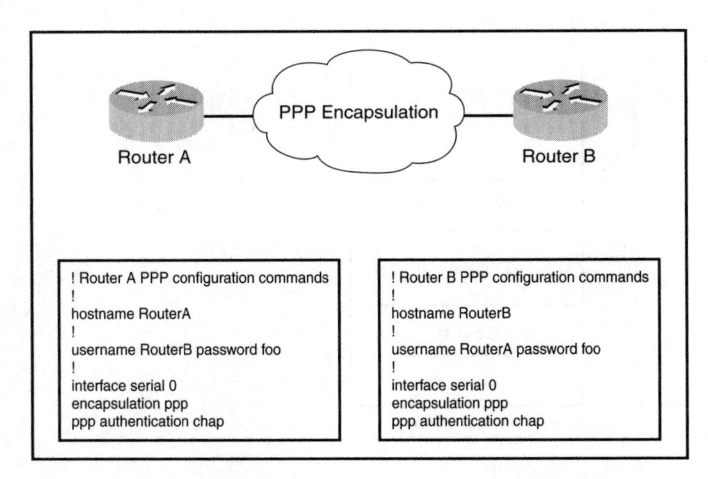


**Figure 10.4** PPP configuration.

# Monitoring PPP

You can monitor PPP activity with the `show interface` and `debug ppp chap` commands. The `show interface` command enables you to view PPP, LCP, and NCP information. The following output shows an example of PPP activity on an interface:

Notice that the "show interface" in the following example is abbreviated to "sh int". Almost all Cisco commands can be abbreviated. However, we recommend you use the full command until you are comfortable with all aspects of configuration. The abbreviations are hard to remember at first, but fairly easy to recognize once written. You will not be asked to provide any abbreviation on the test and you will probably not see any. However, we want to make sure you know they exist and will include some as we go along so you can see what they are like.

```
RouterA#sh int s0
Serial0 is up, line protocol is up
  Hardware is HD64570
  Internet address is 172.16.1.1/16
  MTU 1500 bytes, BW 1544 Kbit, DLY 20000 usec,
    rely 255/255, load 1/255
  Encapsulation PPP, loopback not set, keepalive set (10 sec)
  LCP Open
  Open: IPCP, CDPCP
  Last input 00:00:06, output 00:00:06, output hang never
  Last clearing of "show interface" counters never
  Input queue: 0/75/0 (size/max/drops); Total output drops: 0
  Queueing strategy: weighted fair
  Output queue: 0/1000/64/0 (size/max total/threshold/drops)
     Conversations  0/2/256 (active/max active/max total)
     Reserved Conversations 0/0 (allocated/max allocated)
```

```
   5 minute input rate 0 bits/sec, 0 packets/sec
   5 minute output rate 0 bits/sec, 0 packets/sec
      34 packets input, 1303 bytes, 0 no buffer
      Received 34 broadcasts, 0 runts, 0 giants, 0 throttles
     0 input errors, 0 CRC, 0 frame, 0 overrun, 0 ignored, 0 abort
      72 packets output, 2819 bytes, 0 underruns
      0 output errors, 0 collisions, 14 interface resets
      0 output buffer failures, 0 output buffers swapped out
      41 carrier transitions
      DCD=up  DSR=up  DTR=up  RTS=up  CTS=up
RouterA#
```

The `debug ppp chap` command displays the CHAP packet exchanges and PAP exchanges. The following output displays an example of the authentication handshake sequence:

```
RouterA# debug ppp chap
Serial0: Unable to authenticate. No name received from peer
Serial0: Unable to validate CHAP response.
         USERNAME pioneer not found.
Serial0: Unable to validate CHAP response.
         No password defined for USERNAME pioneer
Serial0: Failed CHAP authentication with remote.
Remote message is Unknown name
Serial0: remote passed CHAP authentication.
Serial0: Passed CHAP authentication with remote.
Serial0: CHAP input code = 4 id = 3 len = 48
```

The **debug ppp chap** command displays the reason why the CHAP request failed.

Once you have finished examining the debug output, use the `no debug all` command to turn off the debugging feature.

# ISDN Overview

*ISDN* refers to the call-processing system that enables voice, data, and video to be transmitted over our existing telephone system. ISDN offers several advantages over existing analog modem lines. For example, ISDN connection speeds begin at 64Kbps, whereas typical modem speeds hover between 28.8Kbps and 56Kbps. The call setup time for an ISDN call is also much quicker. ISDN can transmit data packets, voice, or video. ISDN is a viable solution for remote connectivity (telecommuting) and access to the Internet. ISDN also supports any of the Network layer protocols supported by the Cisco Internetwork Operating System (IOS) and encapsulates other WAN services, such as PPP.

# Configuring ISDN

You must perform both global and interface configuration tasks when configuring a router for ISDN. Global configuration tasks include specifying the type of ISDN switch your router connects to at the provider's central office (CO) and defining what type of traffic is interesting. Table 10.3 lists the ISDN global configuration commands.

**Table 10.3 ISDN Global Configuration Commands**

| Command | Description |
|---|---|
| **ISDN switch-type switch-type** | Defines an ISDN switch type |
| **dialer-list dialer-group protocol** | Defines or restricts (permits or denies) |
| **protocol permit** | Defines any specific protocol traffic as interesting for a particular dialer group |

Table 10.4 shows the ISDN commands that must be configured on an interface.

**Table 10.4 ISDN Interface Configuration Commands**

| Command | Description |
|---|---|
| **interface bri interface number** | Chooses the router interface acting as a TE1 device |
| **encapsulation ppp** | Chooses PPP framing |
| **dialer-group number** | Assigns an interface to a specific dialer group |
| **dialer map protocol next hop** | Maps a Layer 3 protocol to a next hop address with a specific name |
| **address name hostname speed** | Defines the connection speed |
| **number dial-string** | Defines the telephone number to dial |
| **dialer idle-timeout number** | Defines the number of seconds of idle time before the ISDN connection is terminated |

Figure 10.5 presents a simple ISDN DDR configuration for router A and router B.

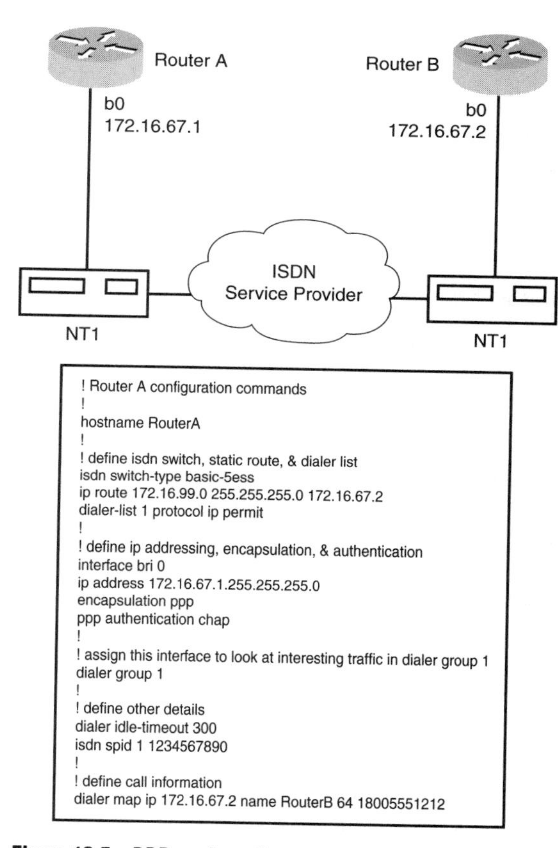


**Figure 10.5** DDR configuration example.

# Monitoring ISDN

The commands listed in this section enable you to monitor the activity and operation of ISDN and DDR configurations.

You can monitor ISDN and DDR configurations with the following commands:

- `show controller bri`
- `show interface bri`
- `show dialer`

Use the `show controller bri` command to display detailed information about the B and D channels. The following output displays an example of the `show controller` command:

```
RouterA# show controller bri 0
BRI unit 0
D Chan Info:
Layer 1 is ACTIVATED
idb 0x32089C, ds 0x3267D8, reset_mask 0x2
buffer size 1524
RX ring with 2 entries at 0x2101600 : Rxhead 0
00 pak=0x4102E8 ds=0x410444 status=D000 pak_size=0
01 pak=0x410C20 ds=0x410D7C status=F000 pak_size=0
TX ring with 1 entries at 0x2101640: tx_count = 0,
  tx_head = 0, tx_tail = 0
00 pak=0x000000 ds=0x000000 status=7C00 pak_size=0
0 missed datagrams, 0 overruns, 0 bad frame addresses
0 bad datagram encapsulations, 0 memory errors
0 transmitter underruns
B1 Chan Info:
Layer 1 is ACTIVATED
idb 0x3224E8, ds 0x3268C8, reset_mask 0x0
buffer size 1524
RX ring with 8 entries at 0x2101400 : Rxhead 0
00 pak=0x421FC0 ds=0x42211C status=D000 pak_size=0
01 pak=0x4085E8 ds=0x408744 status=D000 pak_size=0
02 pak=0x422EF0 ds=0x42304C status=D000 pak_size=0
03 pak=0x4148E0 ds=0x414A3C status=D000 pak_size=0
04 pak=0x424D50 ds=0x424EAC status=D000 pak_size=0
05 pak=0x423688 ds=0x4237E4 status=D000 pak_size=0
06 pak=0x41AB98 ds=0x41ACF4 status=D000 pak_size=0
07 pak=0x41A400 ds=0x41A55C status=F000 pak_size=0
TX ring with 4 entries at 0x2101440: tx_count = 0,
  tx_head = 0, tx_tail = 0
00 pak=0x000000 ds=0x000000 status=5C00 pak_size=0
01 pak=0x000000 ds=0x000000 status=5C00 pak_size=0
02 pak=0x000000 ds=0x000000 status=5C00 pak_size=0
03 pak=0x000000 ds=0x000000 status=7C00 pak_size=0
0 missed datagrams, 0 overruns, 0 bad frame addresses
0 bad datagram encapsulations, 0 memory errors
0 transmitter underruns
B2 Chan Info:
Layer 1 is ACTIVATED
idb 0x324520, ds 0x3269B8, reset_mask 0x2
buffer size 1524
RX ring with 8 entries at 0x2101500 : Rxhead 0
00 pak=0x40FCF0 ds=0x40FE4C status=D000 pak_size=0
01 pak=0x40E628 ds=0x40E784 status=D000 pak_size=0
02 pak=0x40F558 ds=0x40F6B4 status=D000 pak_size=0
03 pak=0x413218 ds=0x413374 status=D000 pak_size=0
04 pak=0x40EDC0 ds=0x40EF1C status=D000 pak_size=0
05 pak=0x4113B8 ds=0x411514 status=D000 pak_size=0
06 pak=0x416ED8 ds=0x417034 status=D000 pak_size=0
07 pak=0x416740 ds=0x41689C status=F000 pak_size=0
TX ring with 4 entries at 0x2101540: tx_count = 0,
  tx_head = 0, tx_tail = 0
00 pak=0x000000 ds=0x000000 status=5C00 pak_size=0
01 pak=0x000000 ds=0x000000 status=5C00 pak_size=0
02 pak=0x000000 ds=0x000000 status=5C00 pak_size=0
03 pak=0x000000 ds=0x000000 status=7C00 pak_size=0
0 missed datagrams, 0 overruns, 0 bad frame addresses
0 bad datagram encapsulations, 0 memory errors
0 transmitter underruns
```

Both B channels and the D channel are active.

Use the `show interface bri` command to display BRI status, encapsulation, and counter information. The following output displays an example of the `show interface` command:

```
RouterA# show interface bri 0
BRI0 is up, line protocol is up (spoofing)
Hardware is BRI
Internet address is 172.16.67.1, subnet mask is 255.255.255.0
MTU 1500 bytes, BW 64 Kbit, DLY 20000 usec,
rely 255/255, load 1/255
Encapsulation PPP, loopback not set, keepalive set (10 sec)
Last input 0:00:07, output 0:00:00, output hang never
Output queue 0/40, 0 drops; input queue 0/75, 0 drops
Five minute input rate 0 bits/sec, 0 packets/sec
Five minute output rate 0 bits/sec, 0 packets/sec
16263 packets input, 1347238 bytes, 0 no buffer
Received 13983 broadcasts, 0 runts, 0 giants
2 input errors, 0 CRC, 0 frame, 0 overrun, 0 ignored, 2 abort
22146 packets output, 2383680 bytes, 0 underruns
0 output errors, 0 collisions, 2 interface resets, 0 restarts
1 carrier transitions
```

The encapsulation type is PPP, and two errors were received on the BRI.

Use the `show dialer bri` command to display general diagnostic information for serial interfaces configured to support DDR. The following output displays an example of the `show dialer` command:

```
RouterA# show dialer interface bri 0
BRI0 - dialer type = IN-BAND NO-PARITY
Idle timer (900 secs), Fast idle timer (20 secs)
Wait for carrier (30 secs), Re-enable (15 secs)
Time until disconnect 838 secs
Current call connected 0:02:16
Connected to 8986

Dial String   Successes Failures  Last called  Last status
8986          0         0         never                   Default
8986          8         3         0:02:16      Success    Default
```

"IN-BAND" indicates that DDR is enabled and the router is currently connected. The Dial String table provides a history of logged calls.

# Configuring Frame Relay

Configuring a Cisco router to serve as a DTE (Data Terminal Equipment) device within a Frame Relay network involves configuring interfaces on the router. Table 10.6 lists the commands you must execute to configure Frame Relay on an interface.

**Table 10.6 Frame Relay Basic Configuration**

| Command | Description |
|---|---|
| **encapsulation frame-relay [cisco I ietf]** | Enables Frame Relay encapsulation; default setting is "cisco"; "ietf" (see RFC 1490) enables connections to non-Cisco equipment |
| **frame-relay lmi-type [ansi I cisco I q933a]** | Sets the Local Management Interface (LMI) type; default setting is "cisco" |

In configurations where inverse ARP is not used to dynamically discover network protocol addresses on the virtual circuit, the `frame-relay map` command must be used to map the Layer 3 protocol address to the Layer 2 DLCI.

Configure the `frame-relay map` command as follows:

```
Frame-relay map protocol protocol-address dlci [broadcast]
[cisco ¦ ietf]
```

In this example, *`protocol`* is a supported protocol, such as IP or IPX, *`protocol-address`* is the destination protocol address, and *`dlci`* is the DLCI number used to connect to the specified protocol address on the interface. Also, `broadcast` (optional) forwards broadcasts to this address (although this is optional, it's usually a good idea to include it), and `ietf` (optional) uses the Internet Engineering Task Force (IETF) form of Frame Relay encapsulation (use this parameter when the router or access server is connected to another vendor's equipment across a Frame Relay network). Finally, `cisco` (optional) is the Cisco encapsulation method.

## NonBroadcast MultiAccess

Because Frame Relay connections are established by direct Permanent Virtual Circuits (PVCs), Frame Relay cannot support broadcast transmissions. If broadcast services are required, a router must copy the broadcast and then transmit it on each of its PVCs. The term that describes this behavior is NonBroadcast MultiAccess (NBMA). NBMA simply describes any multiaccess Layer 2 protocol that does not provide a mechanism for broadcasting messages (such as route updates between routers). For broadcast messages to be communicated in an NBMA network, each router within the network serves as a peer and is part of the same subnet. In a Frame Relay network, broadcast messages must be duplicated and then send out each PVC to each peer.

# Subinterfaces

A single, physical serial interface can be configured with several virtual interfaces called *subinterfaces*. These subinterfaces can be configured on a serial line; different information is sent and received on each serial subinterface. Using subinterfaces, a single router can support PVCs to several other routers. Figure 10.6 depicts a simple Frame Relay network with subinterfaces.

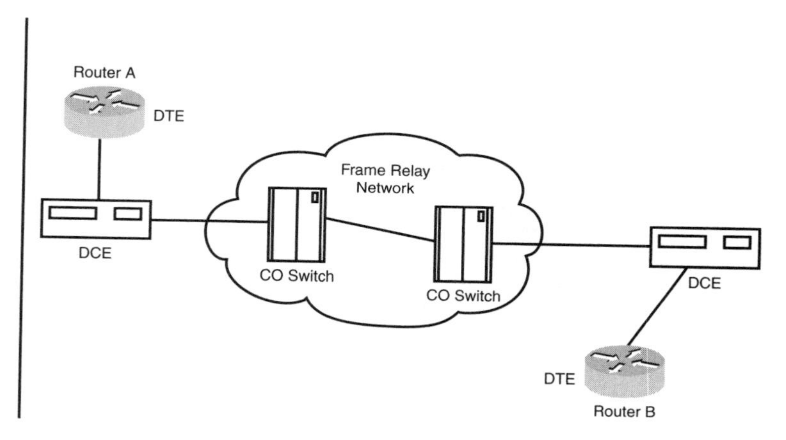


**Figure 10.6** A simple frame relay network.

Before configuring a subinterface for a Frame Relay network, the Frame Relay configuration on the physical interface must be complete. Execute the following command to create a subinterface and assign it a DLCI value:

```
Interface type.subinterface point-to-point
Frame-relay interface-dlci dlci [broadcast]
```

In this command, `type` is the physical serial interface number, `subinterface` is the subinterface number, `dlci` is the DLCI number used to connect to the specified protocol address on the interface, and `broadcast` (optional) forwards broadcasts to this address. A common practice in choosing subinterface numbers is to use the same number as the DLCI value.

The proper syntax for creating and accessing a subinterface is the interface number followed by a period (.) followed by the subinterface number. For example, **serial 0.11** indicates subinterface 11 on serial interface 0.

# Monitoring Frame Relay

After the Frame Relay configuration is complete, you can use the `show interface` and `debug frame-relay` commands to monitor and troubleshoot the configuration. The following output shows the results of the `show interface` command:

```
Router# show interface serial 0
  Serial0 is up, line protocol is up
  Hardware is MCI Serial
  Internet address is 172.59.1.1,
    subnet mask is 255.255.255.252
  MTU 1500 bytes, BW 1544 Kbit, DLY 20000 usec, rely 249/255,
    load 1/255
  Encapsulation FRAME-RELAY, loopback not set,
   keepalive set (10 sec)
  LMI enq sent  4, LMI stat recvd 0, LMI upd recvd 0,
    DTE LMI UP
  LMI enq recvd 268, LMI stat sent  264, LMI upd sent  0
  LMI DLCI 1023  LMI type is CISCO  frame relay DTE
  Last input 0:00:09, output 0:00:07, output hang never
  Last clearing of "show interface" counters 0:44:57
  Output queue 0/40, 0 drops; input queue 0/75, 0 drops
  Five minute input rate 0 bits/sec, 0 packets/sec
 Five minute output rate 0 bits/sec, 0 packets/sec
     309 packets input, 6641 bytes, 0 no buffer
     Received 0 broadcasts, 0 runts, 0 giants
     0 input errors, 0 CRC, 0 frame, 0 overrun,
     0 ignored, 0 abort
     0 input packets with dribble condition detected
     268 packets output, 3836 bytes, 0 underruns
     0 output errors, 0 collisions, 2 interface resets,
     0 restarts
     180 carrier transitions
```

Use the `show frame-relay pvc` command to display the status of the virtual circuit, as shown in the following:

```
RouterA#show frame-relay pvc

PVC Statistics for interface Serial0 (Frame Relay DTE)

DLCI = 222, DLCI USAGE = LOCAL, PVC STATUS = ACTIVE,INTERFACE =
Serial0

  input pkts 50            output pkts 20         in bytes 11431
  out bytes 1474           dropped pkts 2         in FECN pkts 0
  in BECN pkts 0           out FECN pkts 0        out BECN pkts 0
  in DE pkts 0             out DE pkts 0
  pvc create time 04:14:10, last time pvc status changed 00:39:06
RouterA#
```

Use the `show frame-relay lmi` command to determine whether LMI is being transmitted successfully:

```
RouterA#show frame-relay lmi

LMI Statistics for interface Serial0
```

```
(Frame Relay DTE) LMI TYPE = CISCO
  Invalid Unnumbered info 0              Invalid Prot Disc 0
  Invalid dummy Call Ref 0               Invalid Msg Type 0
  Invalid Status Message 0               Invalid Lock Shift 0
  Invalid Information ID 0               Invalid Report IE Len 0
  Invalid Report Request 0               Invalid Keep IE Len 0
  Num Status Enq. Sent 292               Num Status msgs Rcvd 292
  Num Update Status Rcvd 0               Num Status Timeouts 0
RouterA#
```

Use the `show frame-relay map` command to display mappings among protocol, protocol address, and DLCI, as shown in the following:

```
RouterA#show frame-relay map
Serial0 (up): ip 172.59.1.1 dlci 222(0xDE,0x34E0), dynamic,
              broadcast, status defined, active
RouterA#
```

The `debug frame-relay` command enables you to monitor the Frame Relay activity closely. The `debug frame-relay lmi` command enables you to monitor LMI activity on a router closely. The following output shows sample output from the `debug frame-relay lmi` command.

```
RouterA#debug frame-relay lmi
Frame Relay LMI debugging is on

RouterA#
Serial0(out): StEnq, myseq 20, yourseen 67, DTE up
 datagramstart = 0x23A3820, datagramsize = 13

 FR encap = 0xFCF10309
00 75 01 01 01 03 02 14 43

Serial0(in): Status, myseq 20
RT IE 1, length 1, type 1
KA IE 3, length 2, yourseq 68, myseq 20
RouterA#
Serial0(out): StEnq, myseq 21, yourseen 68, DTE up
 datagramstart = 0x23A3820, datagramsize = 13
```

The sequence counters for the LMI transmission are being increased properly. Enabling a single **debug** command on a router does not use much of the router's system resources; however, enabling several **debug** commands may severely affect the router's ability to perform its functions. The **no debug all** command quickly disables all debug commands on a router.

# Upgrading Cisco IOS Software

Cisco IOS is constantly being revised to add new features or to fix bugs in previous versions. The process of upgrading software on a Cisco router can be broken down into three main steps:

1. Back up the current Cisco IOS.

2. Copy the new Cisco IOS to the router.
3. Reload the Cisco router and verify the new IOS.

# Backing Up the Current IOS

The first part of backing up the current IOS involves determining what version of IOS is running on the router and the filename of the software image. It is also necessary to note the size available in Flash memory. The new version of IOS must not be larger than the total Flash memory on the router. The `show version` command displays this information, as shown here:

```
NFLD#sh vers
Cisco Internetwork Operating System Software
IOS (tm) 2500 Software (C2500-J-L), Version 11.2(13),
RELEASE SOFTWARE (fc1)
Copyright (c) 1986-1998 by cisco Systems, Inc.
Compiled Tue 31-Mar-98 10:27 by tlane
Image text-base: 0x0303F1E4, data-base: 0x00001000
ROM: System Bootstrap, Version 11.0(10c)XB1,
PLATFORM SPECIFIC RELEASE SOFTWARE (fc1)
BOOTFLASH: 3000 Bootstrap Software (IGS-BOOT-R),
 Version 11.0(10c)XB1,
PLATFORM SPECIFIC RELEASE SOFTWARE (fc1)

NFLD uptime is 7 minutes
System restarted by reload
System image file is "flash:11-2-13.img", booted via flash

cisco 2500 (68030) processor (revision L)
with 2048K/2048K bytes of memory.
Processor board ID 07110268, with hardware revision 00000000
Bridging software.
SuperLAT software copyright 1990 by Meridian Technology Corp.
X.25 software, Version 2.0, NET2, BFE and GOSIP compliant.
TN3270 Emulation software.
2 Ethernet/IEEE 802.3 interface(s)
2 Serial network interface(s)
32K bytes of non-volatile configuration memory.
16384K bytes of processor board System flash (Read ONLY)
Configuration register is 0x2102
```

From the preceding command listing, we can determine that we have 16,384KB of Flash memory available. Therefore, we can copy any software image less than or equal to 16,384KB to this device. The name of the file is provided as "11-2-13.img." After the memory requirements and the filename have been determined, we need to copy the old image to a TFTP server. This step gives us a fallback procedure in case the new software image is corrupt:

In the following example, the exclamation mark indicates the system is working. In other examples, you will see the letter "e" (erasing) repeated as the system works on a command. The repeated letters simply mean you should be patient and let the system complete the current command before entering another one.

```
NFLD#copy flash TFTP
System flash directory:
File Length  Name/status
 1  7969232 11-2-13.img
[7969296 bytes used, 8807920 available, 16777216 total]
Address or name of remote host [255.255.255.255]? 172.16.24.134
Source file name? 11-2-13.img
Destination file name [11-2-13.img]? <Return>
Verifying checksum for '11-2-13.img' (file # 1)... OK
Copy '11-2-13.img' from Flash to server
 as '11-2-13.img'? [yes/no]y
!!!!!!!!!!!!!!!!!!!!!!!!!!!!!!!!
Upload to server done
Flash copy took 00:04:36 [hh:mm:ss]
```

# Upgrading the IOS

After the current IOS has been backed up to a TFTP server and the available memory on the router has been checked, we can proceed with the upgrade of the IOS. The new IOS must reside on the TFTP server, as shown here:

```
NFLD#copy TFTP flash
Proceed? [confirm]<Return>

System flash directory:
File Length  Name/status
 1  7969232 11-2-14.img
[7969296 bytes used, 8807920 available, 16777216 total]
Address or name of remote host [172.16.24.134]?<RETURN>
Source file name? 11-2-14.img
Destination file name [11-2-14.img]?<RETURN>
Accessing file '11-2-14.img' on 172.16.24.134...
Loading 11-2-14.img from 172.16.24.134 (via Ethernet1): ! [OK]<RETURN>

Erase flash device before writing? [confirm]<RETURN>
Flash contains files. Are you sure you want to erase? [confirm]<RETURN>

System configuration has been modified. Save? [yes/no]: <RETURN>
% Please answer 'yes' or 'no'. Y

System configuration has been modified. Save? [yes/no]: y
Building configuration...
[OK] <RETURN>
```

```
Copy '11-2-14.img' from server
 as '11-2-14.img' into Flash WITH erase? [yes/no]y

%SYS-5-RELOAD: Reload requested
%SYS-4-CONFIG_NEWER: Configurations from version 11.2 may not be
correctly understood.
%FLH: 11-2-14.img from 172.16.24.134 to flash ...

System flash directory:
File Length  Name/status
 1  7969232 11-2-14.img
[7969296 bytes used, 8807920 available, 16777216 total]
Accessing file '11-2-14.img' on 172.16.24.134...
Loading 11-2-14.img from 172.16.24.134 (via Ethernet1): ! [OK]
Erasing device... eeeeeeeeeeeeeeeeeeeeeeeeeeeeeeeeeeeeeeeeeeeeeeeeeee
  ...erased
Loading 11-2-14.img from 172.16.24.134 (via Ethernet1): !!!!!!!!!
!!!!!!!!!!!!!!!!!!!!!!!!!!!!!!!!!!!!!!!!!!!
[OK - 7969232/16777216 bytes]
Verifying checksum... OK (0xF865)
Flash copy took 0:07:00 [hh:mm:ss]
```

## Reloading the Router

Depending on which router model we have, when we copy a new version of software to the router, the router will either reload itself or return with the `Router#` prompt. If the router returns with a prompt, we use the `Router# reload` command to restart the router and load the new software. The router `reload` command is as follows:

```
Router# reload
```

# Routing Protocol Configuration and Review

This section highlights the basic router commands necessary to add the RIP and IGRP to a router configuration.

## RIP

Table 10.6 lists the configuration commands necessary to enable RIP on a router.

**Table 10.6 RIP Configuration Commands**

| Task | Router Command |
|---|---|
| Enter global configuration mode | **RouterA#configure terminal** |
| Enter RIP configuration mode | **RouterA (config)#router rip** |
| Configure network 172.16.0.0 to be advertised | **RouterA (config-router)#network 172.16.0.0** |
| Exit configuration mode | **RouterA (config-router)#<CTRL>Z** |

The `show IP protocol` command displays detailed information about each IP routing protocol that has been configured on the router.

The following output displays the results of the `show IP protocol` command after RIP has been configured:

```
RouterA#show ip protocol
Routing Protocol is "rip"
  Sending updates every 30 seconds, next due in 2 seconds
  Invalid after 180 seconds, hold down 180, flushed after 240
  Outgoing update filter list for all interfaces is not set
  Incoming update filter list for all interfaces is not set
  Redistributing: rip
  Default version control: send version 1, receive any version
    Interface         Send  Recv   Key-chain
    Ethernet0         1     1      2
    Loopback0         1     1      2
    Serial0           1     1      2
  Routing for Networks:
    172.16.0.0
  Routing Information Sources:
    Gateway          Distance      Last Update
    172.16.24.252         120      00:00:12
  Distance: (default is 120)

RouterA#
```

By default, RIP sends updates every 30 seconds. Also, the RIP hold-down timer is set to 180 seconds, and a neighbor router has an IP address of 172.16.24.252.

# IGRP

Table 10.7 lists the configuration commands necessary to enable IGRP on a router.

**Table 10.7 Configuring IGRP**

| Task | Router Syntax |
|---|---|
| Enter global configuration mode | **RouterA#configure terminal** |
| Enter IGRP routing protocol configuration mode for autonomous system 1 | **RouterA(config)#router igrp 1** |
| Configure network 172.16.0.0 to be advertised | **RouterA(config-router)#network 172.16.0.0** |
| Exit configuration mode | **RouterA (config-router)#<CTRL>Z** |

The following output displays the results of the `show IP protocol` command after IGRP has been configured.

```
RouterA#show ip protocol
Routing Protocol is "igrp 1"
  Sending updates every 90 seconds, next due in 7 seconds
  Invalid after 270 seconds, hold down 280, flushed after 630
  Outgoing update filter list for all interfaces is not set
  Incoming update filter list for all interfaces is not set
  Default networks flagged in outgoing updates
  Default networks accepted from incoming updates
  IGRP metric weight K1=1, K2=0, K3=1, K4=0, K5=0
  IGRP maximum hopcount 100
  IGRP maximum metric variance 1
  Redistributing: igrp 1
  Routing for Networks:
    172.16.0.0
  Routing Information Sources:
    Gateway          Distance      Last Update
    172.16.24.252         100      00:00:15
  Distance: (default is 100)
RouterA#
```

By default, IGRP sends updates every 90 seconds. Also, the IGRP maximum hop count is set to 100, and a neighbor router has an IP address of 172.16.24.252.

The next section of this chapter covers access lists for IP and IPX traffic. *Access lists* allow network administrators to restrict access to certain networks, devices, and services. They provide an effective means of applying security within an organization; they also permit or deny specific types of traffic to pass through an interface. The types of IP traffic they filter can be based on source or destination address or address range, protocol, precedence, type of service, icmp-type, icmp-code, icmp-message, igmp-type, port, or state of the TCP connection. A full list of access lists is provided in Table 10.8.

**Table 10.8 Types of Access Lists**

| Numeric Range | Description |
|---|---|
| 1 through 99 | IP standard access list |
| 100 through 199 | IP extended access list |
| 200 through 299 | Ethernet access list |
| 300 through 399 | DECnet access list |
| 600 through 699 | AppleTalk access list |
| 700 through 799 | 48-bit media access control (MAC) address access list |
| 800 through 899 | IPX standard access list |
| 900 through 999 | IPX extended access list |
| 1000 through 1099 | Service Access Point (SAP) access list |

Access lists provide a powerful set of tools that can deny and permit users to access specific applications or hosts. The tradeoff for using access lists, however, is that they require processing power to compare packets entering or exiting an interface with the entries in the list.

A wide variety of access lists can be applied to a router interface. This chapter focuses only on the IP standard and extended access lists, IPX SAP access lists, and IPX standard and extended access lists.

# IP Access Lists

IP access lists are used to deny or permit specific traffic into or out of an interface on a router. They filter IP source and destination addresses and protocol- or service-specific traffic. IP access lists are of two types: standard and extended. The difference between the two is the precision by which each can filter IP traffic.

## IP Standard Access Lists

IP standard access lists filter traffic based on the source IP address or address range. Therefore, administrators can use this tool to restrict access to specific users and allow access to others. The lists are applied to the interface of a router where traffic is to be filtered, and they restrict access into or out of the interface. The direction in which traffic is restricted is determined by the Cisco command used to apply the access list to the interface.

# IP Standard Access List Commands

Creating and applying an access list to an interface consists of two steps, both of which are performed in the configuration mode of a router. First, the access list must be created. A single access list can consist of many access list *statements*. An access list *number* identifies an individual access group, which can consist of many access list *entries*. In addition, the order in which access list entries are created plays an important role in the behavior of the access list. When traffic passes through the interface, it is compared with each access list entry in the order in which the entries were created. If the traffic matches an access list entry, the indicated function (permit or deny) of the access list entry is performed on the traffic. When a packet is permitted entry, the router caches the entry, and any subsequent packets in this session are granted access without being applied against the access list. All access lists have an implicit `deny all` statement at the end. Therefore, if the traffic does not match any entry, it is denied access into or out of the interface. The command to create an access list is as follows:

```
Access-list access-list-number {deny¦permit} source
[source-wildcard]
```

A brief description of each field is provided in Table 10.9.

**Table 10.9 IP Standard Access List Command Field Descriptions**

| Identifier | Description |
|---|---|
| **access-list-number** | A dotted decimal number between 1 and 99 |
| **deny** | Denies access if condition is matched |
| **permit** | Permits access if condition is matched |
| **source** | Number of the network or host from which the packet is being sent |
| **source-wildcard** | Wildcard bits to be applied to the source |

Any time you are working with access lists, remember the implicit deny automatically incorporated into the list. That is, anything you do not specifically identify as accepted is by default denied.

The `source-wildcard` field, referred to as a *wildcard mask*, is used to identify bits in an IP address that have meaning and bits that can be ignored. In this case, the wildcard mask is referred to as a *source-wildcard*, indicating that it is a wildcard mask of the source IP address. A source-wildcard mask is applied to a source IP address to determine a range of addresses to permit or deny.

At first, the best way to learn wildcard masks is to convert them from decimal to binary format. The wildcard mask is applied by comparing the IP address bits with the corresponding IP wildcard bits. A 1 bit in the wildcard mask indicates that the corresponding bit in the IP address can be ignored. Therefore, the IP address bit can be either 1 or 0. A 0 in the wildcard mask indicates that the corresponding bit in the IP address must be strictly followed. Therefore, the value must be exactly the same as specified in the IP address.

Once you have identified the correct access list, you are going to apply your routers interface, you then need to apply it with the following syntax:

```
NFLD(config-if)#ip access-group access-list-number {in¦out}
```

Here, `access-list-number` is the number used to identify the access list. This number must be the same as the one specified in the `access-list` command used to create the previously shown entries. The `in¦out` option indicates whether this list is to filter on inbound or outbound traffic through the interface. It is important to remember that the access list is being applied to a specific interface on a router, rather than to all the interfaces on the router.

# Creating and Applying an IP Standard Access List

The network shown in Figure 10.7 is used to illustrate IP standard access lists.

In this example, suppose you want to permit the following devices to have access to network 172.16.4.0:

- Any device on network 172.16.14.0
- Any device on network 172.16.3.0 except 172.16.3.5
- Only the device with the IP address of 172.16.12.4 on network 172.16.12.0

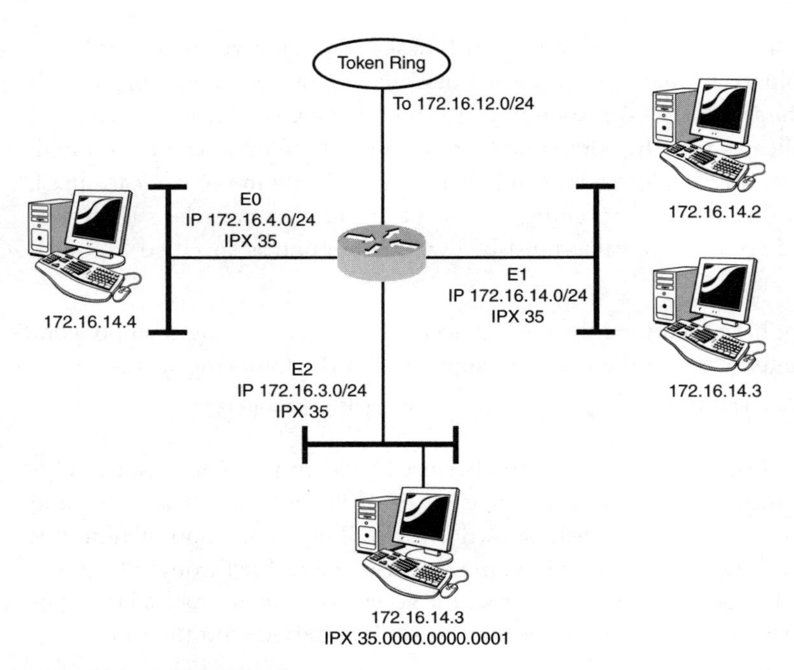


**Figure 10.7** Configuring a standard access list.

Applying an IP standard access list to a router interface involves two steps. The first step is to create the access list to indicate all the source addresses that are permitted or denied access. The second step is to apply the access list to the interface on which you are restricting either outbound or inbound traffic. By applying the `access-group` command to interface Ethernet 0, you can restrict access to network 172.16.4.0. The commands to create this access list are as follows:

```
NFLD#configure terminal
NFLD(config)#access-list 5 permit 172.16.14.0 0.0.0.255
NFLD(config)#access-list 5 deny 172.16.3.5 0.0.0.0
NFLD(config)#access-list 5 permit 172.16.3.0 0.0.0.255
NFLD(config)#access-list 5 permit 172.16.12.4 0.0.0.0
NFLD(config)#access-list 5 deny 0.0.0.0 255.255.255.255
```

These commands restrict and permit the traffic detailed in the requirements. The first `access-list` entry permits access to all users from network 172.16.14.0 to pass through the access list on Ethernet 0. Note that the source-wildcard of 0.0.0.255 indicates that every host ID in the last octet can be ignored, thus allowing all IP addresses between 172.16.14.0 and 172.16.14.255 access. The second `access-list` command denies host ID 172.16.3.5 to pass through the access list. Note that the source-wildcard of 0.0.0.0 indicates that only the source address specified (172.16.3.5) is denied access. The third `access-list` command permits all users on network 172.16.3.0 to pass through the access list. Note that host ID 172.16.3.5 will still not be allowed to pass through the access list, because any traffic from this host was dropped by the previous `deny` command. The order in which a `permit` or `deny` command is placed in an access list is extremely important.

When adding new entries to existing access lists, it is sometimes necessary to reorder the access list so that it will filter traffic correctly. Often, the best way to reorder the entries is to copy all the entries into a text file, add or remove the required entries, and reorder them in that text file. After you have them ordered correctly, add them all to the router configuration.

The fourth `access-list` entry permits only user 172.16.12.4 to pass through the access list. Finally, the last `access-list` command is implicit whenever an access list is created; therefore, any packet not generated by the router with the access list that does not match one of the permit entries is dropped. You do not have to configure this `deny` entry.

Before these access list entries can filter traffic, they must be applied to the interface as an access group. The access lists are going to be applied to outbound packets on Ethernet 0. Therefore, any packet attempting to travel out interface Ethernet 0 must match one of the entries in access group 5. The steps to configure an outbound access list on Ethernet 0 are as follows:

```
NFLD#config t
Enter configuration commands, one per line. End with CNTL/Z.
NFLD(config)#interface ethernet 0
NFLD(config-if)#ip access-group 5 out
```

Here, `access-group 5` has been applied to the outbound Ethernet 0 interface. Now, every packet that is sent out the Ethernet 0 interface will be checked to see if it matches.

More complicated scenarios for restricting access through an interface exist. Sometimes a network administrator wants to permit only a range of IP addresses through an access list. However, it is more complicated to permit access to a range of IP addresses that do not fall exactly on octet bit boundaries. A second example follows to illustrate this scenario.

Continue to use the network provided in Figure 10.7; however, in this case, you want to allow devices to have access only to network 172.16.4.0. Therefore, you want to permit access to any device with the IP address between 172.16.3.32 and 172.16.3.39.

For this scenario, you must determine the proper source-wildcard mask to apply to allow access to devices in the IP address range 172.16.3.32 through 172.16.3.39. Start with the IP address 172.16.3.32 to create this access list.

Next, apply a network mask that allows eight incremental bits in the fourth octet. Table 10.10 illustrates the proper source IP address and source wildcard in binary and decimal format for this example.

Table 10.10 illustrates that by applying the source-wildcard mask of 0.0.0.7, a range of IP addresses that do not fall on an octet boundary has been allowed.

**Table 10.10 Applying a Source-wildcard Mask to a Source IP Address in Binary Format**

| Source Address in Bits | Binary | Decimal |
|---|---|---|
| Source address | 10101100.00010000.00000011.00100000 | 172.16.3.32 |
| Source-wildcard | 00000000.00000000.00000000.00000111 | 0.0.0.7 |
| Permitted address 1 | 10101100.00010000.00010000.00100000 | 172.16.3.32 |
| Permitted address 2 | 10101100.00010000.00010000.00100001 | 172.16.3.33 |
| Permitted address 3 | 10101100.00010000.00010000.00100010 | 172.16.3.34 |
| Permitted address 4 | 10101100.00010000.00010000.00100011 | 172.16.3.35 |
| Permitted address 5 | 10101100.00010000.00010000.00100100 | 172.16.3.36 |
| Permitted address 6 | 10101100.00010000.00010000.00100101 | 172.16.3.37 |
| Permitted address 7 | 10101100.00010000.00010000.00100110 | 172.16.3.38 |
| Permitted address 8 | 10101100.00010000.00010000.00100111 | 172.16.3.39 |

Each permitted address is determined by taking the bits indicated as ignored bits by the source-wildcard mask and listing the possible permutations. Here are a few good rules to know:

- When you're grouping IP addresses, the group size is always a power of 2 (2, 4, 8, 16, and so forth).
- Any time IP addresses are grouped together, the first IP address in the group is divisible by the size of the group. For example, a group of eight IP addresses can start only on multiples of eight (8, 16, 24, and so forth).
- The wildcard mask is always one less than the group size. For example, a group of eight has a wildcard mask of seven. A group of 64 has a wildcard mask of 63.

Although IP standard access lists provide a powerful set of tools for restricting access, they can only restrict access based on the source IP address. IP extended access lists increase the variables that can be used to restrict access through an interface.

# IP Extended Access Lists

IP standard access lists filter traffic based on the source IP address only; therefore, administrators can use this tool to restrict access to specific users only. Because administrators wanted more control of the traffic that could travel through interfaces, Cisco responded with IP extended access lists, which perform the same basic function as standard access lists (permitting and denying IP packets through an interface) but extend the types of IP traffic that can be filtered. Consequently, IP extended access lists allow for more precise filtering of IP traffic. Whereas IP standard access lists allow only source IP address filtering, IP extended access lists provide source and destination IP address filtering. In addition, IP extended access lists filter on Layer 4 protocols, such as Transmission Control Protocol (TCP) and User Datagram Protocol (UDP); look into the TCP or UDP header; and allow filtering on TCP/UDP port numbers.

In addition, IP extended access lists allow filtering based on the IP precedence field, TOS field, icmp-type, icmp-code, icmp-message, igmp-type, and TCP-established connections. This book covers only source and destination address, IP protocol, and TCP/UDP port numbers.

## IP Extended Access List Commands

The steps taken to create and apply an IP extended access list are the same as those used for an IP standard access list. First, create the access list entries. Second, apply the access list group to the interface where you want to filter traffic.

It is important to enter IP extended access list entries in the correct order. Also, an implicit **deny all** traffic entry is at the end of every IP extended access list.

The command to create an IP extended access list is very similar to the command used to create an IP standard access list. However, the additional filtering capabilities require some additional fields in the command. The command to create an access list is as follows:

```
access-list access-list-number {deny¦permit} protocol source
source-wildcard [operator port [port]]  destination [destination-
wildcard] [operator port [port]]
```

Because how to read the command list was covered in the IP standard access list section, only the additional fields are discussed here. The first noticeable difference is the addition of the `protocol` field. This field is typically filled with TCP or UDP (other possibilities exist, but these are beyond the scope of this book and the CCNA exam). The `operator port [port]` field is used to indicate the TCP/UDP port or range of ports for the `source` and `source-wildcard` fields. In addition, the `destination` and `destination-wildcard` fields are added with their corresponding `operator port [port]` field. Basically, the fields necessary to filter traffic on source and destination addresses, the IP protocol (TCP or UDP), and port numbers have been added. In addition, the `access-list-number` field must now be a number between 100 and 199, as indicated in Table 10.8. A complete list of all of the fields in the IP extended access list command is provided in Table 10.11.

**Table 10.11 Access List Command Field Descriptions**

| Access List Command | Description |
|---|---|
| **access list-number** | Identifies the access list for which it belongs |
| **deny** | Denies access if condition is matched |
| **permit** | Permits access if condition is matched |
| **protocol** | Name or number of the IP protocol |
| **source** | Number of the network or host from which the packet is being sent |
| **source-wildcard** | Wildcard bits to be applied to the source |
| **destination** | Number of the network or host from which the packet originated |
| **destination-wildcard** | Wildcard bits to be applied to the destination |
| **precedence** | Filter packets by precedence level |
| **tos** | Filter packets by type of service |
| **icmp-type** | Filter packets by icmp-type |
| **icmp-code** | Filter packets by icmp-code |
| **icmp-message** | Filter packets by icmp-message |
| **igmp-type** | Filter packets by igmp-type |
| **operator** | Compares source or destination ports |
| **port** | Decimal value or name of a TCP or UDP port |
| **established** | Indicates an established connection |
| **log** | Causes an information logging entry |

To apply an IP extended access list, use the same IP access group command that is used for standard access lists. Simply apply the access list to the interface where you want to filter traffic.

## Creating and Applying an IP Extended Access List

To illustrate the use of the IP extended access list functionality, continue to use the network shown in Figure 10.7. In this example, you want to extend the types of traffic being filtered. Suppose you want to permit the following traffic to pass through your access list:

- Any device on network 172.16.14.0 is permitted to communicate with any device on network 172.16.4.0 using IP, TCP, and port number 23 (Telnet).
- Device 172.16.14.2 is permitted to communicate with device 172.16.4.4 using IP, UDP, and UDP port number 69 (TFTP).
- Device 172.16.14.3 is permitted to communicate with any device on any network using IP and TCP for any port number.

The following commands create this access list:

```
NFLD#configure terminal
NFLD(config)#access-list 105 permit tcp 172.16.14.0 0.0.0.255
172.16.4.0 0.0.0.255 eq 23
NFLD(config)#access-list 105 permit udp host 172.16.14.2
host 172.16.4.4 eq 69
NFLD(config)#access-list 105 permit tcp host 172.16.14.3 any
any
NFLD(config)#access-list 105 deny any any
```

Let's discuss these access list entries. The first entry performs the extended functionality by indicating that only TCP traffic from any device on network 172.16.14.0 (indicated by the source-wildcard mask of 0.0.0.255) is permitted to communicate with 172.16.4.0 (indicated by the destination-wildcard of 0.0.0.255) using the TCP port number (indicated by the operator `eq` and the port number 23). The operator `eq` stands for "equal to." A subset of the different possible operators is supplied in Table 10.12.

**Table 10.12 Extended Access List Command Field Descriptions**

| Operator | Meaning |
|---|---|
| **eq** | Match only packets on a given port number |
| **lt** | Match only packets with a lower port number |
| **gt** | Match only packets with a greater port number |
| **range** | Match only packets in the range of port numbers |

The second entry introduces the word "host" into the command; this is a short way of indicating the wildcard mask 0.0.0.0. However, the "host" word precedes the IP address, versus the traditional trailing wildcard mask. So, in this entry, only the device with the IP address 172.16.14.2 has been allowed to communicate with device 172.16.4.4 using the UDP for the port number 69 (TFTP).

The third entry introduces the word "any" into the command. Similar to the word "host" in the preceding condition, the "any" word is a short way of indicating any source or destination address with the wildcard mask 255.255.255.255. This mask indicates that all IP addresses are being described; therefore, it does not matter what source or destination IP address is specified. In this case, all destination addresses have been described. So, in this entry, the device with IP address 172.16.14.3 has been allowed to communicate with any device using the TCP for any port number.

The last entry in italics is the implicit `deny all` statement. It is not necessary to add this entry, because it is always there.

The second step is applying the access list to the interface that you are restricting. Specify whether you are filtering outbound or inbound traffic by adding the keyword "out" or "in" to the end of the command. In this example, apply the access list to Ethernet 1 to illustrate the ability of IP extended access lists to filter traffic based on destination address as well as source address. The command to apply the access group to the interface is as follows:

```
NFLD#config t
Enter configuration commands, one per line. End with CNTL/Z.
NFLD(config)#interface ethernet 1
NFLD(config-if)#ip access-group 105 in
```

Notice that once you have entered configuration mode, you may only enter one command per line. Also notice that you leave configuration mode by pressing Cntl+Z. These two aspects of configuration mode have been favorite test questions.

In summary, extended access lists are used to increase the preciseness of your filtering. The steps performed to create and apply access lists do not change.

# Monitoring and Verifying Access Lists

After you have configured all your access lists, it is important that you review your entries and determine whether you are filtering traffic in the manner intended. Many different methods exist to monitor and verify access lists. For the scope of this book and the CCNA exam, we will illustrate only two of the more basic methods. Refer to the *Cisco Command Reference* to identify some of the other methods used to monitor access lists. To determine which access lists you have applied to specific interfaces, use the `show ip interface` command as follows:

```
NFLD# show ip interface
Ethernet 0 is up, line protocol is up
     Internet address is 172.16.4.4, subnet mask is 255.255.255.0
     Broadcast address is 255.255.255.255
     Address determined by non-volatile memory
     No helper address
     No secondary address
     Outgoing access list 5 is set
     Inbound access list is not set
     Proxy ARP is enabled
     Security level is default
     Split horizon is enabled
     ICMP redirects are always sent
     ICMP unreachables are always sent
     ICMP mask replies are never sent
     IP fast switching is enabled
     Gateway Discovery is disabled
     IP accounting is disabled
     TCP/IP header compression is disabled
NFLD#
```

The entry identifying the outbound access list is highlighted. To get a more detailed look at the type of access lists you have applied, use the `show access-lists` command as follows:

```
NFLD>show access-lists
Standard IP access list 5
permit 172.16.14.0, wildcard bits 0.0.0.255
deny 172.16.3.5, wildcard bits 0.0.0.0
permit 172.16.4.0, wildcard bits 0.0.0.255
permit 172.16.12.4, wildcard bits 0.0.0.0
Extended IP access list 105
permit tcp 172.16.14.0 0.0.0.255 172.16.4.0 eq 23
permit udp host 172.16.14.2 host 172.16.4.4 eq 69
permit tcp host 172.16.14.3 any any
deny 0.0.0.0 255.255.255.255
NFLD>
```

Standard access lists apply to a group of things, whereas extended access lists apply to a specific port or user.

# Prep Questions

## Question 1

Which of the following commands will allow you to review the contents of NVRAM? (Choose the two best answers.)

- ❑ A. **show configuration**
- ❑ B. **show protocols**
- ❑ C. **show version**
- ❑ D. **show running-config**
- ❑ E. **show startup-config**

The correct answers are A and E. The `show configuration` and `show startup-config` commands display the router's backup configuration file from NVRAM. The `show protocols`, `show version`, and `show running-config` commands will allow you to review the contents of RAM, not NVRAM. Therefore, answers B, C, and D are incorrect.

## Question 2

Which of the following router components contains the router's IOS image?

- ❑ A. Flash memory
- ❑ B. NVRAM
- ❑ C. RAM
- ❑ D. Interfaces

The correct answers are A and C. Flash memory and RAM contain the IOS images used by the router. If no image resides in Flash memory, the image in ROM will be used. NVRAM contains the backup configuration and active configuration files, respectively. Therefore, answer B is incorrect. Interfaces provide the network connections for the router. Therefore, answer D is incorrect.

## Question 3

Which of the following router components contain versions of the router's configuration file? (Choose the two best answers.)

- ❑ A. Flash memory
- ❑ B. NVRAM
- ❑ C. RAM
- ❑ D. ROM

The correct answers are B and C. NVRAM contains the backup configuration file for the router, whereas RAM contains the router's active configuration file. Flash memory and ROM do not contain a configuration file; they contain the router's IOS image files. Therefore, answers A and D are incorrect.

## Question 4

Which of the following commands will allow you to review the contents of RAM? (Choose the three best answers.)

- ❑ A. **show configuration**
- ❑ B. **show protocols**
- ❑ C. **show version**
- ❑ D. **show running-config**
- ❑ E. **show startup-config**

The correct answers are B, C, and D. The `show protocols`, `show version`, and `show running-config` commands allow you to review the contents of RAM. The `show configuration` and `show startup-config` commands allow you to review the router's backup configuration file from NVRAM, not RAM. Therefore, answers A and E are incorrect.

## Question 5

Which command would be used to restore a configuration file to RAM on a Cisco router?

- ❍ A. **router#copy TFTP running-config**
- ❍ B. **router>copy TFTP running-config**
- ❍ C. **router#copy TFTP startup-config**
- ❍ D. **router>copy TFTP startup-config**

The correct answer is A. To restore a configuration file, the file must be copied from a TFTP server to the Cisco router. This is a trick question, because you must be in EXEC privileged mode to perform this function. Answers B and D are incorrect because the question implies that the command is initiated from EXEC mode; you can determine this by the > symbol (as opposed to the # symbol) at the end of the word `router` in answers B and D. Answer C is incorrect because the startup configuration file is not in RAM, and the question requires that you copy to the running configuration file, which is in RAM.

## Question 6

Which of the following commands will display the running configuration file to a console terminal?

- ❍ A. **router#show running-config**
- ❍ B. **router#show startup-config**
- ❍ C. **router#show flash**
- ❍ D. **router>show version**
- ❍ E. **None of the above**

The correct answer is A. The command to display a running configuration file to a console terminal is show running-config. Answer B displays the startup configuration file to the console monitor and is therefore incorrect. Answer C is incorrect because it displays any IOS images or configuration files stored in Flash memory. Answer D displays the software version and hardware on this router and is therefore incorrect.

## Question 7

If you need to copy the currently executing configuration file into NVRAM, which command would accomplish this goal?

- ❍ A. **router#copy startup-config running-config**
- ❍ B. **router#copy startup-config TFTP**
- ❍ C. **router#copy running-config startup-config**
- ❍ D. **router>copy startup-config running-config**

The correct answer is C. The startup configuration file exists in NVRAM. So, to copy a configuration file to NVRAM, the current startup configuration file must be overwritten. Answer A is incorrect because the startup configuration file is not the currently executing image, and this command is attempting to write the configuration file to RAM. Answer B is incorrect because the startup configuration file is not the currently executing configuration file, and TFTP does not exist in NVRAM. Answer D is incorrect because the startup configuration file is not the currently executing image and because the command is being executed from EXEC mode.

## Question 8

Which of the following commands would not set a password on a Cisco router?

- ❍ A. **router(config)#enable secret**
- ❍ B. **router(config-line)#password NFLD**
- ❍ C. **router(config)#service encryption password**
- ❍ D. **router(config)#enable password**

The correct answer is C. The `service encryption password` command is used to encrypt passwords in configuration files. Answer A is incorrect because it is used to set the "enable secret password". Answer B is incorrect because this command is used to set the Telnet, auxiliary, or console password, depending on which line configuration mode the router is in when the command is executed. Answer D is incorrect because it is used to set the "enable password".

## Question 9

In which of the following scenarios would a router boot into the initial configuration dialog after its power has been cycled? (Choose the two best answers.)

- ❑ A. When someone copies the startup configuration file to a TFTP server.
- ❑ B. When the running configuration file is copied to the startup configuration file.
- ❑ C. When the router is powered on for the first time.
- ❑ D. When the **write erase** command is executed immediately before the router is powered down.

The correct answers are C and D. The initial configuration dialog starts anytime a configuration file cannot be found in NVRAM. This occurs when a `write erase` command is performed on the startup configuration file or when the router is being powered on for the first time. Answer A is incorrect because copying a startup configuration file to a TFTP server will not cause a router to boot into the initial configuration dialog. Copying the running configuration file to the startup configuration file will not cause the router to boot into the initial configuration dialog. Therefore, answer B is incorrect.

## Question 10

Which of the following configuration register values would force a router to boot from ROM?

- ❍ A. 0x2103
- ❍ B. 0x210F
- ❍ C. 0x2101
- ❍ D. 0x2104

The correct answer is C. A configuration register with the value 0x2101 forces a router to boot from ROM. Only when the boot field has a value of 1 or 0 will the router boot from ROM. Answers A, B, and D are incorrect because all these values would cause the router to look at the boot commands in the configuration file to determine what IOS to load.

## Question 11

Where does the running configuration file exist in a Cisco router?

- ❍ A. NVRAM
- ❍ B. ROM
- ❍ C. RAM
- ❍ D. Flash memory

The correct answer is C. The running configuration file exists in RAM. This file is erased when a router is reloaded or its power is cycled. Answer B cannot be correct because ROM is a read-only device, and configuration files are constantly being updated. Answer A is incorrect because NVRAM is used to maintain the startup configuration file, not the running configuration file. Answer D is incorrect because Flash memory stores a copy of the IOS software, not the running configuration files.

## Question 12

Which is the correct command to back up Cisco IOS software?

- ❍ A. **router#copy running-config startup-config**
- ❍ B. **router(config)#copy TFTP flash**
- ❍ C. **router#copy flash TFTP**
- ❍ D. **router#copy flash NVRAM**

The correct answer is C. To back up Cisco IOS software, you must copy it to a TFTP server or another storage device. Answer A is incorrect because this command deals with configuration files, not Cisco IOS software. Answer B is incorrect because this command would be used to restore the Cisco IOS to a router. Answer D is incorrect because `copy flash NVRAM` is not a valid command.

## Question 13

Which of the following is not a valid Cisco command?

- ❍ A. **router>show version**
- ❍ B. **router#show running-config**
- ❍ C. **router#show startup-config**
- ❍ D. **router#show RAM**

The correct answer is D. `show RAM` is not a Cisco IOS command. Answers A, B, and C are incorrect because they are Cisco commands.

## Question 14

Which of the following can be used to permit or deny traffic with IP standard access lists? (Choose the two best answers.)

- ❑ A. Source IP address
- ❑ B. A range of source IP addresses
- ❑ C. Destination IP address
- ❑ D. A range of destination IP addresses

The correct answers are A and B. IP standard access lists allow IP traffic to be filtered based on source IP addresses; they also allow both individual IP addresses and a range of IP addresses to be specified. Answers C and D are incorrect because IP standard access lists do not filter traffic based on individual IP addresses or a range of destination IP addresses.

## Question 15

Which of the following commands will apply an IP extended access list to an interface?

- ❍ A. **ip access-group 204 in**
- ❍ B. **ip access group 110**
- ❍ C. **ip access-group 115 out**
- ❍ D. **ip access-group 95 out**
- ❍ E. **ipx access-group 805 in**

The correct answer is C. The command in answer C identifies an IP extended access list by the correct numeric range (100 through 199) for IP extended access lists. Answer A is incorrect because it uses the access list number 204, which is reserved for protocol type access lists. Answer B is incorrect because the command is not in the correct format; it should be `ip access-group`, not `ip access group`. In addition, the command should specify whether the access group is being applied to inbound or outbound packets with the "in" or "out" identifier. Answer D is incorrect because it identifies an IP standard access list (access list number 95), not an IP extended access list. Answer E is incorrect because it identifies an IPX standard access list, not an IP extended access list.

## Question 16

What is the valid range for an IP extended access list?

- ❍ A. 1 through 99
- ❍ B. 100 through 199
- ❍ C. 800 through 899
- ❍ D. 900 through 999

The correct answer is B. IP extended access lists are identified by the numeric range of 100 through 199. Answer A is incorrect because the numeric range of 0 through 99 identifies IP standard access lists. Answer C is incorrect because the numeric range of 800 through 899 identifies IPX standard access lists. Answer D is incorrect because the numeric range of 900 through 999 identifies IPX extended access lists.

# Need to Know More?

Sportack, Mark A. *IP Addressing Fundamentals.* Cisco Press, Indianapolis Indiana, 2003. ISBN 1-58705-067-6. IP addressing can be extremely confusing. This book covers the topic from every angle possible. While IP addressing is presented in far more detail than required for the CCNA, it is a good reference to have for the entire Cisco certification program.

Osterloh, Heather. *TCP/IP Primer Plus.* Sams Publishing, Indianapolis, Indiana, 2002. ISBN 0-672-32208-0. Written clearly and concisely, this one book can answer almost any question relating to TCP/IP. It is a good book to have for both this certification and future Cisco certifications.

Castelli, Matthew. *Network Sales and Services Handbook.* Cisco Press, Indianapolis, Indiana, 2003. ISBN 1-58705-090-0. Although this book is targeted at sales, it does a very good job of explaining technologies and Cisco products without getting into mind bogging minutia. A good book to have!

Odom, Wendell. *Cisco CCNA Exam Certification Guide.* Cisco Press, Indianapolis, Indiana, 2000. ISBN 0-7357-0971-8. Cisco is almost always the best place for reference books relating to Cisco. They print incredibly detailed and comprehensive books and this one is excellent. I would not want to read it as a primary text but as a reference it cannot be beat.

# PART III
## Sample Exams

# Sample Exam 640-821

Do not read Chapters 11 to 16 until you have learned and practiced all the material presented in the chapters of this book. These chapters serve a special purpose: They are designed to test whether you are ready to take your CCNA exams. Chapters 11 and 12 deal with exam 640-821, Chapters 13 and 14 deal with exam 640-811, and Chapters 15 and 16 deal with exam 640-801. Each exam is followed by an answer key and brief explanation of correct answers along with an explanation for why the other answers are incorrect. Reading these chapters prior to other chapters is like reading the climax of a story and then going back to find out how the story arrived at that ending. Of course, you don't want to spoil the excitement, do you?

## How to Take the Practice Exams

Like the real Cisco exams, each exam in this book consists of between 55 and 65 questions. Also like the Cisco exams, you should complete each test within 90 minutes. The number of questions and the time duration in the actual exam may vary but should be close to this number.

Which practice exam you take depends on which of the CCNA exams you are preparing for. Once you have read the material presented in the chapters, you should take the practice exam that corresponds to the CCNA exam you are looking to pass. After the exam is complete, evaluate yourself using the answer key in the corresponding answer chapter. In the case of this chapter, the answers are located in Chapter 12, "Answer Key for 640-821." When you evaluate yourself, note the questions you answered incorrectly, identify the corresponding chapters in the book, and then read and understand that material before taking the exam again. The 640-801 exam is in some ways a combination of both the 640-811 and 640-821 exams. Students preparing to take one set of exams can gain something from taking practice exams for the other set of exams. Be aware, though, that not all of the same exam objectives are covered on both sets of exams.

## Exam Taking Tips

Take these exams under your own circumstances, but I strongly suggest that when you take them, you treat them just as you would treat the actual exam at the test center. Use the following tips to get maximum benefit from the exams:

- Before you start, create a quiet, secluded environment where you are not disturbed for the duration of the practice exam.
- Provide yourself a few empty sheets of paper before you start. Use some of these sheets to write your answers, and use the others to organize your thoughts. At the end of the exam, use your answer sheet to evaluate your exam with the help of the answer key that follows the sample exam.
- Don't use any reference material during the exam.
- Some of the questions may be vague and require you to make deductions to come up with the best possible answer from the possibilities given. Others may be verbose, requiring you to read and process a lot of information before you reach the actual question.
- Always read the question carefully. Sometimes a question can seem to be asking one thing when in fact it is asking something entirely different.
- As you progress, keep track of the elapsed time and make sure that you'll be able to answer all the questions in the given time limit.

# Practice Exam #1

## Question 1

Which of the following commands can be issued from the command line on a router to directly check the connectivity between one router and another on a TCP/IP network? (Select all that apply.)

- ❑ A. **ping**
- ❑ B. **enable**
- ❑ C. **trace**
- ❑ D. **show ip arp**

## Question 2

Traffic is not passing between a router at the core of your network and the border router connected to your leased line to the ISP. Your network has several routers. You know the path that packets should take from the core router to the border router. You wish to determine which of the routers may have failed by attempting to view the path that packets take from the core router to the border router. Which of the following IOS commands, used once, will enable you to do this assuming that you are logged in to the console of the core router and know the IP address of the border router?

- ❍ A. **path**
- ❍ B. **trace**
- ❍ C. **show route**
- ❍ D. **ping**

## Question 3

Which of the following are methods via which configuration tasks can be performed on Cisco routers? (Select all that apply.)

- ❑ A. Direct console connection
- ❑ B. Telnet
- ❑ C. SSH
- ❑ D. Terminal server

## Question 4

You wish to configure a Cisco router via a telnet session. Which of the following TCP ports will the router accept a telnet connection on?

❍ A. Console port

❍ B. Port 21

❍ C. Port 23

❍ D. Port 25

❍ E. Port 80

## Question 5

Which of the following Cisco IOS 12.x commands will display the IP address information of all of the interfaces on a Cisco router? (Select one.)

❍ A. **show ip interface brief**

❍ B. **display all ip**

❍ C. **list ip interface all**

❍ D. **show hosts**

## Question 6

Which of the following Cisco IOS 12.x commands will not display IP address information for interface e0? (Select all that apply.)

❑ A. **show ip interface brief**

❑ B. **show interface e0**

❑ C. **show ip interface e0**

❑ D. **show ip arp**

❑ E. **show ip interface e1**

# Question 7

You are connecting to a Cisco router via the console port from a laptop computer, attempting to diagnose a problem with the router's configuration. Which of the following COM settings should you use on the laptop to correctly connect to the router via the console port?

❍ A. 9600bps, 8 data bits, no parity, 1 stop bit, no flow control

❍ B. 9600bps, 7 data bits, parity, 1 stop bit, no flow control

❍ C. 9600bps, 8 data bits, parity, 1 stop bit, flow control

❍ D. 9600bps, 7 data bits, no parity, 1 stop bit, flow control

❍ E. 9600bps, 8 data bits, no parity, 1 stop bit, flow control

# Question 8

You are on site trying to diagnose a problem with a Cisco 2500 series router. To perform this diagnosis, you need to get access to the router. To do this, you will be using a cable to connect to the Cisco router's console port from your laptop via a 9-pin com port. Which of the following cables should you use to make this connection? (Select two.)

❑ A. RJ-45 to RJ-45 rollover cable

❑ B. DB-25 to DB-9 Adapter

❑ C. DB-25 to DB-25 rollover cable

❑ D. RJ-45 to DB-9 Adapter

# Question 9

You are considering upgrading the version of IOS that runs on the routers in your organization. You have stored the newer version of IOS on a TFTP server. Which of the following IOS commands can be used to copy an IOS image from a TFTP server to the flash memory on a router?

❍ A. **copy flash tftp**

❍ B. **download ios image**

❍ C. **copy image flash**

❍ D. **copy tftp flash**

## Question 10

You are interested in backing up a router's running configuration to your TFTP server. This is done so that if alterations are made in the future, the current configuration can quickly be restored. Which of the following IOS commands will allow you to do this?

❍ A. **copy tftp flash**

❍ B. **copy start tftp**

❍ C. **copy running-config tftp**

❍ D. **copy tftp running-config**

## Question 11

You are in the process of assigning hostnames to routers on your network. You have decided that each router on your network requires a different name so that it is obvious to whomever is remotely configuring the router which router they are working on. Which of the following commands will set a router's hostname to ROOSKA?

❍ A. **set name ROOSKA**

❍ B. **configure name ROOKSA**

❍ C. **set mode banner ROOSKA**

❍ D. **configure banner ROOSKA**

❍ E. **hostname ROOSKA**

## Question 12

Which of the following IOS commands will set the message for all terminal connections to the router to "Welcome to Router Rooslan"?

❍ A. **set banner #Welcome to Router Rooslan#**

❍ B. **banner motd #Welcome to Router Rooslan#**

❍ C. **set motd #Welcome to Router Rooslan#**

❍ D. **configure motd #Welcome to Router Rooslan#**

❍ E. **configure banner #Welcome to Router Rooslan#**

# Question 13

You have 10 routers in your network. You believe that one of these routers has failed, but you are not sure which one. You know the IP addresses of interfaces on each of the routers. You are logged in to the console of one of these 10 routers and have verified that this router is fully functional. Which of the following IOS commands can you use to check the network connectivity of other routers in the network? (Select all that apply.)

- ❑ A. **show cdp neighbors**
- ❑ B. **ping**
- ❑ C. **pathping**
- ❑ D. **display network**

# Question 14

Rooslan is configuring a new network and wishes to assign the final IP host address at the end of the IP address range 10.10.224.0 /20 to interface e0 on a Cisco 2500 series router. This should be an addressable host address and only one number below the network broadcast address. Which of the following commands can Rooslan use to do this assuming that he is at the interface configuration prompt for e0?

- ❍ A. **Router(config-if)#ip address 10.10.224.1 255.255.255.0**
- ❍ B. **Router(config-if)#ip address 10.10.224.1 255.255.248.0**
- ❍ C. **Router(config-if)#ip address 10.10.239.254 255.255.248.0**
- ❍ D. **Router(config-if)#ip address 10.10.239.254 255.255.240.0**
- ❍ E. **Router(config-if)#ip address 10.10.255.254 255.255.240.0**

# Question 15

You are configuring a router that will separate the 192.168.20.224 /29 network connected to interface e0 from the 192.168.20.192 /28 network on interface s1. Which of the following, from the interface configuration prompt for e0, will configure the interface with a correct host address? (Select all that apply.)

- ❑ A. **Router(config-if)#ip address 192.168.20.193 255.255.255.240**
- ❑ B. **Router(config-if)#ip address 192.168.20.193 255.255.255.248**
- ❑ C. **Router(config-if)#ip address 192.168.20.225 255.255.255.240**
- ❑ D. **Router(config-if)#ip address 192.168.20.225 255.255.255.248**
- ❑ E. **Router(config-if)#ip address 192.168.20.231 255.255.255.248**
- ❑ F. **Router(config-if)#ip address 192.168.20.129 255.255.255.240**

# Question 16

You are investigating using VLANs to improve the utilization of bandwidth on your company's network. Which of the following hardware devices is used on a local area network to directly provide VLAN functionality?

- ❍ A. Router
- ❍ B. Switch
- ❍ C. Bridge
- ❍ D. Hub

# Question 17

Which of the following operating systems can be installed on a Cisco router, enabling it to be configured to route packets, implement access lists, and provide routing protocol updates to other routers on the network?

- ❍ A. Linux
- ❍ B. IOS
- ❍ C. FreeBSD
- ❍ D. Windows Server 2003
- ❍ E. Solaris

# Question 18

You are attempting to determine the nature of devices connected to your Cisco router while logged in to IOS via the console cable. All devices on your network are Cisco products. Which of the following commands will inform you if the Cisco products present on the network are routers, switches, or repeaters?

- ❍ A. **list network devices**
- ❍ B. **ping devices**
- ❍ C. **identify connections**
- ❍ D. **show cdp neighbors**
- ❍ E. **trace neighbors**

# Question 19

You are connected to a central router that has several other routers connected to it. You wish to generate a list of all of the IOS versions in use on those routers. Which of the following IOS commands can you use from the console to generate this information?

❍ A. **show cdp neighbor detail**

❍ B. **show cdp neighbor**

❍ C. **audit IOS**

❍ D. **show cdp audit**

# Question 20

Which of the following commands will shut down an interface, suspending connectivity between the router and the network connected to that interface as well as informing routing protocols that this interface is unavailable?

❍ A. **Router(config-if)# shutdown**

❍ B. **Router(config-if)# stop**

❍ C. **Router(config-if)# halt**

❍ D. **Router(config-if)# terminate**

❍ E. **Router(config-if)# bootdown**

# Question 21

You are the network administrator of a network that has five routers. You have the following information:

Interface e0 on Router 1 connects to network 192.168.10.0 /28

Interface s1 on Router 1 has an IP address of 192.168.10.18

Interface s1 on Router 2 connects to network 192.168.10.48 /28

Interface s2 on Router 2 connects to network 192.168.10.64

Interface e0 on Router 2 has an IP address of 192.168.10.2

Interface e0 on Router 3 connects to network 192.168.10.16 /28

Interface s1 on Router 3 has an IP address of 192.168.10.33

Interface s1 on Router 4 has an IP address of 192.168.10.50

Interface e0 on Router 4 connects to network 192.168.10.32

Interface s2 on Router 4 connects to network 192.168.10.80

Interface s0 on Router 5 has an IP address of 192.168.10.66

Interface e0 on Router 5 has an IP address of 192.168.10.82

Which of the following commands can be issued while maintaining connectivity between all of the routers?

❍ A. On interface e0 on Router 1 issue the shutdown command. On interface s1 on Router 3 issue the shutdown command.

❍ B. On interface e0 on Router 1 issue the shutdown command. On interface s1 on router 2 issue the shutdown command.

❍ C. On interface e0 on Router 1 issue the shutdown command. On interface e0 on Router 4 issue the shutdown command.

❍ D. On interface e0 on Router 1 issue the shutdown command. On interface e0 on Router 3 issue the shutdown command.

# Question 22

Which of the following numbers are the same in decimal, binary, and hexadecimal? (Perform the conversion without a calculator. Select all that apply.)

❑ A. Decimal: 255, Hexadecimal: FF, Binary: 11111111

❑ B. Decimal: 254, Hexadecimal: FD, Binary: 11111110

❑ C. Decimal: 252, Hexadecimal: FC, Binary: 11111101

❑ D. Decimal: 248, Hexadecimal: F7, Binary: 11111000

❑ E. Decimal: 240, Hexadecimal: F0, Binary: 11110000

❑ F. Decimal: 224, Hexadecimal: E0, Binary: 11100000

# Question 23

Which of the following IP addresses is correctly converted into hexadecimal notation? (Perform the conversion without a calculator. Select all that apply.)

❑ A. 10.23.193.237 = 0A.17.C1.ED

❑ B. 10.178.19.113 = 0A.B1.13.71

❑ C. 10.42.164.211 = 0A.2B.A4.D3

❑ D. 10.191.37.123 = 0A.BF.26.7B

❑ E. 10.77.228.100 = 0A.4D.E4.64

# Question 24

Which of the following network devices configures the network so that each individual host on the LAN is connected to its own individual segment?

❍ A. Router

❍ B. Hub

❍ C. Bridge

❍ D. Repeater

❍ E. Switch

# Question 25

Which of the following statements about WANs and LANs are true? (Select all that apply.)

❑ A. Hosts on WANs are generally connected together via high speed data links.

❑ B. Hosts on LANs are generally connected together via high speed data links.

❑ C. Hosts on WANs share close geographic proximity to each other.

❑ D. Hosts on LANs share close geographic proximity to each other.

❑ E. Frame Relay is a technology likely to be used on a WAN.

❑ F. Frame Relay is a technology likely to be used on a LAN.

# Question 26

You are configuring a local area network in a star topology. Your network will not need to send any traffic to remote networks. Which of the following devices can form the core of a star topology where there are more than 20 hosts? (Select two.)

❑ A. Router

❑ B. Switch

❑ C. Hub

❑ D. Bridge

❑ E. Repeater

## Question 27

Which of the following configuration settings does a host on a TCP/IP network require in order to communicate with hosts on a remote TCP/IP network? (Select all that apply.)

- ❑ A. DNS server address.
- ❑ B. DHCP server address.
- ❑ C. IP address.
- ❑ D. Subnet mask.
- ❑ E. Default gateway address.

## Question 28

In which of the following situations would using CAT 5 UTP cable be inappropriate on a LAN? (Select all that apply.)

- ❑ A. In an environment where there is a large amount of electromagnetic interference.
- ❑ B. Where a host is 90 meters away from the nearest switch.
- ❑ C. On Token Ring networks.
- ❑ D. Where bandwidths of 1 gigabit per second need to be supported.
- ❑ E. Where a host is 340 meters away from the nearest switch.

## Question 29

Which of the following are properties of the 100BASE-FX standard? (Select all that apply.)

- ❑ A. Runs on Cat 6 UTP cable.
- ❑ B. Runs on fiber-optic cable.
- ❑ C. Able to run a maximum length of 200 meters from the switch without signal enhancement.
- ❑ D. Able to run a maximum length of 412 meters from the switch without signal enhancement.
- ❑ E. Runs at 100 Megabit per second.
- ❑ F. Runs at 1 Gigabit per second.

# Question 30

Which of the following technologies are likely to be used when implementing a WAN but not likely to be used when implementing a LAN? (Select all that apply.)

- ❑ A. Leased line
- ❑ B. ATM
- ❑ C. Frame Relay
- ❑ D. PPP
- ❑ E. Gigabit Ethernet

# Question 31

Which of the following technologies are likely to be used to connect two networks in a LAN but not two networks in a WAN?

- ❑ A. ISDN
- ❑ B. Frame Relay
- ❑ C. 100BASE-FX
- ❑ D. 100BASE-TX
- ❑ E. FDDI
- ❑ F. Gigabit Ethernet

# Question 32

Which of the following statements about IOS is false? (Select all that apply.)

- ❑ A. IOS is a graphic interface to configure a Cisco router.
- ❑ B. IOS runs on almost all routers and most switches in the Cisco range.
- ❑ C. IOS images are stored in a router's flash memory.
- ❑ D. IOS contains six exec modes: user mode, delineated mode, privileged mode, extended mode, rescue mode, and control mode.

# Question 33

Which of the following are configuration modes that are available once Privileged EXEC mode is entered when logged into the IOS CLI via the console cable? (Select all that apply.)

- ❑ A. Global configuration mode
- ❑ B. Auxiliary configuration mode
- ❑ C. Router configuration mode
- ❑ D. UTP configuration mode
- ❑ E. Line configuration mode
- ❑ F. Interface configuration mode

# Question 34

Which of the following statements describe roles of a router on a WAN? (Select all that apply.)

- ❑ A. A router determines which packets need to be forwarded to remote networks via the WAN line and which packets should remain on the local network.
- ❑ B. A router can be configured to initiate a WAN connection when traffic meeting specific criteria is encountered.
- ❑ C. Routers on WANs are limited to using the TCP/IP protocol.
- ❑ D. Routers are used to forward broadcast traffic to remote sites.

# Question 35

Which of the following areas of router hardware is used to store the running or active configuration?

- ❍ A. RAM
- ❍ B. ROM
- ❍ C. Flash memory
- ❍ D. NVRAM

# Question 36

Which of the following areas of router hardware is used to store the complete IOS images?

❍ A. RAM

❍ B. ROM

❍ C. Flash memory

❍ D. NVRAM

# Question 37

Which of the following best represents the order in which a router starts up?

❍ A. Load Bootstrap Code; POST; Find and Load IOS Software; Find and Load Configuration.

❍ B. Load Bootstrap Code; Find and Load Configuration; POST; Find and Load IOS Software.

❍ C. POST; Load Bootstrap Code; Find and Load IOS Software; Find and Load Configuration.

❍ D. POST; Load Bootstrap Code; Find and Load Configuration; Find and Load IOS Software.

❍ E. POST; Find and Load IOS Software; Load Bootstrap Code; Find and Load Configuration.

# Question 38

Understanding a router's bootup sequence is essential knowledge for a CCNA candidate. Which of the following occurs immediately before the startup-configuration is located in the router bootup sequence?

❍ A. POST

❍ B. Load Bootstrap Code

❍ C. Find IOS Software

❍ D. Load IOS Software

❍ E. Load Configuration

# Question 39

Which of the following are properties of the configuration register on a modern Cisco 2500 series router? (Select all that apply.)

❑ A. It is a 16-bit software register in the router and its value is set via the **config-register global config** command.

❑ B. It is a 16-bit hardware register in the router and its value is set via jumpers.

❑ C. It is a 64-bit software register in the router and its value is set via the **config-register global config** command.

❑ D. The configuration register instructs the router which of the three operating systems: full function IOS, limited function IOS, or ROMMON to load.

# Question 40

The passwords for a Cisco 7200 series router have been lost. You want to enter ROMMON mode so that you can reset the configuration register, configuring the router to boot ignoring NVRAM, allowing the console user to change the passwords. You are connected to the router via a console cable and laptop running HyperTerminal. You cycle the router's power. Which of the following steps will bring you into ROMMON mode, allowing you to change the configuration registers?

❍ A. Press the <insert> key on the laptop's keyboard within 60 seconds of the power of the router being cycled.

❍ B. Press the <ctrl>, <alt>, and <delete> keys together on the laptop's keyboard within 60 seconds of the power of the router being cycled.

❍ C. Press the <F1> key on the laptop's keyboard within 60 seconds of the power of the router being cycled.

❍ D. Press the <ctrl> and <c> keys together on the laptop's keyboard within 60 seconds of the power of the router being cycled.

❍ E. Press the <break> key on the laptop's keyboard within 60 seconds of the power of the router being cycled.

## Question 41

Which of the following statements about routing is correct?

- ❑ A. Data is forwarded based on its Layer 2 address.
- ❑ B. Data is forwarded based on its Layer 3 address.
- ❑ C. Routing protocols are used to update routing tables.
- ❑ D. Routed protocols are used to update routing tables.
- ❑ E. All routing protocols broadcast route information every 60 seconds to other routers.

## Question 42

Which of the following protocols can be used by routers to determine the best path to a remote network?

- ❑ A. IGRP
- ❑ B. EIGRP
- ❑ C. FTP
- ❑ D. HTTP
- ❑ E. RIP
- ❑ F. OSPF

## Question 43

Oksana has been allocated a single /24 subnet, 172.16.1.0, to divide between four different office locations. The first location has 112 addressable hosts, the second location has 50 addressable hosts, the third location has 28 addressable hosts, and the fourth location has 16 addressable hosts. Which of the following schemes will properly divide the allocated subnet so that each location gets the necessary number of host addresses?

❍ A. SCHEME ONE

Location 1: 172.16.1.0 /25

Location 2: 172.16.1.128 /26

Location 3: 172.16.1.192 /26

Location 4: 172.16.1.224 /27

❍ B. SCHEME TWO

Location 1: 172.16.1.0 /26

Location 2: 172.16.64.0 /26

Location 3: 172.16.128.0 /26

Location 4: 172.16.192.0 /26

❍ C. SCHEME THREE

Location 1: 172.16.1.0 /25

Location 2: 172.16.128.0 /26

Location 3: 172.16.192.0 /27

Location 4: 172.16.224.0 /27

❍ D. SCHEME FOUR

Location 1: 172.16.1.0 /25

Location 2: 172.16.1.128 /26

Location 3: 172.16.1.192 /27

Location 4: 172.16.1.224 /27

# Question 44

Rooslan needs to resubnet a single /24 subnet into 15 networks with a maximum of 12 hosts per network. He wants to use a single consistent subnet mask for all of these networks. He will be using routers running the latest version of IOS. What will be the CIDR notation for the subnet mask that he will use to achieve this?

❍ A. /25

❍ B. /26

❍ C. /27

❍ D. /28

❍ E. /29

# Question 45

You are trying to explain to your boss the difference between bridges and routers, and the situations where each piece of equipment is appropriate. Which of the following statements best summarize these differences?

❑ A. Bridges segment a network into separate collision domains while forwarding broadcast traffic; routers divide networks into different broadcast domains.

❑ B. Bridges divide networks into different broadcast domains. Routers segment a network into separate collision domains while forwarding broadcast traffic.

❑ C. Routers shift traffic at Layer 3 or the OSI model; bridges shift traffic at Layer 2 of the OSI model.

❑ D. Routers shift traffic at Layer 2 or the OSI model; Bridges shift traffic at Layer 3 of the OSI model.

# Question 46

A particular device on the network exhibits the following properties. This device generally has two interfaces, though in some cases can have more. Unicast frames are forwarded to an interface based on a table that remembers which MAC address is connected to each interface. This table is generated by noting the source MAC address of each frame that enters the device through a particular interface. This device forwards broadcast and multicast frames to all interfaces.

Which of the following devices fits this description?

❍ A. Router

❍ B. Bridge

❍ C. Hub

❍ D. Repeater

# Question 47

You have a subnet of 100 hosts on a LAN. All of these hosts are connected to one of two 60-port hubs, each hub connecting 50 of the hosts. The two hubs are connected together directly. Taking which of the following actions will half the size of the collision domain without re-subnetting the network?

❍ A. Removing the two 60-port hubs and replacing them with two 60-port switches.

❍ B. Placing a router between the two hubs.

❍ C. Placing a bridge between the two hubs.

❍ D. Placing a repeater between the two hubs.

## Question 48

You have 120 hosts on a LAN that is increasingly becoming bogged down with broadcast traffic. The LAN is configured with four interconnected 50-port hubs, each with 30 hosts connected. Which of the following methods could you use to reduce the amount of congestion associated with broadcast traffic?

❍ A. Changing the four hubs to four switches.

❍ B. Placing bridges between each hub-to-hub connection.

❍ C. Connecting each of the four hubs to a switch instead of to each other and allow the switch to mediate traffic.

❍ D. Re-subnet the network into two networks. Place a router in the middle. Connect two hubs to one network and two hubs to the other.

## Question 49

A switch has been installed on a LAN where a small, but significant proportion of frames that contain errors are being transmitted. Rather than have these frames be forwarded by the switch, it has been decided that all frames with errors should be dropped by the switch entirely. Which of the following switching methods would allow this to occur?

❍ A. Store and forward

❍ B. Fragment free

❍ C. Cut through

❍ D. Hybrid

## Question 50

You are installing a switch on a LAN where the absolute minimum of latency between a packet entering and leaving the switch is required. Error correction is not an important consideration. Which of the following switching methods would best suit the requirement?

❍ A. Store and Forward

❍ B. Fragment Free

❍ C. Cut Through

❍ D. Hybrid

## Question 51

A segment of ethernet on your network uses CSMA/CD. Which of the following statements about what occurs next, when a collision is detected, is true?

❍ A. The sending host randomizes a timer and waits until that timer expires before attempting to send again.

❍ B. The sending host sends again after a predetermined period.

❍ C. The sending host listens until the segment has no traffic and then retransmits.

❍ D. The sending host analyses the collision frame and retransmits immediately if a broadcast frame is detected.

❍ E. The sending host analyses the collision frame and retransmits immediately if a multicast frame is detected.

## Question 52

When CSMA/CD is in use on an Ethernet network and a host wishes to initiate a unicast transmission to another host, which of the following steps occurs first?

❍ A. The primary host checks the segment to determine if it is currently hosting traffic.

❍ B. The primary host initiates a transmission that switches the network into a hold state.

❍ C. The primary host requests a token from the destination host.

❍ D. The primary host receives a token from the segment.

## Question 53

Host A has an IP address of 10.10.20.55. Host B has an IP address of 10.10.20.60. Both are on the 10.10.20.0 /24 network. Host A has information that it needs to transfer to Host B. Host A does not have the MAC address of Host B, but does know Host B's IP address. Which of the following protocols will Host A use to determine Host B's MAC address?

❍ A. RIPv2

❍ B. IGRP

❍ C. OSPF

❍ D. ARP

❍ E. EIGRP

# Question 54

Which of the following ICMP message names corresponds to the correct description of the message type?

- ❑ A. Destination Unreachable: Source informed that there is a problem delivering the packet.
- ❑ B. Time Exceeded: Packet discarded after the amount of time it takes for the packet to be delivered exceeds a specific value.
- ❑ C. Source Quench: The **ping** command uses a source quench to verify connectivity between two hosts.
- ❑ D. Redirect: Router informs sender that a better route exists.
- ❑ E. Echo: The source is sending data too fast and a request is sent to slow the rate of transmission.

# Question 55

Which of the following WAN services uses packet switching? (Select all that apply.)

- ❑ A. HDLC
- ❑ B. LAPB
- ❑ C. Frame Relay
- ❑ D. ATM
- ❑ E. X.25

# Answer Key 640-821

## Answer Key

1. A and C
2. B
3. A, B, and C
4. C
5. A
6. D and E
7. A
8. A and D
9. D
10. C
11. E
12. B
13. B and C
14. D
15. D and E
16. B
17. B
18. D
19. A
20. A
21. B
22. A, E, and F
23. A and E
24. E
25. B, D, and E
26. B and C
27. C, D, and E
28. A, D, and E
29. B, D, and E
30. A, C, and D
31. C, D, E, and F
32. A and D
33. A, C, E, and F
34. A and B
35. A
36. C
37. C
38. D
39. A and D
40. E
41. B and C
42. A, B, E, and F
43. D
44. D
45. A and C
46. B
47. C
48. D
49. A
50. C
51. A
52. A
53. D
54. A, B, and D
55. C, D, and E

1. Answers A and C are correct. `Ping` and `trace` are used to check connectivity between two routers. `Ping` sends ICMP messages to verify connectivity. `Trace` sends UDP packets to verify the current route to a host. Answer B is incorrect because the `enable` command is used to enter the enable mode. Answer D is incorrect because the `show ip arp` command is used to display the IP ARP cache.

2. Answer B is correct. `Trace` will display as much of the path as is available. Answer A is incorrect because the `path` command is not an IOS command. Answer C is incorrect because the `show route` command will not be useful in diagnosing this fault. Answer D is incorrect; although `ping` could be used by attempting to contact each router in the known path, the question specifies which command can be used once to make this determination.

3. Answers A, B, and C are correct. Direct console connection via a cable, connecting via the network using the Telnet protocol, or connecting via a terminal server (a terminal server is an especially configured router with multiple asynchronous ports that are connected to the console ports of other routers on the network) can be used to perform configuration tasks on Cisco routers. Answer D is incorrect because SSH, an encrypted and secure terminal protocol similar to telnet, is not supported natively by IOS at this time and cannot be used to perform configuration tasks.

4. Answer C is correct. Answer C lists Port 23, which is the Telnet TCP/IP port that routers accept network connections from. Routers can be configured via the network using telnet. Answer A is incorrect because the console port is used for a direct cable uplink to the router, not a connection via the network. The console port is a physical port on the router, Port 23, a TCP/IP port is a logical port. Answers B, D, and E are incorrect because these TCP/IP ports support other protocols rather than Telnet.

5. Answer A is correct. The `show ip interface brief` command will print out a brief summary of each interface's IP addressing information. Answers B and C are not valid Cisco IOS commands. Answer D is incorrect because the `show hosts` command will only display host names and corresponding IP addresses. The show hosts command will display nothing about which router interface uses which IP.

6. Answers D and E are correct. The trick with this question is that it asks which will not display the IP address information for interface e0 rather than which commands will. The false answers (correct in this case) are `show ip arp` and `show ip interface e1`, both of which show the

arp table and the ip information for interface e1 rather than e0. Answer A is incorrect because `show ip interface brief` will display the IP address information for all interfaces on a router, of which e0 is one. Answers B and C are incorrect because the `show interface e0` command and `show ip interface e0` command will display this information.

7. Answer A is correct. The configuration of programs like HyperTerminal or a terminal emulator on Linux require that the console connection be configured with the settings 9600bps, 8 data bits, no parity, 1 stop bit, and no flow control. Answers B, C, D, and E are incorrect because they do not include the required settings.

8. Answers A and D are correct. The console port on Cisco routers uses an RJ-45 connection. A rollover cable is required to connect to a laptop. To connect to the 9-pin com port you will need an RJ-45 to DB-9 Adapter. Answer B is incorrect because a DB-9 adapter is not required. Answer C is incorrect because DB-25 will not connect to the com port and a DB-25 is not required.

9. Answer D is correct. `Copy tftp flash` will initiate the process of copying an IOS file from a TFTP server to the router's flash memory. Other information will need to be specified such as the image name, the address of the TFTP server, and whether or not you wish to erase other images stored in the flash memory. Answer A is incorrect because it attempts to copy data in flash memory to a TFTP server. Answers B and C are also incorrect as neither command can be used to copy an IOS image from a TFTP server.

10. Answer C is incorrect. `Copy running-config tftp` will upload a copy of the running configuration to the TFTP server. Answer D is incorrect because it will download a copy of a configuration into the running-configuration. Answer A is incorrect because it will allow information, generally an IOS image, to be copied from the TFTP server to flash memory. Answer B is incorrect because it will copy the startup config to the TFTP server rather than the running-config. *Although the startup and running configs could possibly be the same, this should not be assumed.*

11. Answer E is correct. The `hostname` command will allow the router's hostname to be set. In this case, hostname ROOSKA will allow the router's hostname to be set to ROOSKA. Answers A, B, C, and D are incorrect. These are invalid IOS commands.

12. Answer B is correct. The `banner motd #BANNER TEXT#` command provides the correct IOS command to set the message for incoming terminal connection clients. Answers A, C, and D are incorrect. The commands are syntactically incorrect.

13. Answers B and C are correct. Both the `ping` and the `pathping` commands can be used to check connectivity between two hosts on a network. Answer A is incorrect, although the `show cdp neighbors` command will display routers directly connected to the router from which the command is issued, it will not show routers several hops away from that router. Answer D is incorrect, Display network does not exist as a command in IOS.

14. Answer D is correct as it is within the specified address range and uses the correct subnet mask. The first part in solving this problem is translating the CIDR notation of /20 into decimal quad notation. /20 is equal to 255.255.240.0. This eliminates answers A, B, and C. The next step is to calculate the network range: 10.10.224.0 has a range of 10.10.224.1 through to 10.10.239.255. 10.10.239.255 is the broadcast address of that network which leaves 10.10.239.254 as the last addressable host address. Answer E is incorrect because it is an IP address outside the network range in question.

15. Answers D and E are correct. They both have the correct subnet mask and have IP addresses which lie within the specified address range (192.168.20.225 through to 192.168.20.231). Interface e0 is connected to network 192.168.20.224 /29. Calculating the range of this network forms the bulk of solving this question. CIDR (Classless Inter Domain Routing) notation /29 translates to 255.255.255.248 in decimal quad. This means that answers that have an alternative subnet mask listed to 255.255.255.248 are incorrect. Answer A is incorrect because it has the subnet mask 255.255.255.240 and hence is incorrect. Answer C is incorrect because it has the subnet mask 255.255.255.240 and hence is incorrect. Answer F is incorrect because it has the subnet mask 255.255.255.240 and hence is incorrect.

16. Answer B is correct. Of the devices listed, only switches can be used on the local area network to directly provide VLAN functionality. Answer A is incorrect because routers cannot be used to provide VLAN functionality directly. Answer B is incorrect because routers cannot be used to provide VLAN functionality directly. Answer C is incorrect as routers cannot be used to provide VLAN functionality directly.

17. Answer B is correct. Only IOS, which was originally based on a variant of Unix, runs on Cisco routers. Answer A is incorrect, Linux will not run on a Cisco router. Answer C is incorrect, FreeBSD will not run on a Cisco router. Answer D is incorrect, Windows Server 2003 will not run on a Cisco router. Answer E is incorrect, Solaris will not run on a Cisco router.

18. Answer D is correct. The `show cdp neighbors` command will not only list the devices that neighbor the router, but, assuming that the devices neighboring the router also use CDP (Cisco Discovery Protocol), which is default for Cisco devices, it will also list whether or not the devices are routers, switches, or repeaters. Answer A is incorrect because it lists network devices and will not display this information. Answer B is incorrect because ping devices will not list this information. Answer C is incorrect because it identifies connections and will not list this information. Answer E is incorrect because it lists trace neighbors and will not list this information.

19. Answer A is correct. The `show cdp neighbor detail` command will provide an in-depth summary of the details of neighboring Cisco devices. This information includes the version of IOS that the neighboring router is running. Answer B is incorrect. Although `show cdp neighbor` does display information about neighboring Cisco devices, it does not include IOS version in its output. The other commands C and D are not valid in IOS.

20. Answer A is correct. The `shutdown` command, issued from the interface configuration mode, will shut down an interface, suspending connectivity and informing routing protocols that this particular interface is now down. Answers B, C, D, and E are incorrect because they will not shut down an interface.

21. Answer B is correct. This question is complex and may require that you draw a diagram to resolve it. Only one set of shutdown commands, e0 on Router 1 and s1 on Router 2, can be implemented while retaining connectivity between all routers. This option is presented in answer B. This question involves working out where the redundant links exist in this network. Three paths exist between routers 2 and 4. A direct path from 2 via interface s1, a two-hop path via router 5, and a three-hop path via router 1 and 3. As the first connection broken in every answer is the one between router 1 and 2, a route between 2 and 4 can be broken while maintaining connectivity to all routers. Answer A is incorrect because it will break connectivity between routers, as no redundant link exists between these interfaces. Answer C is incorrect because it will break connectivity between routers, as no redundant link exists between these interfaces. Answer D is incorrect because it will break connectivity between routers, as no redundant link exists between these interfaces.

22. Answer A, E, and F are correct. A Cisco candidate should be able to convert freely between decimal, binary, and hexadecimal. Answer A

maps correctly with 255 = FF = 11111111. Answer E maps correctly with 240 = F0 = 11110000. Answer F maps correctly with 224 = E0 = 11100000. Answer B is incorrect. The mapping should be: 254 = FE = 11111110. Answer C is incorrect, the mapping should be: 252 = FC = 11111100. Answer D is incorrect, the mapping should be: 248 = F8 = 11111000.

23. Answer A and E are correct. 10.23.193.237 maps to 0A.17.C1.ED and 10.77.228.100 maps to 0A.4D.E4.64. Answer B is incorrect as 10.178.19.113 maps to 0A.B2.13.71. Answer C is incorrect as 10.42.164.211 maps to 0A.2A.A4.D3. Answer D is incorrect as 10.191.37.123 maps to 0A.BF.25.7B.

24. Answer E is correct. A switch is used to configure the network so that each individual host on the LAN is connected to its own individual segment. Answer A is incorrect as routers do not segment a network; they are used to divide logical networks. Answer C is incorrect as bridges do segment networks; however, hosts still share a segment when a bridge is implemented. Answer D is incorrect as repeaters forward all data transmitted to them and do not segment the network.

25. Answers B, D, and E are correct. Hosts on LANs are usually connected via high-speed data links. LANs are often in close geographic proximity to one another, whereas WANs can stretch across a continent. Frame Relay is used for WAN connections. Answer A is incorrect because hosts on WANs are linked at speeds much lower than LAN speeds. Answer C is incorrect because WANs are geographically diverse, the next suburb or the next town rather than the next room or building.

26. Answers B and C are correct. Star networks have a central point to which each host on the network is connected. The two devices that can form the core of star topologies are the hub (B) and the switch (c). Routers are used to send traffic to remote networks. The question states that sending remote traffic is not required. Bridges (D) are generally used to reduce the size of collision domains and do not form the core of star topology LANs. Repeaters (E) are used to lengthen the distance between the switch or hub and the host and do not form the core of star topology LANs.

27. Answers C, D, and E are correct. To communicate with hosts on a remote TCP/IP network, a host requires an IP address, a subnet mask, and a default gateway address. Answer A is incorrect, because though a DNS server can help in resolving FQDN addresses to IP addresses, it is not required for communication to occur between a host and another

host on a remote subnet. Answer B is incorrect. Although DHCP servers are useful in providing address information, this can be configured manually.

28. Answers A, D, and E are correct. CAT 5 UTP does not handle electromagnetic interference well and hence is an inappropriate technology to use in that situation. It supports bandwidths up to 100 megabits per second. Without using a repeater it reaches 100 meters. Depending on which repeaters are used, this can be extended to near 300 meters, not 340. Answers B and C are incorrect. Answer B is incorrect, as CAT 5 UTP can be used without problem on a host only 90 meters from the switch. Answer C is incorrect, as CAT 5 UTP can be used on Token Ring networks.

29. Answers B, D, and E are correct. 100BASE-FX runs on fiber-optic cable. It is able to run a length of 412 meters before needing a repeater and it runs at 100 megabits per second. Answer A is incorrect, 100BASE-FX does not run on UTP. Answer C is incorrect as it will run a maximum of 412, not 200 meters without needing signal enhancement.

30. Answers A, C, and D are correct. Leased lines, Frame Relay, and PPP are WAN technologies. Answer B is incorrect because ATM is limited to LAN distances and cannot provide connectivity over WAN distances (such as between two cities). Answer E is incorrect because Gigabit Ethernet suffers from distance limitations as well.

31. Answers C, D, E, and F are correct. LAN connections are characterized by their proximity to one another. Connected LANs might be in adjacent buildings or on different floors of an office tower. WAN networks often span states if not continents. WAN connections generally operate at lower speed than LAN connections. 100BASE-FX has a maximum range of 412 meters. 100BASE-TX has a maximum range of 100 meters. FDDI has a better range, but cannot span the hundreds of kilometers that some WAN links must. Gigabit Ethernet also provides high bandwidth but is limited in its range. Answers A and B are incorrect because ISDN and frame relay connections can be used not only across the city but across the continent and are the most common types of WAN connections.

32. Answers A and D are correct. This question asks which statements are false. Answer A is correct because its statement is false: IOS is not a graphic interface, it is a text-only interface. Answer D is correct as its statement is false: there are only two modes, privileged and user exec. Answer B is true hence is an incorrect answer. IOS does run on almost all

of Cisco's routers and most of Cisco's switches. Answer C is true hence is an incorrect answer. IOS images are stored in a router's flash memory. Although such a "list the false answer" question is unlikely to occur on the exam, it should remind you to read a question carefully rather than to briefly glance at it assuming you have fully grasped its scope.

**33.** Answers A, C, E, and F are correct. There are four configuration modes available once the Privileged EXEC mode is entered. These four modes are Global, Router, Line, and Interface configuration. Answer B is incorrect, as Auxiliary configuration mode does not exist, even though connections can be initiated through the auxiliary port. Answer D is incorrect, as UTP configuration modes do not exist, even though there are UTP ports. Certain tasks, such as assigning an IP address to an interface, must be done within particular configuration modes.

**34.** Answers A and B are correct. Routers forward packets based on the network address contained within the destination header. This means that routers will determine which packets need to be forwarded to remote networks via the WAN line. Routers can also be configured to initiate WAN connections when traffic meeting specific criteria is encountered. Answer C is incorrect, as routers on WANs are not limited to using TCP/IP. Routers using leased or dial-up lines can transmit other protocols such as IPX. Answer D is incorrect, as routers do not forward broadcast traffic to remote sites.

**35.** Answer A is correct as RAM stores the running/active configuration. Answer B is incorrect, as ROM stores the bootable IOS image that is used until the router locates the full IOS image. Answer C is incorrect, as flash memory stores fully functional IOS images. Answer D is incorrect, as NVRAM stores the initial/startup config file.

**36.** Answer C is correct; Flash Memory stores fully functional IOS images. Answer A is incorrect, as RAM stores the running/active configuration. Answer B is incorrect, as ROM stores the bootable IOS image that is used until the router locates the full IOS image. Answer D is incorrect, as NVRAM stores the initial/startup config file.

**37.** Answer C is correct. The sequence for router bootup is

POST (power on self test)

Load bootstrap code

Find and load IOS software

Find and load configuration

Begin operation

Answer A is incorrect, as it presents the sequence out of order, placing POST after loading bootstrap code. Answer B is incorrect for the same reason. Answer D is incorrect, as the configuration is loaded before the IOS software. Answer E is incorrect, as IOS software is loaded before bootstrap code.

38. Answer D is correct. The IOS software is loaded before the startup-configuration file is located. Answer A is incorrect, as POST occurs before anything else at the start of the sequence. Answer B is incorrect, as loading the bootstrap code occurs well before the startup-configuration is located. Answer C is incorrect, as this occurs two steps before, not immediately before the startup-configuration is located. Answer E is incorrect, as the loading of the configuration is performed after the startup-configuration is located.

39. Answers A and D are correct. The configuration register is a 16-bit software register. It can be set via the config-register global configuration command. Some older routers did use jumpers for the configuration register. The configuration register is used to inform the router which of the three operating systems—full function IOS, limited function IOS, or ROMMON—to load. Limited function IOS is used when images in flash memory have become corrupted and connectivity is required to retrieve a new uncorrupted image from a TFTP server. ROMMON is used for debugging and password recovery. Answer B is incorrect, as the register is in software not in hardware. Answer C is incorrect, as the register is 16 rather than 64 bit.

40. Answer E is correct. The first step in resetting a router's password is to get the router to boot into ROMMON mode so the configuration register can be reconfigured to bypass NVRAM when booting. This is done by holding down the <break> key on the device connected to the console within 60 seconds of the router powering up. Additional steps for completing this task can be found on Cisco's Web site: `http://www.cisco.com`. Answer A is incorrect, as this method will not work. Answer B is incorrect, as this method will not work. Answer C is incorrect, as this method will not work. Answer D is incorrect, as this method will not work.

41. Answers B and C are correct. Answer B is correct because routing uses Layer 3 logical address information to forward data. Answer C is correct, as routing protocols update routing tables. Answer A is incorrect, as switches use Layer 2 information to forward data. Answer D is incorrect as routing rather than routed protocols update routing tables. Answer E is incorrect as only some routing protocols broadcast route information every 60 seconds.

**42.** Answers A, B, E, and F are correct. IGRP (a), EIGRP (b), RIP (e), and OSPF (f) are all routing protocols. Routing protocols find paths through networks, generating routing tables that are used to forward packets expeditiously to their destination. Answers C and D are incorrect. FTP is used for file transfer and HTTP is used for the transfer of Web pages. Both are considered *routed* protocols.

**43.** Answer D is correct. Scheme four allocates four subnets. The first, 172.16.1.0 /25, will allow 126 hosts on the network, meeting the requirement of 112. The second, 172.16.1.128 /26 will allow 62 hosts on the network, meeting the requirement of 50. Networks 172.16.1.192 and 172.16.1.224 will both allow 30 hosts on the network, meeting the requirements of 28 and 16 addressable hosts respectively. Answer A is incorrect as Scheme 1 contains incorrect subnetting information. Answer B is incorrect as Scheme 2 doesn't meet the requirements listed in the question. Answer C is incorrect as scheme 3 deals with subnets other than the original /24 allocated.

**44.** Answer D is correct. A /28 subnetting will provide 16 networks that can host a maximum of 14 hosts per network, meeting the requirement listed in the question. Answer A is incorrect, as /25 network will have 2 networks with 126 hosts. Answer B is incorrect, as a /26 network will have 4 networks of 62 hosts. Answer C is incorrect, as a /27 network will have 8 networks with 30 hosts each. Answer E is incorrect, as a /29 network will have 32 networks with 6 hosts per network.

**45.** Answers A and C are correct. Bridges segment a network into separate collision domains while forwarding broadcast traffic. Routers do not forward broadcast traffic and divide networks into different broadcast domains. This means answer A is correct. Answer C is correct because routers work at Layer 3 of the OSI model and bridges work at Layer 3 of the OSI model. Answer B is incorrect because it is the opposite of answer A and suggests that routers forward broadcast traffic. Answer D is incorrect, as routers work at Layer 3 of the OSI model.

**46.** Answer B is correct. Of the options presented, only a bridge has these characteristics listed in the question. Answer A is incorrect, as routers deal with packets (Layer 3) rather than frames (Layer 2). Answer C is incorrect, as hubs forward all traffic and do not generate tables. Answer D is incorrect, as bridges forward broadcast and multicast frames.

**47.** Answer C is correct. Placing a bridge between the two hubs will reduce the size of the collision domain by 50% as specified in the question. Answer A is incorrect, as replacing the two hubs with switches will reduce the size of the collision domain by far more than half. Answer B is incorrect, as placing a router between the hubs will require re-subnetting the network. Answer D is incorrect, as placing a repeater between the two hubs will not change the size of the broadcast domains.

**48.** Answer D is correct. Only by implementing a router will broadcast traffic be reduced. Answer A is incorrect, as switches forward broadcast traffic. Answer B is incorrect, as bridges do not filter broadcast traffic. Answer C is incorrect, as switches do not forward broadcast traffic.

**49.** Answer A is correct. Store and forward switching has each frame read into a buffer and performs a CRC check on it. Any frame that fails the CRC check is discarded. Answer B is incorrect because fragment free checks the first 64 bytes of a frame, as statistical analysis has shown that if a frame is corrupted, almost always the corruption will be evident in the first 64 bytes. However, this is not true 100% of the time, hence will not satisfy the question condition that all frames with errors should be dropped. Answer C is incorrect, as cut-through switching only checks the frame's destination address and performs no error correction function. Answer D is incorrect, as hybrid is another name for fragment free.

**50.** Answer C is correct. Cut-through switching only checks the frame's destination address and performs no error correction function. This method has the lowest latency. Answer A is incorrect, as store-and-forward switching has each frame read into a buffer and performs a CRC check on it. Any frame that fails the CRC check is discarded. This method has the highest latency. Latency increases with frame size. Answer B is incorrect, as fragment free checks the first 64 bytes of a frame as statistical analysis has shown that if a frame is corrupted, almost always the corruption will be evident in the first 64 bytes. The latency of the 64-byte check, although small, is higher than that imposed by cut-through switching. Answer D is incorrect, as hybrid switching is another name for fragment-free switching, which as explained in answer B has more latency than cut-through switching.

**51.** Answer A is correct. In the CSMA/CD routine on a segment of shared ethernet, if a collision is detected, a random timer is set. Once that timer expires, the process starts again with the host checking the network for traffic and, if the network is clear, initiating transmission. Answer B is incorrect, as the next step is waiting for a random amount of time rather than a fixed amount. Answer C is incorrect because the next step is to wait for a random amount of time, not to check the network. Answer D is incorrect, as the next step is to wait a random amount of time, not to analyze the frame. Answer E is incorrect, as the next step is to wait a random amount of time, not to retransmit if a multicast frame is detected.

**52.** Answer A is correct. When CSMA/CD is in use on Ethernet, the first part of the process is that the host wishing to initiate a transmission checks the network for any current traffic. Answer B is incorrect, as ethernet networks cannot be placed into a hold state. Answers C and D are incorrect, as Ethernet networks do not use tokens.

**53.** Answer D is correct. ARP is the Address Resolution Protocol and is used to determine MAC addresses for a given TCP/IP address. ARP is used when one host wishes to determine the MAC address of another host when it knows its IP address. Answer A is incorrect because RIPv2 is not used when one host wishes to determine the MAC address of another host when it knows its IP address. Answer B is incorrect because IGRP is not used when one host wishes to determine the MAC address of another host when it knows its IP address. Answer C is incorrect because OSPF is not used when one host wishes to determine the MAC address of another host when it knows its IP address. Answer E is incorrect because EIGRP is not used when one host wishes to determine the MAC address of another host when it knows its IP address.

**54.** Answers A, B, and D are correct. Answer A provides the definition of the ICMP Destination Unreachable Message, that there is a problem delivering the packet. Answer B provides the definition of the Time Exceeded message, that the packet has been discarded after the amount of time it takes for a packet to be delivered. Answer C is incorrect; Ping does not use a source quench to verify connectivity. Answer D provides the correct definition of the Redirect message, that a better route exits. Answer E is incorrect; Echo is not generated in response to data being sent too fast.

**55.** Answers C, D, and E are correct. Answer C, frame relay, is classified as a packet-switching technology. Frame relay is sometimes called frame switching, but it is common within Cisco nomenclature to refer to frame relay as a packet-switching technology. Answer D, ATM, is classified as a packet-switching technology. Answer E, X.25, is classified as a packet-switching technology. Answer A, HDLC, is used on leased lines rather than over a packet switched service. Answer B, LAPB, is used on leased lines rather than over a packet-switched service.

# Sample Exam 640-811

## Question 1

You have the following devices to use in constructing a simple LAN on two separate floors of a building. The distance between each floor is 6 meters.

1 2500 Series router.

10 Catalyst 2950 Switches (24 port).

2 Repeaters.

2 Bridges.

You have 200 desktop workstations and 4 servers. 90 workstations and 2 servers will be located on the 5th floor of the building. 110 workstations and 2 servers will be located on the 7th floor of the building. Because of the extensive traffic between the workstations and the servers, you have decided to create a separate TCP/IP subnet for each floor. Which of the following represents the best use of equipment in designing a simple LAN, given the requirements?

❍ A. Place 4 of the Catalyst 2950 switches in stacked configuration on the fifth floor. Connect the 5th floor workstations and the servers to this stack. Place the remaining 6 Catalyst 2960 switches in stacked configuration on the 7th floor. Connect the 7th floor workstations to this stack. Connect the 5th floor stack to one of the bridges. Connect the 7th floor stack to the second bridge. Interconnect the Bridges via the 2 repeaters.

❍ B. Place 4 of the Catalyst 2950 switches in stacked configuration on the 5th floor. Connect the 5th floor workstations and the servers to this stack. Place the remaining 6 Catalyst 2950 switches in stacked configuration on the 7th floor. Connect the 7th floor workstations to this stack. Connect the 5th floor stack to the 2500 series router. Connect the 7th floor stack to the 2500 series router. Configure appropriate static routes.

❍ C. Place 6 of the Catalyst 2950 switches in stacked configuration on the 5th floor. Connect the 5th floor workstations and the servers to this stack. Place the remaining 4 Catalyst 2950 switches in stacked configuration on the 7th floor. Connect the 7th floor workstations to this stack. Connect the 5th floor stack to the 2500 series router. Connect the 7th floor stack to the 2500 series router. Configure appropriate static routes.

❍ D. Place 6 of the Catalyst 2950 switches in stacked configuration on the 5th floor. Connect the 5th floor workstations and the servers to this stack. Place the remaining 4 Catalyst 2950 switches in stacked configuration on the 7th floor. Connect the 7th floor workstations to this stack. Connect the 5th floor stack to the 7th floor stack via repeaters.

# Question 2

Rooslan has been asked to help improve the responsiveness of the LAN at his grandfather's architecture consultancy. At present there are 15 hosts on the network. All of these hosts are connected to a single 20 port 10Mbps hub. Copying files to and from the server, or to other workstations, during normal business hours can take quite a lot of time. Which of the following Cisco devices could Rooslan implement to most improve the responsiveness of this network by reducing congestion?

❍ A. Replace the 10Mbps hub with a Cisco 2500 series router.

❍ B. Replace the 10Mbps hub with a Cisco wireless bridge.

❍ C. Replace the 10Mbps hub with a 100Mbps hub.

❍ D. Replace the 10Mbps hub with a Cisco Catalyst 2950 10/100Mbps switch.

# Question 3

Your Web hosting firm has been allocated a class C IP network address. You have four locations. The first in Phoenix, Arizona hosts 100 servers. The second one in Sydney, Australia hosts 50 servers. The third one in Moscow, Russia hosts 20 servers, and the fourth in Brasilia, Brazil hosts 18 servers. You are tasked with resubnetting the class C IP address space, aware that all of your routers support CIDR. Which of the following subnet masks should be applied to each location?

❍ A. Phoenix: 255.255.255.192, Sydney: 255.255.255.192, Moscow: 255.255.255.224, Brasilia 255.255.255.224.

❍ B. Phoenix: 255.255.255.128, Sydney: 255.255.255.224, Moscow: 255.255.255.240, Brasilia 255.255.255.248.

❍ C. Phoenix: 255.255.255.128, Sydney: 255.255.255.192, Moscow: 255.255.255.224, Brasilia 255.255.255.240.

❍ D. Phoenix: 255.255.255.128, Sydney: 255.255.255.192, Moscow: 255.255.255.224, Brasilia 255.255.255.224.

## Question 4

You are designing an IP addressing scheme for a company that has three branch offices located throughout the country. Each office can be assigned IP addresses from the private address space, as all of their Internet access is handled through proxy servers and none of the hosts needs to be accessed from the public Internet. The first office in Minneapolis requires a single subnet that will support 300 hosts. The second office in Melbourne requires a single subnet that will support 120 hosts. The third office in Vancouver requires a single subnet that will support 28 hosts. Which of the following private IP addressing schemes will meet the needs of each of the offices? (Select all that apply.)

❑ A. Minneapolis: 192.168.1.0 /24
Melbourne: 192.168.2.0 /24
Vancouver: 192.168.3.0 /24

❑ B. Minneapolis: 192.168.2.0 /23
Melbourne: 192.168.4.0 /24
Vancouver: 192.168.5.0 /24

❑ C. Minneapolis: 192.168.1.0 /25
Melbourne: 192.168.2.0 /25
Vancouver: 192.168.3.0 /25

❑ D. Minneapolis: 192.168.2.0 /23
Melbourne: 192.168.4.0 /25
Vancouver: 192.168.6.0 /26

## Question 5

Rooslan is the network engineer for a university. There are three campuses and several remote sites that are all a part of the university network. Using the traceroute utility Rooslan determines that the network diameter is up to 25 hops. Which of the following routing protocols would not be able to map routes of this length? (Choose all that apply.)

❑ A. RIP

❑ B. RIPv2

❑ C. IGRP

❑ D. EIGRP

❑ E. OSPF

## Question 6

Oksana is the network engineer in a network that has routers from multiple vendors. The majority of the routers on the network were manufactured by Cisco systems, but there are routers from other manufacturers that perform critical tasks and cannot be replaced at this time. Which of the following routing protocols are not proprietary to Cisco and hence are likely to be supported by non-Cisco vendors? (Choose all that apply.)

- ❑ A. RIPv2
- ❑ B. OSPF
- ❑ C. IGRP
- ❑ D. EIGRP

## Question 7

Which of the following devices can be used to connect the local LAN to a wide area network (WAN) connection such as an ISDN line to a remote city?

- ❍ A. Bridge
- ❍ B. Layer 2 switch
- ❍ C. Repeater
- ❍ D. Router

## Question 8

Which of the following are most likely to be present in a modern corporate internetwork that spans six cities in four states? (Select 3.)

- ❑ A. Routers
- ❑ B. Switches
- ❑ C. Hubs
- ❑ D. Routing Protocols
- ❑ E. Repeaters
- ❑ F. Bridges

## Question 9

Foley wants to write a standard IP access list to block traffic from all hosts coming from the IP address range 128.250.0.0 through to 128.250.255.255. Which of the following access lists will achieve Foley's goal? (Select all that apply.)

- ❑ A. **access list 1 permit 128.250.0.0 0.0.0.0**
- ❑ B. **access list 1 deny 128.250.0.0 0.0.0.0**
- ❑ C. **access list 1 deny 128.250.255.255 255.255.0.0**
- ❑ D. **access list 1 deny 128.250.254.254 0.0.255.255**
- ❑ E. **access list 1 deny 128.250.0.0 0.0.255.255**

## Question 10

Foley wants to set up an extended IP access list on a Cisco router to block all Telnet access to the host 192.168.81.114. Which of the following access lists will achieve this goal?

- ❍ A. **access list 105 deny tcp any host 192.168.81.114 eq telnet**
- ❍ B. **access list 106 deny tcp 192.168.81.114 any host eq telnet**
- ❍ C. **access list 107 deny tcp 192.168.81.114 0.255.255.255 any host eq telnet**
- ❍ D. **access list 108 deny tcp any host 192.168.81.114 eq http**

## Question 11

Which of the following WAN protocols do not provide error correction?

- ❍ A. SDLC
- ❍ B. LAPB
- ❍ C. HDLC
- ❍ D. PPP

## Question 12

Which of the following WAN protocols support STAC and Predictor compression via Cisco's IOS?

❍ A. PPP, LAPB, and HDLC

❍ B. PPP and LAPB

❍ C. PPP and HDLC

❍ D. HDLC and LAPB

## Question 13

Which of the following protocols are routing rather than routed protocols? (Choose all that apply.)

❑ A. RIPv2

❑ B. IP

❑ C. IPX

❑ D. OSPF

❑ E. EIGRP

## Question 14

Which of the following protocols are routed rather than routing protocols? (Choose all that apply.)

❑ A. NWLink

❑ B. DECnet

❑ C. BGP

❑ D. RIP

❑ E. IGRP

# Question 15

Which of the following sets of IOS commands will set the IP address of router RTR1's ethernet0 interface to 192.168.20.1 /28 and make it active?

- ❍ A. **RTR1(config)#interface ethernet0**

  **RTR1(config-if)#ip address 192.168.20.1 255.255.255.0**

  **RTR1(config-if)#no shut**
- ❍ B. **RTR1(config)#interface ethernet0**

  **RTR1(config-if)#ip address 192.168.20.1 255.255.255.0**

  **RTR1(config-if)#shut**
- ❍ C. **RTR1(config)#interface ethernet0**

  **RTR1(config-if)#ip address 192.168.20.1 255.255.255.240**

  **RTR1(config-if)#no shut**
- ❍ D. **RTR1(config)#interface ethernet0**

  **RTR1(config-if)#ip address 192.168.20.1 255.255.255.240**

  **RTR1(config-if)#shut**
- ❍ E. **RTR1(config)#interface ethernet0**

  **RTR1(config-if)#ip address 192.168.20.1 255.255.240.0**

  **RTR1(config-if)#no shut**

# Question 16

Which of the following sets of IOS commands will set the IP address of router ODLT1's ethernet1 interface to 10.10.40.1 /23 and make it active?

- ❍ A. **ODLT1(config)#interface ethernet0**

  **ODLT1(config-if)#ip address 10.10.40.1 255.255.240.0**

  **ODLT1(config-if)#no shut**
- ❍ B. **ODLT1(config)#interface ethernet0**

  **ODLT1(config-if)#ip address 10.10.40.1 255.255.248.0**

  **ODLT1(config-if)#no shut**
- ❍ C. **ODLT1(config)#interface ethernet0**

  **ODLT1(config-if)#ip address 10.10.40.1 255.255.252.0**

  **ODLT1(config-if)#no shut**
- ❍ D. **ODLT1(config)#interface ethernet0**

  **ODLT1(config-if)#ip address 10.10.40.1 255.255.254.0**

  **ODLT1(config-if)#no shut**

❍ E. **ODLT1(config)#interface ethernet1**
**ODLT1(config-if)#ip address 10.10.40.1 255.255.254.0**
**ODLT1(config-if)#no shut**

❍ F. **ODLT1(config)#interface ethernet1**
**ODLT1(config-if)#ip address 10.10.40.1 255.255.255.0**
**ODLT1(config-if)#no shut**

# Question 17

You are interested in configuring a router so that it can be accessed via a Telnet session from a remote host. Which of the following passwords will you need to set for this option to be enabled?

❍ A. Console password

❍ B. Enable password

❍ C. Auxiliary password

❍ D. VTY password

# Question 18

Which of the following passwords must be set before its corresponding method of accessing the router becomes available?

❍ A. Console password must be set before console access is available.

❍ B. Enable password must be set before console access is available.

❍ C. Auxiliary password must be set before access via the Auxiliary port is available.

❍ D. VTY password must be set before access via Telnet is available.

# Question 19

Which of the following statements about VLANs are true? (Select two.)

❑ A. Each VLAN on a switch must be on a separate subnet.

❑ B. Traffic passing between two ports on a switch that are members of different VLANs must pass through Layer 3 of the OSI model.

❑ C. Traffic passing between two ports on a switch that are members of different VLANs only passes through Layer 2 of the OSI model.

❑ D. Each VLAN on a switch must be on the same subnet.

## Question 20

Which of the following are benefits of instituting VLANs on switches?

❍ A. Broadcast traffic is only forwarded on those ports that are members of the same VLAN.

❍ B. Broadcast traffic is forwarded to all ports on the switch regardless of VLAN membership.

❍ C. Single VLANs can span multiple switches.

❍ D. VLANs are limited to the ports on a single switch.

## Question 21

Which of the following commands can be used to display which particular ports are configured as members of each particular VLAN configured on a Cisco Catalyst 1900 switch?

❍ A. **show vtp**

❍ B. **show running-config**

❍ C. **show spantree**

❍ D. **show start-config**

❍ E. **show vlan-membership**

## Question 22

You are currently configuring a Catalyst 1900 switch's VLANs. You want to configure ports 7–8 to VLAN 2, 9–10 to VLAN 3, and ports 11–12 to VLAN 4. Which of the following sets of command-line instructions will do this?

❍ A.
```
switch(config-if)# interface e 0/7
switch(config-if)# vlan-membership static 2
switch(config-if)# interface e 0/8
switch(config-if)# vlan-membership static 2
switch(config-if)# interface e 0/9
switch(config-if)# vlan-membership static 2
switch(config-if)# interface e 0/10
switch(config-if)# vlan-membership static 2
switch(config-if)# interface e 0/11
switch(config-if)# vlan-membership static 2
switch(config-if)# interface e 0/12
switch(config-if)# vlan-membership static 2
```

❍ B.
```
switch(config-if)# interface e 0/7
switch(config-if)# vlan-membership static 1
switch(config-if)# interface e 0/8
switch(config-if)# vlan-membership static 1
switch(config-if)# interface e 0/9
switch(config-if)# vlan-membership static 2
switch(config-if)# interface e 0/10
switch(config-if)# vlan-membership static 2
switch(config-if)# interface e 0/11
switch(config-if)# vlan-membership static 3
switch(config-if)# interface e 0/12
switch(config-if)# vlan-membership static 3
```

❍ C.
```
switch(config-if)# interface e 0/7
switch(config-if)# vlan-membership static 2
switch(config-if)# interface e 0/8
switch(config-if)# vlan-membership static 2
switch(config-if)# interface e 0/9
switch(config-if)# vlan-membership static 3
switch(config-if)# interface e 0/10
switch(config-if)# vlan-membership static 3
switch(config-if)# interface e 0/11
switch(config-if)# vlan-membership static 4
switch(config-if)# interface e 0/12
switch(config-if)# vlan-membership static 4
```

❍ D.
```
switch(config-if)# interface e 0/7
switch(config-if)# vlan-membership static 4
switch(config-if)# interface e 0/8
switch(config-if)# vlan-membership static 2
switch(config-if)# interface e 0/9
switch(config-if)# vlan-membership static 3
switch(config-if)# interface e 0/10
switch(config-if)# vlan-membership static 4
switch(config-if)# interface e 0/11
switch(config-if)# vlan-membership static 2
switch(config-if)# interface e 0/12
switch(config-if)# vlan-membership static 4
```

# Question 23

Which of the following LAN hosts are most likely to require full rather than half duplex ethernet connections? (Select two.)

❑ A. File server

❑ B. Workstation

❑ C. Proxy server

❑ D. Web server

# Question 24

Which of the following devices can most effectively be used to reduce network congestion caused by unicast transmissions by hosts on the same segment?

❍ A. Gateway

❍ B. Repeater

❍ C. Bridge

❍ D. Router

❍ E. Switch

# Question 25

Which of the following devices can most effectively be used to reduce congestion caused by broadcast transmissions by hosts on the network? (Select all that apply.)

❑ A. Repeater

❑ B. Bridge

❑ C Router

❑ D. Switch (Layer 2)

❑ E. Switch with VLAN

## Question 26

Which of the following, when used while configuring an interface from the command line on a Catalyst 1900 switch, will configure a port into permanent trunk mode and start it negotiating with connected devices to establish a link in trunk mode?

❍ A. **switch1(config-if)# trunking on**

❍ B. **switch1(config-if)# trunk nonegotiate**

❍ C. **switch1(config-if)# switch trunk enable**

❍ D. **switch1(config-if)# switch enable trunk**

❍ E. **switch1(config-if)# trunk on**

## Question 27

Which of the following, when used while configuring a Catalyst 1900 switch from the command line, will set the VTP domain name to ROOSLAN?

❍ A. **vtp enable set domain ROOSLAN**

❍ B. **vtp server domain ROOSLAN**

❍ C. **vtp domain set ROOSLAN**

❍ D. **authenticate VTP domain ROOSLAN**

❍ E. **connect VTP domain ROOSLAN**

## Question 28

Which of the following commands will correctly configure a Catalyst 1900 switch for in-band management on IP address 10.10.10.225 /29?

❍ A. **ip address 10.10.10.225 255.255.255.240**

❍ B. **config ip 10.10.10.225 255.255.255.240**

❍ C. **ip address 10.10.10.225 255.255.255.224**

❍ D. **config ip 10.10.10.225 255.255.255.224**

❍ E. **ip address 10.10.10.225 255.255.255.248**

❍ F. **config ip 10.10.10.225 255.255.255.248**

## Question 29

Which of the following commands will allow a Catalyst 1900 switch to be correctly configured with an addressable (one that is neither broadcast or network address) IPv4 address?

- ❍ A. **ip address 10.10.99.224 255.255.255.240**
- ❍ B. **ip address 10.10.34.239 255.255.255.248**
- ❍ C. **ip address 10.10.154.91 255.255.255.224**
- ❍ D. **ip address 10.10.72.127 255.255.255.224**
- ❍ E. **ip address 10.10.105.31 255.255.255.252**

## Question 30

You have the following access list:

**access-list 1 deny 192.168.10.1 0.255.255.255**

**access-list 1 deny 10.10.20.1 0.0.255.255**

**access-list 1 permit 10.15.30.1 0.0.0.255**

applied to incoming traffic on the ethernet0 interface. No other access lists have been applied on the router. Given this information, which of the following statements is true? (Choose all that apply.)

- ❑ A. Traffic from host address 192.168.10.20 entering the router from interface ethernet0 will be blocked.
- ❑ B. Traffic from host address 192.168.20.1 entering the router from interface ethernet0 will be blocked.
- ❑ C. Traffic from host address 10.10.100.155 entering the router from interface ethernet0 will be allowed.
- ❑ D. Traffic from host address 10.90.100.10 entering the router from interface ethernet0 will be allowed.
- ❑ E. Traffic from host address 10.240.34.8 entering the router from interface ethernet0 will be blocked.

## Question 31

You have the following extended access list applied to inbound traffic on interface Ethernet 0 on a Cisco router.

**access-list 101 allow tcp any host 192.168.10.21 eq 80**

**access-list 101 deny tcp 10.10.20.0 0.0.0.255 192.168.10.21 eq ftp**

**access-list 101 allow tcp 10.10.20.0 0.0.255.255 192.168.10.22 eq telnet**

No other access lists have been applied on Ethernet 0 or any other interfaces on this router. Given this particular access list, which of the following statements are false? (Choose all that apply.)

- ❑ A. All traffic incoming on interface Ethernet 0 for the Web server hosted on host 192.168.10.21 will be allowed.
- ❑ B. All traffic incoming on interface Ethernet 0 for the SSL secured Web site hosted on host 192.168.10.21 will be allowed.
- ❑ C. FTP traffic coming from host 10.100.20.10 to host 192.168.10.21 via interface Ethernet 0 will be blocked.
- ❑ D. FTP traffic coming from host 10.10.20.10 to host 192.168.10.21 via interface Ethernet 0 will be allowed.
- ❑ E. Telnet traffic coming from host 10.10.50.30 to host 192.168.10.21 via interface Ethernet 0 will be allowed.
- ❑ F. Telnet traffic coming from host 10.20.50.30 to host 192.168.10.22 via interface Ethernet 0 will be blocked.

## Question 32

Which of the following are properties of frame relay networks?

- ❑ A. Frame relay networks are multi-access networks.
- ❑ B. In frame relay, routers are called data communications equipment.
- ❑ C. In frame relay, switches are called data terminal equipment.
- ❑ D. The line between a router and the nearest frame relay switch is termed the access link.
- ❑ E. Virtual circuits can only exist between switches of the same make and manufacture.

# Question 33

Which of the following frame relay acronyms matches its definition?

- ❍ A. DTE: Switches in a frame relay service.
- ❍ B. DCE: Routers in a frame relay service.
- ❍ C. SVC: A pre-configured virtual circuit between two DTE.
- ❍ D. CIR: Length of time of which agreed bandwidth can be exceeded.
- ❍ E. DLCI: Frame relay address used to identify a virtual circuit.

# Question 34

Rooslan has the following list of addresses used on a network:

Address 1: 00-10-5A-6D-50-40

Address 2: 00-10-5A-6D-38-24

Address 3: 10.28.12.73

Address 4: 10.12.05.77

Address 5: SERVER1

Address 6: primus.lspace.org

Which of these addresses are examples of Layer 2 addresses as defined in the OSI model? (Select all that apply.)

- ❑ A. Address 1
- ❑ B. Address 2
- ❑ C. Address 3
- ❑ D. Address 4
- ❑ E. Address 5
- ❑ F. Address 6

## Question 35

Which of the following correctly describes a MAC address?

- ❍ A. A 12-character fixed address made up of numerals 0–9 and characters A–F.
- ❍ B. A 12-character dynamic address made up of numerals 0–9 and characters A–F.
- ❍ C. A 32-bit fixed binary address.
- ❍ D. A 32-bit dynamic binary address.
- ❍ E. A 24-character fixed address made up of numerals 0–9 and characters A–F.
- ❍ F. A 24-character dynamic address made up of numerals 0–9 and characters A–F.

## Question 36

Which of the following networking devices is paired with the layer of the OSI model that would best describe its core functionality? (Select all that apply.)

- ❑ A. Repeater, Layer 1.
- ❑ B. Bridge, Layer 2.
- ❑ C. Switch, Layer 4.
- ❑ D. Router, Layer 3.
- ❑ E. Gateway, Layer 3.

## Question 37

You are investigating the OSI model as a way of understanding how different networking devices operate on the LAN. Which of the following descriptions has a correct match between the description of data transferred, the device used, and the layer of the OSI model that this process occurs at? (Select all that apply.)

- ❑ A. Repeaters work with bits at Layer 2.
- ❑ B. Bridges work with packets at Layer 1.
- ❑ C. Switches work with frames at Layer 2.
- ❑ D. Routers work with packets at Layer 3.
- ❑ E. Routers work with frames at Layer 2.
- ❑ F. Bridges work with packets at Layer 3.
- ❑ G. Switches work with packets at Layer 1.

# Question 38

You are the administrator of a LAN that includes four different buildings that are in geographic proximity. Each building has its own router. The router in Building 1 is connected to ISDN lines that go to Building 2 and Building 3. The router in Building 2 is connected to ISDN lines that connect it to Building 1 and Building 4. The router in Building 1 fails. Which of the following statements are true? (Select all that apply.)

- ❑ A. Hosts in Building 4 will be able to contact hosts in Building 2.
- ❑ B. Hosts in Building 2 will be able to contact hosts in Building 3.
- ❑ C. Hosts in Building 1 will be unable to contact hosts in any other buildings.
- ❑ D. Hosts in Building 4 will be able to contact hosts in Building 3.

# Question 39

You are the administrator of a LAN where VLANs have been instituted. Switch 1 has been configured to host VLANs 1 and 2. Switch 2 is connected to switch 1 and hosts VLAN 2. Switch 3 is connected to Switch 1 and hosts VLANs 1 and 3. Switch 4 is connected to Switch 3 and hosts VLANs 3 and 4. Switch 3 fails. Which of the following statements are true? (Select all that apply.)

- ❑ A. Some hosts on VLAN 1 will be able to contact hosts on VLAN 2
- ❑ B. All hosts on VLAN 1 will be able to contact hosts on VLAN 2
- ❑ C. Hosts on VLAN 4 will be able to contact some hosts on VLAN 3
- ❑ D. Hosts on VLAN 2 will be able to contact hosts on VLAN 4

# Question 40

You are interested in logging messages each time a router intercepts or transmits an RIP update on a TCP/IP network. Which of the following IOS commands will do this?

- ❍ A. **debug ip rip**
- ❍ B. **debug ip igrp**
- ❍ C. **log rip updates**
- ❍ D. **log igrp updates**
- ❍ E. **audit ip rip**
- ❍ F. **audit ip igrp**

## Question 41

You want to configure a router to log messages detailing IGRP updates received and sent by the router. Which of the following IOS commands would you use to do this?

- ❍ A. **audit**
- ❍ B. **debug**
- ❍ C. **log**
- ❍ D. **watch**
- ❍ E. **show**

## Question 42

Which of the following IPv4 addresses exist within the private address space? (Select all that apply.)

- ❑ A. 10.99.244.203
- ❑ B. 172.168.33.28
- ❑ C. 172.16.24.193
- ❑ D. 192.169.0.103
- ❑ E. 192.168.23.12

## Question 43

Rooslan is looking at utilizing a private IP address range for a 240-host network. He wants to allocate a single /24 subnet to this task. Which of the following subnets are located within the private IP address space as defined by RFC 1918 and meet Rooslan's requirements? (Select all that apply.)

- ❑ A. 11.128.120.0 /27
- ❑ B. 172.17.119.0 /24
- ❑ C. 172.32.161.0 /24
- ❑ D. 192.168.0.192 /27
- ❑ E. 192.168.101.0 /24

## Question 44

Which of the following IP address/subnet mask combinations cannot be used, as they represent either the network address or broadcast address of that specific network? (Choose all that apply.)

- ❑ A. IP: 10.10.10.255, Subnet Mask: 255.255.255.0
- ❑ B. IP: 10.10.10.224, Subnet Mask: 255.255.255.240
- ❑ C. IP: 10.10.192.224, Subnet Mask: 255.255.224.0
- ❑ D. IP: 10.10.10.192, Subnet Mask: 255.255.255.252
- ❑ E. 1IP: 10.10.252.254, Subnet Mask: 255.255.252.0

## Question 45

You are attempting to debug some IP address/subnet mask combinations that appear not to be working. Which of the following IP addresses are not addressable hosts given the corresponding subnet masks? (Choose all that apply.)

- ❑ A. IP: 192.168.1.0 /24
- ❑ B. IP: 192.168.224.0 /20
- ❑ C. IP: 192.168.224.0 /18
- ❑ D. IP: 192.168.240.0 /19
- ❑ E. IP: 192.168.240.0 /21

## Question 46

You have a host named ALPHA on a TCP/IP subnet that can communicate with other hosts on the same subnet, but cannot communicate with hosts on other subnets. Other hosts on the original TCP/IP subnet can communicate with host ALPHA as well as hosts on remote subnets. Hosts on remote subnets cannot communicate with host ALPHA. Which of the following are possible reasons for this problem? (Select two.)

- ❑ A. The subnet mask on ALPHA is incorrectly set.
- ❑ B. The default gateway on ALPHA is incorrectly set.
- ❑ C. The IP address of ALPHA conflicts with another host on the same subnet.
- ❑ D. The DNS server address on ALPHA is incorrectly set.

# Question 47

You have a LAN with a single TCP/IP subnet. Your network is connected to the Internet via an ISDN line to your ISP. This ISDN line runs via a Cisco router. In the last hour you have noticed that you are unable to browse any Web sites, nor have you received any email from outside your network. You are able to ping your router, but not the ISP's router. Which of the following network devices could be at fault? (Select two.)

❑ A. The UTP cabling between your computer and the switch.

❑ B. The switch at your office may have failed.

❑ C. The router at your office may have failed.

❑ D. The ISDN line between your office and the ISP may have failed.

❑ E. The router at the ISP connected to your ISDN line may have failed.

# Question 48

You are attempting to troubleshoot the following access list which has been applied to inbound traffic on interface Ethernet 0 on a Cisco router.

**access-list 10 permit 10.20.30.0 0.0.255.255**

**access-list 10 permit 10.30.20.0 0.0.255.255**

**access-list 10 permit 10.50.30.0 0.255.255.255**

**access-list 10 deny 10.60.20.0 0.0.255.255**

**access-list 10 deny 10.40.20.0 0.0.255.255**

You are attempting to ascertain why traffic from the host 10.60.20.55 is able to pass through interface Ethernet 0. No other access lists are currently in use on the router. Which of the following reasons explains this?

❍ A. There is an implicit allow at the end of all access lists.

❍ B. Line four of the access list should be re-written as "access-list 10 deny 10.60.20.0 255.255.0.0."

❍ C. Line three of the access list permits all traffic from the 10.x.x.x range of host addresses.

❍ D. Line one of the access list permits all traffic from the 10.x.x.x range of host addresses.

# Question 49

You are attempting to troubleshoot the following extended access list which has been applied to interface Ethernet 0 on a Cisco router:

**access-list 101 permit tcp 10.10.0.0 0.0.255.255 192.168.10.22 eq 80**

**access-list 101 permit tcp 10.20.0.0 0.0.255.255 192.168.10.22 eq 23**

**access-list 101 deny tcp 10.30.0.0 0.0.255.255 192.168.10.22 eq 80**

**access-list 101 deny tcp 10.40.0.0 0.0.255.255 192.168.10.22 eq 23**

**access-list 101 permit tcp 10.50.0.0 0.0.255.255 192.168.10.22 eq 80**

A particular host with IP address 10.40.22.23 is unable to access the Web server hosted on host 192.168.10.22. Which of the following is the reason for this?

❍ A. The fourth line of the access list only grants host on the 10.40.x.x network access to port 23 of host 192.168.10.22.

❍ B. The third line of the access list denies hosts on the 10.40.x.x network access to port 80 of host 192.168.10.22.

❍ C. The first line of the access list denies hosts on the 10.40.x.x network access to port 80 of host 192.168.10.22.

❍ D. The implicit deny statement at the end of all access lists means that packets from network 10.40.x.x destined for port 80 on host 192.168.10.22, which aren't covered by any of the lines in the access list, are discarded.

# Question 50

You are currently using STAC compression on a WAN link but are concerned that CPU utilization might be too high on the routers on either end. Which of the following IOS commands will display the CPU utilization on a router for five seconds, at one-minute and five-minute intervals?

❍ A. **show utilization**

❍ B. **show process**

❍ C. **show compress**

❍ D. **show CPU**

## Question 51

Which of the following statements about PPP authentication protocols are true? (Select two.)

- ❑ A. When PAP is used over a WAN connection, username and password are sent by the dialing router without encryption.
- ❑ B. When CHAP is used over a WAN connection, username and password are sent by the dialing router without encryption.
- ❑ C. When PAP is used over a WAN connection, the router receiving the connection sends a challenge which includes a random number later input into the MD5 hash algorithm.
- ❑ D. When CHAP is used over a WAN connection, the router receiving the connection sends a challenge which includes a random number later input into the MD5 hash algorithm.

## Question 52

Which of the following are benefits of implementing Spanning Tree Protocol (STP) on Cisco switches on a local area network? (Select two.)

- ❑ A. STP stops frames from looping indefinitely in switch-based LANs that have been configured with redundant links.
- ❑ B. STP allows more than one active path to exist at any time between collision domains.
- ❑ C. STP allows only one active path to exist at any time between collision domains.
- ❑ D. STP allows frames to loop indefinitely in switch-based LANs that have been configured with redundant links.

## Question 53

There are five switches in a network, ALPHA, BETA, GAMMA, DELTA, and EPSILON. Each switch is connected to each other switch. Spanning Tree Protocol is in use on this network. STP elects switch BETA as the root bridge. Which of the listed switches will have ports that will not transmit frames received from other ports or forward received frames? (Select all that apply.)

- ❑ A. ALPHA
- ❑ B. BETA
- ❑ C. GAMMA
- ❑ D. DELTA
- ❑ E. EPSILON

# Question 54

One of the LANs that you administrate has STP operational on all of its 16 Cisco Catalyst 1900 switches. You are connected to the switch via the console and would like to display the spanning tree information for VLAN 2. Which of the following commands will enable you to do this?

❍ A. **show spantree 2**

❍ B. **show spantree 1**

❍ C. **show trunk**

❍ D. **show cdp neighbors**

❍ E. **show config vlan 2**

# Question 55

You wish to view the statistics about STP BPDU communications. Which of the following commands can be used while connected to a Catalyst 1900 switch's console port to display this information?

❍ A. **display spantree statistics**

❍ B. **show spantree statistics**

❍ C. **display bpdu statistics**

❍ D. **show bpdu statistics**

❍ E. **show spantree**

# Question 56

LAN A consists of 20 hosts with 100Mbps network cards all connected via Cat 5 UTP to a single 25-port 100Mbps Hub. LAN B consists of 20 hosts with 100Mbps network cards all connected via Cat 5 UTB to a single 25 port 10Mbps switch. Which of the following reasons best explains why LAN B often has better performance than LAN A when all hosts are in use?

❍ A. Under no circumstances will LAN B have better performance than LAN A.

❍ B. Broadcast traffic from every host on LAN A will be transmitted to every other host on LAN A. Broadcast traffic from every host on LAN B will only be transmitted to a single destination host.

❍ C. Unicast traffic from each host on LAN A will be transmitted to every other host on LAN A. Unicast traffic from each host on LAN B will only be transmitted to a single destination host.

❍ D. Unicast traffic from each host on LAN A will be transmitted to a single destination host. Unicast traffic from each host on LAN B will be transmitted to all other hosts on LAN B.

## Question 57

Which of the following routing protocols are classified as “Exterior Routing Protocols”?

❍ A. RIPv2

❍ B. BGP

❍ C. IGRP

❍ D. EIGRP

❍ E. OSPF

## Question 58

Which of the following routing protocols are classified as “Interior Routing Protocols”? (Choose all that apply.)

❑ A. RIPv2

❑ B. BGP

❑ C. IGRP

❑ D. EIGRP

❑ E. OSPF

## Question 59

Which of the following is the maximum routing metric value (non-infinite) of the RIP routing protocol?

❍ A. 10 hops

❍ B. 15 hops

❍ C. 16 hops

❍ D. 255 hops

❍ E. 256 hops

❍ F. 1024 hops

# Question 60

Which of the following can IGRP use in the calculation of its routing metrics? (Choose all that apply.)

- ❑ A. Bandwidth
- ❑ B. Delay
- ❑ C. Load
- ❑ D. Reliability
- ❑ E. MTU
- ❑ F. IOS Version

# Answer Key for 640-811

1. B
2. D
3. D
4. B, D
5. A, B
6. A, B
7. D
8. A, B, D
9. D, E
10. A
11. C
12. B
13. A, D, E
14. A, B
15. C
16. E
17. D
18. C, D
19. A, B
20. A, C
21. E
22. C
23. A, C
24. E
25. C, E
26. E
27. B
28. E
29. C
30. A, B, E
31. B, D, E
32. A, D
33. E
34. A, B
35. A
36. A, B, D
37. C, D
38. A, C
39. A, C
40. A
41. B
42. A, C, E
43. B, E
44. A, B, D
45. A, B, E
46. A, B
47. D, E
48. C
49. D
50. B
51. A, D
52. A, C
53. A, C, D, E
54. A
55. B
56. C
57. B
58. A, C, D, E
59. B
60. A, B, C, D, E

1. Answer B is the correct solution. It assigns the correct number of switches to each floor. Answer C is incorrect because it does not assign the correct number of switches to each floor. Answers A and D are incorrect because they use repeaters to connect the two floors. The distance between the two floors is at most 12 meters, far less than what is required for repeaters. Repeaters will also do nothing to help route traffic. Separate subnets were introduced to remove a congestion problem.

2. Answer D is the correct answer. As congestion from unicast traffic appears to be the problem, the best solution is to replace the 20-port, 10Mbps hub with a Cisco Catalyst 2950 10/100Mbps hub. This will not only improve the bandwidth from 10 to 100Mbps (assuming that the hosts have compliant Ethernet cards) but will also reduce the problem of unicast congestion. Answer B is incorrect because there is no wireless network. Answer A is incorrect because this situation does not call for a router. Answer C is incorrect because although a 100Mbps hub will increase performance, it will not remove the unicast traffic problem, as hubs forward unicast traffic on all ports. The performance difference between a hub and a switch is quite significant.

3. Answer D is correct. Class C address spaces have the subnet mask 255.255.255.0. This allows for a maximum of 254 addressable hosts on the network. When a class C address space is subnetted, a certain amount of hosts are allowed for each particular subnet mask. A subnet mask of 255.255.255.128 allows 126 addressable hosts. A subnet mask of 255.255.255.192 allows 62 addressable hosts. A subnet mask of 255.255.255.224 allows 30 addressable hosts. A subnet mask of 255.255.255.240 allows 14 addressable hosts. Answers A, B, and C are incorrect because the subnet masks for each location and the host addresses are incorrect.

4. Answers B and D are correct. Answer B provides for 510 hosts in Minneapolis, which meets the 300 host requirement. It provides for 254 hosts in Melbourne, which meets the 120 host requirement. It provides for 254 hosts in Vancouver, which meets the 28 host requirement. Answer D is correct as it provides 510 hosts in Minneapolis, 216 in Melbourne, and 62 in Vancouver. To support 300 hosts, a subnet mask of 255.255.254.0 or lower is required. In CIDR notation this is /23 or lower. To support 120 hosts, a subnet mask of 255.255.255.128 or lower is required. In CIDR notation this is /25 or lower. To support 28 hosts, a subnet mask of 255.255.255.224 or lower is required. In CIDR notation this is /27 or lower. Answer A is incorrect because it does not provide enough host addresses for the Minneapolis site.

Answer C is incorrect because it does not provide enough host addresses at the Minneapolis site.

5. Answers A and B are correct. RIP and RIPv2 have a maximum hop count of 15 hops and hence would not be able to map the entire network at this university. Answer C is incorrect, as IGRP can handle routes in excess of 25 hops. Answer D is incorrect, as EIGRP can handle routes with hop counts in excess of 25 hops. Answer E is incorrect, as OSPF can all handle routes with hop counts in excess of 25 hops.
6. Answers A and B are correct. Answer A is correct, as RIPv2 is an open protocol standard supported by a multitude of vendors. Answer B is correct, as OSPF is an open protocol standard supported by a multitude of vendors. Answer C is incorrect, as Interior Gateway Routing Protocol (IGRP) was developed and is owned by Cisco. Answer D is incorrect, as Enhanced Interior Gateway Routing Protocol (EIGRP) is a proprietary routing protocol developed by Cisco. Proprietary means that unless a vendor has specifically licensed the protocol implementation from Cisco, a third-party vendor will not support it.
7. Answer D is correct. Routers generally form the border between a LAN and a WAN link such as an ISDN line or a Frame Relay connection. Answer A is incorrect, as bridges do not perform this function. Answer B is incorrect, as Layer 2 switches cannot perform this function. Answer C is incorrect, as repeaters cannot perform this function.
8. Answers A, B, and D are correct. In this question you are asked to apply your judgment even though more than three answers could be correct. Cisco occasionally does this on its associate level exams. Of the six possibilities listed, routers, switches, and routing protocols are the most likely to be present in a modern corporate internetwork. Answer C is incorrect. Although hubs are possible, in general most networks have upgraded their hubs to switches. Apart from their wireless hubs, Cisco does not sell dedicated hubs anymore. Answer E is incorrect. Although repeaters do appear on corporate networks, they are not as likely to appear as routers, switches, and routing protocols. Answer F is incorrect. Bridges do appear on some modern networks, but like hubs they have been phased out in favor of newer technologies.
9. Answers D and E are correct. Answer D is correct because the first two quads are 128.250 and the mask specifies that they must be fixed. The last two quads are wild according to the mask. This will block the requisite traffic. Answer E is correct because the first two quads are 128.250 and the mask specifies that they must be fixed. The last two

quads are wild according to the mask. This will block the requisite traffic. Access list B is incorrect as this will only block traffic from address 128.250.0.0. Access list C is incorrect as this will block traffic from all hosts except those whose last two quads equal 255. The secret to understanding access lists is to understand how the wildcard masks work. A 0 in the wildcard mask means that the corresponding quad must match. For example, in access list 1, A.B.C.D 0.0.255.255, any IP address that starts A.B will be covered by the access list. There can be any values for C and D but it will still be covered by this list.

10. Answer A is correct. The syntax of an extended IP access list is `access-list [list number] {deny¦permit} protocol source source-wildcard destination destination-wildcard eq port/protocol name` (for example, http, telnet, ftp). Answer A is correct because the source is any host and the destination is the host specified in the question, 192.168.81.114. The protocol specified is telnet. Answer B is incorrect, as this will block telnet traffic from host 192.168.81.114 to any host, but not prevent telnet traffic to this host. Answer C is incorrect as it will block all telnet traffic from network 192.0.0.0 /8. Answer D is incorrect as it deals with http rather than telnet traffic.

11. Answer C is correct. The question asks which protocols do not provide error correction. Although all WAN protocols provide error detection, the HDLC (High Level Data-Link Control) protocol does not provide error correction capability. Essentially HDLC will acknowledge that there is an error, but do nothing further. Answer A is incorrect, as SDLC can correct errors. Answer B is incorrect, as LAPB can correct errors. Answer D is incorrect, as PPP can correct errors.

12. Answer B is correct. PPP and LAPB (Link Access Procedure Balanced) WAN protocols support STAC (named for STAC electronics) and Predictor compression via Cisco's IOS. PPP also supports the MPPC (Microsoft Point to Point Compression) method of compression. Answer A is incorrect, as HDLC only supports the STAC method of compression via Cisco's IOS, it does not support Predictor. Answer C is incorrect, as HDLC only supports the STAC method of compression via Cisco's IOS; it does not support Predictor. Answer D is incorrect, as HDLC only supports the STAC method of compression via Cisco's IOS; it does not support Predictor.

13. Answers A, D, and E are correct. Answer A is correct, as RIPv2 is a routing protocol. Answer D is correct, as OSPF is a routing protocol. Answer E is correct, as EIGRP is a routing protocol. Answer B is incorrect, as IP is a routed protocol. Answer C is incorrect, as IPX is a

routed protocol. Routing protocols inform routers of routes through the network. Routed protocols carry data traffic.

14. Answers A and B are correct. Answer A is correct, as NWLink is a routed protocol. Answer B is correct, as DECnet is a routed protocol. Answer C is incorrect, as BGP is a routing protocol. Answer D is incorrect, as RIP is a routing protocol. Answer E is incorrect, as IGRP is a routing protocol.

15. Answer C is correct. 192.168.20.1 /28 would translate as 192.168.20.1 255.255.255.240 in dotted decimal notation. This eliminates all but answers C and D. NO SHUT makes an interface active, making C the correct answer. Answer A is incorrect because it sets the incorrect subnet mask. Answer B is incorrect because it sets the incorrect subnet mask. Answer D is incorrect because it shuts down the interface. Answer E is incorrect, as it sets the incorrect subnet mask.

16. Answer E is the correct answer. There are two things to look for in answering this question. The first is that the correct Ethernet interface on the router is being addressed—in this case ethernet1 instead of ethernet0. Answer A is incorrect, as Ethernet0 is being configured. Answer B is incorrect, as Ethernet0 is being configured. Answer C is incorrect, as Ethernet0 is being configured. Answer D is incorrect, as Ethernet0 is being configured. The second is to realize that /23 translates into decimal quad notation as 255.255.254.0. Answer F is incorrect, as it has the wrong subnet mask.

17. Answer D is correct The VTY password needs to be set before a router can be accessed remotely via the telnet protocol. Answer A is incorrect; the console password is used for those connections via console cable rather than remote telnet connections. Answer B is incorrect, as the enable password is used to enter privileged mode. Answer C is incorrect, as the auxiliary password is used for access via the auxiliary port.

18. Answers C and D are correct. Answer C is correct. The Auxiliary password must be set before access is available via the auxiliary port. Answer D is correct. The VTY password must be set before access is available via Telnet is available. Answer A is incorrect. Access is available from the console port regardless of whether a console password is set. Answer B is incorrect. Access is available from the console port regardless of whether the enable password has been set.

19. Answers A and B are correct. Answer A is correct. Each VLAN on a switch must reside on a separate logical subnet. Answer B is correct.

Traffic passing between two ports on a switch that are members of separate VLANs must be transferred via a process at Layer 3 of the OSI model. Answer C is incorrect. Intra-VLAN traffic must pass through Layer 3. Answer D is incorrect; VLANs on the same switch must be on separate subnets.

20. Answers A and C are correct. Answer A is correct. One of the benefits of instituting VLANs is that it provides a way of limiting broadcast traffic to those ports that are members of the same VLAN. Answer C is correct. VLANs can also be configured on multiple switches. A broadcast frame transmitted on a port that is a member of VLAN 1 on a particular switch will not only be transmitted to all other ports that are members of VLAN 1 on that switch, but to ports on other switches connected to that switch that are also members of VLAN 1. Answer B is incorrect; broadcast traffic is only forwarded to ports on a switch that are members of the same VLAN. Answer D is incorrect; VLANs can span multiple compatible switches.

21. Answer E is the correct answer. The IOS command to display the membership of VLANS on a switch is `show vlan-membership`. Answer A is incorrect because `show vtp` will display VTP status. Answer B is incorrect. `show running-config` is used on routers to display their configuration. Answer C is incorrect. `Show spantree [vlan]` will display the spanning tree information for a particular VLAN. Answer D is incorrect. `show start-config` is used on routers to display their startup configuration.

22. Answer C is correct. Only answer C assigns each port to its correct VLAN. The other answers assign ports to incorrect VLANs. This question looks exceedingly complex, but can be reduced to the correct answer by eliminating obviously incorrect possibilities. Answer A is incorrect, as port 9 through 12 are assigned to the wrong VLAN. Answer B is incorrect, as port 7 is assigned to VLAN 1 instead of VLAN 2. Answer D is incorrect, as it assigns port 7 to VLAN 4 rather than VLAN 2.

23. Answers A and C are correct. Answer A is correct, as a file server is likely to send and receive a lot of information on the network. Answer C is correct, as a proxy server is likely to send and receive a lot of information on the network. Answer B is incorrect. Although there will be cases where workstations will want to send and receive at the same time, it is less critical than for the file and proxy server. Answer D is incorrect. Web servers tend to receive small amounts of incoming data yet provide large amounts of outgoing data. Even though you would

most likely configure a Web server to also be full duplex, its requirements are not as great as that of the proxy or file server. This question again asked you to exercise a best choice given available options.

**24.** Answer E is correct. A switch will most effectively reduce unicast transmissions by hosts on the same segment by reducing the segment size to only the hosts connected to a single port (usually one). Answer B is incorrect. Repeaters forward all traffic and will do nothing to alter the size of a segment. Answer C is incorrect. Although a bridge will reduce network congestion caused by unicast transmission, it will not do so as effectively as a switch. Answer D is incorrect. Routers can reduce the size of segments, but will not do so as effectively as switches.

**25.** Answers C and E are correct. Answer C is correct. A router can reduce congestion caused by broadcast traffic. Answer E is correct. A switch that is configured with VLANs can reduce congestion caused by broadcast traffic. Answer A is incorrect. Repeaters forward broadcast traffic. Answer B is incorrect. Bridges forward broadcast traffic. Answer D is incorrect. Layer 2 switches forward broadcast traffic.

**26.** Answer E is correct. `Trunk on` will configure a port into trunk mode and start it negotiating with connected devices to establish a link in trunk mode. Answer A is incorrect, as it presents incorrect syntax. Answer B is incorrect, as `Trunk nonegotiate` bypasses this negotiation phase. Answer C is incorrect, as it represents incorrect syntax. Answer D is incorrect, as it represents incorrect syntax. Note that the configuration commands on a Catalyst 1900 switch can be different to those on other switches.

**27.** Answer B is correct. `vtp server domain ROOSLAN` will set the vtp domain name to ROOSLAN on a Catalyst 1900 switch. Answer A has incorrect syntax. Answer C has incorrect syntax. Answer D has incorrect syntax. Answer E has incorrect syntax. Other models of Cisco switch, such as the 6000 series, use the `set vtp domain domainname` command to set the vtp domain.

**28.** Answer E is correct. You need to change the CIDR notation of /29 to dotted decimal subnet notation. /29 is equivalent to 255.255.255.248. IP addresses are set on switches using the `ip address` *`ip-address subnet-mask`* command. Answer A is incorrect, as it presents the wrong subnet mask. Answer B is incorrect, as it presents the wrong subnet mask. Answer C is incorrect, as it presents the wrong subnet mask. Answer D is incorrect, as it presents the wrong subnet mask. Answer F is incorrect, as the `config ip` command will not perform the specified function.

29. Answer C is correct. Answer C represents the only answer where a network or broadcast address for a given network is not listed. Answer A is incorrect, as this is a network address given this subnet mask. Answer B is incorrect, as this is a broadcast address given this subnet mask. Answer D is incorrect, as this is a broadcast address given this subnet mask. Answer E is incorrect, as this is a broadcast address given this subnet mask. This question is answered by calculating which of the IP addresses listed are actually fully addressable given the corresponding subnet masks.

30. Answers A, B, and E are correct. Answer A is correct. Traffic from 192.168.10.20 will be blocked at the first line of the access list. Answer B is correct. Traffic from host 192.168.20.1 will be blocked by the first line of the access list. Answer E is correct. Traffic from host 10.240.34.8 will be blocked, as it is not allowed by the third line of the access list and hence will be implicitly denied. Answer C is incorrect. Traffic from host 10.10.100.155 will be blocked by line 2 of the access list. Answer D is incorrect. Traffic from host address 10.90.100.10 will be blocked by the implicit deny at the end of the access list. The first line of this access list denies traffic coming from any host from 192.X.X.X. That means if the first quad of the host address is 192, the traffic will be discarded. The second line of the access list denies traffic coming from any host with the address 10.10.X.X. The third line of the access list allows traffic from any host with the address 10.15.30.x. At the end of any access list is an implicit deny statement.

31. Answers B, D, and E are correct. Recall that the question asked for which statements are false rather than true. So although these answers are false, they are correct in this context. Answer B is false (hence correct) as traffic accessing the SSL Web site on host 192.168.10.21 will be blocked by the implicit deny at the end of the access list. Answer D is false (hence correct), as line 2 of the access list will block this traffic. Answer A is true (hence incorrect). The first line of the access list makes statement A true. Answer C is true (hence incorrect). Line two of the access list blocks FTP traffic from 10.x.x.x to the FTP server on 192.168.10.21. Answer F is true (hence incorrect). Because of the implicit deny at the end of all access lists, telnet traffic coming from host 10.20.50.30 (not covered by any access list entry) will be blocked.

32. Answers A and D are correct. Answer A is correct. Frame relay networks are multi-access, which means that they can have more than two end points. Answer D is correct. The line between a router and the nearest frame relay switch is the access link. Answer B is incorrect. Routers are referred to as data terminal equipment. Answer C is

incorrect. Switches are referred to as data communications equipment. Answer E is incorrect. Virtual circuits exist between DTE/routers.

33. Answer E is correct. DLCI is the frame relay address used to identify a virtual circuit. Answer A is incorrect. DTE (Data Terminal Equipment) is the routers that form endpoints in a frame relay system. Answer B is incorrect. DCE (Data Communications Equipment) is the switches that carry frame relay traffic. Answer C is incorrect SVC (Switched Virtual Circuit) is a dynamic rather than static virtual circuit that exists as required. Answer D is incorrect. CIR (Committed Information Rate) is the agreed upon bandwidth of the VC.

34. Answers A and B are correct. Answer A is correct as it represents a MAC or Ethernet address. Answer B is correct as it represents a Mac or Ethernet address. Layer 2 addresses are made up of a 12-digit hexadecimal sequence. These addresses are written to the network card. Answer C is incorrect. IP addresses are represented at Layer 4 of the OSI model. Answer D is incorrect. IP addresses are represented at Layer 4 of the OSI model. Answer E is incorrect, as it is a NetBIOS rather than MAC/Ethernet address. Answer F is incorrect, as it is an FQDN address (used by DNS) rather than a MAC address.

35. Answer A is correct. A MAC address is made up of 12 characters consisting of the numerals 0–9 and characters A–F. This can be expressed more simply by saying 12 hexadecimal characters. Hexadecimal is Base16 to decimal's Base10; the extra numbers in hexadecimal are represented by the characters A–F. Answer B is incorrect. MAC addresses are fixed rather than dynamically allocated. Answer C is incorrect. MAC addresses are not binary but hexadecimal. Answer D is incorrect. MAC addresses are not binary but hexadecimal. Answer E is incorrect; MAC addresses are 12 characters in length. Answer F is incorrect, MAC addresses are 12 characters in length and static.

36. Answers A, B, and D are correct. Answer A is correct. Repeaters operate at Layer 1 of the OSI model. Answer B is correct, as bridges operate at Layer 2. Answer D is correct; routers operate at Layer 3 of the OSI model. Answer C is incorrect; switches operate at Layer 2. Answer E is incorrect; gateways (which provide protocol translation) operate at Layers 4, 5, 6, and 7. Some devices such as switches have multiple layer functionality, hence the term Layer 3 switching. However, the question asked about the core functionality, and the core functionality of a switch is to shift frames at Layer 2.

37. Answers C and D are correct. Answer C is correct. Switches work with frames at Layer 2. Answer D is correct. Routers work with packets at

Layer 3. Answer A is incorrect. Repeaters work with bits at Layer 1. Answer B is incorrect; bridges work with frames at Layer 2. Answer E is incorrect; routers work with packets at Layer 3. Answer F is incorrect. Bridges work with frames, and routers work with packets at Layer 3.

38. Answers A and C are correct. Answer A is correct. Even though the router in building one has failed, this does not influence the connectivity of building two to building four which are directly linked. Answer C is correct. If it has no router, hosts in building one cannot contact hosts in other buildings. Answer B is incorrect. The path between buildings two and three goes through building one. If the router in building one fails, these hosts will be unable to communicate. Answer D is incorrect. The path between building four and building three exists through buildings two and one. If building one's router is down, this path is broken.

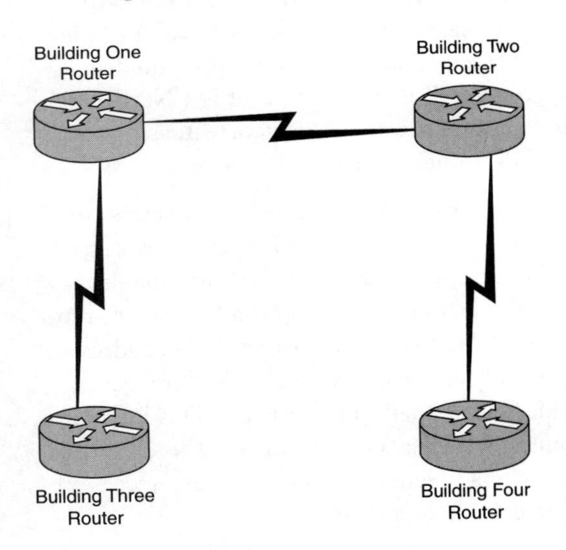


39. Answers A and C are correct. Answer A is correct. Although there are some hosts on VLAN 1 that are hosted off switch 3, there are some that are hosted off switch 1 and switch 2—hence these will still be able to contact each other. Answer C is correct. As switch 4 has hosts on both VLAN 3 and VLAN 4, some of these hosts will be able to contact each other regardless of the status of switch 3. Answer B is incorrect, as some hosts on VLAN 1 were hosted off switch 3. Because the connection between VLAN 2 and VLAN 4 goes through switch 3, answer D is incorrect.

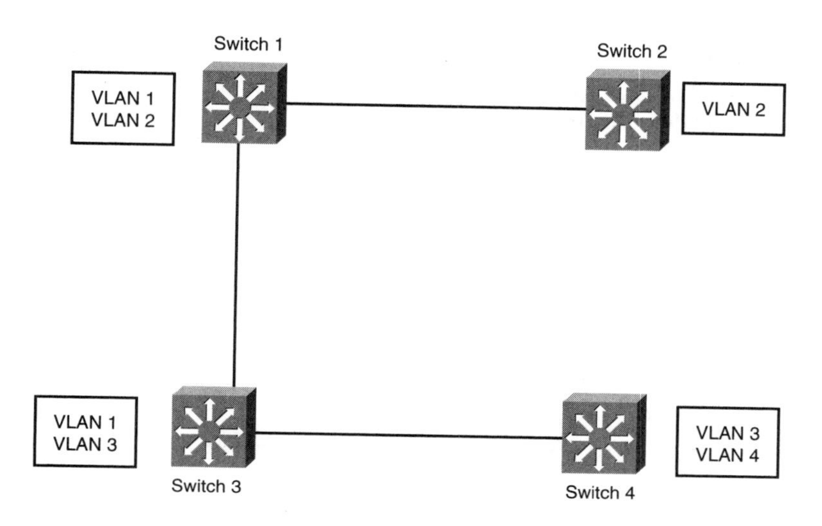


**40.** Answer A is correct. The correct syntax of the IOS command to log a message each time a router intercepts or transmits an RIP update on a TCP/IP network is `debug ip rip`. Answer B is incorrect. IGRP is another routing protocol, Interior Gateway Routing Protocol. Answer C is incorrect; this syntax is invalid. Answer D is incorrect; this syntax is invalid. Answer E is incorrect; this syntax is invalid. Answer F is incorrect; this syntax is invalid.

**41.** Answer B is correct. The `debug` command can be used to write messages to a log file for later examination in understanding a router's performance. Answer A is incorrect, as this command does not exist. Answer C is incorrect, as this command does not exist. Answer D is incorrect, as this command does not exist. Answer E is incorrect; the show command does not perform this function.

**42.** Answers A, C, and E are correct. The private IP address range as defined by RFC 1918 is 10.0.0.0–10.255.255.255 for Class A, 172.16.0.0–172.31.255.255 for Class B, and 192.168.0.0–192.168.255.255 for Class C. Answer A is correct, as this address falls within the Class A private range. Answer C is correct, as this falls within the Class B private range. Answer E is correct, as this falls within the Class C private range. Answer B is incorrect; this address does not fall within the private IP address range. Answer D is incorrect. This address does not fall within the private IP address range.

**43.** Answers B and E are correct. Answer B will provide a 254-host network within the private address range. Answer E is correct. Answer E will provide a 254-host network within the private address range. Answer A is incorrect. This will not provide enough hosts and is not within the private address range. Answer C is incorrect. It does not fall within the private address range. Answer D is incorrect; this network does not provide enough hosts.

44. Answers A, B, and D are correct. Answer A is correct. It represents a network broadcast address and hence cannot be used. Answer B is correct. It represents a network address and hence cannot be used. Answer D is correct. Answer D represents a network address given this particular subnet mask. Answer C is incorrect. This host address can be used given this subnet mask. Answer E is incorrect. This host address can be used given this subnet mask.

45. Answers A, B, and E are correct. Answer A is correct. It is a standard 255.255.255.0 network; hence .0 and .255 are off limits. Answer B is correct. It is a 255.255.240.0 network; hence a range of addresses will be off limits, including 224.0 and 240.0. Answer E is correct. It is a 255.255.248.0, which makes 232.0, 240.0, 248.0 all network addresses. Answer C is incorrect. It is a 255.255.192.0 network; hence 224.0 will not represent a network address but a host address. Answer D is incorrect. It is a 255.255.224.0 network; hence 240.0 will be an addressable host.

46. Answers A and B are correct. Answer A is correct. If the subnet mask were incorrectly set (for example, 255.255.0.0 rather than 255.255.255.0), host ALPHA could have trouble determining which traffic to send to the default gateway and which traffic is on the same subnet. Answer B is correct. If the default gateway is incorrectly set, traffic destined for remote networks will not be forwarded to those networks. Answer C is incorrect. If two hosts had the same IP address, neither would be able to receive traffic. Answer D is incorrect. DNS is irrelevant in this situation.

47. Answers D and E are correct. Answer D is correct. In this situation, you are able to ping your router, which indicates that it has not failed. The inability to ping the ISP's router suggests that either it or the ISDN line connecting your router to the ISP's router may have failed. Answer E is correct. The inability to ping the ISP's router suggests that either it or the ISDN line connecting your router to the ISP's router may have failed. Answer A is incorrect. If your UTP cable had failed, you would not be able to ping your router. Answer B is incorrect. If your switch had failed, you would be unable to ping your router. Answer C is incorrect, as you are able to ping the router.

48. Answer C is correct. Access lists are processed sequentially. Once a packet matches a line of the access list, the access list is no longer processed. Because line three has a mask of 0.255.255.255, it allows all

traffic from hosts in the 10.x.x.x range to pass through. The fourth and fifth lines of the access list will not be processed. Answer A is incorrect. There is an implicit deny at the end of all access lists. Answer B is incorrect; line three is where the problem in this list lies. Answer D is incorrect, as line one only allows traffic starting with 10.20.x.x, rather than 10.x.x.x as suggested in the answer.

**49.** Answer D is correct. None of the lines of the access list directly influence traffic on port 80 from 10.40.22.23 to 192.168.10.22. For this reason, the implicit deny at the end of all access lists blocks this traffic. Answer A is incorrect. Although answer A is factually true, it does not explain why the Web server is unable to be accessed. Answer B is incorrect. The third line does not address hosts on the 10.40.x.x network. Answer C is incorrect. The first line of the access list does not address hosts on the 10.40.x.x network.

**50.** Answer B is correct. The `show process` command will display the processor utilization over the last five seconds, last minute, and last five minutes. This will give an overview figure of how much work the processor is doing at any point in time. Cisco recommends avoiding sustained processor usage exceeding 65%. Answer A is incorrect; this command will not provide the desired output. Answer C is incorrect; this command will not provide the desired output. Answer D is incorrect; this command will not provide the desired output.

**51.** Answer A and D are correct. Answer A is correct. When PAP is used, the username and password are transmitted without encryption from the dialing router. Answer D is correct. When CHAP is used, a challenge which includes a random number is sent from the dialed to router. This random number is input into an MD5 algorithm to provide the encryption key with which to send authentication information between routers. Answer B is incorrect; CHAP uses encryption. Answer C is incorrect; no such challenge occurs when PAP is used over a WAN connection.

**52.** Answers A and C are correct. STP works by locking down all but one active path between any two collision domains on a switch-based LAN. Without this happening, frames could bounce indefinitely from switch to switch, taking a different path back and forth as they attempt to reach their destination. This would render such a network inoperable. Answer B is incorrect; only one path can exist. Answer D is incorrect; STP stops frames from looping indefinitely.

**53.** Answers A, C, D, and E are correct. Only switch BETA will have all ports set to the forwarding state by STP, as it has been elected the root bridge. The ports on the other switches which have the lowest cost to BETA will be set to the forwarding state also. Ports connected to other switches will be set to the blocking state to stop redundant pathways to BETA existing. If the link between BETA and another switch is broken, STP will re-converge the network in such a way as all switches will again be able to communicate with each other without generating switching loops. Answer B is incorrect as all ports on BETA will transmit frames received from other ports and forward received frames as it is the root bridge.

54. Answer A is correct. Spanning tree information for VLAN 2 can be shown using the command

```
show spantree 2
```

Answer B is incorrect. The command `show spantree 1` will show the spanning tree information for VLAN 1. Answer C is incorrect. `show trunk` will show the trunking information on the switch. Answer D is incorrect; `show cdp neighbors` will display information about the CDP neighbors of the switch. Answer E is incorrect. `show config vlan 2` will return an error.

55. Answer B is correct. The `show spantree statistics` command will display the spanning tree protocol BPDU communication statistics. Answer A is incorrect. This is not a legitimate switch command. Answer C is incorrect; this is not a legitimate switch command. Answer D is incorrect; this is not a legitimate switch command. Answer E is incorrect. Answer E will only show basic information about the spanning tree protocol and does not include detailed information such as BPDU statistics.

56. Answer C is correct. The reason why LAN B will often outperform LAN A is that in a switched environment, Unicast traffic is transmitted only to the destination host. Where all hosts are connected to a hub, they will all receive Unicast traffic, whether it is directed to them or not. When one host is transmitting to another host on a switched network, other hosts on the network are also free to start communication. On a network where all hosts are connected via hub, all hosts must wait until a single host making a Unicast transmission finishes that transmission before initiating their own. Answer A is incorrect, as LAN B will always out perform LAN A. Answer B is incorrect. Broadcast traffic on LAN B will reach every host. Answer D is incorrect. Unicast traffic on LAN B will only reach its intended destination host.

57. Answer B is correct. Of the protocols listed, only BGP qualifies as an exterior routing protocol. Exterior routing protocols are used between routers that are not part of the same networks: for example, a router on an ISP's network talking to an upstream provider. Exterior routing protocols deal with the network borders, hence Border Gateway Protocol. Answer A is incorrect. RIPv2 is an interior routing protocol. Answer C is incorrect. IGRP is an interior routing protocol. Answer D is incorrect. EIGRP is an interior routing protocol. Answer E is incorrect. OSPF is an interior routing protocol.

58. Answers A, C, D, and E are correct. RIPv2, IGRP, EIGRP, and OSPF are all interior routing protocols. Interior routing protocols are used on networks where each of the routers on the network is within the control of a single organization. Answer B is incorrect. BGP is an exterior routing protocol.

59. Answer B is correct. The maximum routing metric value of the RIP (and RIPv2) routing protocol is 15 hops. A route with 16 hops is considered of infinite length. Answer A is incorrect; the maximum routing metric is 15 hops. Answer C is incorrect; the maximum routing metric is 15 hops. Answer D is incorrect; the maximum routing metric is 15 hops. Answer E is incorrect; the maximum routing metric is 15 hops. Answer F is incorrect; the maximum routing metric is 15 hops.

60. Answers A, B, C, D, and E are correct. IGRP uses bandwidth, delay, load, reliability, and MTU to generate route metric values. By default, IGRP uses delay and bandwidth in route selection but these other factors can influence the value. Answer F is incorrect; IOS version has no influence on routing metric.

# Sample Exam 640-801

## Question 1

You are designing a simple network for a small publishing company. The company has a single two-story building that houses all 44 employees. The company wishes to be connected to the Internet and an ISDN BRI link will be installed in the coming weeks. The company is using an off-site hosting company to host the corporate Web site. There are five servers located on site, two of which are used for sharing files and printers to the employees, one is used for email, one runs a database server, and the other authenticates logins. All employees have workstations or laptops. The company expects to have 10% more employees within the next two years. Which of the following design decisions would you recommend given this information? (Select two answers, each forms a part of the solution.)

- ❑ A. Purchase four 12-port hubs. Uplink three of the hubs to the fourth. Connect the workstations, laptops, and servers to the hubs.
- ❑ B. Purchase two 24-port Cisco switches with two uplink ports. Uplink the first switch to the second. Connect the workstations, laptops, and servers to the switches.
- ❑ C. Purchase a single 48-port Cisco switch. Connect the ISDN line to the switch's uplink port. Connect the workstations, laptops, and servers to the switch.
- ❑ D. Purchase a single 48-port Cisco switch and a 12-port switch. Use the uplink ports on the switches to connect them together. Connect the workstations, laptops, and servers to the switch.
- ❑ E. Purchase a Cisco router. Connect the ISDN line to the router. Connect the router to the 48-port switch.
- ❑ F. Purchase a Cisco router. Connect the ISDN line to the router. Connect the router to one of the 24 port switches.
- ❑ G. Purchase a Cisco router. Connect the ISDN line to the router. Connect the router to the 12-port hub that has the other three uplinked to it.

# Question 2

You have been asked to design a simple LAN for an accounting company. The accounting company is located in an office park. There are 120 employees located in three buildings. Each employee has a computer. The buildings are each approximately 180 meters from each other. The buildings are named Building A, Building B, and Building C. The largest number of employees, 50, is in Building B. The smallest number, 30, is located in Building A. You wish to network all of these buildings together, provide access for all employees to the network, and connect them to an ISDN PRI line running from Building A to the company's ISP. Which of the following schemes will best do this?

❍ A. Purchase 10 12-port Cisco switches. Place 2 in Building C, 5 in Building B, and 3 in Building C. Use CAT 5 UTP cable to connect all of the hosts to the switches. Use CAT 5 UTP to connect the uplink ports of one of the switches in each building to the switches in the other two. Purchase a Cisco router and install it in Building A. Connect the router to the ISDN line as well as one of the switches.

❍ B. Purchase 3 48-port Cisco switches and a single 12-port Cisco switch. Place one 48-port switch in each building. Place the 12-port switch in Building B. Use CAT 5 UTP to connect all of the hosts to the switches. Use CAT 5 UTP to connect the uplink ports on one of the switches in each building to the switches in the other two. Use the uplink port on the 12-port switch to connect it to that building's 48-port switch. Purchase a Cisco router and install it in Building A. Connect the router to the ISDN line as well as the 48-port switch.

❍ C. Purchase 3 48-port Cisco switches. Place one in each building. Use CAT 5 UTP to connect all of the hosts to the switches. Use CAT 5 UTP to connect the uplink ports on one of the switches in each building to the switches in the other two. Purchase a Cisco router and install it in Building A. Connect the router to the ISDN line as well as the 48-port switch.

❍ D. Purchase 3 48-port Cisco switches and a single 12-port Cisco switch. Place one 48-port switch in each building. Place the 12-port switch in Building B. Use CAT 5 UTP to connect all of the hosts to the switches. Use CAT 5 UTP with repeaters (no segment more than 95 meters) to connect the uplink ports on one of the switches in each building to the switches in the other two. Use the uplink port on the 12-port switch to connect it to that building's 48-port switch. Purchase a Cisco router and install it in Building A. Connect the router to the ISDN line as well as the 48-port switch.

## Question 3

Rooslan has been allocated the network range 192.168.20.0 /24. From this range he needs to create four subnets. The first subnet must support 90 hosts. The second must support 40 hosts. The third must support 30 hosts, and the final network must support 24 hosts. Which of the following schemes will meet Rooslan's needs?

- ❍ A. First: 192.168.20.0 /25, Second: 192.168.20.128 /26, Third: 192.168.20.192 /27, Fourth: 192.168.20.240 /28
- ❍ B. First: 192.168.20.0 /25, Second: 192.168.20.128 /26, Third: 192.168.20.192 /27, Fourth: 192.168.20.224 /27
- ❍ C. First: 192.168.20.0 /26, Second: 192.168.20.64 /26, Third: 192.168.20.192 /27, Fourth: 192.168.20.224 /27
- ❍ D. First: 192.168.20.0 /25, Second: 192.168.20.128 /26, Third: 192.168.20.192 /28, Fourth: 192.168.20.240 /28

## Question 4

Which of the following /24 subnets can be supernetted into a larger network?

- ❑ A. 10.10.20.0 /24 and 10.10.21.0 /24 into 10.10.20.0 /23
- ❑ B. 10.10.21.0 /24 and 10.10.22.0 /24 into 10.10.21.0 /23
- ❑ C. 10.10.130.0 /24, 10.10.131.0 /24, 10.10.132.0 /24, and 10.10.133.0 /24 into 10.10.130.0 /22
- ❑ D. 10.10.164.0 /24, 10.10.165.0 /24, 10.10.166.0 /24, and 10.10.167.0 /24 into 10.10.165.0 /22

## Question 5

You are trying to select a routing protocol to use on a large internetwork. 60% of the routers on the network are Cisco systems running IOS, and 40% are manufactured by other vendors. Which of the following routing protocols are unlikely to be supported by the 40% of routers manufactured by other vendors? (Select all that apply.)

- ❑ A. IGRP
- ❑ B. RIP
- ❑ C. RIPv2
- ❑ D. OSPF
- ❑ E. BGP
- ❑ F. EIGRP

## Question 6

There are 326 routers used in a network for a government department. Some routes are 25 hops in diameter. Which of the following routing protocols could not fully map this network?

❍ A. OSPF

❍ B. IGRP

❍ C. RIPv2

❍ D. EIGRP

## Question 7

You are designing a network for a small bank that has branch offices spread all across the state. There are seven branch offices and a central office. Four of the branch offices have a single TCP/IP subnet, and three of the branch offices have two TCP/IP subnets. Each branch office is connected via ISDN line to the central office. What is the minimum number of routers that will be required for the branch offices if VLANs are not used for branch office hosts to communicate with the central office?

❍ A. 6

❍ B. 7

❍ C. 8

❍ D. 9

## Question 8

You are designing a network for an insurance company that has offices in several capital cities around the country. There is a single head office and six branch offices. You are going to use ISDN BRI leased lines to connect each office to the head office. You also want to configure the network so that it will still operate if a single ISDN BRI line fails. If this occurs, data transmission should be sent via an ISDN BRI line to another branch office, which will then forward the data to the head office. How many ISDN lines will be required to implement such a network?

❍ A. 6

❍ B. 11

❍ C. 9

❍ D. 30

## Question 9

You wish to write an access list that allows access from hosts with IP addresses in the range 10.10.0.0 through to 10.10.255.255. Which of the following access lists will achieve this goal?

- ❍ A. ACCESS LIST 1 PERMIT 10.10.0.0 255.255.255.0
- ❍ B. ACCESS LIST 201 PERMIT 10.10.0.0 255.255.255.0
- ❍ C. ACCESS LIST 1 PERMIT 10.10.0.0 255.255.0.0
- ❍ D. ACCESS LIST 201 PERMIT 10.10.0.0 255.255.0.0
- ❍ E. ACCESS LIST 1 PERMIT 10.10.0.0 0.0.255.255
- ❍ F. ACCESS LIST 201 PERMIT 10.10.0.0 255.255.0.0

## Question 10

You have the following access list:

ACCESS LIST 1 DENY 10.100.45.0 0.0.0.127

ACCESS LIST 1 PERMIT 10.100.20.0 0.0.255.255

Interface e0 is connected to the internal network, which includes the IP range 10.100.0.0 /16. Access list 1 is applied inbound on interface e0. Interface s1 is connected to internal network 10.200.0.0 /16. Which of the following host addresses will not be able to send traffic through the router to the network that is connected to interface s1? (Select all that apply.)

- ❑ A. 10.100.240.223
- ❑ B. 10.100.20.132
- ❑ C. 10.100.45.223
- ❑ D. 10.100.45.25
- ❑ E. 10.100.45.118

## Question 11

One of your clients has asked you to implement a WAN service that will be relatively inexpensive, provide extra data transfer speed if required, and allow new sites to be added to the network quickly. Which of the following WAN technologies will allow this?

- ❍ A. Leased Line—HDLC
- ❍ B. Leased Line—LAPB
- ❍ C. Packet Switched—Frame Relay
- ❍ D. Packet Switched—ATM

# Question 12

Your company has decided to go with a leased-line solution in provisioning WAN connections. They want to use the default leased-line protocol for Cisco systems because Cisco manufactures all of the routers and switches on the corporate network. When on a leased-line WAN service, which of the following data-link protocols is the default used by Cisco routers?

❍ A. SLIP

❍ B. PPP

❍ C. HDLC

❍ D. LAPB

# Question 13

You are working on a network that only supports RIPv1. Which of the following IOS command sequences will force a Cisco router named **router** to only send and receive RIPv1, rather than RIPv1 and RIPv2 routing updates?

❍ A. **router#configure terminal**
**router(config)#router rip**
**router(config-router)#version 1**
**router(config-router)#end**

❍ B. **router#configure terminal**
**router(config)#interface e0**
**router(config-if)#router ripv1**

❍ C. **router#configure terminal**
**router(config)#router ripv1**

❍ D. **router#configure terminal**
**router(config)#interface e0**
**router(config-if)#set rip version 1**

# Question 14

You are adding a router to a network that is entirely made up of Cisco equipment. The routing protocol in use is EIGRP, which is a proprietary protocol from Cisco. The EIGRP's AS (Autonomous System) number is 77. Which of the following IOS command sequences will configure EIGRP with an AS of 77 for the network 10.10.50.0? (Assume that the appropriate interface has already been configured.)

❍ A. **NEWROUTER(config)#router rip 77**

**NEWROUTER(config-router)#network 10.50.10.0**

**NEWROUTER(config-router)#end**

❍ B. **NEWROUTER(config)#router eigrp 77**

**NEWROUTER(config-router)#network 10.50.10.0**

**NEWROUTER(config-router)#end**

❍ C. **NEWROUTER(config)#router eigrp 77**

**NEWROUTER(config-router)#network 10.10.50.0**

**NEWROUTER(config-router)#end**

❍ D. **NEWROUTER(config)#router eigrp 66**

**NEWROUTER(config-router)#network 10.50.10.0**

**NEWROUTER(config-router)#end**

# Question 15

Which of the following sets of IOS commands will set the IP address of router ODLT1's e0 interface to 10.10.40.1 /27, the address of the s1 interface to 10.10.41.1 /29, and the address of the s2 interface to 10.10.40.33 /28? (Select all that apply.)

❑ A. **ODLT1(config)#interface e0**

**ODLT1(config-if)#ip address 10.10.40.1 255.255.240.0**

**ODLT1(config-if)#no shut**

❑ B. **ODLT1(config)#interface e0**

**ODLT1(config-if)#ip address 10.10.40.1255.255.224.0**

**ODLT1(config-if)#no shut**

❑ C. **ODLT1(config)#interface s1**

**ODLT1(config-if)#ip address 10.10.41.1 255.255.240.0**

**ODLT1(config-if)#no shut**

❑ D. **ODLT1(config)#interface s2**

**ODLT1(config-if)#ip address 10.10.40.33 255.255.248.0**

**ODLT1(config-if)#no shut**

❑ E. **ODLT1(config)#interface s2**
**ODLT1(config-if)#ip address 10.10.40.33 255.255.240.0**
**ODLT1(config-if)#no shut**

❑ F. **ODLT1(config)#interface s1**
**ODLT1(config-if)#ip address 10.10.41.1 255.255.248.0**
**ODLT1(config-if)#no shut**

# Question 16

You want to configure the e0 interface of a router with the IP address 10.10.10.31. Which of the following steps taken in IOS will apply this address with a subnet mask, thereby making it addressable on the network to interface e0?

❑ A. **ROUTER(config)#interface e0**
**ROUTER(config-if)#ip address 10.10.10.31 255.255.255.0**
**ROUTER(config-if)#no shut**

❑ B. **ROUTER(config)#interface e0**
**ROUTER(config-if)#ip address 10.10.10.31 255.255.255.192**
**ROUTER(config-if)#no shut**

❑ C. **ROUTER(config)#interface e0**
**ROUTER(config-if)#ip address 10.10.10.31 255.255.255.224**
**ROUTER(config-if)#no shut**

❑ D. **ROUTER(config)#interface e0**
**ROUTER(config-if)#ip address 10.10.10.31 255.255.255.240**
**ROUTER(config-if)#no shut**

❑ E. **ROUTER(config)#interface e0**
**ROUTER(config-if)#ip address 10.10.10.31 255.255.255.248**
**ROUTER(config-if)#no shut**

# Question 17

Which of the following protocols does Cisco recommend that you use to support a router to act as a terminal server to manage other routers?

❍ A. RADIUS

❍ B. TACACS+

❍ C. IGRP

❍ D. OSPF

## Question 18

What is the maximum number of VLANs that have a separate spanning tree supported by Catalyst 1900 switches?

❍ A. 8

❍ B. 16

❍ C. 32

❍ D. 64

❍ E. 128

## Question 19

Which of the following IOS commands issued on a Cisco Catalyst 1900 switch will display the VLAN membership of each of the ports?

❍ A. **list ports**

❍ B. **list VLAN**

❍ C. **show VLAN-membership**

❍ D. **VLAN-membership**

## Question 20

You are designing a LAN for a large manufacturing company's production site. There is a single factory building that is 200 meters long. The first 50 meters are taken up with office space for the administrative staff. The rest of the factory is filled with large equipment that occasionally generates electrical interference. There are 50 workstations and three servers located in the administrative area. Throughout the rest of the factory there are 20 workstations. All of these workstations are located between 120 and 180 meters from the administrative area. All need to be networked to each other. You have the following equipment available:

80 lengths of UTP cable (of whatever is required length)

25 lengths of STP cable (of whatever is required length)

1 48-port Cisco Catalyst switch

2 24-port Cisco Catalyst switches

2 repeaters

What should you do to provide connectivity to all of these hosts given the available equipment?

❍ A. Place the 48-port and one 24-port switch in the administration area. Connect them to each other using a single UTP cable. Connect all of the hosts in the administration area to these two switches with lengths of UTP cable. Place the second 24-port catalyst switch in a safe position 150 meters from the administration area. Connect two 90-meter lengths of UTP cable together with one of the repeaters and use this longer cable to connect the 48-port switch with the 24-port switch out in the factory. Use 20 lengths of STP cable to connect the hosts on the factory floor to the switch.

❍ B. Place the 48-port and one 24-port switch in the administration area. Connect them to each other using a single STP cable. Connect all of the hosts in the administration area to these two switches with lengths of UTP cable. Place the second 24-port catalyst switch in a safe position 150 meters from the administration area. Connect two 90-meter lengths of STP cable together with one of the repeaters and use this longer cable to connect the 48-port switch with the 24-port switch out in the factory. Use 20 lengths of UTP cable to connect the hosts on the factory floor to the switch.

❍ C. Place both 24-port switches in the administration area. Connect them to each other using a single UTP cable. Use lengths of UTP cable to connect all of the hosts in the administration area to these two switches. Place the 48-port catalyst switch in a safe position 150 meters from the administration area. Connect two 90-meter lengths of STP cable together with one of the repeaters and use this longer cable to connect one of the 24-port switches with the 48-port switch out in the factory. Use 20 lengths of UTP cable to connect the hosts on the factory floor to the switch.

❍ D. Place the 48-port and one 24 port-switch in the administration area. Connect them to each other using a single UTP cable. Use lengths of UTP cable to connect all of the hosts in the administration area to these two switches. Place the second 24-port catalyst switch in a safe position 150 meters from the administration area. Connect two 90-meter lengths of STP cable together with one of the repeaters and use this longer cable to connect the 48-port switch with the 24-port switch that is located out in the factory. Use 20 lengths of STP cable to connect the hosts on the factory floor to the switch.

# Question 21

You have been asked to help with a local school's LAN that has become bogged down due to heavy data traffic. The LAN currently has 220 hosts on a single TCP/IP subnet. The school administration does not want this network resubnetted. Which of the following devices can be implemented on the network to reduce the amount of unicast traffic on each segment of the network? (Select all that apply.)

❑ A. Bridge

❑ B. Switch

❑ C. Router

❑ D. Repeater

## Question 22

You wish to configure a switch so that it examines each frame for errors in its entirety before forwarding it on to its destination. For which of the following switching methods should a Catalyst 1900 switch be configured to perform this function?

❍ A. Fragment-free switching

❍ B. Store-and-forward switching

❍ C. Cut-through switching

❍ D. Basic switching

## Question 23

You wish to configure a Cisco Catalyst switch to use a method of switching that will perform some error correction on frames transmitted across the network, but that the latency caused by that error correction will not increase with the size of the frame. Which of the following switching methods should you implement?

❍ A. Fragment-free switching

❍ B. Store-and-forward switching

❍ C. Cut-through switching

❍ D. Basic switching

## Question 24

Which of the following IOS commands will back up the starting configuration to a TFTP server located on IP address 10.10.10.99?

❍ A. **backup start-config tftp 10.10.10.99**

❍ B. **backup running-config tftp 10.10.10.99**

❍ C. **copy tftp startup-config**

❍ D. **copy startup-config tftp**

# Question 25

Which of the following commands can be used to copy the startup configuration to the running configuration on a switch?

❍ A. **copy run start**

❍ B. **copy start run**

❍ C. **overwrite run start**

❍ D. **overwrite start run**

# Question 26

Which of the following commands will set a router's host name to PHOENIX?

❍ A. **hostname PHOENIX**

❍ B. **set name PHOENIX**

❍ C. **configure name PHOENIX**

❍ D. **apply name PHOENIX**

# Question 27

Which of the following IOS command sequences will set the enable password to CAPRICORNUS and the console password to AQUILA on router PHOENIX?

❍ A. **PHOENIX(config)#enable password CAPRICORNUS**
**PHOENIX(config)#line con 0**
**PHOENIX(config-line)#password AQUILA**

❍ B. **PHOENIX(config)#enable password**
**PHOENIX(config)#set password CAPRICORNUS**
**PHOENIX(config)#line con 0**
**PHOENIX(config-line)#password AQUILA**

❍ C. **PHOENIX(config)#enable password CAPRICORNUS**
**PHOENIX(config)#line vty 0 4**
**PHOENIX(config-line)#password AQUILA**

❍ D. **PHOENIX(config)#configure password CAPRICORNUS**
**PHOENIX(config)#line con 0**
**PHOENIX(config-line)#enable password AQUILA**

# Question 28

Which of the following settings are the defaults on a Catalyst 1900 switch when it is first powered on?

- ❍ A. CDP: Enabled
- ❍ B. Console Password: CISCO
- ❍ C. Spanning Tree: Disabled
- ❍ D. Switching Mode: Store and Forward
- ❍ E. 10BaseT port: Full Duplex

# Question 29

You are configuring a Cisco Catalyst 1900 switch from the command line. Which of the following groups of commands will set the IP of the switch to 10.10.10.54 /29 and the default gateway to 10.10.10.49?

❍ A. **switch# configure terminal**

**switch(config)#ip address 10.10.10.54 255.255.255.240**

**switch(config)#ip default-gateway 10.10.10.54**

❍ B. **switch# configure terminal**

**switch(config)#ip address 10.10.10.54 255.255.255.248**

**switch(config)#ip default-gateway 10.10.10.54**

❍ C. **switch# configure terminal**

**switch(config)#ip address 10.10.10.49 255.255.255.240**

**switch(config)#ip default-gateway 10.10.10.54**

❍ D. **switch# configure terminal**

**switch(config)#ip address 10.10.10.54 255.255.255.240**

**switch(config)#ip default-gateway 10.10.10.49**

❍ E. **switch# configure terminal**

**switch(config)#ip address 10.10.10.54 255.255.255.248**

**switch(config)#ip default-gateway 10.10.10.49**

# Question 30

Router Alpha's E0 interface is connected to the Internet. Router Alpha's S1 interface is connected to the internal network that encompasses 30 /24 bit networks from 10.10.10.0 /24 through to 10.10.40.0 /24. You have two goals. First, you want to stop traffic from network 10.10.36.0 /24 from reaching the Internet. Second, you only want traffic from the network 192.168.24.0 /24 to reach the internal network from the Internet. You have the following access lists:

ACCESS LIST 1 PERMIT 192.168.24.0 255.255.255.0

ACCESS LIST 2 PERMIT 192.168.24.0 0.0.0.255

ACCESS LIST 3 DENY 10.10.36.0 255.255.255.0

ACCESS LIST 4 DENY 10.10.36.0 0.0.0.255

Which of the following describes how these access lists can be applied to meet your two goals?

- ❍ A. Apply access list 1 to interface e0 out; apply access list 3 to interface s1 in.
- ❍ B. Apply access list 1 to interface e0 in; apply access list 3 to interface s1 in.
- ❍ C. Apply access list 2 to interface e0 out; apply access list 4 to interface s1 in.
- ❍ D. Apply access list 2 to interface e0 in; apply access list 4 to interface s1 in.

# Question 31

You wish to block users from the network 192.168.20.0 /24, which is a network connected to interface e0, from using the FTP protocol to connect to host 192.168.40.24 on the network that is connected to interface s1. These are the only two configured interfaces on the router, and no other path exists between the networks. Which of the following will achieve this goal?

- ❍ A. Create an access list: **access-list 101 deny tcp 192.168.20.0 255.255.255.0 192.168.40.24 eq ftp** and apply this access list to incoming traffic on interface e0.
- ❍ B. Create an access list: **access-list 101 deny tcp 192.168.20.0 0.0.0.255 192.168.40.24 eq ftp** and apply this access list to outgoing traffic on interface s1.
- ❍ C. Create an access list: **access-list 101 deny tcp 192.168.20.0 0.0.0.255 192.168.40.24 eq ftp** and apply this access list to outgoing traffic on interface e0.
- ❍ D. Create an access list: **access-list 101 deny tcp 192.168.20.0 255.255.255.0 192.168.40.24 eq ftp** and apply this access list to incoming traffic on interface s1.
- ❍ E. None of the above.

# Question 32

You wish to configure interface s0, which will host a frame relay connection to a remote office, to send keepalive packets through the PVC every 20 seconds. Keepalive packets verify that the path is still available. Which of the following IOS sequences will achieve this goal?

❍ A. **WANROUTE(config)#interface s0**

**WANROUTE(config-if)#encapsulation ppp**

**WANROUTE(config-if)#keepalive 20**

**WANROUTE(config-if)#end**

❍ B. **WANROUTE(config)#interface s1**

**WANROUTE(config-if)#encapsulation frame-relay**

**WANROUTE(config-if)#keepalive 20**

**WANROUTE(config-if)#end**

❍ C. **WANROUTE(config)#interface s0**

**WANROUTE(config-if)#encapsulation ppp**

**WANROUTE(config-if)#keepalive 5**

**WANROUTE(config-if)#end**

❍ D. **WANROUTE(config)#interface s0**

**WANROUTE(config-if)#encapsulation frame-relay**

**WANROUTE(config-if)#keepalive 20**

**WANROUTE(config-if)#end**

# Question 33

Which layer of the OSI model represents where you would begin troubleshooting problems with frames?

❍ A. Layer 1

❍ B. Layer 2

❍ C. Layer 3

❍ D. Layer 4

## Question 34

Which layer of the conceptual OSI model represents where you would begin troubleshooting problems with IP addressing?

❍ A. Layer 1

❍ B. Layer 2

❍ C. Layer 3

❍ D. Layer 4

## Question 35

Your local area network is suffering from frequent overloads of broadcast traffic. Which of the following hardware devices could *not* be used to reduce the amount of broadcast traffic on the LAN? (Select two.)

❑ A. Cisco Catalyst 1900 switch

❑ B. Cisco 2500 series router

❑ C. Repeater

❑ D. Hub

## Question 36

You wish to decrease the amount of time that an RIP network takes to converge after a topology change. You want the update period to be 10 seconds. You also want to set the invalid route timer to 100 seconds, the hold-down timer to 100 seconds, and the flush timer to 110 seconds. Which of the following IOS commands, entered after **router rip**, will enable you to achieve this goal?

❍ A. **timers basic 10 100 100 110**

❍ B. **set rip timers 20 100 100 110**

❍ C. **configure rip timers 20 100 100 110**

❍ D. **routing update 10 100 100 95**

## Question 37

You have inherited a /24 network that has been separated into several /29 networks. The original network was 192.168.10.0 /24. You are currently looking at a list of IP addresses that can be assigned to router interfaces. Which of the following IP addresses can be assigned to router interfaces given this networking scheme?

❍ A. 192.168.10.15

❍ B. 192.168.10.223

❍ C. 192.168.10.184

❍ D. 192.168.10.153

## Question 38

Your national company uses the 192.168.0.0 private address space. Your state network has been assigned the 192.168.100.0 /24 and 192.168.101.0 /24 address space. You have subnetted the two address spaces into a total of 16 equal-sized networks. Which of the following IP addresses *cannot* be assigned to hosts on the networks within your state?

❑ A. 192.168.100.31

❑ B. 192.168.101.63

❑ C. 192.168.101.203

❑ D. 192.168.100.227

❑ E. 192.168.100.129

## Question 39

Your network consists of four switches, two repeaters, a single router, two subnets, and 160 hosts. Switches one and two are on subnet 192.168.10.0 /25, and switches three and four are on subnet 192.168.10.128 /25. Hosts 192.168.10.5 through 192.168.10.45 are connected to switch one. Hosts 192.168.10.46 through 192.168.10.86 are connected to switch two. Two segments of UTP, connected via a repeater, connect switch one to switch two. Hosts 192.168.10.130 through hosts 192.168.10.170 are connected to switch three. Hosts 192.168.10.171 through hosts 192.168.10.211 are connected to switch four. Switch three is connected to switch four via two segments of UTP cable connected together via a repeater. Switch four is connected via UTP to the router. Switch one is connected to the router. Host 192.168.10.50 cannot ping host 192.168.10.165. Host 192.168.10.70 can ping host 192.168.10.200. Assuming all of the hosts work, which of the following devices could be faulty? (Select all that apply.)

- ❑ A. The router
- ❑ B. Switch three
- ❑ C. Switch four
- ❑ D. Switch one
- ❑ E. Switch two
- ❑ F. The repeater between switches one and two
- ❑ G. The repeater between switches three and four

# Question 40

You have six switches, 120 hosts, three networks, and one router. Your network configuration can be summarized as follows:

Switches Alpha and Beta service hosts on Network 10.10.10.0 /24. This network is connected to interface e0 on the router. The hosts on switch Alpha have IP addresses between 10.10.10.10 and 10.10.10.30. The hosts on switch Beta have IP addresses between 10.10.10.50 and 10.10.10.70. Switch Alpha is connected to switch Beta. Switch Beta is connected to the router.

Switches Gamma and Delta service hosts on Network 10.10.20.0 /24. This network is connected to interface s1 on the router. The hosts on switch Gamma have IP addresses between 10.10.20.10 and 10.10.20.30. The hosts on switch Delta have IP addresses between 10.10.20.50 and 10.10.20.70. Switch Gamma is connected to switch Delta. Switch Delta is connected to the router.

Switches Epsilon and Omega service hosts on network 10.10.30.0 /24. This network is connected to interface s2 on the router. The hosts on switch Epsilon have IP addresses between 10.10.30.10 and 10.10.30.30. The hosts on switch Omega have IP addresses between 10.10.30.50 and 10.10.30.70. Switch Epsilon is connected to switch Omega. Switch Omega is connected to the router.

See Figure 15.1 for a diagram.

Until yesterday, all hosts were able to communicate with each another. This morning your users have reported some problems. You perform some testing and come up with the following results:

Host 10.10.20.24 can ping host 10.10.20.58

Host 10.10.10.14 can ping host 10.10.30.68

Host 10.10.30.27 can ping host 10.10.10.57

Host 10.10.30.65 cannot ping host 10.10.20.51

Given this information, and assuming that all hosts are functioning properly, which of the following networks might have caused the problem?

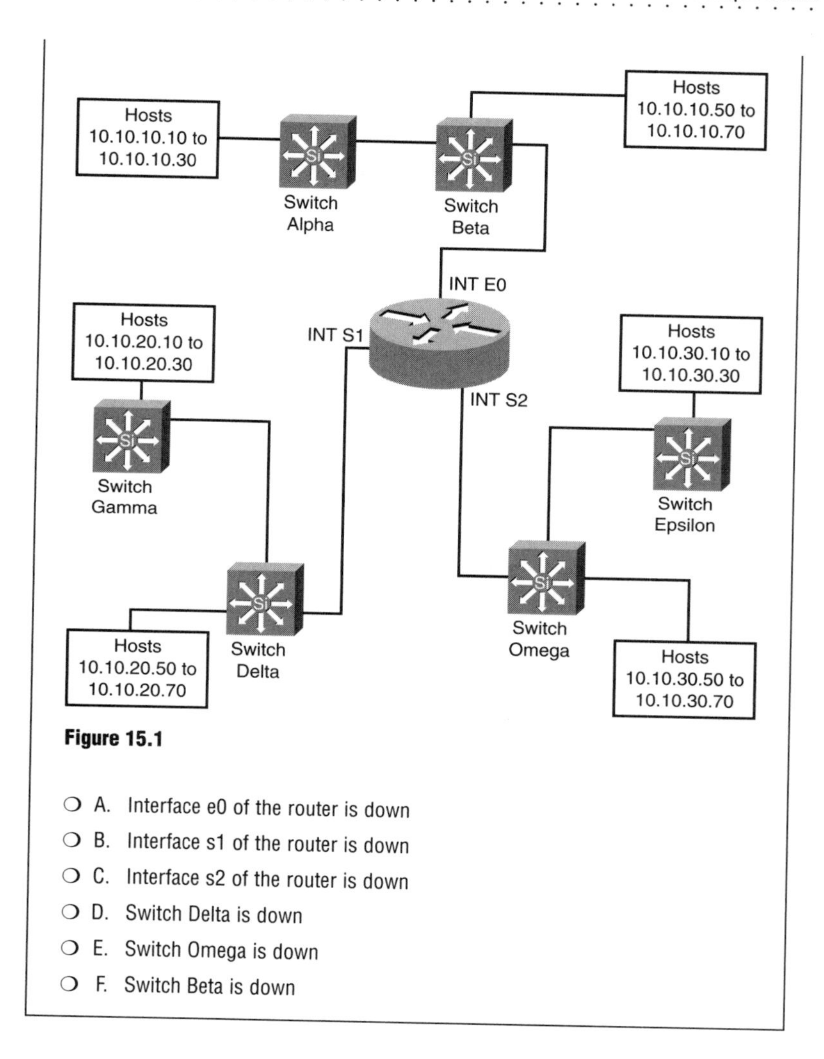


**Figure 15.1**

- ❍ A. Interface e0 of the router is down
- ❍ B. Interface s1 of the router is down
- ❍ C. Interface s2 of the router is down
- ❍ D. Switch Delta is down
- ❍ E. Switch Omega is down
- ❍ F. Switch Beta is down

# Question 41

You have the following access list:

ACCESS LIST 1 PERMIT 10.10.0.0 0.0.255.255

ACCESS LIST 1 DENY 10.10.100.0 0.0.0.255

ACCESS LIST 1 DENY 10.10.130.0 255.255.255.0

ACCESS LIST 1 DENY 10.10.150.0 0.0.0.255

You want to make sure that traffic from the networks 10.10.100.0 /24 and 10.10.150.0 /24 are blocked, but still allow all other traffic from the 10.10.0.0 /16 network. How should you modify the access list? (Select two.)

- ❑ A. Delete line three of the access list.
- ❑ B. Modify line four of the access list to **ACCESS LIST 1 DENY 10.10.150.0 255.255.255.0**.
- ❑ C. Modify line three of the access list to **ACCESS LIST 1 DENY 10.10.130.0 0.0.0.255**.
- ❑ D. Move line one of the access list to the end of the access list.
- ❑ E. Modify line two of the access list to **ACCESS LIST 1 DENY 10.10.100.0 255.255.255.0**.

# Question 42

You have the following access list:

ACCESS LIST 101 deny tcp any host 192.168.10.21 eq 80

ACCESS LIST 101 deny tcp 192.168.20.0 0.0.0.255 eq telnet

ACCESS LIST 101 deny tcp 192.168.0.0 0.0.255.255 192.168.10.22 eq ftp

ACCESS LIST 101 allow tcp 192.168.44.0 0.0.0.255 192.168.10.22 eq ftp

You want to achieve the following:

Block telnet access to any host on the 192.168.10.0 /24 network from the 192.168.20.0 /24 network.

Allow all hosts access to the Web server on host 192.168.10.21.

Allow hosts on network 192.168.44.0 /24 ftp access to host 192.168.10.22 but block ftp access to this host from other networks in the 192.168.0.0 /24 range.

Which of the following modifications do *not* have to be made to the access list? (Select all that apply.)

- ❑ A. Change line one to **ACCESS LIST 101 allow tcp any host 192.168.10.21 eq 80**.
- ❑ B. Change line two to **ACCESS LIST 101 deny tcp 192.168.20.0 0.0.0.255 192.168.10.0 0.0.0.255 eq telnet**.
- ❑ C. Rearrange the access list so that line 4 is above line 3.
- ❑ D. Change line one to **ACCESS LIST 101 allow tcp any host 192.168.10.21 0.0.255.255 eq 80**.
- ❑ E. Change line two to **ACCESS LIST 101 allow tcp 192.168.20.0 0.0.0.255 192.168.10.0 0.0.0.255 eq telnet**.

## Question 43

Which of the following best describes how information progresses up the OSI model from Layer 1 to Layer 5?

❍ A. Bits -> Packets -> Frames -> Datagrams -> Segments

❍ B. Bits -> Datagrams -> Frames -> Packets -> Segments

❍ C. Bits -> Frames -> Packets -> Segments -> Datagrams

❍ D. Bits -> Frames -> Packets -> Datagrams -> Segments

## Question 44

Which of the following correctly map the appropriate layer with the description of information that is transmitted at that layer? (Select all that apply.)

❑ A. Layer 1 = Bits

❑ B. Layer 2 = Packets

❑ C. Layer 3 = Frames

❑ D. Layer 4 = Segments

❑ E. Layer 5 = Datagrams

## Question 45

Which of the following best describes the spanning tree process?

❑ A. Spanning tree creates a series of redundant links between switches.

❑ B. Spanning tree creates a loop network so that data may reach its destination via multiple paths.

❑ C. Spanning tree blocks ports on redundant links so that there is only one path through the LAN from one switch to the next.

❑ D. Spanning tree creates multiple links so that bandwidth can be aggregated creating faster transfer speeds.

## Question 46

How many STP root bridges are on a network that contains two TCP/IP subnets separated by a Cisco router, with each subnet hosting six Cisco Catalyst 1900 switches?

❍ A. 1

❍ B. 2

❍ C. 3

❍ D. 4

## Question 47

Which of the following correctly describes the difference between broadcast, unicast, and multicast transmissions on a LAN?

❍ A. Unicast transmissions are sent from one host to all hosts. Broadcast transmissions are sent from all hosts to one host. Multicast transmissions are sent from some hosts to some other hosts.

❍ B. Unicast transmissions are sent from a single host to another single host. Broadcast transmissions are sent from a single host to all hosts on the LAN. Multicast transmissions are sent from a single host to a group of hosts.

❍ C. Unicast transmissions are sent from a single host to another single host. Broadcast transmissions are sent from a single host to a small group of hosts. Multicast transmissions are sent from a single host to all hosts on the LAN.

❍ D. Unicast transmissions are sent from a single host to a group of hosts. Broadcast transmissions are sent from a single host to all hosts on the LAN. Multicast transmissions are sent from a single host to another single host.

## Question 48

Which of the following statements is true?

❑ A. Switches, without VLANs, reduce the size of broadcast domains.

❑ B. Switches, without VLANs, reduce the size of unicast collision domains.

❑ C. Routers reduce the size of broadcast domains.

❑ D. Switches, when configured with two or more VLANs, reduce the size of broadcast domains.

## Question 49

Which of the following routing protocols are, or make use of, the Distance Vector process?

- ❑ A. RIPv2
- ❑ B. OSPF
- ❑ C. IGRP
- ❑ D. EIGRP

## Question 50

Which of the following routing protocols are exterior routing protocols?

- ❍ A. RIPv2
- ❍ B. IGRP
- ❍ C. OSPF
- ❍ D. BGP

## Question 51

You want to transfer files back and forth across a network, but you are not as concerned about error correction as you are about the speed of the transfer. Which of the following protocols might you utilize?

- ❍ A. HTTP
- ❍ B. Telnet
- ❍ C. TFTP
- ❍ D. FTP

## Question 52

Which of the following ports on a router can be used to initially configure a router via a special cable to a laptop that is running appropriate software?

- ❑ A. console port
- ❑ B. auxiliary port
- ❑ C. UTP port
- ❑ D. serial port

# Question 53

Which of the following Router memory types stores the IOS image?

❍ A. RAM

❍ B. ROM

❍ C. FLASH

❍ D. NVRAM

# Question 54

You have the following access list:

ACCESS LIST 101 deny tcp 10.10.0.0 0.0.255.255 192.168.10.24 eq ftp

ACCESS LIST 101 deny tcp 10.10.10.0 0.0.0.255 192.168.10.24 eq 80

ACCESS LIST 101 allow tcp 10.10.10.0 0.0.0.128 192.168.10.24 eq telnet

ACCESS LIST 101 allow tcp 10.10.10.0 0.0.0.255 192.168.10.25 eq 80

ACCESS LIST 101 allow tcp 10.10.0.0 0.0.255.255 192.168.10.25 eq ftp

Which of the following packets will be discarded while passing through an interface that has this access list applied? (Select all that apply.)

❑ A. FTP packets from host 10.10.234.65 to host 192.168.10.24 will be discarded.

❑ B. HTTP packets from host 10.10.20.0 to host 192.168.10.24 will be discarded.

❑ C. Telnet packets from host 10.10.10.15 to host 192.168.10.24 will be discarded.

❑ D. FTP packets from host 10.10.99.65 to host 192.168.10.25 will be discarded.

❑ E. HTTP packets from host 10.10.10.47 to host 192.168.10.24 will be discarded.

# Question 55

You have the following access list:

ACCESS LIST 102 deny tcp 10.50.0.0 0.0.255.255 192.168.10.24 eq ftp

ACCESS LIST 102 deny tcp 10.60.0.128 0.0.255.127 192.168.10.24 eq ftp

ACCESS LIST 102 deny tcp 10.70.0.0 0.0.0.255 192.168.10.24 eq ftp

ACCESS LIST 102 deny tcp 10.80.0.0 0.0.255.255 192.168.10.24 eq ftp

ACCESS LIST 102 allow tcp 10.100.0.0 0.255.255.255 192.168.10.24 eq ftp

Which of the following FTP packets will be discarded while attempting to travel through an interface where this access list is applied?

❍ A. FTP packets from host 10.100.24.22 to host 192.168.10.24

❍ B. FTP packets from host 10.51.101.223 to host 192.168.10.24

❍ C. FTP packets from host 10.60.103.54 to host 192.168.10.24

❍ D. FTP packets from host 10.60.94.200 to host 192.168.10.24

❍ E. FTP packets from host 10.79.105.22 to host 192.168.10.24

# Answer Key 640-801

## Answer Key

1. D and E
2. D
3. B
4. A and D
5. A and F
6. C
7. B
8. C
9. E
10. D and E
11. C
12. C
13. A
14. C
15. B, E, and F
16. A and B
17. B
18. D
19. C
20. D
21. A and B
22. B
23. A
24. D
25. B
26. A
27. A
28. A
29. E
30. D
31. B
32. D
33. B
34. C
35. C and D
36. A
37. D
38. A and B
39. B and G
40. B
41. A and D
42. D and E
43. C
44. A, D, and E
45. C
46. B
47. B
48. B, C, and D
49. A, C, and D
50. D
51. C
52. A & B
53. C
54. A, B, and E
55. D

1. Answers D and E are correct. D is correct because it allows for company growth providing 60 ports for use on the network. Once answer D is chosen, the only one of the second parts of the solution that mentions a 48-port switch is answer E. The router will mediate all traffic going to networks other than that hosted in the building. Answer A is incorrect, as not enough ports will be available for the company or its growth projection. Answer B is incorrect, as not enough ports will be available given the company's projected growth. Answer C is incorrect, as not enough ports will be available given the company's projected growth. Answer F is wrong, as it can only be true if answer B is true. Answer G is wrong, as it depends on answer A being true.

2. Answer D is correct. It allocates more than the correct number of ports to each building. It also mentions utilizing repeaters to bridge the distance between each building. Answer A is incorrect because it does not provide enough ports for Building C (two 12-port hubs = 24 hosts; Building C has 40 computers). Answer B is incorrect because the distance between buildings exceeds that supported for UTP. Repeaters are needed. Answer C is incorrect because Building B, which has 50 hosts, will not be able to connect all of them to the network. It also suffers from the problem of not having any repeaters on the cables that run between buildings.

3. Answer B is correct. In the subnetting scheme in answer B, 126 hosts are allocated for the first network, 62 are allocated to the second, 30 are allocated to the third, and 30 to the fourth. A quick formula for calculating the number of hosts on a network using its CIDR (Classless Inter Domain Routing) number (the one after the /) is $(2^{(32-\text{CIDR})})-2$. Hence number of hosts when CIDR = 25 is $(2^{(32-25)})-2 = 126$. Answer A is incorrect because it only allocates 14 addresses for the final network and it must support at least 24. Answer C is incorrect because only 62 hosts are allocated for the first network and the first network must support 90 hosts. Answer D is incorrect because only 14 hosts are allocated to the third and 14 hosts allocated to the fourth network. The third network must support 30 hosts and the fourth network must support 24 hosts.

4. Answers A and D are correct because these two networks can be supernetted together. The secret to figuring this out is that the start of the network must be a multiple of four. See the main text for an overview of subnetting. Answer B is incorrect because these two networks cannot be supernetted together; 10.10.21.0 needs to be paired with 10.10.20.0 in a /23 network and 10.10.22.0 with 10.10.23.0. Answer C

is incorrect; 10.10.130.0 and 10.10.131.0 would be part of the 10.10.128.0 /23 network. 10.10.132.0 and 10.10.133.0 would be part of the 10.10.132.0 /23 network.

5. Answers A and F are correct. IGRP and EIGRP are protocols designed and implemented by Cisco. They are not "open" standards, but proprietary and unlikely to be used on non-Cisco equipment. Answer B is incorrect. RIP is an open protocol and is supported by all router manufacturers. Answer C is incorrect. RIPv2 is an open protocol and is supported by all router manufacturers. Answer D is incorrect. OSPF is an open protocol and is supported by all router manufacturers. Answer E is incorrect. BGP is an open protocol and is supported by all router manufacturers. BGP is not used on internal internetworks but is used for routers on the larger internet.

6. Answer C is correct. This question asks which protocols could not map this network. RIPv2 can map routes up to 15 hops in diameter. Routes 16 hops away are considered an infinite distance away. RIPv2 would not be able to map this network. Answer A is incorrect because OSPF could map this network. Answer B is incorrect because IGRP could map this network. Answer D is incorrect because EIGRP could map this network.

7. Answer B is correct. At least one router per branch office is required. Seven branch offices equals seven routers. Even if there are two subnets, only one router is required at the branch office. Answer A is incorrect. At least one router per branch office is required. Even if there are two subnets, only one router is required at the branch office. Answer C is incorrect. At least one router per branch office is required. Even if there are two subnets, only one router is required at the branch office. Answer D is incorrect. At least one router per branch office is required. Even if there are two subnets, only one router is required at the branch office.

8. Answer C is correct. Six lines will be required. The first requirement is one from each branch office to the head office. Each branch office can then be paired with a partner for the sake of redundancy. This creates three pairs and another three lines, for a total of nine lines. Answer A is incorrect. It provides no redundancy if a single ISDN line fails. Answers B and D are incorrect. Six lines, one from each branch office to the head office, compose the first requirement. Each branch office can be then paired with a partner for the sake of redundancy. This creates three pairs and another three lines for a total of nine lines. Tolerance of two lines failing is not required.

9. Answer E is correct. This will allow access from 10.10.x.x, which is the entire range that should be granted access. Answer A is incorrect because it permits hosts from networks x.x.x.0 (where x can be anything from 1 to 255). Answer B is incorrect. Access lists in the 200 range do not deal with TCP/IP, but protocol type codes. Answer C is incorrect because it allows access from networks x.x.0.0 (where x can be anything from 1 to 255). Answers D and F are incorrect because access lists in the 200 range do not deal with TCP/IP, but Ethernet type codes.

10. Answer D is correct. Traffic will be denied if the first 25 bits of the 32-bit binary host address match 00001010.1100100.00101101.0xxxxxxx, as

    ```
    0.0.0.127
    ```

    in binary is equal to

    ```
    00000000.0000000.00000000.01111111
    ```

    The last 7 digits of the final octet are wild. 25 in binary is 00011001. You can see from the decimal that the other first three octets already match, and the first binary digit is the same as well—the list applies and the traffic is denied.

    Answer E is correct. Traffic will be denied if the first 25 bits of the 32-bit binary host address match 00001010.1100100.00101101.0xxxxxxx, as

    ```
    0.0.0.127
    ```

    in binary is equal to

    ```
    00000000.0000000.00000000.01111111
    ```

    The last 7 digits of the final octet are wild. 118 in binary is 01110110. You can see from the decimal that the other first three octets already match, the first binary digit is the same as well—the list applies and the traffic is denied.

    Answers A and B are incorrect. Traffic from these hosts is not stopped by the first line of access list 1 and is permitted by the second. Answer C is incorrect. The first line of access list 1 does not stop traffic from this host, only traffic from hosts on the 10.100.45.0 network with the last quad's value less than 128 (a one must be the first number in the final binary octet for it to not be a match). The second line of the access list permits this traffic.

11. Answer C is correct. Frame relay is relatively inexpensive; can provide the option of bursting, which increases data transfer rate over the agreed upon CIR; and allows new sites to be added to the network quickly. Answer A is incorrect. Leased lines tend to be a lot more expensive than packet-switched networks. It is also often a more involved process to add new sites to such a WAN network than it is with a technology like frame relay. Answer B is incorrect. Leased lines tend to be a lot more expensive than packet-switched networks. It is also often a more involved process to add new sites to such a WAN network than it is with a technology like frame relay. Answer D is incorrect. Although ATM, like frame relay, allows new sites to be added quickly, it is generally more expensive than frame relay and is less likely to offer extra bandwidth above the agreed upon amount.

12. Answer C is correct. HDLC is the default protocol used by Cisco routers. Answer A is incorrect because SLIP is not the default protocol used by Cisco routers. Answer B is incorrect. Although it is pervasive, PPP is not the default protocol used by Cisco routers. Answer D is incorrect. LAPB provides error recovery, but is not the default leased-line protocol used by Cisco routers.

13. Answer A is correct. This is the sequence of IOS commands that you would use to ensure that RIPv1, rather than RIPv1 and RIPv2, is being used on the network. Answer B is incorrect. You do not use the interface configuration mode to set up the specific RIP version that the router should use. Answer C is incorrect because the version of RIP must be specified after the `router rip` command has been entered, not on the same line. Answer D is incorrect because the syntax in this answer is incorrect.

14. Answer C is correct. This answer correctly configures the EIGRP AS (Autonomous System) number and the correct network (10.10.50.0). Answer A is incorrect. This answer attempts to (incorrectly) configure RIP rather than EIGRP. The network is also incorrect. Answer B is incorrect. This answer configures the incorrect network. The network stated in the question is 10.10.50.0, not 10.50.10.0. Answer D is incorrect. This answer configures the wrong AS (Autonomous System) number and the wrong network.

15. Answers B, E, and F are correct because they specify the correct subnet mask and the correct IP address for the interface. Answers A, C, and D are incorrect because they specify an incorrect subnet mask for the network interface.

16. Answer A is correct. 10.10.10.31 is an addressable host if the subnet mask 255.255.255.0 is used. Answer B is correct. 10.10.10.31 is an addressable host if the subnet mask 255.255.255.192 is used. Answer C is incorrect. 10.10.10.31 is a broadcast address if the subnet mask is 255.255.255.224. Answer D is incorrect. 10.10.10.31 is a broadcast address if the subnet mask is 255.255.255.240. Answer E is incorrect. 10.10.10.31 is a broadcast address if the subnet mask is 255.255.255.248.

17. Answer B is correct. TACACS+ is used to support a router that runs as a Terminal Server. Cisco recommends this protocol over RADIUS. TACACS+ is proprietary to Cisco. Answer A is incorrect. Although RADIUS can be used on a terminal server router to manage other routers, Cisco recommends against this because it does not provide the level of administrative granularity that TACACS+ does. Answers C and D are incorrect. IGRP and OSPF are routing protocols, so they cannot be directly used to manage other routers from a router that is configured as a terminal server.

18. Answer D is correct. The Cisco Catalyst 1900 switch supports 64 VLANs with a separate spanning tree. Answer A is incorrect. The Cisco Catalyst 1900 switch supports 64 VLANs with a separate spanning tree. Answer B is incorrect. The Cisco Catalyst 1900 switch supports 64 VLANs with a separate spanning tree. Answer C is incorrect. The Cisco Catalyst 1900 switch supports 64 VLANs with a separate spanning tree. Answer E is incorrect. The Cisco Catalyst 1900 switch supports 64 VLANs with a separate spanning tree.

19. Answer C is correct. `Show VLAN-membership` will display a list of ports and their corresponding VLAN-membership. Answer A is incorrect. The IOS command to display the VLAN membership is `show VLAN-membership`. `List ports` is not a valid IOS command. Answer B is incorrect. The IOS command to display the VLAN membership is `show VLAN-membership`. `List VLAN` is not a valid IOS command. Answer D is incorrect. `VLAN-membership` is used to assign a port to a VLAN. It will not display current port membership status.

20. Answer D is correct. There are adequate ports in the administration area, and all of the cabling on the factory floor is shielded. Answer A is incorrect. The cable running from the administration area switch to the factory floor switch is unshielded. STP should be used rather than UTP because of the documented electromagnetic interference. Answer B is incorrect. The cable running from the factory floor switch to the hosts on the factory floor is unshielded. STP should be used rather than UTP because of the documented electromagnetic interference.

Answer C is incorrect. The two switches that are allocated to the administration area will not have enough ports to handle the 50 workstations and three servers.

21. Answer A is correct because a bridge can segment a network in two, thereby reducing the amount of unicast traffic on a segment. Answer B is correct because a switch reduces the size of a segment to an individual host. Answer C is incorrect. The school asked not to have the network resubnetted, which would be necessary if a router was implemented. Answer D is incorrect because repeater does not reduce the size of a network segment.

22. Answer B is correct. Store-and-forward switching copies the entire frame into a buffer, performs a CRC (cyclic redundancy) check, and then forwards error-free frames to their destination. Answer A is incorrect. Fragment-free switching only examines the first 64 bytes of a frame before forwarding it. Answer C is incorrect because cut-through switching performs no error correction whatsoever on a frame. Answer D is incorrect because basic switching is the same as cut through switching. No error correction occurs using this method.

23. Answer A is correct. Fragment free switching checks the first 64 bytes of a frame for errors. If the frame is error free, it is forwarded to its destination. Because only the first 64 bytes are checked, latency for this method of switching does not increase with the size of the transmitted frame. Answer B is incorrect. Store and forward switching checks the entire frame. This means that latency increases as frame size increases. The larger the frame, the longer it takes to check. Answers C and D are incorrect because basic switching and cut through switching provide no error correction.

24. Answer D is correct. You do not have to enter the IP address of the TFTP server until after this command is issued (it will prompt for one). Answer A is incorrect because `backup` is not an IOS command. Answer B is incorrect because `backup` is not an IOS command. Answer C is incorrect; this will copy a startup-config file stored on the TFTP server to the switch.

25. Answer B is correct. This shorthand is commonly used to copy the startup configuration to the running configuration of a router. Answer A is incorrect. This will copy the running configuration to the startup configuration. Answers C and D are incorrect because `overwrite` is not a command in IOS.

**26.** Answer A is correct. The `hostname` command is used to set the hostname of a router. Answer B is incorrect. The `set name` command does not exist within IOS. Answer C is incorrect. The `configure name` command does not exist within IOS. Answer D is incorrect. The `apply name` command does not exist within IOS.

**27.** Answer A is correct. `Enable password CAPRICORNUS` will set the enable password to CAPRICORNUS. `Line con 0` will put the router into the mode where the console password can be set. `Password AQUILA` will set the appropriate password. Answers B and D are incorrect because `enable password CAPRICORNUS` will set the enable password to CAPRICORNUS. Answer C is incorrect. `Line vty 0 4` will configure the VTY rather than CONSOLE password.

**28.** Answer A is correct. CDP is enabled by default on Cisco Catalyst 1900 switches. Answer B is incorrect. By default, there is no console password on a Cisco Catalyst 1900 switch. Answer C is incorrect. By default, the Spanning Tree protocol is enabled on a Cisco Catalyst 1900 switch. Answer D is incorrect. By default, the switching mode is set to FragmentFree. Answer E is incorrect. By default, the 10BaseT port is set to half duplex.

**29.** Answer E is correct. It assigns the correct IP, default gateway, and the correct subnet mask to the switch. Answer A is incorrect because it assigns the wrong subnet mask and default gateway to the switch. Answer B is incorrect because it assigns the wrong default gateway to the switch. Answer C is incorrect because it assigns the wrong IP address, default gateway, and subnet mask to the switch. Answer D is incorrect because it assigns the wrong subnet mask to the switch.

**30.** Answer D is correct. The first goal is to stop traffic from a particular internal network reaching the Internet. Traffic to the Internet from the internal network travels inbound (into the router) across interface S1 and outbound (out of the router) across interface E0. Access list 4 applied inbound on s1 will meet the first goal, as it blocks the traffic from the specified subnet. To meet the second goal, Access list 2 should be applied to e0 inbound (that is, from the Internet to the router) to restrict traffic from the Internet to that which is specified. Access list 2 could be applied to s1 out and access list 4 to e0 out to achieve the same result; however, this would require more work from the router. It was also not presented as an option in this question. Answer A is incorrect. Traffic from the Internet is inbound on interface e0 and outbound on interface s1. These access lists also use the incorrect wildcard mask

(Access list 1 permits traffic from x.x.x.0 where X is anywhere from 1 to 255). Answer B is incorrect. These access lists use the incorrect wildcard mask (Access list 1 permits traffic from x.x.x.0 where X is anywhere from 1 to 255). Answer C is incorrect. Traffic from the Internet is inbound on interface e0 and outbound on interface s1.

**31.** Answer B is correct. Although this access list should be applied to incoming traffic on interface e0, applying it to outgoing traffic on interface s1 will work as well. Answer A is incorrect because the wildcard mask specifies the first three quads rather than the final quad of 192.168.20.0. Answer C is incorrect. Applying this access list to outgoing traffic on interface e0 will not work because all traffic from that particular network originates on the network that is connected to the interface and will therefore be incoming on e0. Answer D is incorrect because the access list mask specifies the first three quads rather than the final quad of 192.168.20.0. Answer E is incorrect; because answer B will work, there is a correct answer.

**32.** Answer D is correct. The interface is correctly chosen, the encapsulation type is correct, and the keepalive setting is correctly set at 20 seconds. Answer A is incorrect because the encapsulation is set to ppp rather than frame-relay. Answer B is incorrect because the interface is set to s1 instead of s0. Answer C is incorrect because the encapsulation is set to ppp rather than frame-relay, and the keepalive is set to 5 rather than 20.

**33.** Answer B is correct, and answers A, C, and D are incorrect. Layer 1 deals with Bits. Layer 2 deals with Frames. Layer 3 deals with Packets. Layer 4 deals with Segments.

**34.** Answer C is correct. IP addresses are represented by Layer 3 of the OSI model. Answers A, B, and D are incorrect, as they represent IP addresses occurring at other layers of the OSI model.

**35.** Answers C and D are correct. Repeaters and hubs do nothing to stop or filter broadcast traffic; therefore, these devices could not be used to reduce this type of congestion on the LAN. Answer A is incorrect. The Catalyst 1900 switch can be configured with VLANs. VLANs do not forward broadcast traffic; therefore, segmenting the network into several VLANs might alleviate this problem. Answer B is incorrect. Routers do not forward broadcast traffic. Segmenting the network with a router may alleviate the broadcast traffic problem.

36. Answer A is correct because it provides the correct syntax and is also the only one that has the correct series of numbers. Answers B, C, and D are incorrect because the syntax and number series are incorrect.

37. Answer D is correct. To answer this question you must work out what the network address and broadcast address will be for each of the /29 networks that this /24 network has been divided into. You can only assign an address that is neither a network nor a broadcast address to a router interface. In answer D, this address is the first available host address on network 192.168.10.152 /29. Answer A is incorrect. 192.168.10.15 is the broadcast address of network 192.168.10.8 /29. Legitimate addresses would have been from .9 through to .14. Answer B is incorrect. 102.168.10.223 is the broadcast address of network 192.168.10.116 /29. Legitimate addresses would have been from .117 through to .222. Answer C is incorrect. 192.168.10.184 is the network address of network 192.168.10.184 /29. Legitimate addresses would have been from .185 through to .190.

38. Answers A and B are correct. To find which hosts are addressable and which hosts are not, you must find what the networks are. To do this divide the two /24 address spaces into a total of 16 equal-sized networks. This comes to 8 equal sized networks per /24 address space. As the networks are of equal size, the subnet mask of this new network is straightforward to calculate. A /24 network is 1 network of 254 hosts. A /24 network divided in two is 2 networks at /25 with 126 hosts. A /24 network divided in four is at /26 and has 62 hosts. A /24 network divided in eight is at /27 and has 30 hosts per network division. So in this question, taking two /24 networks and putting them into 16 equal-sized networks results in 16 networks of 30 possible hosts. The final octet network addresses of these networks will be .0, .32, .64, .96, .128, .160, .192, and .224. If any of the answers have these numbers in the final address, they cannot be assigned to hosts on the network. Similarly the broadcast addresses of .31., .63, .95, .127, .159, .191, .223, and .255 cannot be addressed. Any answer that has these numbers in the final octet cannot be assigned to a host. The question is looking for which addresses cannot be assigned. Answer A (192.168.100.31) cannot be assigned, as 192.168.100.31 is the broadcast address of network 192.168.100.0 /27. Therefore, answer A is a correct answer. Answer B is a correct answer. 192.168.100.63 is the broadcast address of network 192.168.100.32 /27. Answer C is incorrect because it is a host address on the 192.168.101.192 /27 network. This address can be assigned and hence is a wrong answer. Answer D is incorrect because it is a host address on the 192.168.100.224 /27 network. This address can be

assigned and hence is a wrong answer. Answer E is incorrect because it is a host address on the 192.168.100.128 /27 network. This address can be assigned and hence is a wrong answer.

**39.** Answer B and Answer G are correct. See Figure 16.1 for a diagram.

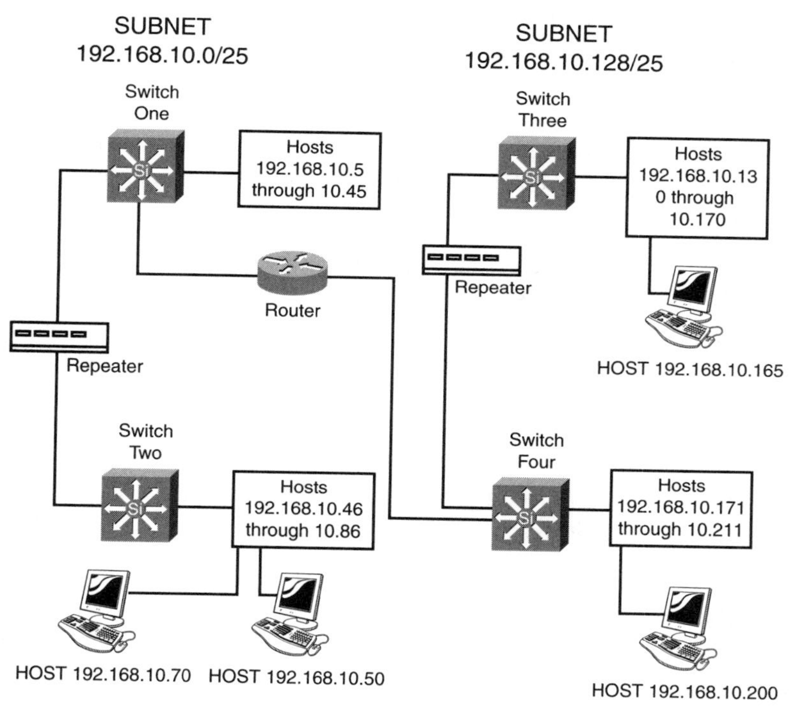


**Figure 16.1**

Answer B is correct. As host 192.168.10.165 is hosted off switch three, this host would not be able to be pinged if switch three went down. Answer G is correct. Although host 192.168.10.165 is hosted off switch three and is unreachable, the break could have occurred on the repeater or the switch. Answer A is incorrect. Host 192.168.10.80 can ping host 192.168.10.200, thereby indicating that the router is functional. Answer C is incorrect. Host 192.168.10.200 is contactable. This means that switch four must be active. Answer D is incorrect. Switch one lies between host 192.168.10.70 and host 192.168.10.200, and these hosts can contact each other. Answer E is incorrect. Switch two hosts 192.168.10.70, which is able to communicate across the network. Answer F is incorrect. The repeater between switches one and two lies between host 192.168.10.70 and host 192.168.10.200, and these hosts can contact each other.

40. Answer B is correct. At no point do packets successfully traverse interface s1 of the router. Use the diagram with the question to trace each ping path. Of the options presented, this is the most likely from the information you are given in the question. Answer A is incorrect. Interface e0 is functional because packets can pass from host 10.10.10.14 to host 10.10.30.68. Answer C is incorrect. Interface s2 is functional because packets can pass from host 10.10.10.14 to host 10.10.30.68. Answer D is incorrect. Host 10.10.20.58 can be pinged; this would be impossible if the switch was down. Answer E is incorrect. Switch Omega is functional because packets can pass from host 10.10.10.14 to host 10.10.30.68. Answer F is incorrect. Switch Beta is functional because packets can pass from host 10.10.10.14 to host 10.10.30.68.

41. Answer A is correct. All other traffic bar 10.10.100.0 /24 and 10.10.150.0 /24 should be allowed. This line is irrelevant to our purpose. Answer D is correct. A router "reads" an access list from top to bottom. Once traffic matches, the router stops "reading." Access list 1 matches all traffic from the network 10.10.0.0 /16, hence the traffic we are interested in denying has already been permitted. Answers B and E are incorrect. These lines do what we want them to, but they do not have a chance to do so until line one is moved to the bottom of the list. Answer C is incorrect. Line three is irrelevant to our purpose and should be deleted.

42. Answer D is correct. This change will allow HTTP access to all hosts on the 192.168.0.0 /24 network; this was not specified in the goals. Answer E is correct. This will allow, rather than deny as specified, telnet access from target network to the destination network. Answer A is incorrect. This modification must be made to meet the goal of allowing all hosts access to the Web server on host 192.168.10.21. Answer B is incorrect. This modification must be made to achieve the goal of blocking telnet access to any host on the 192.168.10.0 /24 network from the 192.168.20.0 /24 network. Answer C is incorrect. This modification is required, or else hosts on 192.168.44.0 /24 will not be able to FTP to host 192.168.10.22.

43. Answer C is correct, and answers A, B, and D are incorrect. Bits represent Layer 1 communication. Frames represent Layer 2 communication. Packets represent Layer 3 communication. Segments represent Layer 4 communication and Datagrams represent Layer 5 (and above) communication.

44. Answer A is correct because Bits represent Layer 1 communication. Answer D is correct because Segments represent Layer 4 communication. Answer E is correct because Datagrams represent Layer 5 (and

above) communication. Answer B is incorrect. Frames represent Layer 2 communication. Packets represent Layer 3 communication. Answer C is incorrect. Frames represent Layer 2 communication. Packets represent Layer 3 communication.

**45.** Answer C is correct because spanning tree is designed to ensure that there is only one path through the network. If multiple paths exist, data can loop through the network indefinitely until it expires. Answers A, B, and D are incorrect because spanning tree is designed to ensure that there is only one path through the network.

**46.** Answer B is correct, and answers A, C, and D are incorrect. There will be an STP root bridge for each broadcast domain. Two TCP/IP subnets separated by a Cisco router equals two broadcast domains.

**47.** Answer B is correct, and answers A, C, and D are incorrect. Unicast is 1:1. Multicast is 1:Many. Broadcast is 1:All.

**48.** Answer B is correct. Switches do reduce the size of unicast collision domains. Answer C is correct. Routers do reduce the size of broadcast domains as they do not forward broadcast packets. Answer D is correct. VLANs do not forward broadcast packets to other VLANs. Implementing VLANs on a switch reduces the size of the broadcast domain. Answer A is incorrect. Switches, without VLANs, forward broadcast packets on all interfaces; therefore, they do not reduce the size of the broadcast domain.

**49.** Answer A is correct. RIPv2 uses distance vector logic to determine routes. Answer C is correct. IGRP uses distance vector logic to determine routes. Answer D is correct. EIGRP is a hybrid protocol that makes use of both distance vector and link-state logic to determine routes. Answer B is incorrect. OSPF uses link-state logic to determine routes.

**50.** Answer D is correct. BGP is an exterior routing protocol. Answer A is incorrect. RIPv2 is an interior routing protocol. Answer B is incorrect. IGRP is an interior routing protocol. Answer C is incorrect. OSPF is an interior routing protocol.

**51.** Answer C is correct. TFTP is used for high-speed/low overhead file transfer. It is commonly used on Cisco systems for backing up and restoring config files and IOS images. Answer A is incorrect. HTTP is generally not used for bidirectional file transfer. It also has greater overhead than TFTP. Answer B is incorrect. Telnet is generally not used for bidirectional file transfer. Answer D is incorrect. Although FTP can be used to transfer files, TFTP is a better choice in this scenario because FTP has a greater overhead than TFTP.

52. Answer A is correct. A laptop running appropriate software can connect via a special cable to the console port for direct router configuration. Answer B is correct. A laptop running appropriate software can connect via a special cable to the auxiliary port for direct router configuration. Answer C is incorrect. A laptop cannot configure a router's initial setup via the UTP port. Later, when the router is configured, a Telnet session may be established via this port. Answer D is incorrect. A laptop cannot configure a router's initial setup via the serial port.

53. Answer C is correct. FLASH stores the IOS as well as additional configuration files and alternate IOS images (depending on the size of FLASH memory). Answer A is incorrect. RAM stores the running configuration file, working memory, and routing tables. Answer B is incorrect. The POST and Bootstrap are stored in ROM. Answer D is incorrect. NVRAM stores the startup config file and the config register, but does not store the IOS image.

54. Answer A is correct. According to line one of the access list, FTP traffic from 10.10.x.x to host 192.168.10.24 will be discarded. Answer B is correct. Although none of the access lists specifically mention this traffic, all access lists have an implicit deny statement at the end for any traffic that does not match. Answer E is correct. According to line 2 of the access list, these packets will be discarded. Answer C is incorrect. According to line 3 of the access list, these packets will be allowed to pass through. Answer D is incorrect. According to line 5 of the access list, these packets will be allowed to pass through.

55. Answer D is correct. This is a difficult question that requires you to understand access lists and their masks extremely well. The mask on the second line of the access list:

```
ACCESS LIST 102 deny tcp 10.60.0.128 0.0.255.127 192.168.10.24 eq ftp
```

stipulates that the first bit in the final octet is set but that other bits are wild (127 = 011111111). The first bit is set by the access list at 1 (as it is 128 in decimal, 10000000 in binary), meaning that this line of the list will catch all values in the final decimal quad over and including 128. In real life, you would not write an access list like this. The third quad is wild. The final decimal quad is 200; therefore, the packet is discarded. Answer A is incorrect. The fifth line of the access list will allow FTP packets from this host to traverse the interface when this list is applied. Once a packet matches a line in the access list, it stops being processed. Answer B is incorrect. The fifth line of the access list will allow FTP packets from this host to traverse the interface when this list is applied. Once a packet matches a line in the access list, it stops being processed. Answer C is incorrect. The mask on the second line of the access list stipulates that the first bit in the final octet is set but that other bits are wild (127 = 011111111). The first bit is set by the access list at 1, meaning that this line of the list will catch all values in the final decimal quad over and including 128. In real life, you would not write an access list like this. The third quad is wild. The final decimal quad is 57; therefore, the packet passes. If the final decimal quad had been over 128, like in answer D, then this packet would have been discarded. Answer E is incorrect. The fifth line of the access list will allow ftp packets from this host to traverse the interface when this list is applied. Once a packet matches a line in the access list, it stops being processed.

# PART IV
# Appendices

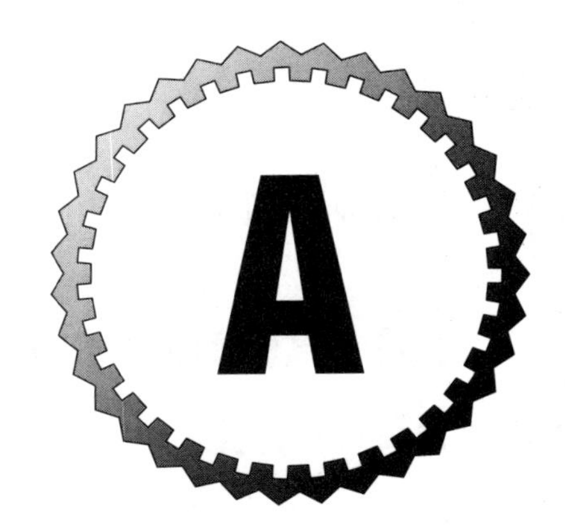


# What's on the CD-ROM

This appendix is a brief rundown of what you'll find on the CD-ROM that comes with this book. For a more detailed description of the PrepLogic Practice Exams, Preview Edition exam simulation software, see Appendix B, "Using the PrepLogic Practice Exams, Preview Edition Software." In addition to the PrepLogic Practice Exams, Preview Edition, the CD-ROM includes an electronic version of the book, in Portable Document Format (PDF), and the source code used in the book.

## PrepLogic Practice Tests, Preview Edition

PrepLogic is a leading provider of certification training tools. Trusted by certification students worldwide, PrepLogic is, we believe, the best practice exam software available. In addition to providing a means of evaluating your knowledge of the Exam Cram material, PrepLogic Practice Exams, Preview Edition features several innovations that help you to improve your mastery of the subject matter.

For example, the practice tests allow you to check your score by exam area or domain to determine which topics you need to study more. Another feature allows you to obtain immediate feedback on your responses in the form of explanations for the correct and incorrect answers.

PrepLogic Practice Exams, Preview Edition exhibits most of the full functionality of the Premium Edition but offers only a fraction of the total questions. To get the complete set of practice questions and exam functionality, visit PrepLogic.com and order the Premium Edition for this and other challenging exam titles.

Again, for a more detailed description of the PrepLogic Practice Exams, Preview Edition features, see Appendix B.

## An Exclusive Electronic Version of the Text

As mentioned previously, the CD-ROM that accompanies this book also contains an electronic PDF version of this book. This electronic version comes complete with all figures as they appear in the book. You can use Acrobat's handy search capability for study and review purposes.

# Using PrepLogic Practice Exams, Preview Edition Software

This Exam Cram includes a special version of PrepLogic Practice Exams—a revolutionary test engine designed to give you the best in certification exam preparation. PrepLogic offers sample and practice exams for many of today's most in-demand and challenging technical certifications. This special Preview Edition is included with this book as a tool to use in assessing your knowledge of the Exam Cram material while also providing you with the experience of taking an electronic exam.

This appendix describes in detail what PrepLogic Practice Exams, Preview Edition is, how it works, and what it can do to help you prepare for the exam. Note that although the Preview Edition includes all the test simulation functions of the complete, retail version, it contains only a single practice test. The Premium Edition, available at PrepLogic.com, contains the complete set of challenging practice exams designed to optimize your learning experience.

## Exam Simulation

One of the main functions of PrepLogic Practice Exams, Preview Edition is exam simulation. To prepare you to take the actual vendor certification exam, PrepLogic is designed to offer the most effective exam simulation available.

# Question Quality

The questions provided in the PrepLogic Practice Exams, Preview Edition are written to highest standards of technical accuracy. The questions tap the content of the Exam Cram chapters and help you review and assess your knowledge before you take the actual exam.

# Interface Design

The PrepLogic Practice Exams, Preview Edition exam simulation interface provides you with the experience of taking an electronic exam. This enables you to effectively prepare for taking the actual exam by making the test experience a familiar one. Using this test simulation can help eliminate the sense of surprise or anxiety you might experience in the testing center because you will already be acquainted with computerized testing.

# Effective Learning Environment

The PrepLogic Practice Exams, Preview Edition interface provides a learning environment that not only tests you through the computer, but also teaches the material you need to know to pass the certification exam. Each question comes with a detailed explanation of the correct answer and often provides reasons the other options are incorrect. This information helps to reinforce the knowledge you already have and also provides practical information you can use on the job.

# Software Requirements

PrepLogic Practice Exams requires a computer with the following:

- Microsoft Windows 98, Windows Me, Windows NT 4.0, Windows 2000, or Windows XP
- A 166MHz or faster processor is recommended
- A minimum of 32MB of RAM
- As with any Windows application, the more memory, the better your performance
- 10MB of hard drive space

# Installing PrepLogic Practice Exams, Preview Edition

Install PrepLogic Practice Exams, Preview Edition by running the setup program on the PrepLogic Practice Exams, Preview Edition CD. Follow these instructions to install the software on your computer:

1. Insert the CD into your CD-ROM drive. The Autorun feature of Windows should launch the software. If you have Autorun disabled, click Start and select Run. Go to the root directory of the CD and select setup.exe. Click Open, and then click OK.
2. The Installation Wizard copies the PrepLogic Practice Exams, Preview Edition files to your hard drive; adds PrepLogic Practice Exams, Preview Edition to your Desktop and Program menu; and installs test engine components to the appropriate system folders.

## Removing PrepLogic Practice Exams, Preview Edition from Your Computer

If you elect to remove the PrepLogic Practice Exams, Preview Edition product from your computer, an uninstall process has been included to ensure that it is removed from your system safely and completely. Follow these instructions to remove PrepLogic Practice Exams, Preview Edition from your computer:

1. Select Start, Settings, Control Panel.
2. Double-click the Add/Remove Programs icon.
3. You are presented with a list of software installed on your computer. Select the appropriate PrepLogic Practice Exams, Preview Edition title you want to remove. Click the Add/Remove button. The software is then removed from your computer.

# Using PrepLogic Practice Exams, Preview Edition

PrepLogic is designed to be user friendly and intuitive. Because the software has a smooth learning curve, your time is maximized because you start practicing almost immediately. PrepLogic Practice Exams, Preview Edition has two major modes of study: Practice Test and Flash Review.

Using Practice Test mode, you can develop your test-taking abilities as well as your knowledge through the use of the Show Answer option. While you are taking the test, you can expose the answers along with a detailed explanation of why the given answers are right or wrong. This gives you the ability to better understand the material presented.

Flash Review is designed to reinforce exam topics rather than quiz you. In this mode, you will be shown a series of questions but no answer choices. Instead, you will be given a button that reveals the correct answer to the question and a full explanation for that answer.

# Starting a Practice Test Mode Session

Practice Test mode enables you to control the exam experience in ways that actual certification exams do not allow:

- **Enable Show Answer Button**—Activates the Show Answer button, allowing you to view the correct answer(s) and full explanation(s) for each question during the exam. When not enabled, you must wait until after your exam has been graded to view the correct answer(s) and explanation.
- **Enable Item Review Button**—Activates the Item Review button, allowing you to view your answer choices, marked questions, and to facilitate navigation between questions.
- **Randomize Choices**—Randomize answer choices from one exam session to the next. Makes memorizing question choices more difficult therefore keeping questions fresh and challenging longer.

To begin studying in Practice Test mode, click the Practice Test radio button from the main exam customization screen. This enables the options detailed in the preceding list.

To your left, you are presented with the option of selecting the preconfigured Practice Test or creating your own Custom Test. The preconfigured test has a fixed time limit and number of questions. Custom Tests allow you to configure the time limit and the number of questions in your exam.

The Preview Edition included with this book includes a single preconfigured Practice Test. Get the complete set of challenging PrepLogic Practice Tests at PrepLogic.com and make certain you're ready for the big exam.

Click the Begin Exam button to begin your exam.

## Starting a Flash Review Mode Session

Flash Review mode provides you with an easy way to reinforce topics covered in the practice questions. To begin studying in Flash Review mode, click the Flash Review radio button from the main exam customization screen. Either select the preconfigured Practice Test or create your own Custom Test.

Click the Best Exam button to begin your Flash Review of the exam questions.

## Standard PrepLogic Practice Exams, Preview Edition Options

The following list describes the function of each of the buttons you see. Depending on the options, some of the buttons will be grayed out and inaccessible or missing completely. Buttons that are appropriate are active. The buttons are as follows:

- **Exhibit**—This button is visible if an exhibit is provided to support the question. An exhibit is an image that provides supplemental information necessary to answer the question.
- **Item Review**—This button leaves the question window and opens the Item Review screen. From this screen you will see all questions, your answers, and your marked items. You will also see correct answers listed here when appropriate.
- **Show Answer**—This option displays the correct answer with an explanation of why it is correct. If you select this option, the current question is not scored.
- **Mark Item**—Check this box to tag a question you need to review further. You can view and navigate your Marked Items by clicking the Item Review button (if enabled). When grading your exam, you will be notified if you have marked items remaining.
- **Previous Item**—View the previous question.
- **Next Item**—View the next question.
- **Grade Exam**—When you have completed your exam, click to end your exam and view your detailed score report. If you have unanswered or marked items remaining, you will be asked if you would like to continue taking your exam or view your exam report.

## Time Remaining

If the test is timed, the time remaining is displayed on the upper-right corner of the application screen. It counts down minutes and seconds remaining to complete the test. If you run out of time, you will be asked if you want to continue taking the test or if you want to end your exam.

## Your Examination Score Report

The Examination Score Report screen appears when the Practice Test mode ends—as the result of time expiration, completion of all questions, or your decision to terminate early.

This screen provides you with a graphical display of your test score with a breakdown of scores by topic domain. The graphical display at the top of the screen compares your overall score with the PrepLogic Exam Competency Score.

The PrepLogic Exam Competency Score reflects the level of subject competency required to pass this vendor's exam. Although this score does not directly translate to a passing score, consistently matching or exceeding this score does suggest you possess the knowledge to pass the actual vendor exam.

## Review Your Exam

From Your Score Report screen, you can review the exam that you just completed by clicking on the View Items button. Navigate through the items, viewing the questions, your answers, the correct answers, and the explanations for those questions. You can return to your score report by clicking the View Items button.

# Get More Exams

Each PrepLogic Practice Exams, Preview Edition that accompanies your Exam Cram contains a single PrepLogic Practice Test. Certification students worldwide trust PrepLogic Practice Tests to help them pass their IT certification exams the first time. Purchase the Premium Edition of PrepLogic Practice Exams and get the entire set of all new challenging Practice Tests for this exam. PrepLogic Practice Tests—Because You Want to Pass the First Time.

## Contacting PrepLogic

If you would like to contact PrepLogic for any reason including information about our extensive line of certification practice tests, we invite you to do so. Please contact us online at www.preplogic.com.

# Customer Service

If you have a damaged product and need a replacement or refund, please call the following phone number:

800-858-7674

## Product Suggestions and Comments

We value your input! Please email your suggestions and comments to the following address:

feedback@preplogic.com

## License Agreement

YOU MUST AGREE TO THE TERMS AND CONDITIONS OUTLINED IN THE END USER LICENSE AGREEMENT ("EULA") PRESENTED TO YOU DURING THE INSTALLATION PROCESS. IF YOU DO NOT AGREE TO THESE TERMS, DO NOT INSTALL THE SOFTWARE.

# Glossary

### access list

Rules applied to a router that will determine traffic patterns for data.

### administrative distance

A value that ranges from 0 through 255 that determines the priority of a source's routing information.

### advanced distance vector protocol

A routing protocol that combines the strengths of the distance vector and link state routing protocols. Cisco's Enhanced Interior Gateway Routing Protocol (EIGRP) is considered an advanced distance vector protocol.

### Application layer

The highest layer of the OSI model (Layer 7). It is closest to the end user and selects appropriate network services to support end-user applications such as email and FTP.

### area

See *autonomous system*.

### ARP (Address Resolution Protocol)

Used to map a known logical address to an unknown physical address. A device performs an ARP broadcast to identify the physical address of a destination device. This physical address is then stored in cache memory for later transmissions.

### Asynchronous Transfer Mode (ATM)

A dedicated-connection switching technology that organizes digital data into 53-byte cell units and transmits them over a physical medium using digital signal technology.

### attenuation

A term that refers to the reduction in strength of a signal. Attenuation occurs with any type of signal, whether digital or analog. Sometimes referred to as *signal loss*.

### autonomous system (AS)

A group of networks under common administration that share a routing strategy. An autonomous system is sometimes referred to as a *domain* or *area*.

### bandwidth

The available capacity of a network link over a physical medium.

### BGP (Border Gateway Protocol)

An exterior routing protocol that exchanges route information between autonomous systems.

### boot field

The lowest four binary digits of a configuration register. The value of the boot field determines the order in which a router searches for Cisco IOS software.

### BRI (Basic Rate Interface)

An ISDN interface that contains two B channels and one D channel for circuit-switched communication for data, voice, and video.

### bridge

A device used to segment a LAN into multiple physical segments. A bridge uses a forwarding table to determine which frames need to be forwarded to specific segments. Bridges isolate local traffic to the originating physical segment but forward all non-local and broadcast traffic.

### Bridge Protocol Data Unit (BDPU)

Data messages that are exchanged across the switches within an extended LAN that uses a spanning tree protocol topology.

### broadcast

A data frame that every node on a local segment will be sent.

### buffering

A method of flow control used by the Transport layer that involves the memory buffers on the receiving hosts. The Transport layer of the receiving system ensures that sufficient buffers are available and that data is not transmitted at a rate that exceeds the rate at which the receiving system can process it.

### carrier detect signal

A signal received on a router interface that indicates whether the Physical layer connectivity is operating properly.

### CDP (Cisco Discovery Protocol)

A Cisco proprietary protocol that operates at the Data Link layer. CDP enables network administrators to view a summary protocol and address information about other directly connected Cisco routers (and some Cisco switches).

### channel

A single communications path on a system. In some situations, channels can be multiplexed over a single connection.

### CHAP (Challenge Handshake Authentication Protocol)

An authentication protocol for the Point-to-Point Protocol (PPP) that uses a three-way, encrypted handshake to force a remote host to identify itself to a local host.

### checksum

A field that performs calculations to ensure the integrity of data.

### CIDR (Classless Interdomain Routing)

Implemented to resolve the rapid depletion of IP address space on the Internet and to minimize the number of routes on the Internet. CIDR provides a more efficient method of allocating IP address space by removing the concept of classes in IP addressing. CIDR enables routes to be summarized on powers-of-two boundaries, thus reducing multiple routes into a single prefix.

### CIR (Committed Information Rate)

The rate at which a Frame Relay link transmits data, averaged over time. CIR is measured in bits per second.

### classful addressing

Categorizes IP addresses into ranges that are used to create a hierarchy in the IP addressing scheme. The most common classes are A, B, and C, which can be identified by looking at the first three binary digits of an IP address.

### classless addressing

Also commonly known as *supernetting*. The limited number of IP addresses was causing major concern and there was a huge waste of addressing as well, as routing became an issue. Because of a new hierarchical distribution of addresses, classless addressing resolved many concerns.

### CO (central office)

The local telephone company office where all local loops in an area connect.

### configuration register

A numeric value (typically displayed in hexadecimal form) used to specify certain actions on a router.

### congestion

A situation that occurs during data transfer if one or more computers generate network traffic faster than it can be transmitted through the network.

### connectionless network services

Connectionless network services involve using a permanently established link. Path selection and bandwidth allocation are done dynamically.

### connection-oriented network services

Connection-oriented network services involve using a nonpermanent path for data transfer between systems. In order for two systems to communicate, they must establish a path that will be used for the duration of their connection.

### console
A terminal attached directly to the router for configuring and monitoring the router.

### convergence
The process by which all routers within an internetwork route information and eventually agree on optimal routes through the internetwork.

### counting to infinity
A routing problem in which the distance metric for a destination network is continually increased because the internetwork has not fully converged.

### CPE (customer premise equipment)
Terminating equipment such as telephones and modems supplied by the service provider, installed at the customer site, and connected to the network.

### CRC (cyclic redundancy check)
An error-checking mechanism by which the receiving node calculates a value based on the data it receives and compares it with the value stored within the frame from the sending node.

### CSMA/CD (Carrier Sense Multiple Access/Collision Detection)
A physical specification used by Ethernet to provide contention-based frame transmission. CSMA/CD specifies that a sending device must share physical transmission media and listen to determine whether a collision occurs after transmitting. In simple terms, this means that an Ethernet card has a built-in capability to detect a potential packet collision on the internetwork.

### cut-through switching
A method of forwarding frames based on the first 6 bytes contained in the frame. Cut-through switching provides higher throughput than store-and-forward switching because it requires only 6 bytes of data to make the forwarding decision. Cut-through switching does not provide error checking like its counterpart store-and-forward switching.

### DARPA (Defense Advanced Research Projects Agency)
A government agency that develops advanced defense capabilities. It is now known as *ARPA*.

### DCE (data communications equipment)
The device at the network end of a user-to-network connection that provides a physical connection to the network, forwards traffic, and provides a clocking signal used to synchronize data transmission between the DCE and DTE devices.

### DDR (dial-on-demand routing)
The technique by which a router can initiate and terminate a circuit-switched connection over ISDN or telephone lines to meet network traffic demands.

### de-encapsulation

The process by which a destination peer layer removes and reads the control information sent by the source peer layer in another network host.

### default mask

A binary or decimal representation of the number of bits used to identify an IP network. The class of the IP address defines the default mask. A default mask is represented by four octets of binary digits. The mask can also be presented in dotted decimal notation.

### default route

A network route (that usually points to another router) established to receive and attempt to process all packets for which no route appears in the route table.

### delay

The amount of time necessary to move a packet through the internetwork from source to destination.

### demarc

The point of demarcation is between the carrier's equipment and the customer premise equipment (CPE).

### discard eligibility bit

A bit that can be set to indicate that a frame may be dropped if congestion occurs within the Frame Relay network.

### distance vector protocol

An interior routing protocol that relies on distance and vector or direction to choose optimal paths. A distance vector protocol requires each router to send all or a large part of its route table to its neighboring routers periodically.

### DLCI (data link connection identifier)

A value that specifies a permanent virtual circuit (PVC) or switched virtual circuit (SVC) in a Frame Relay network.

### DNS (Domain Name System)

A system used to translate fully qualified hostnames or computer names into IP addresses, and vice versa.

### domain

See *autonomous system*.

### dotted decimal notation

A method of representing binary IP addresses in a decimal format. Dotted decimal notation represents the four octets of an IP address in four decimal values separated by decimal points.

### DTE (data terminal equipment)

The device at the user end of the user-to-network connection that connects to a data network through a data communications equipment (DCE) device.

### dynamic route

A network route that adjusts automatically to changes within the internetwork.

### EGP (Exterior Gateway Protocol)

An exterior routing protocol that exchanges route information between autonomous systems. EGP has become obsolete and is being replaced by the Border Gateway Protocol (BGP).

### EIGRP (Enhanced Interior Gateway Routing Protocol)

A Cisco proprietary routing protocol that includes features of both distance vector and link state routing protocols. EIGRP is considered an advanced distance vector protocol.

### encapsulation

Generally speaking, encapsulation is the process of wrapping data in a particular protocol header. In the context of the OSI model, encapsulation is the process by which a source peer layer includes header and/or trailer control information with a Protocol Data Unit (PDU) destined for its peer layer in another network host. The information encapsulated instructs the destination peer layer how to process the information.

### EXEC

The user interface for executing Cisco router commands.

### exterior routing protocol

A routing protocol that conveys information between autonomous systems; it is widely used within the Internet. The Border Gateway Protocol (BGP) is an example of an exterior routing protocol.

### FCS (frame check sequence)

Extra characters added to a frame for error control purposes. FCS is the result of a cyclic redundancy check (CRC).

### Flash

Router memory that stores the Cisco IOS image and associated microcode. Flash is erasable, reprogrammable ROM that retains its content when the router is powered down or restarted.

### flat routing protocol

A routing environment in which all routers are considered peers and can communicate with any other router in the network as directly as possible. A flat routing protocol functions well in simple and predictable network environments.

### flow control

A mechanism that throttles back data transmission to ensure that a sending system does not overwhelm the receiving system with data.

### Forward Explicit Congestion Notification (FECN)

A Frame Relay message that notifies the receiving device that there is congestion in the network. An FECN bit is sent in the same direction in which the frame was traveling, toward its destination.

### Frame Relay

A switched Data Link layer protocol that supports multiple virtual circuits using High-level Data Link Control (HDLC) encapsulation between connected devices.

### frame tagging

A method of tagging a frame with a unique user-defined virtual local area network (VLAN). The process of tagging frames allows VLANs to span multiple switches.

### FTP (File Transfer Protocol)

A protocol used to copy a file from one host to another host, regardless of the physical hardware or operating system of each device. FTP identifies a client and server during the file-transfer process. In addition, it provides a guaranteed transfer by using the services of the Transmission Control Protocol (TCP).

### full-duplex

The physical transmission process on a network device by which one pair of wires transmits data while another pair of wires receives data. Full-duplex transmission is achieved by eliminating the possibility of collisions on an Ethernet segment, thereby eliminating the need for a device to sense collisions.

### function

A term that refers to the different devices and the hardware tasks these devices perform within ISDN.

### global configuration mode

A router mode that enables simple router configuration commands, such as router names, banners, and passwords, to be executed. Global configuration commands affect the whole router rather than a single interface or component.

### GNS (Get Nearest Server)

A request sent by an Internetwork Packet Exchange (IPX) client to locate the closest active server of a particular service. Depending on where the service can be located, either a server or a router can respond to the request.

### half-duplex

The physical transmission process whereby one pair of wires is used to transmit information and the other pair of wires is used to receive information or to sense collisions on the physical media. Half-duplex transmission is required on Ethernet segments with multiple devices.

### handshake

The process of one system making a request to another system prior to a connection being established. Handshakes occur during the establishment of a connection between two systems, and they address matters such as synchronization and connection parameters.

### HDLC (High-level Data Link Control)

A bit-oriented, synchronous Data Link layer protocol that specifies data encapsulation methods on serial links.

### Header

Control information placed before the data during the encapsulation process.

### hierarchical routing protocol

A routing environment that relies on several routers to compose a backbone. Most traffic from non-backbone routers traverses the backbone routers (or at least travels to the backbone) to reach another non-backbone router. This is accomplished by breaking a network into a hierarchy of networks, where each level is responsible for its own routing.

### hold-down

The state into which a route is placed so that routers will not advertise or accept updates for that route until a timer expires.

### hop count

The number of routers a packet passes through on its way to the destination network.

### hostname

A logical name given to a router.

### HSSI (High-Speed Serial Interface)

A physical standard designed for serial connections that require high data transmission rates. The HSSI standard allows for high-speed communication that runs at speeds up to 52Mbps.

### ICMP (Internet Control Message Protocol)

A protocol that communicates error messages and controls messages between devices. Thirteen different types of ICMP messages are defined. ICMP allows devices to check the status of other devices, to query the current time, and to perform other functions such as `ping` and `traceroute`.

### IEEE (Institute of Electrical and Electronics Engineers)

An organization that defines standards for network LANs, among other things. The IEEE is the industry standard used in today's computing world.

### IGRP (Interior Gateway Routing Protocol)

A Cisco proprietary distance vector routing protocol that uses hop count as its metric.

### initial configuration dialog

The dialog used to configure a router the first time it is booted or when no configuration file exists. The initial configuration dialog is an optional tool used to simplify the configuration process.

### integrated routing

A technique in which a router that is routing multiple routed protocols shares resources. Rather than using several routing protocols to support multiple routed protocols, a network administrator can use a single routing protocol to support multiple routed protocols. The Enhanced Interior Gateway Routing Protocol (EIGRP) is an example of a routing protocol that supports integrated routing.

### interdomain router

A router that uses an exterior routing protocol, such as the Border Gateway Protocol (BGP), to exchange route information between autonomous systems.

### interfaces

Router components that provide the network connections where data packets move in and out of the router. Depending on the model of router, interfaces exist either on the motherboard or on separate, modular interface cards.

### interior routing protocol

A routing protocol that exchanges information within an autonomous system. Routing Information Protocol (RIP), Interior Gateway Routing Protocol (IGRP), and Open Shortest Path First (OSPF) are examples of interior routing protocols.

### intradomain router

A router that uses an interior routing protocol, such as the Interior Gateway Routing Protocol (IGRP), to convey route information within an autonomous system.

### IP (Internet Protocol)

One of the many protocols maintained in the TCP/IP suite of protocols. IP is the transport mechanism for Transmission Control Protocol (TCP), User Datagram Protocol (UDP), and Internet Control Message Protocol (ICMP) data. It also provides the logical addressing necessary for complex routing activity.

### IP extended access list

An access list that provides a way of filtering IP traffic on a router interface based on the source and destination IP address or port, IP precedence field, TOS field, ICMP-type, ICMP-code, ICMP-message, IGMP-type, and TCP-established connections.

### IP standard access list

An access list that provides a way of filtering IP traffic on a router interface based on the source IP address or address range.

### IPX (Internetwork Packet Exchange)

The Layer 3 protocol used within NetWare to transmit data between servers and workstations.

### IPX extended access list

An access list that provides a way of filtering IPX traffic on a router interface based on the source and destination IPX address or address range, IPX protocol, and source and destination sockets.

### IPX SAP filter

A method of filtering SAP traffic on a router interface. SAP filters are used to filter SAP traffic origination or traffic destined for specific IPX addresses or address ranges.

### IPX standard access list

An access list that provides a way of filtering IPX traffic on a router interface based on the source IPX address or address range.

### ISDN (Integrated Services Digital Network)

A communications protocol offered by telephone companies that permits telephone networks to carry data, voice, and other traffic.

### ISL (interswitch link)

A protocol used to allow virtual local area networks (VLANs) to span multiple switches. ISL is used between switches to communicate common VLANs between devices.

### keepalive frames

Protocol Data Units (PDUs) transmitted at the Data Link layer that indicate whether the proper frame type is configured.

### LAN protocols

Protocols that identify Layer 2 protocols used for the transmission of data within a local area network (LAN). The three most popular LAN protocols used today are Ethernet, token ring, and Fiber Distributed Data Interface (FDDI).

### LCP (Link Control Protocol)

A protocol that configures, tests, maintains, and terminates Point-to-Point Protocol (PPP) connections.

### link state packet

A broadcast packet that contains the status of a router's links or network interfaces.

### link state protocol

An interior routing protocol in which each router sends only the state of its own network links across the network, but sends this information to every router within its autonomous system or area. This process enables routers to learn and maintain full knowledge of the network's exact topology and how it is interconnected. Link state protocols use a "shortest path first" algorithm.

### LLC (Logical Link Control) sublayer

A sublayer of the Data Link layer. The LLC sublayer provides the software functions of the Data Link layer.

### LMI (Local Management Interface)

A set of enhancements to the Frame Relay protocol specifications used to manage complex networks. Some key Frame Relay LMI extensions include global addressing, virtual circuit status messages, and multicasting.

### load

An indication of how busy a network resource is. CPU utilization and packets processed per second are two indicators of load.

### local loop

The line from the customer's premises to the telephone company's central office (CO).

### logical addressing

Network layer addressing is most commonly referred to as *logical addressing* (versus the physical addressing of the Data Link layer). A logical address consists of two parts: the network and the node. Routers use the network part of the logical address to determine the best path to the network of a remote device. The node part of the logical address is used to identify the specific node to forward the packet on the destination network.

### logical ANDing
A process of comparing two sets of binary numbers to result in one value representing an IP address network. Logical ANDing is used to compare an IP address against its subnet mask to yield the IP subnet on which the IP address resides. ANDing is also used to determine whether a packet has a local or remote destination.

### MAC address
A physical address used to define a device uniquely.

### MAC (Media Access Control) layer
A sublayer of the Data Link layer that provides the hardware functions of the Data Link layer.

### metric
The relative cost of sending packets to a destination network over a specific network route. Examples of metrics include bandwidth, delay, and reliability.

### MIB (management information database)
A database that maintains statistics on certain data items. The Simple Network Management Protocol (SNMP) uses MIBs to query information about devices.

### multicasting
A process of using one IP address to represent a group of IP addresses. Multicasting is used to send messages to a subset of IP addresses in a network or networks.

### multipath routing protocol
A routing protocol that load-balances over multiple optimal paths to a destination network when the costs of the paths are equal.

### multiplexing
A method of flow control used by the Transport layer in which application conversations are combined over a single channel by interleaving packets from different segments and transmitting them.

### NBMA (nonbroadcast multiaccess)
A multiaccess network that either does not support broadcasts or for which sending broadcasts is not feasible.

### NCP (NetWare Core Protocol)
A collection of upper-layer server routines that satisfy requests from other applications.

### NCP (network control protocol)
A collection of protocols that establishes and configures different Network layer protocols for use over a Point-to-Point Protocol (PPP) connection.

### NetBIOS (Network Basic Input/Output System)
A common Session layer interface specification from IBM and Microsoft that enables applications to request lower-level network services.

### NetWare
A popular LAN operating system developed by Novell Corporation that runs on a variety of different types of LANs.

### NetWare shell
An upper-layer NetWare service that determines whether application calls require additional network services.

### network discovery
When a router starts up, this is the process by which it learns of its internetwork environment and begins to communicate with other routers.

### NIC (network interface card)
A board that provides network communication capabilities to and from a network host.

### NLSP (NetWare Link State Protocol)
A link state routing protocol used for routing Internetwork Package Exchange (IPX).

### NOS (network operating system)
A term used to describe distributed file systems that support file sharing, printing, database access, and other similar applications.

### NVRAM (nonvolatile random access memory)
A memory area of the router that stores permanent information, such as the router's backup configuration file. The contents of NVRAM are retained when the router is powered down or restarted.

### OSI (Open Systems Interconnection) model
A layered networking framework developed by the International Organization for Standardization. The OSI model describes seven layers that correspond to specific networking functions.

### OSPF (Open Shortest Path First)
A hierarchical link state routing protocol that was developed as a successor to the Routing Information Protocol (RIP).

### packet switching
A process by which a router moves a packet from one interface to another.

### PAP (Password Authentication Protocol)
An authentication protocol for the Point-to-Point Protocol (PPP) that uses a two-way, unencrypted handshake to enable a remote host to identify itself to a local host.

### parallelization
A method of flow control used by the Transport layer in which multiple channels are combined to increase the effective bandwidth for the upper layers; synonymous with *multilink*.

### path length
The sum of the costs of each link traversed up to the destination network. Some routing protocols refer to path length as *hop count*.

### PDU (Protocol Data Unit)
A unit of measure that refers to data that is transmitted between

two peer layers within different network devices. Segments, packets, and frames are examples of PDUs.

### peer-to-peer communication
A form of communication that occurs between the same layers of two different network hosts.

### physical connection
A direct connection between two devices.

### ping
A tool for testing IP connectivity between two devices. Ping is used to send multiple IP packets between a sending and a receiving device. The destination device responds with an Internet Control Message Protocol (ICMP) packet to notify the source device of its existence.

### POP (point of presence)
A physical location where a carrier has installed equipment to interconnect with a local exchange carrier.

### PPP (Point-to-Point Protocol)
A standard protocol that enables router-to-router and host-to-network connectivity over synchronous and asynchronous circuits such as telephone lines.

### Presentation layer
Layer 6 of the OSI model. The Presentation layer is concerned with how data is represented to the Application layer.

### PRI (Primary Rate Interface)
An ISDN interface that contains 23 B channels and 1 D channel for circuit-switched communication for data, voice, and video. In North America and Japan, a PRI contains 23 B channels and 1 D channel. In Europe, it contains 30 B channels and 1 D channel.

### privileged mode
An extensive administrative and management mode on a Cisco router. This router mode permits testing, debugging, and commands to modify the router's configuration.

### protocol
A formal description of a set of rules and conventions that defines how devices on a network must exchange information.

### PSTN (public switched telephone network)
The circuit-switching facilities maintained for voice analog communication.

### PVC (permanent virtual circuit)
A virtual circuit that is permanently established and ready for use.

### RAM (random access memory)
A memory area of a router that serves as a working storage area. RAM contains data such as route tables, various types of caches and buffers, as well as input and output queues and the router's active configuration file. The contents of RAM are lost when the router is powered down or restarted.

### RARP (Reverse Address Resolution Protocol)

This protocol provides mapping that is exactly opposite to the Address Resolution Protocol (ARP). RARP maps a known physical address to a logical address. Diskless machines that do not have a configured IP address when started typically use RARP. RARP requires the existence of a server that maintains physical-to-logical address mappings.

### reference point

An identifier of the logical interfaces between functions within ISDN.

### reliability

A metric that allows the network administrator to assign arbitrarily a numeric value to indicate a reliability factor for a link. The reliability metric is a method used to capture an administrator's experience with a given network link.

### RIP (Routing Information Protocol)

A widely used distance vector routing protocol that uses hop count as its metric.

### ROM (read-only memory)

An area of router memory that contains a version of the Cisco IOS image—usually an older version with minimal functionality. ROM also stores the bootstrap program and power-on diagnostic programs.

### ROM monitor

A mode on a Cisco router in which the executing software is maintained in ROM.

### ROM monitor mode (RXBOOT)

A router-maintenance mode that enables router recovery functions when the IOS file in Flash has been erased or is corrupt.

### route aggregation

The process of combining multiple IP address networks into one superset of IP address networks. Route aggregation is implemented to reduce the number of route table entries required to forward IP packets accurately in an internetwork.

### route poisoning

A routing technique by which a router immediately marks a network as unreachable as soon as it detects that the network is down. The router broadcasts the update throughout the network and maintains this poisoned route in its route table for a specified period of time.

### route table

An area of a router's memory that stores the network topology information used to determine optimal routes. Route tables contain information such as destination network, next hop, and associated metrics.

### routed protocol

A protocol that provides the information required for the routing protocol to determine the topology of the internetwork and the best path to a destination. The routed protocol provides this information in the form of a logical address and other fields within a packet. The information contained in the packet allows the router to direct user traffic. The most common routed protocols include Internet Protocol (IP) and Internetwork Packet Exchange (IPX).

### router modes

Modes that enable the execution of specific router commands and functions. User, privileged, and setup are examples of router modes that allow you to perform certain tasks.

### routing algorithms

Well-defined rules that aid routers in the collection of route information and the determination of the optimal path.

### routing loop

An event in which two or more routers have not yet converged and are propagating their inaccurate route tables. In addition, they are probably still switching packets based on their inaccurate route tables.

### routing protocols

Routing protocols use algorithms to generate a list of paths to a particular destination and the cost associated with each path. Routers use routing protocols to communicate among each other the best route to use to reach a particular destination.

### RS-232

A physical standard used to identify cabling types for serial data transmission for speeds of 19.2Kbps or less. RS-232 connects two devices communicating over a serial link with either a 25-pin (DB-25) or 9-pin (DB-9) serial interface. RS-232 is now known as *EIA/TIA-232*.

### running configuration file

The executing configuration file on a router.

### SAP (Service Advertisement Protocol)

An Internetwork Package Exchange (IPX) protocol that serves as a means to inform network clients of available network resources and services.

### SDLC (Synchronous Data Link Control)

Primarily used for terminal-to-mainframe communication, SDLC requires that one device be labeled as the primary station and all other devices be labeled as secondary stations. Communication can only occur between the primary station and a secondary station.

### session

A dialogue between two or more different systems.

### Session layer

As Layer 5 of the OSI model, the Session layer is concerned with establishing, managing, and terminating sessions between applications on different network devices.

### setup mode
The router mode triggered on startup if no configuration file resides in nonvolatile random access memory (NVRAM).

### shortest path first
See *link state protocol.*

### single-path routing protocol
A routing protocol that uses only one optimal path to a destination.

### sliding windows
A method by which TCP dynamically sets the window size during a connection, allowing either device involved in the communication to slow down the sending data rate based on the other device's capacity.

### SMTP (Simple Mail Transfer Protocol)
A protocol used to pass mail messages between devices, SMTP uses Transmission Control Protocol (TCP) connections to pass the email between hosts.

### socket
The combination of the sending and destination Transmission Control Protocol (TCP) port numbers and the sending and destination Internet Protocol (IP) addresses defines a socket. Therefore, a socket can be used to define any User Datagram Protocol (UDP) or TCP connection uniquely.

### Spanning Tree Protocol
A protocol used to eliminate all circular routes in a bridged or switched environment while maintaining redundancy. Circular routes are not desirable in Layer 2 networks because of the forwarding mechanism employed at this layer.

### split horizon
A routing mechanism that prevents a router from sending information that it received about a network back to its neighbor that originally sent the information. This mechanism is very useful in preventing routing loops.

### SPX (Sequenced Packet Exchange)
The Layer 4 protocol used within NetWare to ensure reliable, connection-oriented services.

### startup configuration file
The backup configuration file on a router.

### static route
A network route that is manually entered into the route table. Static routes function well in very simple and predictable network environments.

### store-and-forward switching
A method of forwarding frames by copying an entire frame into the buffer of a switch and making a forwarding decision. Store-and-forward switching does not achieve the same throughput as its counterpart, cut-through switching, because it copies the entire frame into the buffer instead of copying only the first 6 bytes. Store-and-forward

switching, however, provides error checking that is not provided by cut-through switching.

### subinterface

One of possibly many virtual interfaces on a single physical interface.

### subnetting

A process of splitting a classful range of IP addresses into multiple IP networks to allow more flexibility in IP addressing schemes. Subnetting overcomes the limitation of address classes and allows network administrators the flexibility to assign multiple networks with one class of IP addresses.

### switch

A switch provides increased port density and forwarding capabilities as compared to bridges. The increased port densities of switches allow LANs to be microsegmented, thereby increasing the amount of bandwidth delivered to each device.

### TCP (Transmission Control Protocol)

One of the many protocols maintained in the TCP/IP suite of protocols. TCP provides a connection-oriented and reliable service to the applications that use it.

### TCP three-way handshake

A process by which TCP connections send acknowledgments between each other when setting up a TCP connection.

### TCP windowing

A method of increasing or reducing the number of acknowledgments required between data transmissions. This allows devices to throttle the rate at which data is transmitted.

### Telnet

A standard protocol that provides a virtual terminal. Telnet enables a network administrator to connect to a router remotely.

### TFTP (Trivial File Transfer Protocol)

A protocol used to copy files from one device to another. TFTP is a stripped-down version of FTP.

### tick

A measure of network delay time about 1/18th of a second. In RIP version 2, ticks serve as the primary value used to determine the best path.

### traceroute

An IP service that allows a user to utilize the services of the User Datagram Protocol (UDP) and the Internet Control Message Protocol (ICMP) to identify the number of hops between sending and receiving devices and the paths taken from the sending to the receiving device. Traceroute also provides the IP address and DNS name of each hop. Typically, traceroute is used to troubleshoot IP connectivity between two devices.

### trailer

Control information placed after the data during the encapsulation process. See *encapsulation* for more detail.

### Transport layer

As Layer 4 of the OSI model, it is concerned with segmenting upper-layer applications, establishing end-to-end connectivity through the network, sending segments from one host to another, and ensuring the reliable transport of data.

### trunk

A switch port that connects to another switch to allow virtual local area networks (VLANs) to span multiple switches.

### tunnel

A tunnel takes packets or frames from one protocol and places them inside frames from another network system. See *encapsulation*.

### UDP (User Datagram Protocol)

One of the many protocols maintained in the TCP/IP suite of protocols, UDP is a Layer 4, best-effort delivery protocol and, therefore, maintains connectionless network services.

### user mode

A display-only mode on a Cisco router. Only limited information about the router can be viewed within this router mode; no configuration changes are permitted.

### V.35

A physical standard used to identify cabling types for serial data transmission for speeds up to 4Mbps. The V.35 standard was created by the International Telecommunication Union-Telecommunication (ITU-T) standardization sector.

### virtual connection

A logical connection between two devices created through the use of acknowledgments.

### VLAN (virtual local area network)

A technique of assigning devices to specific LANs based on the port to which they attach on a switch rather than the physical location. VLANs extend the flexibility of LANs by allowing devices to be assigned to specific LANs on a port-by-port basis versus a device basis.

### VLSM (variable-length subnet masking)

VLSM provides more flexibility in assigning IP address space. (A common problem with routing protocols is the necessity of all devices in a given routing protocol domain to use the same subnet mask.) Routing protocols that support VLSM allow administrators to assign IP networks with different subnet masks. This increased flexibility saves IP address space because administrators can assign IP networks based on the number of hosts on each network.

## VTP

With VTP, an administrator can make configuration changes centrally on a single Catalyst series switch and have those changes automatically communicated to all the other switches in the network.

## WANs (wide area networks)

WANs use data communications equipment (DCE) to connect multiple LANs. Examples of WAN protocols include but are not limited to Frame Relay, Point-to-Point Protocol (PPP), High-level Data Link Control (HDLC), and Integrated Services Digital Network (ISDN).

## well-known ports

A set of ports between 1 and 1,023 that are reserved for specific TCP/IP protocols and services.

# Index

## NUMBERS



## A



## B

## C



## D

## E



## F



## G - H



## I

## J - K - L

## M



## N



## O

# P

## Q - R

## S

## T

## U - V



## W - X - Y - Z